EVERYMAN'S LIBRARY

185

POETRY

Everyman, I will go with thee, and be thy guide
In thy most need to go by thy side

RICHARD HARRIS BARHAM, born in Canterbury in 1788, son of a country gentleman. Educated at St Paul's School and Brasenose College, Oxford, he took orders, held various livings, and became a minor canon of St Paul's Cathedral and priest of the Chapels Royal. Wrote under the name Thomas Ingoldsby. Died in London in 1845.

RICHARD HARRIS BARHAM

THE INGOLDSBY
LEGENDS

OR MIRTH & MARVELS

EDITED WITH
AN INTRODUCTION BY

D. C. BROWNING
M.A.(Glasgow), B.A., B.Litt.(Oxon.)

LONDON   J. M. DENT & SONS LTD
NEW YORK   E. P. DUTTON & CO INC

© Introduction and editing, J. M. Dent & Sons Ltd, 1960
All rights reserved
Made in Great Britain
at the
Aldine Press · Letchworth · Herts
for
J. M. DENT & SONS LTD
Aldine House · Bedford Street · London
First published in this edition 1960

INTRODUCTION

RICHARD HARRIS BARHAM, who wrote under the name Thomas Ingoldsby, was born in Canterbury on 6th December 1788. The Barhams were an old Kentish family, who claimed descent from one Ursus, who came over with the Conqueror. A less shadowy forbear was Sir Randal Fitzurse, one of the four knights who murdered Thomas à Becket, the archbishop, in Canterbury Cathedral in 1170; the murder is referred to in one of the *Ingoldsby Legends*, 'The Brothers of Birchington,' where St Thomas comes off best in an encounter with the Devil. Sir Randal was the owner of Barham Court in Kent, and his brother Robert founded the Barham family. But the family seat mentioned frequently in the *Legends*, and illustrated on page x of this volume, is Tappington or Tapton Everard, between Canterbury and Folkestone, the property of the poet's father, whose name was the same as his. Richard Harris Barham senior was a man of substance in a very literal sense, for he weighed twenty-seven stone when middle-aged, and drank a bottle of port every night; he died when the poet was six years old.

Three years later young Richard was sent to school at St Paul's, where one of his schoolfellows was Richard Bentley, in whose *Miscellany* most of the *Ingoldsby Legends* were later to appear. A good classical scholar, Barham was captain of the school for two years; his talent for rhyming appeared even at this early stage, and he was a favourite of the high master, Dr Roberts, and his wife. In 1802 the boy met with a serious accident when coming back in the Dover stage coach from his holidays; it overturned, and as he tried to open the door his arm was pinned beneath it and terribly mangled. Amputation seemed inevitable, but the arm was ultimately saved, though it was always to some extent crippled.

In 1807 Barham went to Brasenose College, Oxford, then, as now, a sporting and boisterous college. Among his friends there was Theodore Hook, the inveterate hoaxer and wit, of whom he was to see much in later life. Two stories of his college days throw an interesting light on his character. Gambling was rife in the Oxford of those days, and Barham found himself owing more than he could pay. An appeal to his guardian brought the necessary sum, together with a serious admonition, which he took so much to heart that ever afterwards he avoided all forms of speculation. The other story has a more humorous side. Taken to task by his tutor for his absence from morning chapel, he told the bewildered don that the hour of seven o'clock was *too late* for him. 'Unless I get to bed by four—or five at latest,' he explained, 'I am really fit for nothing next day.' All his life he was a late riser, but worked far into the night, when his mind was at its most alert.

On graduating in 1811, his first aim was the law, but after a few months of study he turned instead to the Church. Taking orders in 1813, he became curate of Ashford, then of Westwell, and in 1817 was appointed rector of Snargate and curate of Warehorn; this was the Romney Marsh country, a centre of smuggling; mysterious horsemen would appear at lonely spots, but melt into the darkness with the words, 'Good night! It's only parson,' and rumour had it that contraband was even stored in the church. In 1819 Barham produced his first published work. While confined to bed with a broken leg, the result of another road accident—a gig overturned this time—he wrote a novel, *Baldwin*, for which the publishers gave him £20, but neither it nor his later *My Cousin Nicholas* won much popularity.

In 1821 he applied for a minor canonry that fell vacant at St Paul's, and was appointed to it. This meant moving to London, and he settled in Lincoln's Inn Fields. It also meant that his earnings were less, so he became, to use his own words, 'a slave of the lamp.' He wrote for *Blackwood's* and other magazines, and for a time edited the *London Chronicle*. In 1824 he was appointed a priest of the Chapels Royal and rector of St Gregory. He had now to reside within the City limits, and took the house in St Paul's Churchyard which was his home for the remainder of his life. He continued to write for various periodicals, including *John Bull*, which was edited by his former college friend, Theodore Hook; to *Bentley's Miscellany*, founded by his old schoolfellow, Richard Bentley, he contributed the pieces known as the *Ingoldsby Legends*. In 1842 he was elected president of Sion College for a year, and was appointed rector of St Faith's, but a series of bereavements—of his nine children only three survived their parents—saddened the latter part of his life; a blow from which he never fully recovered was the sudden death of his son Edward from cholera in 1840.

In October of 1844 the Queen paid a state visit to London, and Barham, while watching the procession from a friend's window, caught a chill which was neglected and turned to bronchitis. He kept on working through the periods of varying health and relapse during the months that followed, even writing an amusing sketch of his confusing talk with the doctor when he tried to find out the precise purpose of the different treatments he was getting. Visits to Bath and Clifton in search of health were unsuccessful, and the lines 'As I Laye A-thynkynge' which form a tail-piece to the present volume were inspired partly by the deaths of his children and partly by the thought that he was soon to follow them. He died in London on 17th June 1845, and was buried in the church of St Mary Magdalen, but later his remains were removed to Kensal Green.

Most of the *Ingoldsby Legends* appeared in *Bentley's Miscellany*, which began in 1837 with Dickens as editor; after it expired in 1843 the series was transferred to the *New Monthly Magazine*. 'The "Monstre" Balloon,' included in Bentley's first number, was unsigned, but from the second number onwards the contributions appeared over the name Thomas Ingoldsby. Although the account given of the Ingoldsby family is fictitious, the name is found in a branch of the Barham family genealogy, and, as we have seen, their seat of Tappington Everard was genuine. For several of the tales of which he made use Barham was indebted to Mrs Hughes, wife of Dr Hughes, grandfather of the author of *Tom Brown's Schooldays*. Of the *Legends* Dr Hughes observed: 'Many of these effusions were written while waiting for a cup of tea, a railroad train, or an unpunctual acquaintance, on some stray cover of a letter in his pocket-book; one in particular served to relieve the tedium of a hot walk up Richmond Hill. It was rather a piece of luck if he found time to join together the *disjecta membra* in a fair copy.'

The ease with which Barham wrote was in large measure due to his extraordinary command of rhyme and rhythm, which he could apply to the most refractory material. All was grist that came to his poetic mill. As his son remarks: 'Popular phrases, sentences the most prosaic, even the cramped technicalities of legal diction, and snatches from various languages, are wrought in with an apparent absence of all art, that surprises, pleases, and convulses the reader at every turn.' The materials for the tales of ancient superstition were got from monkish chronicles, including the *Golden Legend*. But quite a few of the Latin extracts with which the poems are headed are 'phoney,' and were the product of Barham's fertile brain and accomplished scholarship. The anti-Catholic tone of so many of the pieces is due to the spirit of controversy that prevailed at the time they were written, the Church of England being apprehensive at the tendency of its members to go over to Rome. During his last days Barham became worried about some of the *Legends* that seemed to hold certain aspects of religion up to ridicule, and kept insisting that they were directed only against error and imposture and the reactionary unbelief to which these may give rise.

The best-known of the *Legends* are in verse; those in prose, half a dozen in number, are of less interest and have been omitted from the present volume. Barham's work, though reckoned old-fashioned, is much in sympathy with the trends of the present day. His taste for the brutal and horrible is fitted to the mood of a country disillusioned by two titanic wars, while his ingenious rhymes and his practice of interlarding his verses with quotations from both English and foreign writers can both be paralleled among our modern poets. Word-play was fashionable in his time; his translation—and transliteration—of 'circumspice' by 'Sir, come-spy-see,' and his line 'But when the Crier cried "O Yes!" the people cried "O No!"' are as happy as anything in Hood. An often-quoted example of his macaronics, not in the *Legends*, is the epigram beginning:

> What Horace says is, *Eheu fugaces*
> *Anni labuntur, Postume, Postume!*
> Years glide away, and are lost to me, lost to me!

Of his grislier pieces, the most horrible is 'Bloudie Jacke of Shrewsberrie, the Shropshire Bluebeard,' which he himself latterly thought rather too shocking. But a strong element of comedy redeems even his most sanguinary tales, and one feels that his corpses are bleeding sawdust instead of gore. The most famous of the *Legends* is a mild one with no murders, 'The Jackdaw of Rheims,' and next to it we might put 'Misadventures at Margate,' an equally innocuous tale of how one Mr Simpkinson was victimized by 'that vulgar little boy.' But everyone has his own favourites in this classic of the comic and grotesque.

An informative life of Barham was written by his son, Richard Harris Dalton Barham, and there is a homely memoir by his daughter, Mrs Bond. The latter gives a delightful picture of him as canon of St Paul's, marrying eloping couples who had obtained the necessary authorization at nearby Doctors' Commons; visiting almshouses at Mile End and composing the squabbles of the old women who lived in them; buying trinkets for his wife, to whom he was devoted; browsing in the old libraries of St Paul's Cathedral or of Sion College; and often winding up at the Garrick Club, of which he had been a member since its foundation in 1831. Short and broad, he was not active, being handicapped by the effect of his two accidents, but had great powers of endurance. His face was expressive of good humour and fun, unlike that of his great contemporary Hood, who, like many comedians, had always a lugubrious air. Next to his wife and children he loved cats, and often had one sitting on his table or even on his shoulder while he wrote; one of his last injunctions was 'Take care of Chance' (a cat he had adopted). One may fitly end with the lines of his 'self-epitaph,' so typical in their whimsical absurdity:

> Trav'ler pass—nor vainly scan
> Fate's dark decree, which hence withdrew
> So wise, so good, so great a man,
> And left so sad a scamp as you.

1960.   D. C. BROWNING.

SELECT BIBLIOGRAPHY

WORKS. *The Ingoldsby Legends, or Mirth and Marvels,* by Thomas Ingoldsby, Esquire, 3 series, 1840, 1842, 1847, edited with memoir by R. H. D. Barham, 1860.

VERSE. *Ingoldsby Lyrics,* by Thomas Ingoldsby, edited by his son, 1881.

NOVELS. *Baldwin, or a Miner's Heir,* by an Old Bachelor, 1820; *Some Account of My Cousin Nicholas,* 1841.

LIFE. R. H. D. Barham: *The Life and Letters of Richard Harris Barham,* 2 vols., 1870.

Tappington Everard

CONTENTS

PREFACE TO FIRST SERIES

To Richard Bentley, Esq.

MY DEAR SIR,

You wish me to collect into one single volume certain rambling extracts from our family memoranda, many of which have already appeared in the pages of your Miscellany. At the same time you tell me that doubts are entertained in certain quarters as to the authenticity of their details.

Now with respect to their genuineness, the old oak chest, in which the originals are deposited, is not more familiar to my eyes than it is to your own; and if its contents have any value at all, it consists in the strict veracity of the facts they record.

To convince the most incredulous, I can only add, that should business—pleasure is out of the question—ever call them into the neighbourhood of Folkestone, let them take the high road from Canterbury to Dover till they reach the eastern extremity of Barham Downs. Here a beautiful green lane diverging abruptly to the right will carry them through the Oxenden plantations and the unpretending village of Denton, to the foot of a very respectable hill—as hills go in this part of Europe. On reaching its summit let them look straight before them—and if among the hanging woods which crown the opposite side of the valley, they cannot distinguish an antiquated Manor-house of Elizabethan architecture, with its gable ends, stone stanchions, and tortuous chimneys rising above the surrounding trees, why —the sooner they procure a pair of Dollard's patent spectacles the better.

If, on the contrary, they can manage to descry it, and, proceeding some five or six furlongs through the avenue, will ring at the Lodge-gate—they cannot mistake the stone lion with the Ingoldsby escutcheon (Ermine, a saltire engrailed Gules) in his paws—they will be received with a hearty old English welcome.

The papers in question having been written by different parties, and at various periods, I have thought it advisable to reduce the more ancient of them into a comparatively modern phraseology, and to make my collateral ancestor, Father John,

especially, 'deliver himself like a man of this world'; Mr
Maguire, indeed, is the only Gentleman who, in his account of
the late Coronation, retains his own rich vernacular.

As to arrangement, I shall adopt the sentiment expressed by
the Constable of Bourbon four centuries ago, *teste* Shakspeare,
one which seems to become more fashionable every day,

> The Devil take all order!!—I'll to the throng!

Believe me to be,

My dear Sir,

Your, most indubitably and immeasurably,

THOMAS INGOLDSBY.

TAPPINGTON EVERARD,
  20th. Jan. 1840.

PREFACE TO THE SECOND EDITION

To Richard Bentley, Esq.

MY DEAR SIR,

I SHOULD have replied sooner to your letter, but that the last three days in January are, as you are aware, always dedicated, at the Hall, to an especial *battue*, and the old house is full of shooting-jackets, shot-belts, and 'double Joes.' Even the women wear percussion caps, and your favourite (?) Rover, who, you may remember, examined the calves of your legs with such suspicious curiosity at Christmas, is as pheasant-mad as if he were a biped, instead of being a genuine four-legged scion of the Blenheim breed. I have managed, however, to avail myself of a lucid interval in the general hallucination, (how the rain *did* come down on Monday!) and as you tell me the excellent friend whom you are in the habit of styling 'a Generous and Enlightened Public' has emptied your shelves of the first edition, and 'asks for more,' why, I agree with you, it *would* be a want of *respect* to that very *respectable* personification, when furnishing him with a farther supply, not to endeavour at least to amend my faults, which are few, and your own, which are more numerous. I have, therefore, gone to work *con amore*, supplying occasionally on my own part a deficient note, or elucidatory stanza, and on yours knocking out, without remorse, your superfluous *i*'s, and now and then eviscerating your *colon*.

My duty to our illustrious friend thus performed, I have a crow to pluck with him,—Why will he persist—as you tell me he does persist—in calling me by all sorts of names but those to which I am entitled by birth and baptism—my 'Spondorial and Patronymic appellations,' as Dr Pangloss has it?—Mrs Malaprop complains, and with justice, of an 'assault upon her parts of speech': but to attack one's very existence—to deny that one *is* a person *in esse*, and scarcely to admit that one *may be* a person *in posse*, is tenfold cruelty;—'it is pressing to death, whipping, and hanging!'—let me entreat all such likewise to remember that, as Shakespeare beautifully expresses himself elsewhere—I

give his words as quoted by a very worthy Baronet in a neighbouring county, when protesting against a defamatory placard
at a general election—

> Who steals my purse steals stuff!—
> 'Twas mine—'tisn't his—nor nobody elses!
> But he who runs away with my GOOD NAME,
> Robs me of what does not do him any good,
> And makes me deuced poor!! [1]

In order utterly to squabash and demolish every gainsayer, I
had thought, at one time, of asking my old and esteemed friend,
Richard Lane, to crush them at once with his magic pencil, and
to transmit my features to posterity, where all his works are sure
to be 'delivered according to the direction'; but somehow the
noble-looking profiles which he has recently executed of the
Kemble family put me a little out of conceit with my own, while
the undisguised amusement which my 'Mephistopheles Eyebrow,' as he termed it, afforded him, in the 'full face,' induced
me to lay aside the design. Besides, my dear Sir, since, as has
well been observed, 'there never was a married man yet who had
not somebody remarkably like him walking about town,' it is a
thousand to one but my lineaments might, after all, out of sheer
perverseness be ascribed to anybody rather than to the real
owner. I have therefore sent you, instead thereof, a very fair
sketch of Tappington, taken from the Folkestone road (I tore it
last night out of Julia Simpkinson's *album*); get Gilks to make a
woodcut of it. And now, if any miscreant (I use the word only
in its primary and 'Pickwickian' sense of 'Unbeliever') ventures
to throw any further doubt upon the matter, why, as Jack Cade's
friend says in the play, 'There are the chimneys in my father's
house, and the bricks are alive at this day to testify it!'

'Why, very well then—we hope here be truths!'

Heaven be with you, my dear Sir!—I was getting a little
excited; but you, who are mild as the milk that dews the soft
whisker of the new-weaned kitten, will forgive me when, wiping
away the nascent moisture from my brow, I 'pull in,' and subscribe myself,

Yours quite as much as his own,

THOMAS INGOLDSBY.

TAPPINGTON EVERARD,
  2nd Feb. 1843.

---

[1] A reading which seems most unaccountably to have escaped the researches of all modern Shakespearians, including the rival editors of the new
and illustrated versions.

FIRST SERIES

THE NURSE'S STORY

THE HAND OF GLORY

'Malefica quaedam auguriatrix in Angliâ fuit, quam demones horribiliter extraxerunt, et imponentes super equum terribilem, per aera rapuerunt; Clamoresque terribiles (ut ferunt) per quatuor fermè miliaria audiebantur.' [1]

NUREMB. CHRON.

On the lone bleak moor,   At the midnight hour,
Beneath the Gallows Tree,
    Hand in hand   The Murderers stand
By one, by two, by three!
    And the Moon that night   With a grey, cold light
Each baleful object tips;
    One half of her form   Is seen through the storm,
The other half's hid in Eclipse!
    And the cold Wind howls,   And the Thunder growls,
    And the Lightning is broad and bright;
        And altogether   It's very bad weather,
    And an unpleasant sort of a night!
        'Now mount who list,   And close by the wrist
Sever me quickly the Dead Man's fist!—
    Now climb who dare   Where he swings in air,
And pluck me five locks of the Dead Man's hair!'

There's an old woman dwells upon Tappington Moor,
She hath years on her back at the least fourscore,
And some people fancy a great many more;
    Her nose it is hook'd,   Her back it is crook'd,
    Her eyes blear and red: On the top of her head
Is a mutch, and on that   A shocking bad hat,
Extinguisher-shaped, the brim narrow and flat!
Then,—My Gracious!—her beard!—it would sadly perplex
A spectator at first to distinguish her sex;
    Nor, I'll venture to say, without scrutiny could he
Pronounce her, off-handed, a Punch or a Judy.

---

[1] 'There was in England a certain evil witch, whom demons dragged forth in a horrible manner, and setting her upon a dreadful horse carried her off through the air. Dreadful cries, so they say, were heard over nearly four miles.'

Did you see her, in short, that mud-hovel within,
With her knees to her nose, and her nose to her chin,
Leering up with that queer indescribable grin,
You'd lift up your hands in amazement, and cry,
'—Well!—I never *did* see such a regular Guy!'

And now before   That old Woman's door,
Where nought that's good may be,
Hand in hand   The Murderers stand
By one, by two, by three!
Oh! 'tis a horrible sight to view,
In that horrible hovel, that horrible crew,
By the pale blue glare of that flickering flame,
Doing the deed that hath never a name!
'Tis awful to hear   Those words of fear!
The pray'r mutter'd backwards, and said with a sneer!
(Matthew Hopkins himself has assured us that when
A witch says her pray'rs, she begins with 'Amen.')—
—'Tis awful to see   On that Old Woman's knee
The dead, shrivell'd hand, as she clasps it with glee!—
And now, with care,   The five locks of hair
From the skull of the Gentleman dangling up there,
With the grease and the fat   Of a black Tom Cat
She hastens to mix,   And to twist into wicks,
And one on the thumb, and each finger to fix.—
(For another receipt the same charm to prepare,
Consult Mr Ainsworth and *Petit Albert*.)

'Now open lock   To the Dead Man's knock!
Fly bolt, and bar, and band!—
Nor move, nor swerve   Joint, muscle, or nerve,
At the spell of the Dead Man's hand!
Sleep all who sleep!—Wake all who wake!—
But be as the Dead for the Dead Man's sake!!'

All is silent! all is still,
Save the ceaseless moan of the bubbling rill
As it wells from the bosom of Tappington Hill;
And in Tappington Hall   Great and Small,
Gentle and Simple, Squire and Groom,
Each one hath sought his separate room,
And sleep her dark mantle hath o'er them cast,
For the midnight hour hath long been past!

All is darksome in earth and sky,
Save, from yon casement, narrow and high,
A quivering beam   On the tiny stream
Plays, like some taper's fitful gleam
By one that is watching wearily.

Within that casement, narrow and high,
In his secret lair, where none may spy,
Sits one whose brow is wrinkled with care,
And the thin grey locks of his failing hair
Have left his little bald pate all bare;
    For his full-bottom'd wig Hangs bushy and big,
On the top of his old-fashion'd, high-back'd chair.
    Unbraced are his clothes, Ungarter'd his hose,
His gown is bedizened with tulip and rose,
Flowers of remarkable size and hue,
Flowers such as Eden never knew;
—And there, by many a sparkling heap
    Of the good red gold, The tale is told
What powerful spell avails to keep
That care-worn man from his needful sleep!

Haply, he deems no eye can see
As he gloats on his treasure greedily,—
    The shining store Of glittering ore,
The fair Rose-Noble, the bright Moidore,
And the broad Double-Joe from ayont the sea,—
But there's one that watches as well as he;
    For, wakeful and sly, In a closet hard by,
On his truckle-bed lieth a little Foot-page,
A boy who's uncommonly sharp of his age,
    Like young Master Horner, Who erst in a corner
    Sat eating a Christmas pie:
And while that Old Gentleman's counting his hoards,
Little Hugh peeps through a crack in the boards!

    There's a voice in the air, There's a step on the stair,
The old man starts in his cane-back'd chair;
    At the first faint sound He gazes around,
And holds up his dip of sixteen to the pound.
    Then half arose From beside his toes
His little pug-dog with his little pug nose,
But, ere he can vent one inquisitive sniff,
That little pug-dog stands stark and stiff,
    For low, yet clear, Now fall on the ear,
—Where once pronounced for ever they dwell,—
The unholy words of the Dead Man's spell!
    'Open lock To the Dead Man's knock!
    Fly bolt, and bar, and band!
    Nor move, nor swerve Joint, muscle, or nerve,
At the spell of the Dead Man's hand!
Sleep all who sleep!—Wake all who wake!—
But be as the Dead for the Dead Man's sake!'

Now lock, nor bolt, nor bar avails,
Nor stout oak panel thick-studded with nails.
Heavy and harsh the hinges creak,
Though they had been oil'd in the course of the week;
The door opens wide as wide may be,
 And there they stand, That murderous band,
  Lit by the light of the GLORIOUS HAND,
   By one!—by two!—by three!

They have pass'd through the porch, they have pass'd through
 the hall,
Where the Porter sat snoring against the wall;
 The very snore froze In his very snub nose,
You'd have verily deem'd he had snored his last
When the GLORIOUS HAND by the side of him passed!
E'en the little wee mouse, as it ran o'er the mat
At the top of its speed to escape from the cat,
 Though half dead with affright, Paused in its flight;
And the cat that was chasing that little wee thing
Lay crouch'd as a statue in act to spring!
 And now they are there, On the head of the stair,
And the long crooked whittle is gleaming and bare!
—I really don't think any money would bribe
Me the horrible scene that ensued to describe,
 Or the wild, wild glare Of that old man's eye,
  His dumb despair, And deep agony.

The kid from the pen, and the lamb from the fold,
Unmoved may the blade of the butcher behold;
They dream not—ah, happier they!—that the knife,
Though uplifted, can menace their innocent life;
It falls;—the frail thread of their being is riven,
They dread not, suspect not, the blow till 'tis given.—
But, oh! what a thing 'tis to see and to know
That the bare knife is raised in the hand of the foe,
Without hope to repel, or to ward off the blow!—
—Enough!—let's pass over as fast as we can
The fate of that grey, that unhappy old man!

 But fancy poor Hugh, Aghast at the view
 Powerless alike to speak or to do!
 In vain doth he try To open the eye
That is shut, or close that which is clapt to the chink,
Though he'd give all the world to be able to wink!—
No!—for all that this world can give or refuse,
I would not be now in that little boy's shoes,
Or indeed any garment at all that is Hugh's!

—'Tis lucky for him that the chink in the wall
He has peep'd through so long, is so narrow and small!
 Wailing voices, sounds of woe
  Such as follow departing friends,
 That fatal night round Tappington go,
  Its long-drawn roofs and its gable ends:
 Ethereal Spirits, gentle and good,
 Aye weep and lament o'er a deed of blood.

'Tis early dawn—the morn is grey,
And the clouds and the tempest have pass'd away,
And all things betoken a very fine day;
But, while the lark her carol is singing,
Shrieks and screams are through Tappington ringing!
 Upstarting all Great and small,
Each one who's found within Tappington Hall,
Gentle and Simple, Squire or Groom,
All seek at once that old Gentleman's room;
 And there on the floor, Drench'd in its gore,
A ghastly corpse lies exposed to the view,
Carotid and jugular both cut through!
 And there, by its side, 'Mid the crimson tide,
Kneels a little Foot-page of tenderest years;
Adown his pale cheeks the fast-falling tears
Are coursing each other round and big,
And he's staunching the blood with a full-bottomed wig!
Alas! and alack for his staunching!—'tis plain,
As anatomists tell us, that never again
Shall life revisit the foully slain,
When once they've been cut through the jugular vein.

There's a hue and a cry through the County of Kent,
And in chase of the cut-throats a Constable's sent,
But no one can tell the man which way they went,
There's a little Foot-page with that Constable goes,
And a little pug-dog with a little pug nose.

 In Rochester town, At the sign of the Crown,
Three shabby-genteel men are just sitting down
To a fat stubble-goose, with potatoes done brown;
 When a little Foot-page Rushes in, in a rage,
Upsetting the apple-sauce, onions, and sage.
That little Foot-page takes the first by the throat,
And a little pug-dog takes the next by the coat,
And a Constable seizes the one more remote;
And fair rose-nobles and broad moidores,
The Waiter pulls out of their pockets by scores,

And the Boots and the Chambermaids run in and stare;
And the Constable says, with a dignified air,
'You're *wanted*, Gen'lemen, one and all,
For that 'ere precious lark at Tappington Hall!'

There's a black gibbet frowns upon Tappington Moor,
Where a former black gibbet has frown'd before:
　　It is as black as black may be,
　　　　And murderers there　Are dangling in air,
　　By one!—by two! by three!

There's a horrid old hag in a steeple-crown'd hat,
Round her neck they have tied to a hempen cravat
A Dead Man's hand and a dead Tom Cat!
They have tied up her thumbs, they have tied up her toes,
　　They have tied up her eyes, they have tied up her limbs!
Into Tappington mill-dam souse she goes,
　　With a whoop and a halloo—'She swims!—She swims!'
　　　　They have dragg'd her to land,
　　　　And every one's hand,
　　Is grasping a faggot, a billet, or brand,
When a queer looking horseman, dressed all in black,
Snatches up that old harridan just like a sack
To the crupper behind him, puts spurs to his hack,
Makes a dash through the crowd, and is off in a crack!—
　　No one can tell,　Though they guess pretty well,
Which way that grim rider and old woman go,
For all see he's a sort of infernal Ducrow;
　　And she scream'd so, and cried,　We may fairly decide
That the old woman did not much relish her ride!

MORAL

This truest of stories confirms beyond doubt
That truest of adages—'Murder will out!'
In vain may the blood-spiller 'double' and fly,
In vain even witchcraft and sorcery try:
Although for a time he may 'scape, by-and-by
He'll be sure to be caught by a Hugh and a Cry!

PATTY MORGAN THE MILKMAID'S STORY

'LOOK AT THE CLOCK'

FYTTE I

'LOOK at the Clock!' quoth Winifred Pryce,
  As she open'd the door to her husband's knock,
Then paus'd to give him a piece of advice,
  'You nasty Warmint, look at the Clock!
  Is this the way, you   Wretch, every day you
Treat her who vow'd to love and obey you?—
  Out all night!   Me in a fright!
Staggering home as it's just getting light!
You intoxified brute!—you insensible block!—
Look at the Clock!—Do!—Look at the Clock!'

Winifred Pryce was tidy and clean,
Her gown was a flower'd one, her petticoat green,
Her buckles were bright as her milking cans,
And her hat was a beaver, and made like a man's;
Her little red eyes were deep set in their socket-holes,
Her gown-tail was turn'd up, and tuck'd through the pocket-
    holes;
  A face like a ferret   Betoken'd her spirit:
To conclude, Mrs Pryce was not over young,
Had very short legs, and a very long tongue.

  Now David Pryce   Had one darling vice;
Remarkably partial to anything nice,
Nought that was good to him came amiss,
Whether to eat, or to drink, or to kiss!
  Especially ale—   If it was not too stale
I really believe he'd have emptied a pail;
  Not that in Wales   They talk of their Ales;
To pronounce the word they make use of might trouble you,
Being spelt with a C, two Rs, and a W.

  That particular day,   As I've heard people say,
Mr David Pryce had been soaking his clay,
And amusing himself with his pipe and cheroots,
The whole afternoon, at the Goat-in-Boots,
  With a couple more soakers,   Thoroughbred smokers,
Both, like himself, prime singers and jokers;
And long after day had drawn to a close,
And the rest of the world was wrapp'd in repose,
They were roaring out 'Shenkin!' and 'Ar hydd y nos';

While David himself, to a Sassenach tune,
Sang, 'We've drunk down the Sun, boys! let's drink down the
    Moon!
    What have we with day to do?
    Mrs Winifred Pryce, 'twas made for you.'
At length, when they couldn't well drink any more,
Old 'Goat-in-Boots' showed them the door:
    And then came that knock,   And the sensible shock
David felt when his wife cried, 'Look at the Clock!'
For the hands stood as crooked as crooked might be,
The long at the Twelve, and the short at the Three!

That selfsame clock had long been a bone
Of contention between this Darby and Joan,
And often, among their pother and rout,
When this otherwise amiable couple fell out,
    Pryce would drop a cool hint,   With an ominous squint
At its case, of an 'Uncle' of his, who'd a 'Spout.'
    That horrid word 'Spout'   No sooner came out
Than Winifred Pryce would turn her about,
    And with scorn on her lip,   And a hand on each hip,
'Spout' herself till her nose grew red at the tip.
    'You thundering Willin,   I know you'd be killing
Your wife—ay, a dozen of wives—for a shilling!
    You may do what you please,   You may sell my chemise,
(Mrs P. was too well-bred to mention her smock)
But I never will part with my Grandmother's Clock!'

Mrs Pryce's tongue ran long and ran fast;
But patience is apt to wear out at last,
And David Pryce in temper was quick,
So he stretched out his hand, and caught hold of a stick;
Perhaps in its use he might mean to be lenient,
But walking just then wasn't very convenient,
    So he threw it, instead,   Direct at her head;
    It knock'd off her hat;   Down she flat;
Her case, perhaps, was not much mended by that:
But whatever it was,—whether rage and pain
Produced apoplexy, or burst a vein,
Or her tumble induced a concussion of brain,
I can't say for certain,—but *this* I can,
When, sober'd by fright, to assist her he ran,
Mrs Winifred Pryce was as dead as Queen Anne!

    The fearful catastrophe   Named in my last strophe
As adding to grim Death's exploits such a vast trophy,
Made a great noise; and the shocking fatality,
Ran over, like wildfire, the whole Principality,

And then came Mr Ap Thomas, the Coroner,
With his jury to sit, some dozen or more, on her.
   Mr Pryce to commence   His 'ingenious defence,'
Made a 'powerful appeal' to the jury's 'good sense':
   'The world he must defy   Ever to justify
Any presumption of "Malice Prepense"';—
   The unlucky lick   From the end of his stick
He 'deplored,'—he was 'apt to be rather too quick';—
   But, really, her prating   Was so aggravating:
Some trifling correction was just what he meant;—all
The rest, he assured them, was 'quite accidental'!

   Then he calls Mr Jones,   Who depones to her tones,
And her gestures, and hints about 'breaking his bones.'
While Mr Ap Morgan, and Mr Ap Rhys
   Declared the Deceased   Had styled him 'a Beast,'
And swear they had witness'd, with grief and surprise,
The allusion she made to his limbs and his eyes.

The jury, in fine, having sat on the body
The whole day, discussing the case, and gin toddy,
Return'd about half past eleven at night
The following verdict, 'We find, *Sarve her right!*'

Mr Pryce, Mrs Winifred Pryce being dead,
Felt lonely, and moped; and one evening he said
He would marry Miss Davis at once in her stead.

   Not far from his dwelling,
   From the vale proudly swelling,
Rose a mountain; it's name you'll excuse me from telling,
For the vowels made use of in Welsh are so few
That the A and the E, the I, O, and the U,
Have really but little or nothing to do;
And the duty, of course, falls the heavier by far,
On the L, and the H, and the N, and the R.
   Its first syllable 'PEN,'   Is pronounceable;—then
Come two L Ls, and two H Hs, two F Fs, and an N
About half a score Rs, and some Ws follow,
Beating all my best efforts at euphony hollow:
But we shan't have to mention it often, so when
We do, with your leave, we'll curtail it to 'PEN.'

   Well—the moon shone bright
   Upon 'Pen' that night,
When Pryce, being quit of his fuss and his fright,
   Was scaling its side   With that sort of stride
A man puts out when walking in search of a bride.

Mounting higher and higher,   He began to perspire,
Till, finding his legs were beginning to tire,
    And feeling opprest   By a pain in his chest,
He paus'd, and turn'd round to take breath, and to rest;
A walk all up hill is apt, we know.
To make one, however robust, puff and blow,
So he stopp'd and look'd down on the valley below.

O'er fell, and o'er fen,   Over mountain and glen,
All bright in the moonshine, his eye roved, and then
All the Patriot rose in his soul, and he thought
Upon Wales, and her glories, and all he'd been taught
    Of her Heroes of old,   So brave and so bold—,
Of her Bards with long beards, and harps mounted in gold;
    Of King Edward the First,   Of memory accurst;
And the scandalous manner in which he behaved,
    Killing Poets by dozens,
    With their uncles and cousins,
Of whom not one in fifty had ever been shaved—
Of the Court Ball, at which by a lucky mishap,
Owen Tudor fell into Queen Katherine's lap;
    And how Mr Tudor   Successfully woo'd her,
Till the Dowager put on a new wedding ring,
And so made him Father-in-law to the King.

He thought upon Arthur, and Merlin of yore,
On Gryffith ap Conan, and Owen Glendour;
On Pendragon, and Heaven knows how many more.
He thought of all this, as he gazed, in a trice,
And on all things, in short, but the late Mrs Pryce;
When a lumbering noise from behind made him start,
And sent the blood back in full tide to his heart,
    Which went pit-a-pat
    As he cried out 'What's that?'—
    That very queer sound?—
    Does it come from the ground?
Or the air,—from above,—or below,—or around?—
    It is not like Talking,   It is not like Walking,
It's not like the clattering of pot or of pan,
Or the tramp of a horse,—or the tread of a man,—
Or the hum of a crowd,—or the shouting of boys,—
It's really a deuced odd sort of a noise!
Not unlike a cart's,—but that can't be; for when
Could 'all the King's horses, and all the King's men,'
With Old Nick for a wagoner, drive one up 'Pen'?—

Pryce, usually brimful of valour when drunk,
Now experienced what schoolboys denominate 'funk.'

In vain he look'd back   On the whole of the track
He had traversed; a thick cloud, uncommonly black,
At this moment obscured the broad disk of the moon,
And did not seem likely to pass away soon;
   While clearer and clearer,   'Twas plain to the hearer,
Be the noise what it might, it drew nearer and nearer,
And sounded, as Pryce to this moment declares,
Very much 'like a Coffin a-walking up stairs.'

   Mr Pryce had begun   To 'make up' for a run,
As in such a companion he saw no great fun,
   When a single bright ray   Shone out on the way
He had passed, and he saw, with no little dismay,
Coming after him, bounding o'er crag and o'er rock,
The deceased Mrs Winifred's 'Grandmother's Clock!!'
'Twas so!—it had certainly moved from its place,
And come, lumbering on thus, to hold him in chase;
'Twas the very same Head, and the very same Case,
And nothing was altered at all—but the Face!
In that he perceived, with no little surprise,
The two little winder-holes turned into eyes
   Blazing with ire,   Like two coals of fire;
And the 'Name of the Maker' was changed to a Lip,
And the Hands to a Nose with a very red tip.
No!—he could not mistake it,—'twas SHE to the life!
The identical face of his poor defunct Wife!

   One glance was enough   Completely '*Quant. suff.*'
As the doctors write down when they send you their 'stuff,'—
Like a Weather-cock whirled by a vehement puff,
   David turned himself round;   Ten feet of ground
He clear'd, in his start, at the very first bound!

I've seen people run at West-End Fair for cheeses—
I've seen Ladies run at Bow Fair for chemises—
At Greenwich Fair twenty men run for a hat,
And one from a Bailiff much faster than that—
At football I've seen lads run after the bladder—
I've seen Irish Bricklayers run up a ladder—
I've seen little boys run away from a cane—
And I've seen (that is, *read of*) good running in Spain; [1]
   But I never did read   Of, or witness, such speed
As David exerted that evening.—Indeed
All I have ever heard of boys, women, or men,
Falls far short of Pryce, as he ran over 'PEN!'

[1] I-run is a town said to have been so named from something of this sort.

He reaches its brow,— He has passed it,—and now
Having once gained the summit, and managed to cross it, he
Rolls down the side with uncommon velocity;
　　But, run as he will,　Or roll down the hill,
That bugbear behind him is after him still!
And close at his heels, not at all to his liking,
The terrible clock keeps on ticking and striking,
　　Till, exhausted and sore,　He can't run any more
But falls as he reaches Miss Davis's door,
And screams when they rush out, alarm'd at his knock,
'Oh! Look at the Clock!—Do!—Look at the Clock!!'

Miss Davis look'd up, Miss Davis look'd down,
She saw nothing there to alarm her;—a frown
　　Came o'er her white forehead,　She said, 'It was horrid
A man should come knocking at that time of night,
And give her Mamma and herself such a fright;—
　　To squall and to bawl　About nothing at all!'
She begg'd 'he'd not think of repeating his call:
　　His late wife's disaster　By no means had passed her,'
She'd 'have him to know she was meant for his Master!'
Then regardless alike of his love and his woes,
She turn'd on her heel and she turn'd up her nose.

　　Poor David in vain　Implored to remain,
He 'dared not,' he said, 'cross the mountain again.'
　　Why the fair was obdurate
　　None knows,—to be sure, it
Was said she was setting her cap at the Curate;—
Be that as it may, it is certain the sole hole
Pryce found to creep into that night was the Coal-hole!
　　In that shady retreat　With nothing to eat,
And with very bruised limbs, and with very sore feet,
　　All night close he kept;　I can't say he slept;
But he sigh'd, and he sobb'd, and he groan'd, and he wept;
　　Lamenting his sins,　And his two broken shins,
Bewailing his fate with contortions and grins,
And her he once thought a complete *Rara Avis*,
Consigning to Satan,—viz., cruel Miss Davis!

Mr David has since had a 'serious call,'
He never drinks ale, wine, or spirits, at all,
And they say he is going to Exeter Hall
　　To make a grand speech,　And to preach and to teach
People that 'they can't brew their malt liquor too small'!
That an ancient Welsh Poet, one PYNDAR AP TUDOR,
Was right in proclaiming 'ARISTON MEN HUDOR!'

Which means 'The pure Element
   Is for Man's belly meant!'
And that *Gin*'s but a *Snare* of Old Nick the deluder!

And 'still on each evening when pleasure fills up,'
At the old Goat-in-Boots, with Metheglin, each cup,
   Mr Pryce, if he's there,   Will get into 'The Chair,'
And make all his quondam associates stare
By calling aloud to the Landlady's daughter,
'Patty, bring a cigar, and a glass of Spring Water!'
The dial he constantly watches; and when
The long hand's at the 'XII,' and the short at the 'X'
   He gets on his legs,   Drains his glass to the dregs,
Takes his hat and greatcoat off their several pegs,
With his President's hammer bestows his last knock,
And says solemnly—'Gentlemen!
                     LOOK AT THE CLOCK!!!'

THE GHOST

THERE stands a City,—neither large nor small,
   Its air and situation sweet and pretty;
It matters very little—if at all—
   Whether its denizens are dull or witty,
Whether the ladies there are short or tall,
   Brunettes or blondes, only, there stands a city!—
Perhaps 'tis also requisite to minute
That there's a Castle and a Cobbler in it.

A fair Cathedral, too, the story goes,
   And kings and heroes lie entomb'd within her;
There pious saints, in marble pomp repose,
   Whose shrines are worn by knees of many a Sinner;
There, too, full many an Aldermanic nose
   Roll'd its loud diapason after dinner;
And there stood high the holy sconce of Becket,
—Till four assassins came from France to crack it.

The Castle was a huge and antique mound,
   Proof against all th' artillery of the quiver,
Ere those abominable guns were found,
   To send cold lead through gallant warrior's liver.
It stands upon a gently rising ground,
   Sloping down gradually to the river,
Resembling (to compare great things with smaller)
A well-scooped, mouldy Stilton cheese,—but taller.

The keep, I find, 's been sadly alter'd lately,
 And, 'stead of mail-clad knights, of honour jealous,
In martial panoply so grand and stately,
 Its walls are filled with money-making fellows,
And stuff'd, unless I'm misinformed greatly,
 With leaden pipes, and coke, and coals, and bellows;
In short, so great a change has come to pass,
'Tis now a manufactory of Gas.

But to my tale.—Before this profanation,
 And ere its ancient glories were cut short all,
A poor hard-working Cobbler took his station
 In a small house, just opposite the portal;
His birth, his parentage, and education,
 I know but little of—a strange, odd mortal;
His aspect, air, and gait, were all ridiculous;
His name was Mason—he'd been christened Nicholas.

Nick had a wife possessed of many a charm,
 And of the Lady Huntingdon persuasion;
But, spite of all her piety, her arm
 She'd sometimes exercise when in a passion;
And, being of a temper somewhat warm,
 Would now and then seize, upon small occasion,
A stick, or stool, or anything that round did lie,
And baste her lord and master most confoundedly.

No matter!—'tis a thing that's not uncommon,
 'Tis what we all have heard, and most have read of,—
I mean, a bruising, pugilistic woman,
 Such as I own I entertain a dread of,
—And so did Nick,—whom sometimes there would come on
 A sort of fear his Spouse might knock his head off,
Demolish half his teeth, or drive a rib in,
She shone so much in 'facers' and in 'fibbing.'

'There's time and place for all things,' said a sage
 (King Solomon, I think), and this I can say,
Within a well-roped ring, or on a stage,
 Boxing may be a very pretty *Fancy*,
When Messrs Burke or Bendigo engage;
 —'Tis not so well in Susan, Jane, or Nancy:—
To get well mill'd by any one's an evil,
But by a lady—'tis the very Devil.

And so thought Nicholas, whose only trouble
 (At least his worst) was this his rib's propensity,
For sometimes from the alehouse he would hobble,
 His senses lost in a sublime immensity

Of cogitation—then he couldn't cobble—
    And then his wife would often try the density
Of his poor skull, and strike with all her might,
As fast as kitchen-wenches strike a light.

Mason, meek soul, who ever hated strife,
    Of this same striking had a morbid dread,
He hated it like poison—or his wife—
    A vast antipathy!—but so he said—
And very often, for a quiet life,
    On these occasions he'd sneak up to bed,
Grope darkling in, and, soon as at the door
He heard his lady—he'd pretend to snore.

One night, then, ever partial to society,
    Nick, with a friend (another jovial fellow),
Went to a Club—I should have said Society—
    At the City Arms, once call'd the Porto Bello;
A Spouting party, which, though some decry it, I
    Consider no bad lounge when one is mellow;
There they discuss the tax on salt, and leather,
And change of ministers and change of weather.

In short, it was a kind of British Forum,
    Like John Gale Jones's, erst in Piccadilly,
Only they managed things with more decorum,
    And the Orations were not *quite* so silly;
Far different questions, too, would come before 'em,
    Not always Politics, which, will ye nill ye,
Their London prototypes were always willing,
To give one *quantum suff.* of—for a shilling.

It more resembled one of later date,
    And tenfold talent, as I'm told in Bow Street,
Where kindlier natured souls do congregate,
    And, though there are who deem that same a low street,
Yet, I'm assured, for frolicsome debate
    And genuine humour it's surpassed by no street,
When the 'Chief Baron' enters, and assumes
To 'rule' o'er mimic 'Thesigers' and 'Broughams.'

Here they would oft forget their Ruler's faults,
    And waste in ancient lore the midnight taper,
Inquire if Orpheus first produced the Waltz,
    How Gas-lights differ from the Delphic Vapour,
Whether Hippocrates gave Glauber's Salts,
    And what the Romans wrote on ere they'd paper;—
This night the subject of their disquisitions
Was Ghosts, Hobgoblins, Sprites, and Apparitions.

One learned gentleman, a 'sage grave man,'
   Talk'd of the Ghost in Hamlet, 'sheath'd in steel';—
His well-read friend, who next to speak began,
   Said, 'That was Poetry, and nothing real';
A third, of more extensive learning, ran
   To Sir George Villiers' Ghost, and Mrs Veal;
Of Sheeted Spectres spoke with shorten'd breath,
And thrice he quoted 'Drelincourt on Death.'

Nick smoked, and smoked, and trembled as he heard
   The point discuss'd, and all they said upon it,
How, frequently, some murder'd man appear'd,
   To tell his wife and children who had done it;
Or how a Miser's ghost, with grisly beard,
   And pale lean visage, in an old Scotch bonnet,
Wander'd about to watch his buried money!
When all at once Nick heard the clock strike One,—he

Sprang from his seat, not doubting but a lecture
   Impended from his fond and faithful She;
Nor could he well to pardon him expect her,
   For he had promised to 'be home to tea';
But having luckily the key o' the back door,
   He fondly hoped that, unperceived, he
Might creep up stairs again, pretend to doze,
And hoax his spouse with music from his nose.

Vain, fruitless hope!—The wearied sentinel
   At eve may overlook the crouching foe,
Till, ere his hand can sound the alarum-bell
   He sinks beneath the unexpected blow;
Before the whispers of Grimalkin fell,
   When slumb'ring on her post, the mouse may go;—
But woman, wakeful woman, 's never weary,
—Above all, when she waits to thump her deary.

Soon Mrs Mason heard the well-known tread;
   She heard the key slow creaking in the door,
Spied, through the gloom obscure, towards the bed
   Nick creeping soft, as oft he had crept before;
When, bang, she threw a something at his head,
   And Nick at once lay prostrate on the floor;
While she exclaim'd with her indignant face on,—
'How dare you use your wife so, Mr Mason?'

Spare we to tell how fiercely she debated,
   Especially the length of her oration,—

Spare we to tell how Nick expostulated,
 Roused by the bump into a good set passion,
So great, that more than once he execrated,
 Ere he crawl'd into bed in his usual fashion;
—The Muses hate brawls; suffice it then to say,
He duck'd below the clothes—and there he lay!

'Twas now the very witching time of night,
 When churchyards groan, and graves give up their dead,
And many a mischievous, enfranchised Sprite
 Had long since burst his bonds of stone or lead,
And hurried off, with schoolboy-like delight,
 To play his pranks near some poor wretch's bed,
Sleeping perhaps serenely as a porpoise,
Nor dreaming of this fiendish Habeas Corpus.

Not so our Nicholas, his meditations
 Still to the same tremendous theme recurred,
The same dread subject of the dark narrations,
 Which, back'd with such authority, he'd heard;
Lost in his own horrific contemplations,
 He ponder'd o'er each well-remember'd word;
When at the bed's foot, close beside the post,
He verily believed he saw—a Ghost!

Plain and more plain the unsubstantial Sprite
 To his astonish'd gaze each moment grew;
Ghastly and gaunt, it rear'd its shadowy height,
 Of more than mortal seeming to the view,
And round its long, thin, bony fingers drew
 A tatter'd winding sheet, of course *all white*;—
The moon that moment peeping through a cloud,
Nick very plainly saw it *through the shroud*!

And now those matted locks, which never yet
 Had yielded to the comb's unkind divorce,
Their long-contracted amity forget,
 And spring asunder with elastic force;
Nay, e'en the very cap, of texture coarse,
 Whose ruby cincture crown'd that brow of jet,
Uprose in agony—the Gorgon's head
Was but a type of Nick's up-squatting in the bed.

From every pore distill'd a clammy dew,
 Quaked every limb,—the candle too no doubt,
En règle, would have burnt extremely blue,
 But Nick unluckily had put it out;

And he, though naturally bold and stout,
    In short, was in a most tremendous stew;—
The room was fill'd with a sulphureous smell,
But where that came from Mason could not tell.

All motionless the Spectre stood,—and now
    Its rev'rend form more clearly shone confest;
From the pale cheek a beard of purest snow
    Descended o'er its venerable breast;
The thin grey hairs, that crown'd its furrow'd brow,
    Told of years long gone by.—An awful guest
It stood, and with an action of command,
Beckon'd the Cobbler with its wan right hand.

'Whence, and what art thou, Execrable Shape?'
    Nick *might* have cried, could he have found a tongue,
But his distended jaws could only gape,
    And not a sound upon the welkin rung:
His gooseberry orbs seem'd as they would have sprung
    Forth from their sockets,—like a frightened Ape
He sat upon his haunches, bolt upright,
And shook, and grinn'd, and chatter'd with affright.

And still the shadowy finger, long and lean,
    Now beckon'd Nick, now pointed to the door;
And many an ireful glance, and frown, between,
    The angry visage of the Phantom wore,
As if quite vex'd that Nick would do no more
    Than stare, without e'en asking, 'What d'ye mean?'
Because, as we are told,—a sad old joke too,—
Ghosts, like the ladies, 'never speak till spoke to.'

Cowards, 'tis said, in certain situations,
    Derive a sort of courage from despair,
And then perform, from downright desperation,
    Much more than many a bolder man would dare.
Nick saw the Ghost was getting in a passion,
    And therefore, groping till he found the chair,
Seized on his awl, crept softly out of bed,
And follow'd quaking where the Spectre led.

And down the winding stair, with noiseless tread,
    The tenant of the tomb pass'd slowly on,
Each mazy turning of the humble shed
    Seem'd to his step at once familiar grown,
So safe and sure the labyrinth did he tread
    As though the domicile had been his own,
Though Nick himself, in passing through the shop,
Had almost broke his nose against the mop.

Despite its wooden bolt, with jarring sound,
　　The door upon its hinges open flew;
And forth the Spirit issued,—yet around
　　It turn'd as if its follower's fears it knew,
And, once more beckoning, pointed to the mound,
　　The antique Keep, on which the bright moon threw
With such effulgence her mild silvery gleam,
The visionary form seem'd melting in her beam.

Beneath a pond'rous archway's sombre shade,
　　Where once the huge portcullis swung sublime,
'Mid ivied battlements in ruin laid,
　　Sole, sad memorials of the olden time,
The Phantom held its way,—and though afraid
　　Even of the owls that sung their vesper chime,
Pale Nicholas pursued, its steps attending,
And wondering what on earth it all would end in.

Within the mouldering fabric's deep recess
　　At length they reach a court obscure and lone;—
It seem'd a drear and desolate wilderness,
　　The blacken'd walls with ivy all o'ergrown;
The night-bird shriek'd her note of wild distress,
　　Disturb'd upon her solitary throne,
As though indignant mortal step should dare,
So led, at such an hour, to venture there!

—The Apparition paused, and would have spoke,
　　Pointing to what Nick thought an iron ring,
But then a neighbouring chanticleer awoke,
　　And loudly 'gan his early matins sing;
And then 'it started like a guilty thing,'
　　As that shrill clarion the silence broke.
—We know how much dead gentlefolks eschew
The appalling sound of 'Cock-a-doodle-do!'

The vision was no more—and Nick alone—
　　'His streamers waving' in the midnight wind,
Which through the ruins ceased not to groan;
　　—His garment, too, was somewhat short behind,—
And, worst of all, he knew not where to find
　　The ring,—which made him most his fate bemoan;—
The iron ring,—no doubt of some trap door,
'Neath which the old dead Miser kept his store.

'What's to be done?' he cried, ''Twere vain to stay
　　Here in the dark without a single clue—
Oh, for a candle now, or moonlight ray!
　　'Fore George, I'm vastly puzzled what to do,'

(Then clapped his hand behind)—''Tis chilly too—
  I'll mark the spot, and come again by day.
What can I mark it by?—Oh, here's the wall—
The mortar's yielding—here I'll stick my awl!'

Then rose from earth to sky a withering shriek,
  A loud, a long protracted note of woe,
Such as when tempests roar, and timbers creak,
  And o'er the side the masts in thunder go;
While on the deck resistless billows break,
  And drag their victims to the gulfs below;—
Such was the scream when, for the want of candle,
Nick Mason drove his awl in up to the handle.

Scared by his Lady's heart-appalling cry,
  Vanished at once poor Mason's golden dream—
For dream it was;—and all his visions high,
  Of wealth and grandeur, fled before that scream—
And still he listens with averted eye,
  When gibing neighbours make 'the Ghost' their theme;
While ever from that hour they all declare
That Mrs Mason used a cushion in her chair!

THE CYNOTAPH

'Poor Tray charmant!
Poor Tray de mon Ami!'

DOG-BURY AND VERGERS.

OH! where shall I bury my poor dog Tray,
Now his fleeting breath has passed away?—
Seventeen years, I can venture to say,
Have I seen him gambol, and frolic, and play,
Evermore happy, and frisky, and gay,
As though every one of his months was May,
And the whole of his life one long holiday—
Now he's a lifeless lump of clay,
Oh! where shall I bury my faithful Tray?

I am almost tempted to think it hard
That it may not be there, in yon sunny churchyard,
  Where the green willows wave O'er the peaceful grave,
Which holds all that once was honest and brave,
Kind, and courteous, and faithful, and true;
Qualities, Tray, that were found in you.

But it may not be—yon sacred ground,
By holiest feelings fenced around,
May ne'er within its hallow'd bound
Receive the dust of a soul-less hound.

I would not place him in yonder fane,
Where the midday sun through the storied pane
Throws on the pavement a crimson stain;
Where the banners of chivalry heavily swing
O'er the pinnacled tomb of the Warrior King,
With helmet and shield, and all that sort of thing.

   No!—come what may. My gentle Tray
Shan't be an intruder on bluff Harry Tudor,
Or panoplied monarchs yet earlier and ruder,
   Whom you see on their backs, In stone or in wax,
Though the Sacristans now are 'forbidden to ax'
For what Mister Hume calls 'a scandalous tax';
While the Chartists insist they've a right to go snacks.—
No!—Tray's humble tomb would look but shabby
'Mid the sculptured shrines of that gorgeous Abbey.
   Besides, in the place They say there's no space
To bury what wet-nurses call 'a Babby.'
Even 'Rare Ben Jonson,' that famous wight,
I am told, is interr'd there bolt upright,
In just such a posture, beneath his bust,
As Tray used to sit in to beg for a crust.
   The epitaph, too, Would scarcely do;
For what could it say, but, 'Here lies Tray,
A very good kind of a dog in his day' ?
And satirical folks might be apt to imagine it
Meant as a quiz on the House of Plantagenet.

No! no!—The Abbey may do very well
For a feudal 'Nob,' or poetical 'Swell,'
'Crusaders,' or 'Poets,' or 'Knights of St John,'
Or Knights of St John's Wood, who once went on
To the Castle of Goode Lorde Eglintonne.
Count Fiddle-fumkin, and Lord Fiddle-faddle,
'Sir Craven,' 'Sir Gael,' and 'Sir Campbell of Saddell'
(Who, as poor Hook said, when he heard of the feat,
'Was somehow knock'd out of his family-seat'):
   The Esquires of the body To my Lord Tomnoddy;
   'Sir Fairlie,' 'Sir Lambe,'
   And the 'Knight of the Ram,'
The 'Knight of the Rose,' and the 'Knight of the Dragon,'
   Who, save at the flagon, And prog in the wagon,
The newspapers tell us did little 'to brag on';

And more, though the Muse knows but little concerning 'em,
'Sir Hopkins,' 'Sir Popkins,' 'Sir Gage,' and 'Sir Jerningham,'
All *Preux Chevaliers*, in friendly rivalry
Who should best bring back the glory of Chi-valry.—
—(Pray be so good, for the sake of my song,
To pronounce here the ante-penultimate long;
Or some hyper-critic will certainly cry,
'The word "Chivalry" is but a "rhyme to the eye."'
    And I own it is clear A fastidious ear
Will be, more or less, always annoy'd with you when you in-
sert any rhyme that's not perfectly genuine.
    As to pleasing the 'eye,' 'Tisn't worth while to try,
Since Moore and Tom Campbell themselves admit 'Spinach'
Is perfectly antiphonetic to 'Greenwich.')—
But stay!—I say! Let me pause while I may—
This digression is leading me sadly astray
From my object—A grave for my poor dog Tray!

I would not place him beneath thy walls,
And proud o'ershadowing dome, St Paul's!
Though I've always consider'd Sir Christopher Wren,
As an architect, one of the greatest of men;
And,—talking of Epitaphs,—much I admire his,
'*Circumspice, si Monumentum requiris*';
Which an erudite Verger translated to me,
'If you ask for his monument, *Sir-come-spy-see!*'—
    No!—I should not know where To place him there;
I would not have him by surly Johnson be;—
Or that queer-looking horse that is rolling on Ponsonby;—
    Or those ugly minxes The sister Sphynxes,
Mix'd creatures, half lady, half lioness, *ergo*,
(Denon says), the emblems of *Leo* and *Virgo*;
On one of the backs of which singular jumble,
Sir Ralph Abercrombie is going to tumble,
With a thump which alone were enough to dispatch him,
If the Scotchman in front shouldn't happen to catch him,

No! I'd not have him there,—nor nearer the door,
Where the man and the Angel have got Sir John Moore,[1]
And are quietly letting him down through the floor,
By Gillespie, the one who escaped, at Vellore,
    Alone from the row;— Neither he, nor Lord Howe
Would like to be plagued with a little Bow-wow.
    No, Tray, we must yield, And go further afield;
To lay you by Nelson were downright effront'ry;—
—We'll be off from the City, and look at the country.

[1] See note at end of 'The Cynotaph.'

It shall not be there,   In that sepulchred square,
Where folks are interr'd for the sake of the air
(Though, pay but the dues, they could hardly refuse
To Tray what they grant to Thuggs, and Hindoos,
Turks, Infidels, Heretics, Jumpers, and Jews),
    Where the tombstones are placed   In the very *best taste*
At the feet and the head   Of the elegant Dead,
And no one's received who's not 'buried in lead':
For, there lie the bones   Of Deputy Jones,
Whom the Widow's tears, and the orphan's groans
Affected as much as they do the stones
His executors laid on the Deputy's bones;
    Little rest, poor knave!   Would Tray have in his grave;
    Since Spirits, 'tis plain,   Are sent back again,
To roam round their bodies,—the bad ones in pain—
Dragging after them sometimes a heavy jack-chain;
Whenever they met, alarm'd by its groans, his
Ghost all night long would be barking at Jones's.

Nor shall he be laid   By that cross Old Maid,
Miss Penelope Bird,—of whom it is said
All the dogs in the Parish were ever afraid.
    He must not be placed   By one so strait-laced
    In her temper, her taste,   And her morals, and waist.
For, 'tis said, when she went up to Heaven, and St Peter,
    Who happened to meet her,   Came forward to greet her,
She pursed up with scorn every vinegar feature,
And bade him 'Get out for a horrid Male Creature!'
So, the Saint, after looking as if he could eat her,
Nor knowing, perhaps, very well how to treat her,
And not being willing,—or able,—to beat her,
Sent her back to her grave till her temper grew sweeter,
With an epithet—which I decline to repeat here.
    No,—if Tray were interred   By Penelope Bird,
No dog would be e'er so be-'whelp'd and be-'cur'r'd—
All the night long her cantankerous Sprite
Would be running about in the pale moonlight,
Chasing him round, and attempting to lick
The ghost of poor Tray with the ghost of a stick.

Stay!—let me see!—   Ay—here it shall be
At the root of this gnarled and time-worn tree,
    Where Tray and I   Would often lie,
And watch the bright clouds as they floated by
In the broad expanse of the clear blue sky,
When the sun was bidding the world good-bye;
And the plaintive Nightingale, warbling nigh,
Pour'd forth her mournful melody;

While the tender Wood-pigeon's cooing cry
Has made me to say to myself, with a sigh,
'How nice you would eat with a steak in a pie!'
Ay, here it shall be!—far, far from the view
Of the noisy world and its maddening crew.
   Simple and few,   Tender and true
The lines o'er his grave.—They have, some of them, too,
The advantage of being remarkably new.

EPITAPH

Affliction sore   Long time he bore,
  Physicians were in vain!—
   Grown blind, alas! he'd   Some Prussic Acid,
And that put him out of his pain!

NOTE, PAGE 22

In the autumn of 1824, Captain Medwin having hinted that certain beautiful lines on the burial of that gallant officer might have been the production of Lord Byron's Muse, the late Mr Sydney Taylor, somewhat indignantly, claimed them for their rightful owner, the late Rev. Charles Wolfe. During the controversy a third claimant started up in the person of a *soi-disant* 'Doctor Marshall,' who turned out to be a Durham blacksmith, and his pretensions a hoax. It was then that a certain 'Doctor Peppercorn' put forth *his* pretensions, to what he averred was the only 'true and original' version, viz:

Not a *sou* had he got,—not a guinea or note,
  And he look'd confoundedly flurried,
As he bolted away without paying his shot,
  And the Landlady after him hurried.

We saw him again at dead of night,
  When home from the Club returning;
We twigg'd the Doctor beneath the light
  Of the gas-lamp brilliantly burning.

All bare, and exposed to the midnight dews,
  Reclined in the gutter we found him;
And he look'd like a gentleman taking a snooze,
  With his *Marshall* cloak around him.

'The Doctor's as drunk as the d——,' we said,
  And we managed a shutter to borrow;
We raised him, and sigh'd at the thought that his head
  Would 'consumedly ache' on the morrow.

We bore him home, and we put him to bed,
  And we told his wife and his daughter
To give him, next morning, a couple of red
  Herrings, with soda-water.—

Loudly they talk'd of his money that's gone,
   And his Lady began to upbraid him;
But little he reck'd, so they let him snore on
   'Neath the counterpane just as we laid him.

We tuck'd him in, and had hardly done
   When, beneath the window calling,
We heard the rough voice of a son of a gun
   Of a watchman 'One o'clock!' bawling.

Slowly and sadly we all walk'd down
   From his room in the uppermost storey;
A rushlight we placed on the cold hearth-stone.
   And we left him alone in his glory!!

'Hos ego versiculos feci, tulit alter honores.'—VIRGIL.
'I wrote the lines—* * owned them—he told stories!'

THOMAS INGOLDSBY

LEGEND OF HAMILTON TIGHE

THE Captain is walking his quarter-deck,
With a troubled brow and a bended neck;
One eye is down through the hatchway cast,
The other turns up to the truck on the mast;
Yet none of the crew may venture to hint
'Our skipper hath gotten a sinister squint!'

The Captain again the letter hath read
Which the bum-boat woman brought out to Spithead—
Still, since the good ship sail'd away,
He reads that letter three times a day;
Yet the writing is broad and fair to see
As a Skipper may read in his degree,
And the seal is as black, and as broad, and as flat,
As his own cockade in his own cock'd hat:
He reads, and he says, as he walks to and fro,
'Curse the old woman—she bothers me so!'

He pauses now, for the topmen hail—
'On the larboard quarter a sail! a sail!'
That grim old Captain he turns him quick,
And bawls through his trumpet for Hairy-faced Dick.
'The breeze is blowing—huzza! huzza!
The breeze is blowing—away! away!
* B 185

The breeze is blowing—a race! a race!
The breeze is blowing—we near the chase!
Blood will flow, and bullets will fly,—
Oh where will be then young Hamilton Tighe?'

—'On the foeman's deck, where a man should be,
With his sword in his hand, and his foe at his knee.
Cockswain, or boatswain, or reefer may try,
But the first man on board will be Hamilton Tighe!'

Hairy-faced Dick hath a swarthy hue,
Between a gingerbread-nut and a Jew,
And his pigtail is long, and bushy, and thick,
Like a pump-handle stuck on the end of a stick.
Hairy-faced Dick understands his trade;
He stands by the breech of a long carronade,
The linstock glows in his bony hand,
Waiting that grim old Skipper's command.

'The bullets are flying—huzza! huzza!
The bullets are flying—away! away!'—
The brawny boarders mount by the chains,
And are over their buckles in blood and in brains.
On the foeman's deck, where a man should be,
    Young Hamilton Tighe   Waves his cutlass high,
And *Capitaine Crapaud* bends low at his knee.

Hairy-faced Dick, linstock in hand,
Is waiting that grim-looking Skipper's command:—
    A wink comes sly   From that sinister eye—
Hairy-faced Dick at once lets fly,
And knocks off the head of young Hamilton Tighe!

There's a lady sits lonely in bower and hall,
Her pages and handmaidens come at her call:
'Now, haste ye, my handmaidens, haste and see
How he sits there and glow'rs with his head on his knee!'
The maidens smile, and, her thought to destroy,
They bring her a little, pale, mealy-faced boy;
And the mealy-faced boy says, 'Mother dear,
Now Hamilton's dead, I've a thousand a year!'

The lady has donn'd her mantle and hood,
She is bound for shrift at St Mary's Rood:—
'Oh! the taper shall burn, and the bell shall toll,
And the mass shall be said for my stepson's soul,
And the tablet fair shall be hung on high,
Orate pro animâ Hamilton Tighe!'

Her coach and four   Draws up to the door,
With her groom, and her footman, and half a score more;
The lady steps into her coach alone,
And they hear her sigh, and they hear her groan;
They close the door, and they turn the pin,
But there's One rides with her that never stepped in!
All the way there, and all the way back,
The harness strains, and the coach-springs crack,
The horses snort, and plunge, and kick,
Till the coachman thinks he is driving Old Nick;
And the grooms and the footmen wonder, and say
'What makes the old coach so heavy to-day?'
But the mealy-faced boy peeps in, and sees
A man sitting there with his head on his knees!

'Tis ever the same,—in hall or in bower,
Wherever the place, whatever the hour,
That Lady mutters, and talks to the air,
And her eye is fix'd on an empty chair;
But the mealy-faced boy still whispers with dread,
'She talks to a man with never a head!'

There's an old Yellow Admiral living at Bath,
As grey as a badger, as thin as a lath;
And his very queer eyes have such very queer leers,
They seem to be trying to peep at his ears;
That old Yellow Admiral goes to the Rooms,
And he plays long whist, but he frets and he fumes,
For all his Knaves stand upside down,
And the Jack of Clubs does nothing but frown;
And the Kings, and the Aces, and all the best trumps
Get into the hands of the other old frumps;
While, close to his partner, a man he sees
Counting the tricks with his head on his knees.

In Ratcliffe Highway there's an old marine store,
And a great black doll hangs out of the door;
There are rusty locks, and dusty bags,
And musty phials, and fusty rags,
And a lusty old woman, call'd Thirsty Nan,
And her crusty old husband's a Hairy-faced man!

That Hairy-faced man is sallow and wan,
And his great thick pigtail is wither'd and gone;
And he cries, 'Take away that lubberly chap
That sits there and grins with his head in his lap!'
And the neighbours say, as they see him look sick,
'What a rum old covey is Hairy-faced Dick!'

That Admiral, Lady, and Hairy-faced man
May say what they please, and may do what they can;
But one thing seems remarkably clear,—
They may die to-morrow, or live till next year,—
But wherever they live, or whenever they die,
They'll never get quit of young Hamilton Tighe!

THE WITCHES' FROLIC

[Scene, the 'Snuggery' at Tappington.—Grandpapa in a high-backed
cane-bottomed elbow-chair of carved walnut-tree, dozing; his nose at an
angle of forty-five degrees—his thumbs slowly perform the rotatory motion
described by lexicographers as 'twiddling.'—The 'Hope of the family'
astride on a walking-stick, with burnt-cork moustaches, and a pheasant's tail
pinned in his cap, solaceth himself with martial music.—Roused by a strain
of surpassing dissonance, Grandpapa *loquitur*.]

COME hither, come hither, my little boy Ned!
    Come hither unto my knee—
I cannot away with that horrible din,
That sixpenny drum, and that trumpet of tin.
Oh, better to wander frank and free
Through the Fair of good Saint Bartlemy,
Than list to such awful minstrelsie.
Now lay, little Ned, those nuisances by,
And I'll rede ye a lay of Grammarye

[Grandpapa riseth, yawneth like the crater of an extinct volcano, proceedeth
slowly to the window, and apostrophizeth the Abbey in the distance.]

I love thy tower, Grey Ruin,
    I joy thy form to see,
    Though reft of all,   Cell, cloister, and hall,
Nothing is left save a tottering wall
That, awfully grand and darkly dull,
Threaten'd to fall and demolish my skull,
As, ages ago, I wander'd along
Careless thy grass-grown courts among,
In sky-blue jacket, and trousers laced,
The latter uncommonly short in the waist.

Thou art dearer to me, thou Ruin grey,
Than the Squire's veranda over the way;
    And fairer, I ween,   The ivy sheen
    That thy mouldering turret binds,
Than the Alderman's house about half a mile off,
    With the green Venetian blinds.

Full many a tale would my Grandam tell,
    In many a bygone day,
Of darksome deeds, which of old befell
    In thee, thou Ruin grey!
And I the readiest ear would lend,
    And stare like frighten'd pig!
While my Grandfather's hair would have stood up on end,
    Had he not worn a wig.

One tale I remember of mickle dread—
Now lithe and listen, my little boy Ned!

Thou mayest have read, my little boy Ned,
    Though thy mother thine idlesse blames,
In Doctor Goldsmith's history book,
    Of a gentleman called King James,
In quilted doublet, and great trunk breeches,
Who held in abhorrence Tobacco and Witches.

Well,—in King James's golden days,—
    For the days were golden then,—
They could not be less, for good Queen Bess
    Had died, aged threescore and ten,
        And her days we know, Were all of them so;
While the Court poets sung, and the Court gallants swore
That the days were as golden still as before.

Some people, 'tis true, a troublesome few,
    Who historical points would unsettle,
Have lately thrown out a sort of a doubt
    Of the genuine ring of the metal;
But who can believe to a monarch so wise
People would dare tell a parcel of lies!

—Well, then, in good King James's days,—
Golden or not does not matter a jot,—
Yon Ruin a sort of a roof had got;
For though, repairs lacking, its walls had been cracking
Since Harry the Eighth sent its people a-packing,
    Though joists, and floors, And windows, and doors
Had all disappear'd, yet pillars by scores
Remain'd, and still propp'd up a ceiling or two,
While the belfry was almost as good as new;
You are not to suppose matters look'd just so
In the Ruin some two hundred years ago.

Just in that farthermost angle, where
There are still the remains of a winding stair,
One turret especially high in air
   Uprear'd its tall gaunt form;
As if defying the power of Fate, or
The hand of 'Time the Innovator';
   And though to the pitiless storm
Its weaker brethren all around
Bowing, in ruin had strew'd the ground,
Alone it stood, while its fellows lay strew'd,
Like a four-bottle man in a company 'screw'd,'
Not firm on his legs, but by no means subdued.

One night—'twas in Sixteen hundred and six,—
I like when I can, Ned, the date to fix,—
   The month was May,   Though I can't well say
At this distance of time the particular day—
But oh! that night, that horrible night!
—Folks ever afterwards said with affright
That they never had seen such a terrible sight.

The Sun had gone down fiery red;
And if, that evening, he laid his head
In Thetis's lap beneath the seas,
He must have scalded the goddess's knees.
He left behind him a lurid track
Of blood-red light upon clouds so black,
That Warren and Hunt, with the whole of their crew,
Could scarcely have given them a darker hue.

There came a shrill and a whistling sound,
Above, beneath, beside, and around,
   Yet leaf ne'er moved on tree!
So that some people thought old Beelzebub must
Have been lock'd out of doors, and was blowing the dust
From the pipe of his street-door key.
And then a hollow moaning blast
Came, sounding more dismally still than the last,
And the lightning flash'd, and the thunder growl'd,
And louder and louder the tempest howl'd,
And the rain came down in such sheets as would stagger a
Bard for a simile short of Niagara.

     Rob Gilpin 'was a citizen';
       But, though of some 'renown,'
     Of no great 'credit' in his own,
       Or any other town.

He was a wild and roving lad,
   For ever in the alehouse boozing;
Or romping,—which is quite as bad,—
   With female friends of his own choosing.

And Rob this very day had made,
   Not dreaming such a storm was brewing,
An assignation with Miss Slade,—
   Their trysting-place that same grey Ruin.

But Gertrude Slade became afraid,
   And to keep her appointment unwilling,
When she spied the rain on her window-pane
   In drops as big as a shilling;
She put off her hat and her mantle again,—
'He'll never expect me in all this rain!'

But little he recks of the fears of the sex,
   Or that maiden false to her tryst could be,
He had stood there a good half-hour
Ere yet had commenced that perilous shower,
   Alone by the trysting-tree!

Robin looks east, Robin looks west,
But he sees not her whom he loves the best;
Robin looks up, and Robin looks down,
But no one comes from the neighbouring town.

The storm came at last,—loud roar'd the blast,
And the shades of evening fell thick and fast;
The tempest grew; and the straggling yew,
His leafy umbrella, was wet through and through;
Rob was half dead with cold and with fright,
When he spies in the Ruins a twinkling light—
A hop, two skips, and a jump, and straight
Rob stands within that postern gate.

And there were gossips sitting there,
   By one, by two, by three:
   Two were an old ill-favour'd pair;
   But the third was young, and passing fair,
With laughing eyes, and with coal-black hair;
   A daintie quean was she!
Rob would have given his ears to sip
But a single salute from her cherry lip.

As they sat in that old and haunted room,
In each one's hand was a huge birch broom,
On each one's head was a steeple-crown'd hat,
On each one's knee was a coal-black cat;
Each had a kirtle of Lincoln green—
It was, I trow, a fearsome scene.

'Now riddle me, riddle me right, Madge Gray,
What foot unhallow'd wends this way?
Goody Price, Goody Price, now areed me aright,
Who roams the old Ruins this drearysome night?'

Then up and spake that sonsie quean,
   And she spake both loud and clear:
'Oh, be it for weal, or be it for woe,
Enter friend, or enter foe,
   Rob Gilpin is welcome here!'—

'Now tread we a measure! a hall! a hall!
Now tread we a measure,' quoth she—
   The heart of Robin   Beat thick and throbbing—
'Roving Rob, tread a measure with me!'
'Ay, lassie!' quoth Rob, as her hand he gripes,
'Though Satan himself were blowing the pipes!'

Now around they go, and around, and around,
With hop-skip-and-jump, and frolicsome bound,
   Such sailing and gliding,   Such sinking and sliding,
   Such lofty curvetting,   And grand pirouetting;
Ned, you would swear that Monsieur Gilbert
And Miss Taglioni were capering there!

And oh! such awful music! ne'er
Fell sounds so uncanny on mortal ear,
There were the tones of a dying man's groans
Mix'd with the rattling of dead men's bones:
Had you heard the shrieks, and the squeals, and the squeaks,
You'd not have forgotten the sound for weeks.

And around, and around, and around they go,
Heel to heel, and toe to toe,
Prance and caper, curvet and wheel,
Toe to toe, and heel to heel.
''Tis merry, 'tis merry, Cummers, I trow,
To dance thus beneath the nightshade bough!'—

'Goody Price, Goody Price, now riddle me right,
Where may we sup this frolicsome night?'

'Mine host of the Dragon hath mutton and veal!
The Squire hath partridge, and widgeon, and teal;
But old Sir Thopas hath daintier cheer,
A pasty made of the good red deer,
A huge grouse pie, and a fine Florentine,
A fat roast goose, and a turkey and chine.'

—'Madge Gray, Madge Gray,
Now tell me, I pray,
Where's the best wassail bowl to our roundelay?'

—'There is ale in the cellars of Tappington Hall,
But the Squire [1] is a churl, and his drink is small;
   Mine host of the Dragon   Hath many a flagon
Of double ale, lamb's wool, and *eau de vie*,
   But Sir Thopas, the Vicar,   Hath costlier liquor,—
A butt of the choicest Malvoisie.
   He doth not lack   Canary or sack;
And a good pint stoup of Clary wine
Smacks merrily off with a Turkey and Chine!'

'Now away! and away! without delay,
Hey *Cockalorum*! my Broomstick gay!
We must be back ere the dawn of the day:
Hey up the chimney! away! away!'—
   Old Goody Price   Mounts in a trice,
In showing her legs she is not over nice;
   Old Goody Jones,   All skin and bones,
Follows 'like winking.'—Away go the crones,
Knees and nose in a line with the tows,
Sitting their brooms like so many Ducrows;
   Latest and last   The damsel pass'd.
One glance of her coal-black eye she cast;
She laugh'd with glee loud laughters three,
'Dost fear, Rob Gilpin, to ride with me?'—
Oh, never might man unscath'd espy
One single glance from that coal-black eye.
   —Away she flew!—   Without more ado
Rob seizes and mounts on a broomstick too,
'Hey! up the chimney, lass! Hey after you!'

---

[1] Stephen Ingoldsby, surnamed 'The Niggard,' second cousin and successor to 'The Bad Sir Giles.' (Visitation of Kent, 1666.) For an account of his murder by burglars, and their subsequent execution, *see* Dodsley's *Remarkable Trials*, etc., London, 1776, vol. ii, p. 264, also the present volume, 'The Nurse's Story.'

It's a very fine thing, on a fine day in June,
To ride through the air in a Nassau Balloon;
But you'll find very soon, if you aim at the Moon
In a carriage like that, you're a bit of a 'Spoon,'
    For the largest can't fly   Above twenty miles high,
And you're not half-way then on your journey, nor nigh;
    While no man alive   Could ever contrive,
Mr Green has declared, to get higher than five.
And the soundest Philosophers hold that, perhaps,
If you reach'd twenty miles your balloon would collapse,
    Or pass by such action   The sphere of attraction,
Getting into the track   Of some comet—Good-lack!
'Tis a thousand to one that you'd never come back;
And the boldest of mortals a danger like that must fear,
Rashly protruding beyond our own atmosphere.
    No, no; when I try   A trip to the sky,
I shan't go in that thing of yours, Mr Gye,
Though Messieurs Monk Mason, and Spencer, and Beazly,
All join in saying it travels so easily.
    No; there's nothing so good   As a pony of wood—
Not like that which, of late,   They stuck up on the gate
At the end of the Park, which caused so much debate,
And gave so much trouble to make it stand straight,—
But a regular Broomstick—you'll find that the favourite—
Above all, when, like Robin, you haven't to pay for it.
    —Stay—really I dread—   I am losing the thread
Of my tale; and it's time you should be in your bed,
So lithe now, and listen, my little boy Ned!

The Vicarage walls are lofty and thick,
And the copings are stone, and the sides are brick,
The casements are narrow, and bolted and barr'd,
And the stout oak door is heavy and hard;
Moreover, by way of additional guard,
A great big dog runs loose in the yard,
And a horse-shoe is nailed on the threshold sill,—
To keep out aught that savours of ill,—
But, alack! the chimney-pot's open still!
—That great big dog begins to quail,
Between his hind-legs he drops his tail,
Crouch'd on the ground, the terrified hound
Gives vent to a very odd sort of a sound;
It is not a bark, loud, open, and free,
As an honest old watch-dog's bark should be;
It is not a yelp, it is not a growl,
But a something between a whine and a howl;

And, hark!—a sound from the window high
Responds to the watch-dog's pitiful cry:
    It is not a moan,   It is not a groan;
It comes from a nose,—but is not what a nose
Produces in healthy and sound repose.
Yet Sir Thopas the Vicar is fast asleep,
And his respirations are heavy and deep!

He snores, 'tis true, but he snores no more
As he's aye been accustom'd to snore before,
And as men of his kidney are wont to snore
(Sir Thopas's weight is sixteen stone four),
He draws his breath like a man distress'd
By pain or grief, or like one oppress'd
By some ugly old Incubus perch'd on his breast.
    A something seems   To disturb his dreams,
And thrice on his ear, distinct and clear,
Falls a voice as of somebody whispering near
In still small accents, faint and few,
'Hey down the chimney-pot!—Hey after you!'

Throughout the Vicarage, near and far,
There is no lack of bolt or of bar;
    There are plenty of locks   To closet and box,
Yet the pantry wicket is standing ajar!
And the little low door, through which you must go,
Down some half-dozen steps, to the cellar below,
Is also unfastened, though no one may know
By so much as a guess, how it comes to be so;
    For wicket and door,   The evening before,
Were both of them lock'd, and the key safely placed
On the bunch that hangs down from the Housekeeper's waist.

Oh! 'twas a jovial sight to view
In that snug little cellar that frolicsome crew!—
    Old Goody Price   Had got something nice,
A turkey-poult larded with bacon and spice;—
    Old Goody Jones
    Would touch nought that had bones,—
She might just as well mumble a parcel of stones.
Goody Jones, in sooth, hath got never a tooth,
And a New-College pudding of marrow and plums
Is the dish of all others that suiteth her gums.

Madge Gray was picking   The breast of a chicken,
Her coal-black eye, with its glance so sly,
Was fixed on Rob Gilpin himself, sitting by
With his heart full of love, and his mouth full of pie;

Grouse pie, with hare　In the middle, is fare
Which, duly concocted with science and care,
Doctor Kitchener says, is beyond all compare;
　　And a tenderer leveret　Robin had never ate;
So, in after times, oft he was wont to asseverate.

'Now pledge we the wine-cup!—a health! a health!
Sweet are the pleasures obtain'd by stealth!
Fill up! fill up!—the brim of the cup
Is the part that aye holdeth the toothsomest sup!
Here's to thee, Goody Price!—Goody Jones, to thee!—
To thee, Roving Rob! and again to me!
Many a sip, never a slip
Come to us four 'twixt the cup and the lip!'

　　The cups pass quick,　The toasts fly thick,
Rob tries in vain out their meaning to pick,
But hears the words 'Scratch,' and 'Old Bogey,' and 'Nick.'
　　More familiar grown,　Now he stands up alone,
Volunteering to give them a toast of his own.
　　'A bumper of wine!　Fill thine!　Fill mine!
Here's a health to old Noah who planted the Vine!'
　　Oh then what sneezing,
　　　　What coughing and wheezing,
Ensued in a way that was not over pleasing!
Goody Price, Goody Jones, and the pretty Madge Gray,
All seem'd as their liquor had gone the wrong way.

But the best of the joke was, the moment he spoke
Those words which the party seem'd almost to choke,
As by mentioning Noah some spell had been broke,
Every soul in the house at that instant awoke!
And, hearing the din from barrel and bin,
Drew at once the conclusion that thieves had got in.
Up jump'd the Cook and caught hold of her spit;
Up jump'd the Groom and took bridle and bit;
Up jump'd the Gardener and shoulder'd his spade;
Up jump'd the Scullion,—the Footman,—the Maid
(The two last, by the way, occasioned some scandal,
By appearing together with only one candle,
Which gave for unpleasant surmises some handle);
Up jump'd the Swineherd,—and up jump'd the big boy,
A nondescript under him, acting as Pig-boy;
Butler, Housekeeper, Coachman—from bottom to top
Everybody jump'd up without parley or stop,
With the weapon which first in their way chanced to drop—
Whip, warming-pan, wig-block, mug, musket, and mop.

Last of all doth appear,
  With some symptoms of fear,
Sir Thopas in person to bring up the rear,
In a mix'd kind of costume half *Pontificalibus*,
Half what scholars denominate pure *Naturalibus*;
    Nay, the truth to express, As you'll easily guess,
They have none of them time to attend much to dress;
    But He, or She, As the case may be,
He or She seizes what He or She pleases,
Trunk-hosen or kirtles, and shirts or chemises,
And thus one and all, great and small, short and tall,
Muster at once in the Vicarage hall,
With upstanding locks, starting eyes, shorten'd breath,
Like the folks in the Gallery Scene in Macbeth,
When Macduff is announcing their Sovereign's death.
And hark!—what accents clear and strong,
To the listening throng came floating along!
'Tis Robin encoring himself in a song—
    'Very good song! very well sung!
    Jolly companions every one!'

On, on to the cellar! away! away!
On, on to the cellar without more delay!
The whole posse rush onwards in battle array—
Conceive the dismay of the party so gay,
Old Goody Jones, Goody Price, and Madge Gray,
When the door bursting wide, they descried the allied
Troops, prepared for the onslaught, roll in like a tide,
And the spits, and the tongs, and the pokers beside!—
'Boot and saddle's the word! mount, Cummers, and ride!'—
Alarm was ne'er caused more strong and indigenous
By cats among rats, or a hawk in a pigeon-house;
    Quick from the view Away they all flew,
With a yell, and a screech, and a hullaballoo,
'Hey up the chimney! Hey after you!'—
The Volscians themselves made an exit less speedy
From Corioli, 'flutter'd like doves' by Macready.

    They are gone,—save one, Robin alone!
Robin whose high state of civilization
Precludes all idea of aërostation,
    And who now has no notion Of more locomotion
Than suffices to kick, with much zeal and devotion,
Right and left at the party, who pounced on their victim,
And maul'd him, and kick'd him, And lick'd him, and prick'd
    him,

As they bore him away scarce aware what was done,
And believing it all but a part of the fun,
Hic—hiccoughing out the same strain he'd begun,
'Jol—jolly companions every one!'

    Morning grey   Scarce bursts into day
Ere at Tappington Hall there's the deuce to pay;
The tables and chairs are all placed in array
In the old oak-parlour, and in and out
Domestics and neighbours, a motley rout,
Are walking, and whispering, and standing about;
    And the Squire is there.   In his large arm-chair,
Leaning back with a grave magisterial air;
    In the front of a seat a   Huge volume, called Fleta,
And Bracton, a tome of an old-fashion'd look,
And Coke upon Lyttelton, then a new book;
    And he moistens his lips   With occasional sips
From a luscious sack-posset that smiles in a tankard
Close by on a side-table—not that he drank hard,
    But because at that day,   I hardly need say,
The Hong Merchants had not yet invented How Qua,
Nor as yet would you see Souchong or Bohea
At the tables of persons of any degree:
How our ancestors managed to do without tea
I must fairly confess is a mystery to me;
    Yet your Lydgates and Chaucers
    Had no cups and saucers;
Their breakfast, in fact, and the best they could get,
Was a sort of a *déjeuner à la fourchette*;
    Instead of our slops   They had cutlets and chops,
And sack-possets, and ale in stoups, tankards, and pots;
And they wound up the meal with rumpsteaks and 'schalots.

    Now the Squire lifts his hand
    With an air of command,
And gives them a sign, which they all understand,
To bring in the culprit; and straightway the carter
And huntsman drag in that unfortunate martyr,
Still kicking, and crying, 'Come,—what are you arter?'
The charge is prepared, and the evidence clear,
'He was caught in the cellar a-drinking the beer!
And came there, there's very great reason to fear,
With companions,—to say but the least of them,—queer;
    Such as Witches, and creatures
    With horrible features,
    And horrible grins,   And hook'd noses and chins,
Who'd been playing the deuce with his Reverence's bins.'

The face of his worship grows graver and graver,
As the parties detail Robin's shameful behaviour;
Mister Buzzard, the clerk, while the tale is reciting,
Sits down to reduce the affair into writing,
   With all proper diction,   And due 'legal fiction';
Viz.: 'That he, the said prisoner, as clearly was shown,
Conspiring with folks to deponents unknown,
With divers, that is to say, two thousand people,
In two thousand hats, each hat peak'd like a steeple,
   With force and with arms,
   And with sorcery and charms,
   Upon two thousand brooms;
   Enter'd four thousand rooms,
To wit, two thousand pantries, and two thousand cellars,
Put in bodily fear twenty thousand in-dwellers,
And with sundry,—that is to say, two thousand,—forks,
Drew divers,—that is to say, ten thousand—corks,
And, with malice prepense, down their two thousand throttles,
Emptied various,—that is to say, ten thousand—bottles;
All in breach of the peace,—moved by Satan's malignity—
And in spite of King James, and his Crown, and his Dignity.'

   At words so profound   Rob gazes around,
But no glance sympathetic to cheer him is found.
   —No glance, did I say? Yes, one!—Madge Gray!—
She is there in the midst of the crowd standing by,
And she gives him one glance from her coal-black eye,
One touch to his hand, and one word to his ear,—
(That's a line which I've stolen from Sir Walter, I fear,)—
   While nobody near   Seems to see her or hear;
As his worship takes up, and surveys, with a strict eye,
The broom now produced as the *corpus delicti*,
   Ere his fingers can clasp,   It is snatch'd from his grasp,
The end poked in his chest with a force makes him gasp,
And, despite the decorum so due to the *Quorum*,
His worship's upset, and so too is his iorum,
And Madge is astride on the broomstick before 'em.
'*Hocus Pocus!   Quick, Presto!* and *Hey Cockalorum!*
Mount, mount for your life, Rob!—Sir Justice, adieu!—
—Hey up the chimney-pot! hey after you!'

   Through the mystified group,
   With a halloo and a whoop,
Madge on the pommel, and Robin *en croupe*,
The pair through the air ride as if in a chair,
While the party below stand mouth open and stare!

'Clean bumbaized' and amazed, and fix'd, all the room stick,
'Oh! what's gone with Robin,—and Madge,—and the broom-
    stick?'
Ay, 'what's gone' indeed, Ned?—of what befell
Madge Gray, and the broomstick, I never heard tell:
But Robin was found, that morn, on the ground,
In yon old grey Ruin again, safe and sound,
Except that at first he complained much of thirst,
And a shocking bad headache, of all ills the worst,
    And close by his knee   A flask you might see,
But an empty one, smelling of *eau-de-vie*.

Rob from this hour is an alter'd man;
He runs home to his lodgings as fast as he can,
    Sticks to his trade,   Marries Miss Slade,
Becomes a Teetotaller—that is the same
As Teetotallers now, one in all but the name;
Grows fond of Small-beer, which is always a steady sign,
Never drinks spirits except as a medicine;
    Learns to despise   Coal-black eyes,
Minds pretty girls no more than so many Guys;
Has a family, lives to be sixty, and dies!

    Now, my little boy Ned   Brush off to your bed,
Tie your night-cap on safe, or a napkin instead,
Or these terrible nights you'll catch cold in your head;
And remember my tale, and the moral it teaches,
Which you'll find much the same as what Solomon preaches:
Don't flirt with young ladies; don't practise soft speeches;
Avoid waltzes, quadrilles, pumps, silk hose, and knee-
    breeches;—
Frequent not grey Ruins,—shun riot and revelry,
Hocus Pocus, and Conjuring, and all sorts of devilry;—
Don't meddle with broomsticks,—they're Beelzebub's switches;
Of cellars keep clear,—they're the devil's own ditches;
And beware of balls, banquetings, brandy, and—witches!
Above all! don't run after black eyes!—if you do,—
Depend on't you'll find what I say will come true,—
Old Nick, some fine morning, will 'hey after you'!

THE JACKDAW OF RHEIMS

'Tunc miser Corvus adeo conscientiae stimulis compunctus fuit, et execratio eum tantopere excarneficavit, ut exinde tabescere inciperet, maciem contraheret, omnem cibum aversaretur, nec ampliùs crocitaret : pennae praeterea ei defluebant, et alis pendulis omnes facetias intermisit, et tam macer apparuit ut omnes ejus miserescent.

'Tunc abbas sacerdotibus mandavit ut rursus furem absolverent ; quo facto, Corvus, omnibus mirantibus, propediem convaluit, et pristinam sanitatem recuperavit.' [1]   DE ILLUST. ORD. CISTERC.

THE Jackdaw sat on the Cardinal's chair!
Bishop and abbot, and prior were there;
  Many a monk, and many a friar,
  Many a knight, and many a squire,
With a great many more of lesser degree,—
In sooth a goodly company;
And they served the Lord Primate on bended knee.
  Never, I ween,   Was a prouder seen,
Read of in books, or dreamt of in dreams,
Than the Cardinal Lord Archbishop of Rheims!

  In and out   Through the motley rout
That little Jackdaw kept hopping about;
  Here and there.   Like a dog in a fair,
  Over comfits and cates,   And dishes and plates,
Cowl and cope, and rochet and pall,
Mitre and crosier! he hopp'd upon all!
  With a saucy air,   He perch'd on the chair
Where, in state, the great Lord Cardinal sat
In the great Lord Cardinal's great red hat;
  And he peer'd in the face   Of his Lordship's Grace,
With a satisfied look, as if he would say,
'We Two are the greatest folks here to-day!'
  And the priests, with awe,   As such freaks they saw,
Said, 'The Devil must be in that little Jackdaw!!'

The feast was over, the board was clear'd,
The flawns and the custards had all disappear'd,

[1] 'Then the wretched Raven was so stung by the pricks of conscience, and the curse so tortured him, that thenceforward he began to waste away, became emaciated, refused all food, and no longer croaked; his feathers too began to fall out, and with drooping wings he gave over all his saucy tricks and had such a lean look that all began to pity him.

'Then the abbot gave commands to the priests that they should absolve the thief; when this was done, the Raven, to the amazement of all, very soon got better and recovered his former health.'

And six little Singing-boys,—dear little souls!
In nice clean faces, and nice white stoles,
   Came, in order due.   Two by two,
Marching that grand refectory through!
A nice little boy held a golden ewer,
Emboss'd and fill'd with water, as pure
As any that flows between Rheims and Namur,
Which a nice little boy stood ready to catch
In a fine golden hand-basin made to match.
Two nice little boys, rather more grown,
Carried lavender-water, and eau de Cologne;
And a nice little boy had a nice cake of soap,
Worthy of washing the hands of the Pope.
   One little boy more   A napkin bore,
Of the best white diaper, fringed with pink,
And a Cardinal's Hat mark'd in 'permanent ink.'

The great Lord Cardinal turns at the sight
Of these nice little boys dress'd all in white:
   From his finger he draws   His costly turquoise:
And, not thinking at all about little Jackdaws,
   Deposits it straight   By the side of his plate,
While the nice little boys on his Eminence wait;
Till, when nobody's dreaming of any such thing,
That little Jackdaw hops off with the ring!

There's a cry and a shout,   And a deuce of a rout,
And nobody seems to know what they're about,
But the monks have their pockets all turn'd inside out;
   The friars are kneeling,   And hunting, and feeling
The carpet, the floor, and the walls, and the ceiling.
   The Cardinal drew   Off each plum-coloured shoe,
And left his red stockings exposed to the view;
He peeps, and he feels   In the toes and the heels;
They turn up the dishes,—they turn up the plates,—
They take up the poker and poke out the grates,
   —They turn up the rugs,   They examine the mugs:—
   But, no!—no such thing;—   They can't find THE RING!
And the Abbot declared that, 'when nobody twigg'd it,
Some rascal or other had popp'd in, and prigg'd it!'

The Cardinal rose with a dignified look,
He call'd for his candle, his bell, and his book!
   In holy anger, and pious grief,
He solemnly cursed that rascally thief!
He cursed him at board, he cursed him in bed;
From the sole of his foot to the crown of his head;

He cursed him in sleeping, that every night
He should dream of the devil, and wake in a fright;
He cursed him in eating, he cursed him in drinking,
He cursed him in coughing, in sneezing, in winking;
He cursed him in sitting, in standing, in lying;
He cursed him in walking, in riding, in flying,
He cursed him in living, he cursed him dying!—
Never was heard such a terrible curse!!
  But what gave rise   To no little surprise,
Nobody seem'd one penny the worse!

  The day was gone,   The night came on,
The Monks and the Friars they search'd till dawn;
  When the Sacristan saw,   On crumpled claw,
Come limping a poor little lame Jackdaw!
  No longer gay,   As on yesterday;
His feathers all seem'd to be turn'd the wrong way:—
His pinions droop'd—he could hardly stand,—
His head was as bald as the palm of your hand;
  His eye so dim,   So wasted each limb,
That, heedless of grammar, they all cried, 'THAT'S HIM!—
That's the scamp that has done this scandalous thing!
That's the thief that has got my Lord Cardinal's Ring!'
  The poor little Jackdaw,   When the monks he saw,
Feebly gave vent to the ghost of a caw;
And turn'd his bald head, as much as to say,
'Pray, be so good as to walk this way!'
  Slower and slower   He limp'd on before,
Till they came to the back of the belfry-door,
  Where the first thing they saw,
  Midst the sticks and the straw,
Was the RING, in the nest of that little Jackdaw!

Then the great Lord Cardinal call'd for his book,
And off that terrible curse he took;
  The mute expression   Served in lieu of confession,
And, being thus coupled with full restitution,
The Jackdaw got plenary absolution!
  —When those words were heard,
  That poor little bird
Was so changed in a moment, 'twas really absurd.
  He grew sleek, and fat;   In addition to that,
A fresh crop of feathers came thick as a mat!
  His tail waggled more   Even than before;
But no longer it wagg'd with an impudent air,
No longer he perch'd on the Cardinal's chair.

He hopp'd now about   With a gait devout;
At Matins, at Vespers, he never was out;
And, so far from any more pilfering deeds,
He always seem'd telling the Confessor's beads.
If any one lied,—or if any one swore,—
Or slumber'd in pray'r-time and happen'd to snore,
    That good Jackdaw   Would give a great 'Caw!'
As much as to say, 'Don't do so any more!'
While many remark'd, as his manners they saw,
That they 'never had known such a pious Jackdaw!'
    He long lived the pride   Of that country side,
And at last in the odour of sanctity died;
    When, as words were too faint   His merits to paint
The Conclave determined to make him a Saint;
And on newly-made Saints and Popes, as you know,
It's the custom, at Rome, new names to bestow,
So they canonized him by the name of Jem Crow!

A LAY OF ST DUNSTAN

'This holy childe Dunstan was borne in yᵉ yere of our Lorde ix. hondred & xxv. that tyme regnynge in this londe Kinge Athelston. * * *

'Whan it so was that Saynt Dunstan was wery of prayer than used he to werke in goldsmythes werke with his owne handes for to eschewe ydelnes.'

GOLDEN LEGEND.

St Dunstan stood in his ivied tower,
    Alembic, crucible, all were there;
When in came Nick to play him a trick,
    In guise of a damsel passing fair.
        Every one knows   How the story goes:
He took up the tongs and caught hold of his nose.
But I beg that you won't for a moment suppose
That I mean to go through, in detail, to you
A story at least as trite as it's true;
    Nor do I intend   An instant to spend
On the tale, how he treated his monarch and friend,
When, bolting away to a chamber remote,
Inconceivably bored by his Witen-gemote,
    Edwy left them all joking,   And drinking, and smoking,
So tipsily grand, they'd stand nonsense from no King,
    But sent the Archbishop   Their Sovereign to fish up,
With a hint that perchance on his crown he might feel taps,
Unless he came back straight and took off his heel-taps.

You must not be plagued with the same story twice,
And perhaps have seen this one, by W. DYCE,
At the Royal Academy, very well done,
And mark'd in the catalogue, Four, seven, one.

You might there view the Saint, who in sable array'd is,
Coercing the Monarch away from the ladies;
His right hand has hold of his Majesty's jerkin;
His left shows the door, and he seems to say, 'Sir King.
Your most faithful Commons won't hear of your shirking!
Quit your tea, and return to your Barclai and Perkyn,
Or, by Jingo,[1] ere morning, no longer alive, a
Sad victim you'll lie to your love for Elgiva!'

No farther to treat   Of his ungallant feat,
What I mean to do now is succinctly to paint
One particular fact in the life of the Saint,
Which somehow, for want of due care, I presume,
Has escaped the researches of Rapin and Hume,
In recounting a miracle, both of them men, who a
Great deal fall short of Jaques Bishop of Genoa,
An Historian who likes deeds like these to record—
See his *Aurea Legenda*, by 𝔚𝔶𝔫𝔨𝔶𝔫 𝔡𝔢 𝔚𝔬𝔯𝔡𝔢.

St Dunstan stood again in his tower,
    Alembic, crucible, all complete;
He had been standing a good half-hour,
And now he utter'd the words of power,
    And call'd to his Broomstick to bring him a seat.

The words of power!—and
    what be they
To which e'en Broomsticks
    bow and obey?
Why,—'twere uncommonly
    hard to say,
As the prelate I name has
    recorded none of them,
What they may be,   But I
    know they are three,
And ABRACADABRA, I
    take it, is one of them:
For I'm told that most Cabal-
    ists use that identical
Word, written thus in what
    they call 'a Pentacle.'

[1] St Jingo, or Gengo (Gengulphus), sometimes styled 'The Living Jingo,'
from the great tenaciousness of vitality exhibited by his severed members.
See his Legend, as recorded hereafter in the present volume.

However that be,   You'll doubtless agree
It signifies little to you or to me,
As not being dabblers in Grammarye;
Still, it must be confess'd, for a Saint to repeat
Such language aloud is scarcely discreet;
For, as Solomon hints to folks given to chatter,
'A bird of the air may carry the matter';
    And in sooth,   From my youth   I remember a truth
Insisted on much in my earlier years,
To wit, 'Little Pitchers have very long ears!'
Now, just such a 'Pitcher' as those I allude to
Was outside the door, which his 'ears' appeared glued to.

    Peter, the Lay-brother, meagre and thin,
        Five feet one in his sandal-shoon,
    While the saint thought him sleeping,
    Was listening and peeping,
        And watching his master the whole afternoon.

This Peter the Saint had pick'd out from his fellows,
To look to his fire, and to blow with the bellows,
To put on the Wall's-Ends and Lambtons whenever he
Chose to indulge in a little *orfevrerie*;
    —Of course you have read,
    That St Dunstan was bred
A Goldsmith, and never quite gave up the trade!
The Company—richest in London, 'tis said—
Acknowledge him still as their Patron and Head;
    Nor is it so long   Since a capital song
In his praise—now recorded their archives among—
Delighted the noble and dignified throng
Of their guests, who, the newspapers told the whole town,
With cheers 'pledged the wine-cup to Dunstan's renown,'
When Lord Lyndhurst, THE DUKE, and Sir Robert were dining
At the Hall some time since with the Prime Warden Twining.—
—I am sadly digressing—a fault which sometimes
One can hardly avoid in these gossiping rhymes—
A slight deviation's forgiven! but then this is
Too long, I fear, for a decent parenthesis,
So I'll rein up my Pegasus sharp, and retreat, or
You'll think I've forgotten the Lay-brother Peter,
    Whom the Saint, as I said,   Kept to turn down his bed,
    Dress his palfreys and cobs,   And do other odd jobs,—
        As reducing to writing   Whatever he might, in
The course of the day or the night, be inditing,
And cleaning the plate of his mitre with whiting;
Performing, in short, all those duties and offices
Abbots exact from Lay-brothers and Novices.

It occurs to me here   You'll perhaps think it queer
That St Dunstan should have such a personage near,
  When he'd only to say   Those words,—be what they may,—
And his Broomstick at once his commands would obey.—
  That's true—but the fact is   'Twas rarely his practice
Such aid to resort to, or such means apply,
Unless he'd some 'dignified knot' to untie,
Adopting, though sometimes, as now, he'd reverse it,
Old Horace's Maxim '*nec Broomstick intersit.*'—
—Peter, the Lay-brother, meagre and thin,
Heard all the Saint was saying within;
Peter, the Lay-brother, sallow and spare,
Peep'd through the key-hole, and—what saw he there?—
Why,—A BROOMSTICK BRINGING A RUSH-BOTTOM'D CHAIR.
What Shakespeare observes, in his play of King John,
  Is undoubtedly right,   That 'ofttimes the sight
Of means to do ill deeds will make ill deeds done.'
Here's Peter, the Lay-brother, pale-faced and meagre,
A good sort of man, only rather too eager
To listen to what other people are saying,
When he ought to be minding his business or praying,
Gets into a scrape,—and an awkward one too,—
As you'll find, if you've patience enough to go through
  The whole of the story   I'm laying before ye,—
Entirely from having 'the means' in his view
Of doing a thing which he ought not to do!

  Still rings in his ear,   Distinct and clear,
Abracadabra! that word of fear!
And the two which I never yet happen'd to hear.
  Still doth he spy,   With Fancy's eye,
The Broomstick at work, and the Saint standing by;
And he chuckles, and says to himself with glee,
'Aha! that Broomstick shall work for *me*!'

  Hark! that swell   O'er flood and o'er fell,
Mountain, and dingle, and moss-cover'd dell!
List!—'tis the sound of the Compline bell,
And St Dunstan is quitting his ivied cell;
  Peter, I wot,   Is off like a shot,
Or a little dog scalded by something that's hot,
For he hears his Master approaching the spot
Where he'd listened so long, though he knew he ought not:
Peter remember'd his Master's frown—
He trembled—he'd not have been caught for a crown;
  Howe'er you may laugh,   He had rather by half,
Have run up to the top of the tower and jump'd down.

The Compline hour is past and gone,
Evening service is over and done;
   The monks repair   To their frugal fare,
A snug little supper of something light
And digestible, ere they retire for the night.
For, in Saxon times, in respect to their cheer,
St Austin's Rule was by no means severe,
But allowed from the Beverley Roll 'twould appear,
Bread and cheese, and spring onions, and sound table beer,
And even green peas, when they were not too dear;
Not like the rule of La Trappe, whose chief merit is
Said to consist in its greater austerities;
And whose monks, if I rightly remember their laws,
   Ne'er are suffer'd to speak,   Think only in Greek,
And subsist, as the Bears do, by sucking their paws.
   Astonish'd I am   The gay Baron Geramb,
With his head sav'ring more of the Lion than Lamb,
Could e'er be persuaded to join such a set—I
Extend the remark to Signor Ambrogetti.—
For a monk of La Trappe is as thin as a rat,
While an Austin Friar was jolly and fat;
Though, of course, the fare to which I allude,
With as good table-beer as ever was brew'd,
Was all 'caviare to the multitude,'
Extending alone to the clergy, together in
Hall assembled,—and not to Lay-brethren.
St Dunstan himself sits there at his post,
   On what they say is   Called a Dais,
O'erlooking the whole of his clerical host,
And eating poached eggs with spinach and toast;
Five Lay-brothers stand behind his chair,
But where is the sixth?—Where's Peter!—Ay, WHERE?

'Tis an evening in June,   And a little half moon,
A brighter no fond lover ever set eyes on,
   Gleaming and beaming,   And dancing the stream in,
Has made her appearance above the horizon;
Just such a half moon as you see, in a play,
On the turban of Mustapha Muley Bey,
Or the fair Turk who weds with the 'Noble Lord Bateman';
—*Vide* plate in George Cruickshank's memoirs of that great man.

She shines on a turret remote and lone,
A turret with ivy and moss overgrown,
And lichens that thrive on the cold dank stone;
Such a tower as a poet of no mean calibre

I once knew and loved, poor, dear Reginald Heber,
Assigns to oblivion [1]—a den for a She bear;
   Within it are found,   Strew'd above and around,
On the hearth, on the table, the shelves, and the ground,
All sorts of instruments, all sorts of tools,
To name which, and their uses, would puzzle the Schools,
And make very wise people look very like fools;
   Pincers and hooks,   And black-letter books,
All sorts of pokers, and all sorts of tongs,
And all sorts of hammers, and all that belongs
To Goldsmith's work, chemistry, alchymy,—all,
   In short that a Sage,   In that erudite age,
Could require, was at hand, or at least within call.
In the midst of the room lies a Broomstick!—and there
A Lay-brother sits in a rush-bottom'd chair!

Abracadabra, that fearful word,
And the two which, I said, I have never yet heard,
   Are utter'd.—'Tis done!   Peter, full of his fun,
Cries, 'Broomstick! you lubberly son of a gun!
Bring ale?—bring a flagon—a hogshead—a tun!
   'Tis the same thing to you; I have nothing to do;
And, 'fore George, I'll sit here, and I'll drink till all's blue!'

No doubt you've remark'd how uncommonly quick
A Newfoundland puppy runs after a stick,
Brings it back to his master, and gives it him—Well,
   So potent the spell,
The Broomstick perceived it was vain to rebel,
So ran off like that puppy;—some cellar was near,
For in less than ten seconds 'twas back with the beer!
Peter seizes the flagon; but ere he can suck
Its contents, or enjoy what he thinks his good luck,
The Broomstick comes in with a tub in a truck;
   Continues to run   At the rate it begun,
And, *au pied de lettre*, next brings in a tun!
A fresh one succeeds, then a third, then another,
Discomfiting much the astounded Lay-brother;
Who, had he possess'd fifty pitchers or stoups,
They all had been too few: for, arranging in groups
The barrels, the Broomstick next *started the hoops*;
   The ale deluged the floor,
   But, still, through the door,
Said Broomstick kept bolting, and bringing in more.

[1] 'And cold oblivion, midst the ruin laid,
Folds her dank wing beneath the ivy shade.'
PALESTINE.

E'en Macbeth to Macduff
Would have cried 'Hold! enough!'
If half as well drench'd with such 'perilous stuff,'
And, Peter, who did not expect such a rough visit,
Cried lustily, 'Stop!—That will do, Broomstick!—*Sufficit!*'

But ah, well-a-day! The Devil, they say,
'Tis easier at all times to raise than to lay.
Again and again Peter roar'd out in vain
His Abracadabra, and t'other words twain:—
As well might one try A pack in full cry
To check, and call off from their headlong career,
By bawling out, 'Yoicks!' with one's hand at one's ear.
The longer he roar'd, and the louder and quicker,
The faster the Broomstick was bringing in liquor.

The poor Lay-Brother knew Not on earth what to do—
He caught hold of the Broomstick and snapped it in two.—
Worse and Worse!—Like a dart Each part made a start,
And he found he'd been adding more fuel to fire,
For *both* now came loaded with Meux's entire;
Combe's, Delafield's, Hanbury's, Truman's—no stopping—
Goding's, Charenton's, Whitbread's continued to drop in,
With Hodson's pale ale, from the Sun Brewhouse, Wapping,
The firms differ'd then, but I can't put a tax on
My memory to say what their names were in Saxon.
To be sure the best beer Of all did not appear;
For I've said 'twas in June, and so late in the year
The 'Trinity Audit Ale' is not come-at-able,
—As I've found to my great grief when dining at that table.

Now extremely alarm'd, Peter scream'd without ceasing,
For a flood of brown-stout he was up to his knees in,
Which, thanks to the Broomstick, continued increasing;
He fear'd he'd be drown'd,
And he yell'd till the sound
Of his voice, wing'd by terror, at last reach'd the ear
Of St Dunstan himself, who had finish'd *his* beer,
And had put off his mitre, dalmatic, and shoes,
And was just stepping into his bed for a snooze.

His Holiness paused when he heard such a clatter;
He could not conceive what on earth was the matter.
Slipping on a few things, for the sake of decorum,
He issued forthwith from his *Sanctum sanctorum*,
And calling a few of the Lay-brothers near him,
Who were not yet in bed, and who happen'd to hear him,
At once led the way Without further delay,
To the tower where he'd been in the course of the day.

Poor Peter!—alas!—though St Dunstan was quick,
There were two there before him—Grim Death, and Old Nick!—
When they open'd the door out the malt-liquor flow'd,
Just as when the great Vat burst in Tot'n'am Court Road;
The Lay-brothers nearest were up to their necks
In an instant, and swimming in strong double X;
While Peter, who, spite of himself now had drank hard,
After floating awhile, like a toast in a tankard,
   To the bottom had sunk,   And was spied by a monk,
Stone-dead, like poor Clarence, half drown'd and half drunk.
In vain did St Dunstan exclaim, '*Vade retro
Strongbeerum!—discede a Lay-fratre Petro!*'—
   Queer Latin, you'll say,   That prefix of '*Lay*,'
And *Strongbeerum!*—I own they'd have call'd me a blockhead if
At school I had ventured to use such a Vocative;
'Tis a barbarous word, and to me it's a query
If you'll find it in Patrick, Morell, or Moreri;
But, the fact is, the Saint was uncommonly flurried,
And apt to be loose in his Latin when hurried;
The Brown-stout, however, obeys to the letter,
Quite as well as if talk'd to, in Latin much better,
   By a grave Cambridge Johnian,   Or graver Oxonian
Whose language, we all know, is quite Ciceronian.
It retires from the corpse, which is left high and dry;
But, in vain do they snuff and hot towels apply,
And other means used by the faculty try.
   When once a man's dead   There's no more to be said;
Peter's 'Beer with an *e*' was his 'Bier with an *i*!!'

Moral

By way of a moral, permit me to pop in
The following maxims:—Beware of eaves-dropping!—
Don't make use of language that isn't well scann'd!—
Don't meddle with matters you don't understand!—
Above all, what I'd wish to impress on both sexes
Is,—Keep clear of Broomsticks, Old Nick, and three XXXs.

L'Envoye

In Goldsmiths' Hall there's a handsome glass case,
And in it a stone figure, found on the place,
When, thinking the old Hall no longer a pleasant one,
They pull'd it all down, and erected the present one.
If you look, you'll perceive that this stone figure twists
A thing like a broomstick in one of its fists.
It's so injured by time, you can't make out a feature;
But it is not St Dunstan,—so doubtless it's Peter.

Gengulphus, or, as he is usually styled in this country, 'Jingo,' was perhaps more in the mouths of the 'general' than any other saint, on occasions of adjuration (see note, page 45). Mr Simpkinson from Bath had kindly transmitted me a portion of a primitive ballad, which has escaped the researches of Ritson and Ellis, but is yet replete with beauties of no common order. I am happy to say that, since these Legends first appeared, I have recovered the whole of it.—*Vide infra.*

> 'A Franklyn's dogge leped ober a style,
> And hys name was littel Byngo
> B wyth a Y—Y wyth an N,—
> N wyth a G—G wyth an O,—
> They call'd hym littel Byngo!
>
> Thys Franklyn, Syrs, he brewed goode ayle,
> And he called it Rare goode Styngo!
> S, T, Y, N, G, O!
> He call'd it Rare goode Styngo!
>
> Nowe is notte thys a prettie song?
> I thinke it is bye Jyngo!
> I wythe a Y—N, G, O—
> I sweare yt is, by Jyngo!'

A LAY OF ST GENGULPHUS

'Non multò post, Gengulphus, in domo suâ dormiens, occisus est à quodam clerico qui cum uxore suâ adulterare solebat. Cujus corpus dum, in fereto, in sepulturam portaretur, multi infirmi de tactu sanati sunt.

'Cum hoc illius uxori referretur ab ancillâ sua, scilicet dominum suum, quam martyrem sanctum, miracula facere, irridens illa, et subsurrans, ait, "Ita Gengulphus miracula facitat ut pulvinarium meum cantat,"' etc.[1]

WOLFII MEMORAB.

GENGULPHUS comes from the Holy Land,
    With his scrip, and his bottle, and sandal shoon,
Full many a day hath he been away,
    Yet his lady deems him return'd full soon.

[1] 'Not long afterwards Gengulphus, while sleeping in his house, was murdered by a clerk who was wont to commit adultery with his wife. While his body was being borne on a bier to sepulture, many sick were cured by touching it.

'When this was reported to his wife by her maid, namely that her husband was working miracles like a holy martyr, she scoffingly said in an undertone: "Gengulphus is as likely to work miracles as my couch is to sing."'

Full many a day hath he been away,
   Yet scarce had he crossed ayont the sea,
Ere a spruce young spark of a Learned Clerk
   Had called on his Lady, and stopp'd to tea.

This spruce young guest, so trimly drest,
   Stay'd with that Lady, her revels to crown;
They laugh'd, and they ate and they drank of the best,
   And they turn'd the old castle quite upside down.

They would walk in the park, that spruce young Clerk,
   With that frolicsome Lady so frank and free,
Trying balls and plays, and all manner of ways,
   To get rid of what French people called Ennui.

Now the festive board with viands is stored,
   Savoury dishes be there, I ween,
Rich puddings and big, and a barbecued pig,
   And oxtail soup in a China tureen.

There's a flagon of ale as large as a pail—
   When, cockle on hat, and staff in hand,
While on nought they are thinking save eating and drinking,
   Gengulphus walks in from the Holy Land!

'You must be pretty deep to catch weasels asleep,'
   Says the proverb: that is 'take the Fair unawares';
A maid o'er the banisters chancing to peep,
   Whispers, 'Ma'am, here's Gengulphus a-coming upstairs.'

Pig, pudding, and soup, the electrified group,
   With the flagon, pop under the sofa in haste,
And contrive to deposit the Clerk in the closet,
   As the dish least of all to Gengulphus's taste.

Then oh! what rapture, what joy was exprest,
   When 'poor dear Gengulphus' at last appear'd!
She kiss'd and she press'd 'the dear man' to her breast,
   In spite of his great, long, frizzly beard.

Such hugging and squeezing! 'twas almost unpleasing,
   A smile on her lip, and a tear in her eye;
She was so very glad, that she seem'd half mad,
   And did not know whether to laugh or to cry.

Then she calls up the maid and the table-cloth's laid,
   And she sends for a pint of the best Brown Stout;
On the fire, too, she pops some nice mutton-chops,
   And she mixes a stiff glass of 'Cold Without.'

Then again she began at the 'poor dear' man;
    She press'd him to drink, and she press'd him to eat,
And she brought a foot-pan, with hot water and bran,
    To comfort his 'poor dear' travel-worn feet.

'Nor night nor day since he'd been away,
    Had she had any rest,' she 'vow'd and declared.'
She 'never could eat one morsel of meat,
    For thinking how "poor dear" Gengulphus fared.'

She 'really did think she had not slept a wink
    Since he left her, although he'd been absent so long';
He here shook his head,—right little he said,
    But he thought she was 'coming it rather too strong.'

Now his palate she tickles with the chops and the pickles,
    Till, so great the effect of that stiff gin grog,
His weaken'd body, subdued by the toddy,
    Falls out of his chair, and he lies like a log.

Then out comes the Clerk from his secret lair;
    He lifts up the legs, and she lifts up the head,
And, between them, this most reprehensible pair
    Undress poor Gengulphus and put him to bed.

Then the bolster they place athwart his face,
    And his night-cap into his mouth they cram;
And she pinches his nose underneath the clothes,
    Till the 'poor dear soul' goes off like a lamb.

And now they tried the deed to hide;
    For a little bird whisper'd, 'Perchance you may swing;
Here's a corpse in the case with a sad swell'd face,
    And a Medical Crowner's a queer sort of thing!'

So the Clerk and his wife, they each took a knife,
    And the nippers that nipp'd the loaf-sugar for tea;
With the edges and points they sever'd the joints
    At the clavicle, elbow, hip, ankle, and knee.

Thus, limb from limb, they dismember'd him
    So entirely, that e'en when they came to his wrists,
With those great sugar-nippers they nipped off his 'flippers,'
    As the Clerk, very flippantly, termed his fists.

When they'd cut off his head, entertaining a dread
  Lest folks should remember Gengulphus's face,
They determined to throw it where no one could know it,
  Down the well,—and the limbs in some different place.

But first the long beard from the chin they shear'd,
  And managed to stuff that sanctified hair,
With a good deal of pushing, all into the cushion
  That filled up the seat of a large arm-chair.

They contriv'd to pack up the trunk in a sack,
  Which they hid in an osier-bed outside the town,
The Clerk bearing arms, legs and all on his back,
  As that vile Mr Greenacre served Mrs Brown.

But to see now how strangely things sometimes turn out,
  And that in a manner the least expected!
Who could surmise a man ever could rise
  Who'd been thus carbonado'd, cut up, and dissected?

No doubt 'twould surprise the pupils at Guy's;
  I am no unbeliever—no man can say that o' me—
But St Thomas himself would scarce trust his own eyes
  If he saw such a thing in his School of Anatomy.

You may deal as you please with Hindoos and Chinese,
  Or a Mussulman making his heathen salaam, or
A Jew or a Turk; but it's other guess work
  When a man has to do with a Pilgrim or Palmer.

By chance the Prince Bishop, a Royal Divine,
  Sends his cards round the neighbourhood next day, and urges his
Wish to receive a snug party to dine,
  Of the resident clergy, the gentry, and burgesses.

At a quarter past five they are all alive,
  At the palace, for coaches are fast rolling in;
And to every guest his card had express'd
  'Half past' as the hour for 'a greasy chin.'

Some thirty are seated, and handsomely treated
  With the choicest Rhine wines in his Highness's stock;
When a Count of the Empire, who felt himself heated,
  Requested some water to mix with his Hock.

The Butler, who saw it, sent a maid out to draw it,
    But scarce had she given the windlass a twirl,
Ere Gengulphus's head, from the well's bottom, said
    In mild accents, 'Do help us out, that's a good girl!'

Only fancy her dread when she saw a great head
    In her bucket;—with fright she was ready to drop:—
Conceive, if you can, how she roar'd and she ran,
    With the head rolling after her, bawling out 'Stop!'

She ran and she roar'd, till she came to the board
    Where the Prince Bishop sat with his party around,
When Gengulphus's poll, which continued to roll
    At her heels, on the table bounced up with a bound.

Never touching the cates, or the dishes or plates,
    The decanters or glasses, the sweetmeats or fruits,
The head smiles, and begs them to bring him his legs,
    As a well-spoken gentleman asks for his boots.

Kicking open the casement, to each one's amazement,
    Straight a right leg steps in, all impediment scorns,
And near the head stopping, a left follows hopping
    Behind,—for the left leg was troubled with corns.

Next, before the beholders, two great brawny shoulders,
    And arms on their bent elbows dance through the throng,
While two hands assist, though nipp'd off at the wrist,
    The said shoulders in bearing a body along.

They march up to the head, not one syllable said,
    For the thirty guests all stare in wonder and doubt,
As the limbs in their sight arrange and unite,
    Till Gengulphus, though dead, looks as sound as a trout.

I will venture to say, from that hour to this day,
    Ne'er did such an assembly behold such a scene;
Or a table divide fifteen guests of a side
    With a dead body placed in the centre between.

Yes, they stared—well they might, at so novel a sight:
    No one utter'd a whisper, a sneeze, or a hem,
But sat all bolt upright, and pale with affright;
    And they gazed at the dead man, the dead man at them.

The Prince Bishop's Jester, on punning intent,
　　As he view'd the whole thirty, in jocular terms
Said, 'They put him in mind of a Council of *Trente*
　　Engaged in reviewing the Diet of Worms.'

But what should they do?—Oh! nobody knew
　　What was best to be done, either stranger or resident;
The Chancellor's self read his Puffendorf through
　　In vain, for his books could not furnish a precedent.

The Prince Bishop mutter'd a curse, and a prayer,
　　Which his double capacity hit to a nicety:
His Princely, or Lay, half induced him to swear,
　　His Episcopal moiety said '*Benedicite!*'

The Coroner sat on the body that night,
　　And the jury agreed,—not a doubt could they harbour,—
'That the chin of the corpse—the sole thing brought to light—
　　Had been recently shaved by a very bad barber.'

They sent out Von Taünsend, Von Bürnie, Von Roe,
　　Von Maine, and Von Rowantz—through châlets and châteaux,
Towns, villages, hamlets, they told them to go,
　　And they stuck up placards on the walls of the Stadthaus.

'MURDER!!

'WHEREAS, a dead gentleman, surname unknown,
　　Has been recently found at his Highness's banquet,
Rather shabbily dressed in an Amice, or gown
　　In appearance resembling a second-hand blanket;

'AND WHEREAS, there's great reason indeed to suspect
　　That some ill-disposed person, or persons, with malice
Aforethought, have kill'd, and begun to dissect
　　The said Gentleman, not very far from the palace;

'THIS IS TO GIVE NOTICE!—Whoever shall seize,
　　And such person or persons, to justice surrender,
Shall receive—such REWARD—as his Highness shall please,
　　On conviction of him, the aforesaid offender.

'And, in order the matter more clearly to trace
　　To the bottom, his Highness, the Prince Bishop, further,
Of his clemency, offers free PARDON and Grace
　　To all such as have *not* been concern'd in the murther.
　　* C 185

'Done this day, at our palace,—July twenty-five,—
  By Command,
            (Signed)
                    Johann Von Rüssell,

                                                      N.B.

Deceased rather in years—had a squint when alive:
  And smells slightly of gin—linen mark'd with a "G."'

The Newspapers, too, made no little ado,
  Though a different version each managed to dish up;
Some said 'The Prince Bishop had run a man through,'
  Others said 'an assassin had kill'd the Prince Bishop.'

The *Ghent Herald* fell foul of the *Bruxelles Gazette*,
  The *Bruxelles Gazette* with much sneering ironical,
Scorned to remain in the *Ghent Herald*'s debt,
  And the *Amsterdam Times* quizz'd the *Nuremberg Chronicle*.

In one thing, indeed, all the journals agreed,
  Spite of 'politics,' 'bias,' or 'party collision';
Viz.: to 'give,' when they'd 'further accounts' of the deed,
  'Full particulars' soon, in 'a later Edition.'

But now, while on all sides they rode and they ran,
  Trying all sorts of means to discover the caitiffs,
Losing patience, the holy Gengulphus began
  To think it high time to 'astonish the natives.'

First, a Rittmeister's Frau, who was weak in both eyes,
  And supposed the most short-sighted woman in Holland,
Found greater relief, to her joy and surprise,
  From one glimpse of his 'squint' than from glasses by Dollond.

By the slightest approach to the tip of his Nose,
  Megrims, headache, and vapours were put to the rout;
And one single touch of his precious Great Toes
  Was a certain specific of chilblains and gout.

Rheumatics,—sciatica,—tic-douloureux!
  Apply to his shin-bones—not one of them lingers;—
All bilious complaints in an instant withdrew,
  If the patient was tickled with one of his fingers.

Much virtue was found to reside in his thumbs;
  When applied to the chest, they cured scantness of breathing,
Sea-sickness, and colic; or rubb'd on the gums,
  Were 'A blessing to Mothers,' for infants in teething.

Whoever saluted the nape of his neck,
　Where the mark remain'd visible still of the knife,
Notwithstanding east winds perspiration might check,
　Was safe from sore throat for the rest of his life.

Thus, while each acute and each chronic complaint
　Giving way, proved an influence clearly divine,
They perceived the dead Gentleman must be a Saint,
　So they lock'd him up, body and bones, in a shrine.

Through country and town his new Saintship's renown
　As a first-rate physician kept daily increasing,
Till, as Alderman Curtis told Alderman Brown,
　It seem'd as if 'Wonders had never *done ceasing*.'

The Three Kings of Cologne began, it was known,
　A sad falling off in their off'rings to find,
His feats were so many—still the greatest of any,—
　In every sense of the word, was—behind;

For the German Police were beginning to cease
　From exertions which each day more fruitless appear'd,
When Gengulphus himself, his fame still to increase,
　Unravell'd the whole by the help of—his beard!

If you look back you'll see the aforesaid *barbe gris*,
　When divorced from the chin of its murder'd proprietor,
Had been stuff'd in the seat of a kind of settee,
　Or double-arm'd chair, to keep the thing quieter

It may seem rather strange, that it did not arrange
　Itself in its place when the limbs join'd together;
P'rhaps it could not get out, for the cushion was stout,
　And constructed of good, strong, maroon-colour'd leather

Or, what is more likely, Gengulphus might choose,
　For Saints, e'en when dead, still retain their volition,
It should rest there, to aid some particular views,
　Produced by his very peculiar position.

Be that as it may, on the very first day
　That the widow Gengulphus sat down on that settee,
What occurr'd almost frighten'd her senses away,
　Beside scaring her hand-maidens, Gertrude and Betty.

They were telling their mistress the wonderful deeds
    Of the new Saint, to whom all the Town said their orisons:
And especially how as regards invalids,
    His miraculous cures far outrivall'd Von Morison's.

'The cripples,' said they, 'fling their crutches away,
    And people born blind now can easily see us!'—
But she (we presume, a disciple of Hume)
    Shook her head, and said angrily, '*Credat Judaeus!*

'Those rascally liars, the Monks and the Friars,
    To bring grist to their mill, these devices have hit on.—
He works miracles!—pooh!—I'd believe it of you
    Just as soon, you great Geese,—or the Chair that I sit on!'

The Chair!—at that word—it seems really absurd,
    But the truth must be told,—what contortions and grins
Distorted her face!—She sprang up from her place
    Just as though she'd been sitting on needles and pins!

For, as if the Saint's beard the rash challenge had heard
    Which she utter'd, of what was beneath her forgetful,
Each particular hair stood on end in the chair,
    Like a porcupine's quills when the animal's fretful.

That stout maroon leather, they pierced altogether,
    Like tenter-hooks holding when clench'd from within,
And the maids cried 'Good gracious! how very tenacious!'
    —They as well might endeavour to pull off her skin!—

She shriek'd with the pain, but all efforts were vain;
    In vain did they strain every sinew and muscle,—
The cushion stuck fast!—From that hour to her last
    She could never get rid of that comfortless 'Bustle'!

And e'en as Macbeth, when devising the death
    Of his King, heard 'the very stones prate of his whereabouts';
So this shocking bad wife heard a voice all her life
    Crying 'Murder!' resound from the cushion,—or thereabouts.

With regard to the Clerk, we are left in the dark
    As to what his fate was; but I cannot imagine he
Got off scot-free, though unnoticed it be
    Both by Ribadaneira and Jacques de Voragine:

For cut-throats, we're sure, can be never secure,
    And 'History's Muse' still to prove it her pen holds,
As you'll see, if you look in a rather scarce book,
    God's Revenge against Murder, by one Mr Reynolds.

MORAL

Now, you grave married Pilgrims, who wander away,
    Like Ulysses of old [1] (*vide* Homer and Naso),
Don't lengthen your stay to three years and a day,
    And when you *are* coming home, just write and say so!

And you, learned Clerks, who're *not* given to roam,
    Stick close to your books, nor lose sight of decorum;
Don't visit a house when the Master's from home!
    Shun drinking,—and study the *Vitae Sanctorum*!

Above all, you gay ladies, who fancy neglect
    In your spouses, allow not your patience to fail;
But remember Gengulphus's wife!—and reflect
    On the moral enforced by her terrible tale!

THE LAY OF ST ODILLE

ODILLE was a maid of a dignified race;
Her father, Count Otto, was lord of Alsace;
    Such an air, such a grace,   Such a form, such a face,
All agreed, 'twere a fruitless endeavour to trace
In the Court, or within fifty miles of the place.
Many ladies in Strasburg were beautiful, still
They were beat all to sticks by the lovely Odille.

But Odille was devout, and, before she was nine,
Had 'experienced a call' she consider'd divine,
To put on the veil at St Ermengarde's shrine.—
Lords, Dukes, and Electors, and Counts Palatine
Came to seek her in marriage from both sides the Rhine;
    But vain their design,   They are all left to pine,
Their oglings and smiles are all useless; in fine,
Not one of these gentlefolks, try as they will,
Can draw 'Ask my papa' from the cruel Odille.

At length one of her suitors, a certain Count Herman,
A highly respectable man as a German,

---

[1] 'Qui mores hominum multorum vidit et urbes' ('Who saw the manners and cities of many men').

Who smoked like a chimney, and drank like a Merman,
Paid his court to her father, conceiving his firman
    Would soon make her bend,   And induce her to lend
An ear to a love-tale in lieu of a sermon.
He gain'd the old Count, who said, 'Come, Mynheer, fill!—
Here's luck to yourself and my daughter Odille!'

The Lady Odille was quite nervous with fear,
When a little bird whisper'd that toast in her ear;
    She murmur'd 'O, dear! My Papa has got queer,
I am sadly afraid, with that nasty strong beer!
He's so very austere, and severe, that it's clear,
If he gets in his "tantrums," I can't remain here;
But St Ermengarde's convent is luckily near;
    It were folly to stay   *Pour prendre congé,*
I shall put on my bonnet, and e'en run away!'
—She unlock'd the back door and descended the hill,
On whose crest stood the towers of the sire of Odille.

—When he found she'd levanted, the Count of Alsace
At first turn'd remarkably red in the face;
He anathematized, with much unction and grace,
Every soul who came near, and consign'd the whole race
Of runaway girls to a very warm place;
    With a frightful grimace He gave orders for chase;
His vassals set off at a deuce of a pace,
And of all whom they met, high or low, Jack or Jill,
Ask'd, 'Pray have you seen anything of Lady Odille?'

Now I think I've been told,—for I'm no sporting man,—
That the 'Knowing ones' call this by far the best plan,
'Take the lead and then keep it!'—that is, if you can.—
Odille thought so too, so she set off and ran,
    Put her best leg before,   Starting at score,
As I said some lines since, from that little back door,
And not being miss'd until half after four,
    Had what hunters call 'law' for a good hour and more;
Like 'young Lochinvar who came out of the West.'
''Tis done!—I am gone!—over briar, brook, and rill!
They'll be sharp lads who catch me!' said young Miss Odille.

But you've all read in Aesop, or Phaedrus, or Gay,
How a tortoise and hare ran together one day;
    How the hare, making play,
    'Progress'd right slick away,'

As 'them tarnation chaps' the Americans say;
While the tortoise, whose figure is rather *outré*
For racing, crawl'd straight on, without let or stay,
Having no post-horse duty or turnpikes to pay,
 Till, ere noon's ruddy ray
 Changed to eve's sober grey,
Though her form and obesity caused some delay,
Perseverance and patience brought up her leeway,
And she chased her fleet-footed 'praycursor' until
She o'ertook her at last;—so it fared with Odille!

For although, as I said, she ran gaily at first,
And show'd no inclination to pause, if she durst;
She at length felt oppressed with the heat and with thirst,
Its usual attendant; nor was that the worst,
Her shoes went down at heel; at last one of them burst.
 Now a gentleman smiles At a trot of ten miles;
But not so the Fair; then consider the stiles,
And as then ladies seldom wore things with a frill
Round the ankle, these stiles sadly bother'd Odille.

Still, despite all the obstacles placed in her track,
She kept steadily on, though the terrible crack
In her shoe made of course her progression more slack,
Till she reach'd the Swartz Forest (in English the Black);
 I cannot divine How the boundary line
Was pass'd which is somewhere there form'd by the Rhine—
 Perhaps she'd the knack To float o'er on her back—
Or, perhaps, cross'd the old bridge of boats at Brisach
(Which Vauban, some years after, secured from attack
By a bastion of stone which the Germans call 'Wacke').
All I know is, she took not so much as a snack,
Till, hungry and worn, feeling wretchedly ill,
On a mountain's brow sank down the weary Odille.

I said on its 'brow,' but I should have said 'crown,'
For 'twas quite on the summit, bleak, barren, and brown,
And so high that 'twas frightful indeed to look down
Upon Friburg, a place of some little renown,
That lay at its foot; but imagine the frown
That contracted her brow, when full many a clown
She perceived coming up from that horrid post-town.
 They had follow'd her trail,
 And now thought without fail,
As little boys say, to 'lay salt on her tail';
While the Count, who knew no other law but his will,
Swore that Herman that evening should marry Odille.

Alas, for Odille! poor dear! what could she do?
Her father's retainers now had her in view,
As she found from their raising a joyous halloo;
While the Count, riding on at the head of his crew,
In their snuff-colour'd doublets and breeches of blue,
Was huzzaing and urging them on to pursue.—
   What, indeed, *could* she do? She very well knew
If they caught her how much she should have to go through;
But then—she'd so shocking a hole in her shoe!
And to go further on was impossible;—true,
She might jump o'er the precipice;—still there are few
In her place, who could manage their courage to screw
Up to bidding the world such a sudden adieu:—
Alack! how she envied the birds as they flew;
No Nassau balloon, with its wicker canoe,
Came to bear her from him she loath'd worse than a Jew;
So she fell on her knees in a terrible stew,
   Crying 'Holy St Ermengarde!
Oh, from these vermin guard
Her whose last hope rests entirely on you;—
Don't let papa catch me, dear Saint!—rather kill
At once, *sur-le-champ*, your devoted Odille!'

It's delightful to see those who strive to oppress
Get baulk'd when they think themselves sure of success.
The Saint came to the rescue!—I fairly confess
I don't see, as a Saint, how she well could do less
Than to get such a votary out of her mess.
Odille had scarce closed her pathetic address,
When the rock, gaping wide as the Thames at Sheerness,
Closed again, and secured her within its recess,
   In a natural grotto, Which puzzled Count Otto,
Who could not conceive where the deuce she had got to.
'Twas her voice!—but 'twas *Vox et praeterea Nil!*
Nor could anyone guess what was gone with Odille!

Then burst from the mountain a splendour that quite
Eclipsed, in its brilliance, the finest Bude light,
And there stood St Ermengarde, dressed all in white,
A palm-branch in her left hand, her beads in her right;
While, with faces fresh gilt, and with wings burnish'd bright,
A great many little boys' heads took their flight
Above and around to a very great height,
   And seem'd pretty lively considering their plight,
Since everyone saw, With amazement and awe,
They could never sit down, for they hadn't *de quoi*.—

All at the sight,   From the knave to the knight,
Felt a very unpleasant sensation, call'd fright;
    While the Saint, looking down,
    With a terrible frown,
Said, 'My Lords, you are done most remarkably brown!—
I am really ashamed of you both;—my nerves thrill
At your scandalous conduct to poor, dear Odille!

'Come, make yourselves scarce!—it is useless to say,
You will gain nothing here by a longer delay.
"Quick! Presto! Begone!" as the conjurors say;
For as to the Lady, I've stow'd her away
In this hill, in a stratum of London blue clay;
And I shan't, I assure you, restore her to-day
Till you faithfully promise no more to say "Nay,"
But declare, "If she will be a nun, why, she may."
For this you've my word, and I never yet broke it,
So put that in your pipe, my Lord Otto, and smoke it!—
One hint to your vassals,—a month at the "Mill"
Shall be nuts to what they'll get who worry Odille!'

The Saint disappear'd as she ended, and so
Did the little boys' heads, which, above and below,
As I told you a very few stanzas ago,
Had been flying about her, and jumping Jem Crow;
Though, without any body, or leg, foot, or toe,
How they managed such antics, I really don't know;
Be that as it may, they all 'melted like snow
Off a dyke,' as the Scotch say in sweet Edinbro'.
    And there stood the Count,
    With his men on the mount,
Just like 'twenty-four jackasses all on a row.'
What was best to be done—'twas a sad bitter pill—
But gulp it he must, or else lose his Odille.

The lord of Alsace therefore alter'd his plan,
And said to himself, like a sensible man,
'I can't do as I would,—I must do as I can;
It will not do to lie under any Saint's ban,
For your hide, when you do, they all manage to tan;
So Count Herman must pick up some Betsy or Nan,
Instead of my girl,—some Sue, Polly, or Fan;—
If he can't get the corn he must do with the bran,
And make shift with the pot if he can't have the pan.'

With such proverbs as these
   He went down on his knees,
And said, 'Blessed St Ermengarde, just as you please—
They shall build a new convent,—I'll pay the whole bill
(Taking discount), its Abbess shall be my Odille!'

There are some of my readers, I'll venture to say,
Who have never seen Friburg, though some of them may,
And others, 'tis likely may go there some day.
Now, if ever you happen to travel that way,
I do beg and pray, 'twill your pains well repay,—
That you'll take what the Cockney folk call a 'poshay'
(Though in Germany these things are more like a dray),
You may reach this same hill with a single relay,—
   And do look how the rock,
   Through the whole of its block,
Is split open, as though by some violent shock
From an earthquake, or lightning, or horrid hard knock
From the club-bearing fist of some jolly old cock
Of a germanized giant, Thor, Woden, or Lok:
   And see how it rears   Its two monstrous great ears,
For when once you're between them such each side appears;
And list to the sound of the water one hears
Drip, drip, from the fissures, like rain-drops or tears,
—Odille's, I believe,—which have flowed all these years;
—I think they account for them so;—but the rill
I am sure is connected some way with Odille.

MORAL

Now then, for a moral, which always arrives
At the end, like the honey bees take to their hives,
And the more one observes it the better one thrives,—
We have all heard it said in the course of our lives,
'Needs must when a certain old gentleman drives';
'Tis the same with a lady,—if once she contrives
To get hold of the ribands, how vainly one strives
To escape from her lash, or to shake off her gyves!
Then let's act like Count Otto, and while one survives,
Succumb to *our* She-Saints—videlicet wives!
   (*Aside.*)
That is if one has not a 'good bunch of fives.'—
(I can't think how that last line escaped from my quill.
For I am sure it has nothing to do with Odille.)
   Now, young ladies, to you!—
   Don't put on the shrew!

And don't be surprised if your father looks blue
When you're pert, and won't act as he wants you to do!
Be sure that you never elope;—there are few,—
Believe me, you'll find what I say to be true,—
Who run restive, but find as they bake they must brew,
And come off at last with 'a hole in their shoe';
Since not even Clapham, that sanctified ville,
Can produce enough saints to save *every* Odille.

A LAY OF ST NICHOLAS

'Statim sacerdoti apparuit diabolus in specie puellae pulchritudinis mirae, et ecce Divus, fide catholicâ, et cruce, et aquâ benedicta armatus venit, et aspersit aquam in nomine Sanctae et Individuae Trinitatis, quam, quasi ardentem, diabolus, nequaquam sustinere valens, mugitibus fugit.' [1]   ROGER HOVEDEN.

'LORD ABBOT! Lord Abbot! I'd fain confess;
    I am a-weary, and worn with woe;
Many a grief doth my heart oppress,
    And haunt me withersoever I go!'

On bended knee spake the beautiful Maid;
    'Now lithe and listen, Lord Abbot, to me!'—
'Now naye, Fair Daughter,' the Lord Abbot said,
    'Now naye, in sooth it may hardly be;

'There is Mess Michael, and holy Mess John,
    Sage Penitauncers I ween be they!
And hard by doth dwell, in St Catherine's cell,
    Ambrose, the anchorite old and grey!'

'—Oh, I will have none of Ambrose or John,
    Though sage Penitauncers I trow they be;
Shrive me may none save the Abbot alone,
    Now listen, Lord Abbot, I speak to thee.

'Nor think foul scorn, though mitre adorn
    Thy brow, to listen to shrift of mine!
I am a Maiden royally born,
    And I come of old Plantagenet's line.

[1] 'Straightway the devil appeared to the priest in the shape of a maiden of marvellous beauty, and lo! the saint came armed with the Catholic faith, the cross, and holy water, and sprinkled the water in the name of the sacred and indivisible Trinity. The devil, wholly unable to withstand this, fled howling from it as though it was burning.'

'Though hither I stray, in lowly array,
   I am a damsel of high degree;
And the Compte of Eu, and the Lord of Ponthieu,
   They serve my father on bended knee!

'Counts a many, and Dukes a few,
   A suitoring came to my father's Hall;
But the Duke of Lorraine, with his large domain,
   He pleased my father beyond them all.

'Dukes a many, and Counts a few,
   I would have wedded right cheerfullie;
But the Duke of Lorraine was uncommonly plain,
   And I vow'd that he ne'er should my bridegroom be!

'So hither I fly, in lowly guise,
   From their gilded domes and their princely halls;
Fain would I dwell is some holy cell,
   Or within some Convent's peaceful walls!'

—Then out and spake that proud Lord Abbot,
   'Now rest thee, Fair Daughter, withouten fear;
Nor Count nor Duke but shall meet the rebuke
   Of Holy Church an he seek thee here:

'Holy Church denieth all search
   'Midst her sanctified ewes and her saintly rams;
And the wolves doth mock who would scathe her flock,
   Or, especially, worry her little pet lambs.

'Then lay, Fair Daughter, thy fears aside,
   For here this day shalt thou dine with me!'—
'Now naye, now naye,' the fair maiden cried;
   'In sooth, Lord Abbot, that scarce may be.

'Friends would whisper, and foes would frown,
   Sith thou art a Churchman of high degree,
And ill mote it match with thy fair renown
   That a wandering damsel dine with thee!

'There is Simon the Deacon hath pulse in store,
   With beans and lettuces fair to see;
His lenten fare now let me share,
   I pray thee, Lord Abbot, in charitie!'

—'Though Simon the Deacon hath pulse in store,
  To our patron Saint foul shame it were
Should wayworn guest, with toil oppress'd,
  Meet in his Abbey such churlish fare.

'There is Peter the Prior, and Francis the Friar,
  And Roger the Monk shall our convives be;
Small scandal I ween shall then be seen;
  They are a goodly companie!'

The Abbot hath donn'd his mitre and ring,
  His rich dalmatic, and maniple fine;
And the choristers sing, as the lay-brothers bring
  To the board a magnificent turkey and chine.

The turkey and chine, they are done to a nicety;
  Liver, and gizzard, and all are there;
Ne'er mote Lord Abbot pronounce *Benedicite*
  Over more luscious or delicate fare.

But no pious stave he, no *Pater* or *Ave*
  Pronounced, as he gazed on that maiden's face:
She ask'd him for stuffing, she ask'd him for gravy,
  She asked him for gizzard:—but not for Grace!

Yet gaily the Lord Abbot smiled, and press'd,
  And the blood-red wine in the wine-cup fill'd;
And he help'd his guest to a bit of the breast,
  And he sent the drumsticks down to be grill'd.

There was no lack of old Sherris sack,
  Of Hippocras fine, or of Malmsey bright;
And aye, as he drain'd off his cup with a smack,
  He grew less pious and more polite.

She pledged him once, and she pledged him twice,
  And she drank as Lady ought not to drink;
And he press'd her hand 'neath the table thrice,
  And he wink'd as Abbot ought not to wink.

And Peter the Prior, and Francis the Friar,
  Sat each with a napkin under his chin;
But Roger the Monk got excessively drunk,
  So they put him to bed, and they tuck'd him in!

The lay-brothers gazed on each other, amazed;
    And Simon the Deacon, with grief and surprise,
As he peep'd through the key-hole, could scarcely fancy **real**
    The scene he beheld, or believe his own eyes.

In his ear was ringing the Lord Abbot singing,—
    He could not distinguish the words very plain,
But 'twas all about 'Cole,' and 'jolly old Soul,'
    And 'Fiddlers,' and 'Punch,' and things quite as profane.

Even Porter Paul, at the sound of such revelling,
    With fervour himself began to bless;
For he thought he must somehow have let the devil in,—
    And perhaps was not very much out in his guess.

The Accusing Buyers [1] 'flew up to Heaven's Chancery,'
    Blushing like scarlet with shame and concern;
The Archangel took down his tale, and in answer he
    Wept—(See the works of the late Mr Sterne).

Indeed, it is said, a less taking both were in
    When, after a lapse of a great many years,
They book'd Uncle Toby five shillings for swearing,
    And blotted the fine out again with their tears!

But St Nicholas' agony who may paint?
    His senses at first were wellnigh gone;
The beautiful saint was ready to faint
    When he saw in his Abbey such sad goings on!

For never, I ween, had such doings been seen
    There before, from the time that most excellent Prince
Earl Baldwin of Flanders, and other Commanders,
    Had built and endowed it some centuries since.

—But hark!—'tis a sound from the outermost gate!
    A startling sound from a powerful blow.—
Who knocks so late?—it is half after eight
    By the clock,—and the clock's five minutes too slow.

Never, perhaps, had such loud double raps
    Been heard in St Nicholas' Abbey before;
All agreed 'it was shocking to keep people knocking,'
    But none seem'd inclined to 'answer the door.'

---

[1] The Prince of Peripatetic Informers, and terror of Stage Coachmen when such things were. Alack! alack! the Railroads have ruined his 'vested interest.'

Now a louder bang through the cloisters rang,
   And the gate on its hinges wide open flew;
And all were aware of a Palmer there,
   With his cockle, hat, staff, and his sandal shoe.

Many a furrow, and many a frown,
   By toil and time on his brow were traced;
And his long loose gown was of ginger brown,
   And his rosary dangled below his waist.

Now seldom, I ween, in such costume seen,
   Except at a stage-play or masquerade;
But who doth not know it was rather the go
   With Pilgrims and Saints in the second Crusade?

With noiseless stride did that Palmer glide
   Across that oaken floor;
And he made them all jump, he gave such a thump
   Against the Refectory door!

Wide open it flew, and plain to the view
   The Lord Abbot they all mote see;
In his hands was a cup, and he lifted it up,
   'Here's the Pope's good health with three!!'

Rang in their ears three deafening cheers,
   'Huzza! huzza! huzza!'
And one of the party said, 'Go it, my hearty!'—
   When outspake that Pilgrim grey—

'A boon, Lord Abbot! a boon! a boon!
   Worn is my foot, and empty my scrip;
And nothing to speak of since yesterday noon
   Of food, Lord Abbot, hath pass'd my lip.

'And I am come from a far countree,
   And have visited many a holy shrine;
And long have I trod the sacred sod
   Where the Saints do rest in Palestine!'—

'An thou art come from a far countree,
   And if thou in Paynim lands hast been,
Now rede me aright the most wonderful sight
   Thou Palmer grey, that thine eyes have seen.

'Arede me aright the most wonderful sight,
    Grey Palmer, that ever thine eyes did see,
And a manchette of bread, and a good warm bed,
    And a cup o' the best shall thy guerdon be!'

'Oh! I have been east, and I have been west,
    And I have seen many a wonderful sight;
But never to me did it happen to see
    A wonder like that which I see this night!

'To see a Lord Abbot, in rochet and stole,
    With Prior and Friar,—a strange mar-velle!—
O'er a jolly full bowl, sitting cheek by jowl,
    And hob-nobbing away with a Devil from Hell!

He felt in his gown of ginger-brown,
    And he pull'd out a flask from beneath;
It was rather tough work to get out the cork,
    But he drew it at last with his teeth.

O'er a pint and a quarter of holy water
    He made the sacred sign;
And he dashed the whole on the *soi-disant* daughter
    Of old Plantagenet's line!

Oh! then did she reek, and squeak, and shriek,
    With a wild, unearthly scream;
And fizzl'd, and hiss'd, and produced such a mist,
    They were all half-choked by the steam.

Her dove-like eyes turn'd to coals of fire,
    Her beautiful nose to a horrible snout,
Her hands to paws, with nasty great claws,
    And her bosom went in, and her tail came out.

On her chin there appear'd a long Nanny-goat's beard
    And her tusks and her teeth no man mote tell;
And her horns and her hoofs gave infallible proofs
    'Twas a frightful Fiend from the nethermost Hell!

The Palmer threw down his ginger gown,
    His hat and his cockle; and, plain to sight,
Stood St Nicholas' self, and his shaven crown
    Had a glow-worm halo of heavenly light.

The Fiend made a grasp, the Abbot to clasp;
  But St Nicholas lifted his holy toe,
And, just in the nick, let fly such a kick
  On his elderly Namesake, he made him let go.

And out of the window he flew like a shot,
  For the foot flew up with a terrible thwack,
And caught the foul demon about the spot
  Where his tail joins on to the small of his back.

And he bounded away, like a football at play,
  Till into the bottomless pit he fell slap,
Knocking Mammon the meagre o'er pursy Belphegor,
  And Lucifer into Beëlzebub's lap.

Oh! happy the slip from his Succubine grip,
  That saved the Lord Abbot,—though breathless with fright
In escaping he tumbled and fractured his hip,
  And his left leg was shorter thenceforth than his right!

On the banks of the Rhine, as he's stopping to dine,
  From a certain Inn-window the traveller is shown
Most picturesque ruins, the scene of these doings,
  Some miles up the river, south-east of Cologne.

And, while '*sour-kraut*' she sells you, the Landlady tells you
  That there, in those walls, now all roofless and bare,
One Simon, a Deacon, from a lean grew a sleek one,
  On filling a *ci-devant* Abbot's state chair.

How a *ci-devant* Abbot, all clothed in drab, but
  Of texture the coarsest, hair shirt, and no shoes
(His mitre and ring, and all that sort of thing
  Laid aside), in yon Cave lived a pious recluse;

How he rose with the sun, limping 'dot and go one,'
  To yon rill of the mountain, in all sorts of weather,
Where a Prior and a Friar, who lived somewhat higher
  Up the rock, used to come and eat cresses together;

How a thirsty old codger, the neighbours called Roger,
  With them drank cold water in lieu of old wine!
What its quality wanted he made up in quantity,
  Swigging as though he would empty the Rhine!

And how, as their bodily strength fail'd, the mental man
   Gain'd tenfold vigour and force in all four;
And how, to the day of their death, the 'Old Gentleman'
   Never attempted to kidnap them more.

And how, when at length, in the odour of sanctity,
   All of them died without grief or complaint;
The Monks of St Nicholas said 'twas ridiculous
   Not to suppose every one was a Saint.

And how, in the Abbey, no one was so shabby
   As not to say yearly four masses a head,
On the eve of that supper, and kick on the crupper
   Which Satan received, for the souls of the dead!

How folks long held in reverence their reliques and memories,
   How the *ci-devant* Abbot's obtain'd greater still,
When some cripples, on touching his fractured *os femoris*,
   Threw down their crutches, and danced a quadrille!

And how Abbot Simon (who turn'd out a prime one)
   These words, which grew into a proverb full soon,
O'er the late Abbot's grotto, stuck up as a motto,
   '𝔚𝔥𝔬 𝔰𝔲𝔭𝔭𝔢𝔰 𝔴𝔦𝔱𝔥 𝔱𝔥𝔢 𝔇𝔢𝔳𝔦𝔩𝔩𝔢 𝔰𝔥𝔬𝔩𝔡𝔢 𝔥𝔞𝔳𝔢 𝔞 𝔩𝔬𝔫𝔤 𝔰𝔭𝔬𝔬𝔫𝔢!!'

THE TRAGEDY

'*Quaeque ipse miserrima vidi.*' [1]—VIRGIL.

CATHERINE of Cleves was a Lady of rank,
She had lands and fine houses, and cash in the Bank;
   She had jewels and rings,
   And a thousand smart things;
   Was lovely and young, With a *rather* sharp tongue,
And she wedded a Noble of high degree
With the star of the order of *St Esprit*;
   But the Duke de Guise   Was, by many degrees,
Her senior, and not very easy to please;
He'd a sneer on his lip, and a scowl with his eye,
And a frown on his brow,—and he look'd like a Guy,—
   So she took to intriguing   With Monsieur St Megrin,
A young man of fashion, and figure, and worth,
But with no great pretensions to fortune or birth;

[1] 'Pitiful sights which I myself saw.'

He would sing, fence, and dance
  With the best man in France,
And took his rappee with genteel nonchalance;
He smiled, and he flatter'd, and flirted with ease,
And was very superior to Monseigneur de Guise.

Now Monsieur St Megrin was curious to know
If the Lady approved of his passion or no;
    So without more ado,
    He put on his surtout,
And went to a man with a beard like a Jew,
    One Signor Ruggieri,
    A Cunning-man near, he
Could conjure, tell fortunes, and calculate tides,
Perform tricks on the cards, and Heaven knows what besides,
Bring back a stray'd cow, silver ladle, or spoon,
And was thought to be thick with the Man in the Moon.
    The Sage took his stand
    With his wand in his hand,
Drew a circle, then gave the dread word of command,
Saying solemnly—'*Presto!*—*Hey, quick!*—*Cock-a-lorum!!*'
When the Duchess immediately popp'd up before 'em.

Just then a Conjunction of Venus and Mars,
Or something peculiar above in the stars,
Attracted the notice of Signor Ruggieri,
Who 'bolted,' and left him alone with his deary.—
Monsieur St Megrin went down on his knees,
And the Duchess shed tears large as marrow-fat peas,
    When,—fancy the shock,— A loud double knock,
Made the Lady cry 'Get up, you fool!—there's De Guise!'—
    'Twas his Grace, sure enough;
    So Monsieur, looking bluff,
Strutted by, with his hat on, and fingering his ruff,
While, unseen by either, away flew the Dame
Through the opposite key-hole, the same way she came;
    But, alack! and alas!   A mishap came to pass,
In her hurry she, somehow or other, let fall
A new silk Bandanna she'd worn as a shawl;
    She used it for drying   Her bright eyes while crying,
And blowing her nose, as her Beau talk'd of dying!

Now the Duke, who had seen it so lately adorn her,
And he knew the great C with the Crown in the corner,
The instant he spied it, smoked something amiss,
And said, with some energy, 'D—— it! what's this?'

He went home in a fume,　And bounced into her room,
Crying, 'So, Ma'am, I find I've some cause to be jealous!
Look here!—here's a proof you run after the fellows!
—Now take up that pen,—if it's bad choose a better,—
And write, as I dictate, this moment a letter
　　To Monsieur—you know who!'
　　The Lady look'd blue;
But replied with much firmness—'Hang me if I do!'
　De Guise grasped her wrist　With his great bony fist,
And pinched it, and gave it so painful a twist,
That his hard, iron gauntlet the flesh went an inch in,—
She did not mind death, but she could not stand pinching;
　So she sat down and wrote　This polite little note:—

'Dear Mister St Megrin,　The Chiefs of the League in
　Our house mean to dine　This evening at nine;
　I shall, soon after ten,　Slip away from the men,
And you'll find me upstairs in the drawing-room then;
Come up the back way, or those impudent thieves
Of Servants will see you;　Yours
　　　　　　　　　　　CATHERINE OF CLEVES.'

She directed and sealed it, all pale as a ghost,
And De Guise put it into the Twopenny Post.

St Megrin had almost jumped out of his skin
For joy that day when the post came in;
　He read the note through,　Then began it anew,
And thought it almost too good news to be true.—
　He clapp'd on his hat,　And a hood over that,
With a cloak to disguise him, and make him look fat;
So great his impatience, from half after Four
He was waiting till Ten at De Guise's backdoor.
When he heard the great clock of St Genevieve chime,
He ran up the back staircase six steps at a time.
　He had scarce made his bow,　He hardly knew how,
　When alas! and alack!　There was no getting back,
For the drawing-room door was bang'd to with a whack;—
　In vain he applied　To the handle and tried,
Somebody or other had locked it outside!
And the Duchess in agony mourn'd her mishap,
'We are caught like a couple of rats in a trap.'

　Now the Duchess's Page,　About twelve years of age,
For so little a boy was remarkably sage;
And, just in the nick, to their joy and amazement,
Popp'd the Gas-lighter's ladder close under the casement.

But all would not do,—
  Though St Megrin got through
The window,—below stood De Guise and his crew.
And though never a man was more brave than St Megrin,
Yet fighting a score is extremely fatiguing;
  He thrust carte and tierce Uncommonly fierce,
But not Beelzebub's self could their cuirasses pierce;
  While his doublet and hose, Being holiday clothes,
Were soon cut through and through from his knees to his nose.
Still an old crooked sixpence the Conjuror gave him
From pistol and sword was sufficient to save him,
  But, when beat on his knees,
  That confounded De Guise
Came behind with the 'fogle' that caused all this breeze,
Whipp'd it tight round his neck, and, when backward he'd
    jerk'd him,
The rest of the rascals jump'd on him and Burked him.
The poor little Page, too, himself got no quarter, but
  Was served the same way,
  And was found the next day
With his heels in the air, and his head in the water-butt;
  Catherine of Cleves
  Roar'd 'Murder!' and 'Thieves!'
  From the window above
  While they murder'd her love;
Till, finding the rogues had accomplish'd his slaughter,
She drank Prussic acid without any water,
And died like a Duke-and-a-Duchess's daughter!

MORAL

Take warning, ye Fair, from this tale of the Bard's,
And don't go where fortunes are told on the cards,
But steer clear of Conjurors,—never put query
To 'Wise Mrs Williams,' or folks like Ruggieri.
When alone in your room, shut the door close, and lock it;
Above all,—KEEP YOUR HANDKERCHIEF SAFE IN YOUR POCKET!
Lest you too should stumble, and Lord Leveson Gower, he
Be call'd on,—sad poet!—to tell your sad story!

MR BARNEY MAGUIRE'S ACCOUNT
OF THE CORONATION

AIR—'The Groves of Blarney'

OCH! the Coronation! what celebration
    For emulation can with it compare?
When to Westminster the Royal Spinster,
    And the Duke of Leinster, all in order did repair!
'Twas there you'd see the new Polishemen.
    Making a skrimmage at half after four,
And the Lords and Ladies, and the Miss O'Gradys,
    All standing round before the Abbey door.

Their pillows scorning, that selfsame morning
    Themselves adorning, all by the candle-light,
With roses and lilies, and daffy-down-dillies,
    And gould, and jewels, and rich di'monds bright.
And then approaches five hundred coaches,
    With Gineral Dullbeak.—Och! 'twas mighty fine
To see how asy bould Corporal Casey,
    With his sword drawn, prancing, made them kape the line.

Then the Guns' alarums, and the King of Arums,
    All in his Garters and his Clarence shoes,
Opening the massy doors to the bould Ambassydors,
    The Prince of Potboys, and great haythen Jews;
'Twould have made you crazy to see Esterhazy
    All joo'ls from his jasey to his di'mond boots,
With Alderman Harmer, and that swate charmer,
    The famale heiress, Miss Anjā-ly Coutts.

And Wellington, walking with his swoord drawn, talking
    To Hill and Hardinge, haroes of great fame;
And Sir De Lacy, and the Duke Dalmasey
    (They call'd him Sowlt afore he changed his name),
Themselves presading Lord Melbourne, lading
    The Queen, the darling, to her royal chair,
And that fine ould fellow, the Duke of Pell-Mello,
    The Queen of Portingal's Chargy-de-fair.

Then the Noble Prussians, likewise the Russians,
    In fine laced jackets with their goulden cuffs,
And the Bavarians, and the proud Hungarians,
    And Everythingarians all in furs and muffs.

Then Misthur Spaker, with Misthur Pays the Quaker,
   All in the Gallery you might persave;
But Lord Brougham was missing, and gone a-fishing,
   Ounly crass Lord Essex would not give him lave.

There was Baron Alten himself exalting,
   And Prince Von Swartzenburg, and many more,
Och! I'd be bother'd, and entirely smother'd
   To tell the half of 'em was to the fore;
With the swate Peeresses, in their crowns and dresses,
   And Aldermanesses, and the Boord of Works;
But Mehemet Ali said, quite gintaly,
   'I'd be proud to see the likes among the Turks!'

Then the Queen, Heaven bless her! och! they did dress her
   In her purple garments and her goulden Crown;
Like Venus or Hebe, or the Queen of Sheby,
   With eight young ladies houlding up her gown,
Sure 'twas grand to see her also for to he-ar
   The big drums bating, and the trumpets blow,
And Sir George Smart! Oh! he play'd a Consarto,
   With his four-and-twenty fiddlers all on a row!

Then the Lord Archbishop held a goulden dish up,
   For to resave her bounty and great wealth,
Saying, 'Plase your Glory, great Queen Vic-tory!
   Ye'll give the Clargy lave to dhrink your health!'
Then his Riverence, retrating, discoorsed the mating;
   'Boys! Here's your Queen! deny it if you can!
And if any bould traitour, or infarior craythur,
   Sneezes at that, I'd like to see the man!'

Then the Nobles kneeling to the Pow'rs appealing,
   'Heaven send your Majesty a glorious reign!'
And Sir Claudius Hunter he did confront her,
   All in his scarlet gown and goulden chain.
The great Lord May'r, too, sat in his chair, too,
   But mighty sarious, looking fit to cry,
For the Earl of Surrey, all in his hurry,
   Throwing the thirteens, hit him in his eye.

Then there was preaching, and good store of speeching,
   With Dukes and Marquises on bended knee;
And they did splash her with raal Macasshur,
   And the Queen said, 'Ah! then thank ye all for me!—'
Then the trumpets braying, and the organ playing,
   And sweet trombones with their silver tones;
But Lord Rolle was rolling;—'twas mighty consoling
   To think his Lordship did not break his bones

Then the crames and custard, and the beef and mustard,
   All on the tombstones like a poulterer's shop;
With lobsters and whitebait, and other swatemeats,
   And wine and nagus, and Imparial Pop!
There was cakes and apples in all the Chapels,
   With fine polonies, and rich mellow pears,—
Och! the Count Von Strogonoff, sure he got prog enough,
   The sly ould Divil, undernathe the stairs.

Then the cannons thunder'd, and the people wonder'd,
   Crying, 'God save Victoria, our Royal Queen!'
Och! if myself should live to be a hundred
   Sure it's the proudest day that I'll have seen!
And now, I've ended, what I pretended,
   This narration splendid in swate poe-thry,
Ye dear bewitcher, just hand the pitcher,
   Faith, it's myself that's getting mighty dhry!

THE 'MONSTRE' BALLOON

OH! the balloon, the great balloon,
It left Vauxhall one Monday at noon,
And everyone said we should hear of it soon
With news from Aleppo or Scanderoon,
But very soon after folks changed their tune:
'The netting had burst—the silk—the shalloon;—
It had met with a trade-wind—an awful monsoon—
It was blown out to sea—it was blown to the moon—
They ought to have put off their journey till June;
Sure none but a donkey, a goose, or baboon
Would go up in November in any balloon!'

Then they talk'd about Green—'Oh! where's Mister Green?
And where's Mister Hollond who hired the machine?
And where is Monk Mason, the man that has been
Up so often before—twelve times or thirteen—
And who writes such nice letters describing the scene?
And where's the cold fowl, and the ham, and poteen?
The press'd beef, with the fat cut off—nothing but lean,
And the portable soup in the patent tureen?
Have they got to Grand Cairo, or reach'd Aberdeen?
Or Jerusalem—Hamburg—or Ballyporeen?
No! they have not been seen! Oh! they haven't been seen!'

Stay! here's Mister Gye—Mr Frederick Gye—
'At Paris,' says he, 'I've been up very high,
A couple of hundred of toises, or nigh,
A cockstride the Tuileries' pantiles, to spy,
With Dollond's best telescope stuck at my eye,
And my umbrella under my arm like Paul Pry,
But I could see nothing at all but the sky;
So I thought with myself 'twas of no use to try
Any longer: and, feeling remarkably dry
From sitting all day stuck up there, like a Guy,
I came down again, and—you see—here am I!'

But here's Mr Hughes!—What says young Mr Hughes?—
'Why, I'm sorry to say we've not got any news
Since the letter they threw down in one of their shoes,
Which gave the mayor's nose such a deuce of a bruise,
As he popp'd up his eye-glass to look at their cruise
Over Dover; and which the folks flock'd to peruse
At Squiers's bazaar, the same evening, in crews—
Politicians, newsmongers, town council and blues,
Turks, Heretics, Infidels, Jumpers, and Jews,
Scorning Bachelor's papers, and Warren's reviews;
But the wind was then blowing towards Helvoetsluys,
And my father and I are in terrible stews,
For so large a balloon is a sad thing to lose!'—

Here's news come at last!—Here's news come at last!
A vessel's come in, which has sail'd very fast;
And a gentleman serving before the mast—
Mister Nokes—has declared that 'the party has passed
Safe across to The Hague, where their grapnel they cast,
As a fat burgomaster was staring aghast
To see such a monster come borne on the blast,
And it caught in his waistband, and there it stuck fast?'—
Oh! fie! Mister Nokes,—for shame, Mr Nokes!
To be poking your fun at us plain-dealing folks—
Sir, this isn't a time to be cracking your jokes,
And such jesting your malice but scurvily cloaks;
Such a trumpery tale every one of us smokes,
And we know very well your whole story's a hoax!—

'Oh! what shall we do?—Oh! where will it end?—
Can nobody go?—Can nobody send
To Calais—or Bergen-op-zoom—or Ostend?
Can't you go there yourself?—Can't you write to a friend,
For news upon which we may safely depend?'

D 185

Huzza! huzza! one and eightpence to pay
For a letter from Hamborough, just come to say
They descended at Weilburg, about break of day;
And they've lent them the palace there, during their stay,
And the town is becoming uncommonly gay
And they're feasting the party, and soaking their clay
With Johannisberg, Rudesheim, Moselle, and Tokay!
And the Landgraves, and Margraves, and Counts beg and pray
That they won't think, as yet, about going away;
Notwithstanding, they don't mean to make much delay,
But pack up the balloon in a wagon, or dray,
And pop themselves into a German 'po-shay,'
And get on to Paris by Lisle and Tournay;
Where they boldly declare, any wager they'll lay,
If the gas people there do not ask them to pay
Such a sum as must force them at once to say 'Nay,'
They'll inflate the balloon in the Champs-Élysées,
And be back again here the beginning of May.—

Dear me! what a treat for a juvenile fête
What thousands will flock their arrival to greet!
There'll be hardly a soul to be seen in the street,
For at Vauxhall the whole population will meet,
And you'll scarcely get standing-room, much less a seat,
For this all preceding attraction must beat:
Since, they'll unfold, what we want to be told,
How they cough'd,—how they sneez'd,—how they shiver'd
    with cold,—
How they tippled the 'cordial' as racy and old
As Hodges, or Deady, or Smith ever sold,
And how they all then felt remarkably bold:
How they thought the boil'd beef worth its own weight in gold
And how Mr Green was beginning to scold
Because Mr Mason would try to lay hold
Of the moon, and had very near overboard roll'd!

And there they'll be seen—they'll be all to be seen!
The greatcoats, the coffee-pot, mugs, and tureen!
With the tightrope, and fireworks, and dancing between,
If the weather should only prove fair and serene,
And there, on a beautiful transparent screen,
In the middle you'll see a large picture of Green.
Mr Hollond on one side, who hired the machine,
Mr Mason on t'other, describing the scene;
And Fame, on one leg, in the air, like a queen,
With three wreaths and a trumpet, will over them lean;

While Envy, in serpents and black bombazin,
Looks on from below with an air of chagrin!
Then they'll play up a tune in the Royal Saloon,
And the people will dance by the light of the moon,
And keep up the ball till the next day at noon;
And the peer and the peasant, the lord and the loon,
The haughty grandee, and the low picaroon,
The six-foot life-guardsman, and little gossoon,
Will all join in three cheers for the 'Monstre' Balloon.

HON. MR SUCKLETHUMBKIN'S STORY

THE EXECUTION

A SPORTING ANECDOTE

My Lord Tomnoddy got up one day;
  It was half after two, He had nothing to do,
So his Lordship rang for his cabriolet.
  Tiger Tim Was clean of limb,
His boots were polish'd, his jacket was trim;
With a very smart tie in his smart cravat,
And a smart cockade on the top of his hat;
Tallest of boys, or shortest of men,
He stood in his stockings just four foot ten;
And he ask'd, as he held the door on the swing,
'Pray, did your Lordship please to ring?'

My Lord Tomnoddy he raised his head,
And thus to Tiger Tim he said,
  'Malibran's dead, Duvernay's fled,
Taglioni has not yet arrived in her stead;
Tiger Tim, come tell me true,
What may a Nobleman find to do?'—

Tim look'd up, and Tim look'd down,
He paused, and he put on a thoughtful frown,
And he held up his hat, and he peep'd in the crown;
He bit his lip, and he scratch'd his head,
He let go the handle, and thus he said,
As the door, released, behind him bang'd:
'An't please you, my Lord, there's a man to be hang'd.'

My Lord Tomnoddy jump'd up at the news,
  'Run to M'Fuze, And Lieutenant Tregooze,
And run to Sir Carnaby Jenks, of the Blues.

Rope-dancers a score   I've seen before—
Madame Sacchi, Antonio, and Master Black-more;
    But to see a man swing   At the end of a string,
With his neck in a noose, will be quite a new thing!'

My Lord Tomnoddy stepped into his cab—
Dark rifle green, with a lining of drab;
    Through street, and through square,
    His high-trotting mare,
Like one of Ducrow's, goes pawing the air.
Adown Piccadilly and Waterloo Place
Went the high-trotting mare at a very quick pace;
    She produced some alarm,   But did no great harm,
Save frightening a nurse with a child on her arm,
    Spattering with clay   Two urchins at play,
Knocking down—very much to the sweeper's dismay—
An old woman who wouldn't get out of the way,
    And upsetting a stall   Near Exeter Hall,
Which made all the pious Church-Mission folks squall.
    But eastward afar,   Through Temple Bar,
My Lord Tomnoddy directs his car;
    Never heeding their squalls,
    Or their calls, or their bawls,
He passes by Waithman's Emporium for shawls,
And, merely just catching a glimpse of St Paul's,
    Turns down the Old Bailey,
    Where in front of the gaol, he
Pulls up at the door of the gin-shop, and gaily
Cries, 'What must I fork out to-night, my trump,
For the whole first floor of the Magpie and Stump?'

The clock strikes twelve—it is dark midnight—
Yet the Magpie and Stump is one blaze of light.
    The parties are met;   The tables are set;
There is 'punch,' 'cold *without*,' 'hot *with*,' 'heavy wet,'
    Ale-glasses and jugs,   And rummers and mugs,
And sand on the floor, without carpets or rugs,
    Cold fowl and cigars,   Pickled onions in jars,
Welsh rabbits and kidneys—rare work for the jaws!—
And very large lobsters, with very large claws;
    And there is M'Fuze,   And Lieutenant Tregooze,
And there is Sir Carnaby Jenks, of the Blues,
    All come to see a man 'die in his shoes'!

The clock strikes One!   Supper is done.
And Sir Carnaby Jenks is full of his fun,
Singing 'Jolly companions every one!'

My Lord Tomnoddy   Is drinking gin-toddy,
And laughing at ev'ry thing, and ev'ry body,—
The clock strikes Two! and the clock strikes Three!
—'Who so merry, so merry as we?'
Save Captain M'Fuze,   Who is taking a snooze,
While Sir Carnaby Jenks is busy at work,
Blacking his nose with a piece of burnt cork.

The clock strikes Four!—   Round the debtors' door
Are gather'd a couple of thousand or more;
As many await   At the press-yard gate,
Till slowly its folding doors open, and straight
The mob divides, and between their ranks
A wagon comes loaded with posts and with planks.

The clock strikes Five!   The Sheriffs arrive,
And the crowd is so great that the street seems alive;
But Sir Carnaby Jenks   Blinks, and winks,
A candle burns down in the socket, and stinks,
Lieutenant Tregooze   Is dreaming of Jews,
And acceptances all the bill-brokers refuse;
My Lord Tomnoddy   Has drunk all his toddy
And just as the dawn is beginning to peep,
The whole of the party are fast asleep.

Sweetly, oh! sweetly, the morning breaks,
With roseate streaks,
Like the first faint blush on a maiden's cheeks;
Seem'd as that mild and clear blue sky
Smiled upon all things far and nigh,
On all—save the wretch condemn'd to die!
Alack! that ever so fair a Sun
As that which its course has now begun,
Should rise on such a scene of misery!—
Should gild with rays so light and free
That dismal, dark-frowning Gallows-tree!

And hark!—a sound comes, big with fate;
The clock from St Sepulchre's tower strikes—Eight!—
List to that low funereal bell:
It is tolling, alas! a living man's knell!—
And see!—from forth that opening door
They come—HE steps that threshold o'er
Who never shall tread upon threshold more!
—God! 'tis a fearsome thing to see
That pale wan man's mute agony,—

The glare of that wild, despairing eye,
Now bent on the crowd, now turn'd to the sky,
As though 'twere scanning, in doubt and in fear,
The path of the Spirit's unknown career;
Those pinion'd arms, those hands that ne'er
Shall be lifted again—not even in prayer;
That heaving chest!—Enough—'tis done!
The bolt has fallen!—the spirit is gone—
For weal or for woe is known but to One!
—Oh!' twas a fearsome sight!—Ah me!
A deed to shudder at,—not to see.

Again that clock! 'tis time, 'tis time!
The hour is past:—with its earliest chime
The cord is severed, the lifeless clay
By 'dungeon villains' is borne away:
Nine!—'twas the last concluding stroke!
And then—my Lord Tomnoddy awoke!
And Tregooze and Sir Carnaby Jenks arose,
And Captain M'Fuze, with the black on his nose:
And they stared at each other, as much as to say,
    'Hollo! Hollo!   Here's a rum Go!
Why, Captain!—my Lord!—Here's the devil to pay!
The fellow's been cut down and taken away!—
    What's to be done?   We've miss'd all the fun!—
Why, they'll laugh at and quiz us all over the town,
We are all of us done so uncommonly brown!'

What *was* to be done?—'twas perfectly plain
That they could not well hang the man over again:
What *was* to be done?—The man was dead!
Nought *could* be done—nought could be said;
So—my Lord Tomnoddy went home to bed!

SOME ACCOUNT OF A NEW PLAY

IN A FAMILIAR EPISTLE TO MY BROTHER-IN-LAW, LIEUT.
SEAFORTH, H.P., LATE OF THE HON. E.I.C.'S 2ND REGT OF
BOMBAY FENCIBLES

'The play's the thing!'—HAMLET

Tavistock Hotel, Nov. 1839.

DEAR CHARLES,
  —In reply to your letter, and Fanny's,
Lord Brougham, it appears, isn't dead,—though Queen Anne is;
'Twas a 'plot' and a 'farce'—you hate farces, you say—
Take another 'plot,' then, viz., the plot of the Play.

The Countess of Arundel, high in degree,
As a lady possess'd of an earldom in fee,
Was imprudent enough, at fifteen years of age,
—A period of life when we're not over sage,—
To form a liaison—in fact, to engage
Her hand to a Hop-o'-my-thumb of a Page.
  This put her Papa— She had no Mamma—
As may well be supposed, in a deuce of a rage.

Mr Benjamin Franklin was wont to repeat,
In his budget of proverbs, 'Stol'n kisses are sweet!'
  But they have their alloy— Fate assumed, to annoy
Miss Arundel's peace, and embitter her joy,
The equivocal shape of a fine little Boy.

When, through 'the young Stranger,' her secret took wind,
The old Lord was neither 'to haud nor to bind.'
  He bounced up and down, And so fearful a frown
Contracted his brow, you'd have thought he'd been blind.
  The young lady, they say, Having fainted away
Was confin'd to her room for the whole of that day;
While her beau—no rare thing in the old feudal system—
Disappear'd the next morning, and nobody miss'd him.

The fact is, his Lordship, who hadn't, it seems,
Form'd the slightest idea, not ev'n in his dreams,
That the pair had been wedded according to law,
Conceived that his daughter had made a *faux pas*;
  So he bribed at a high rate A sort of a Pirate
To knock out the poor dear young Gentleman's brains,
And gave him a handsome *douceur* for his pains.

The Page thus disposed of, his Lordship now turns
His attention at once to the Lady's concerns;
    And, alarm'd for the future,   Looks out for a suitor,
One not fond of raking, nor giv'n to 'the pewter,'
But adapted to act both the husband and tutor—
Finds a highly respectable, middle-aged widower,
Marries her off, and thanks Heaven that he's rid of her.
    Relieved from his cares,   The old Peer now prepares
To arrange in good earnest his worldly affairs;
Has his will made anew by a Special Attorney,
Sickens,—takes to his bed,—and sets out on his journey.
    Which way he travell'd   Has not been unravell'd;
To speculate much on the point were too curious,
If the climate he reach'd were serene or sulphureous.
To be sure in his balance-sheet all must declare
One item—the Page—was an awkward affair;
But *per contra*, he'd lately endowed a new Chantry
For Priests, with ten marks, and the run of the pantry.
    Be that as it may,   It's sufficient to say
That his tomb in the chancel stands there to this day,
Built of Bethersden marble—a dark bluish grey.
The figure, a fine one of pure alabaster,
Some cleanly churchwarden has covered with plaster;
    While some Vandal or Jew,   With a taste for virtu,
Has knock'd off his toes, to place, I suppose,
In some Pickwick Museum, with part of his nose;
    From his belt and his sword   And his misericorde
The enamel's been chipp'd out, and never restored;
His *ci-gît* in old French is inscribed all around,
And his head's in his helm, and his heel's on his hound,
The palms of his hands, as if going to pray,
Are joined and upraised o'er his bosom—But stay!
I forgot that his tomb's not described in the Play!

Lady Arundel, now in her own right a Peeress,
Perplexes her noddle with no such nice queries,
But produces in time, to her husband's great joy,
Another remarkably 'fine little boy.'
    As novel connections   Oft change the affections,
And turn all one's love into different directions,
Now to young 'Johnny Newcome' she seems to confine hers,
Neglecting the poor little dear out at dry-nurse;
    Nay, far worse than that,
    She considers 'the brat'
As a bore—fears her husband may smell out a rat.
    For her legal adviser   She takes an old Miser,
A sort of 'poor cousin.'   She might have been wiser;

For this arrant deceiver, By name Maurice Beevor,
A shocking old scamp, should her own issue fail,
By the law of the land stands the next in entail;
So, as soon as she ask'd him to hit on some plan
To provide for her eldest, away the rogue ran
To that selfsame unprincipled seafaring man;
In his ear whisper'd low . . .—'Bully Gaussen' said 'Done!—
I Burked the papa, now I'll Bishop the son!'
   'Twas agreed; and, with speed
   To accomplish the deed,
He adopted a scheme he was sure would succeed.
   By long cock-and-bull stories Of Candish and Noreys,
Of Drake, and bold Raleigh (then fresh in his glories,
Acquired 'mongst the Indians, and Rapparee Tories),
   He so worked on the lad, That he left, which was bad,
The only true friend in the world that he had,
Father Onslow, a priest, though to quit him most loth,
Who in childhood had furnish'd his pap and his broth,
At no small risk of scandal, indeed, to his cloth.

   The kidnapping crimp Took the foolish young imp
On board of his cutter so trim and so jimp,
Then, seizing him just as you'd handle a shrimp,
Twirl'd him thrice in the air with a whirligig motion,
And soused him at once neck and heels in the ocean;
   This was off Plymouth Sound,
   And he must have been drown'd,
For 'twas nonsense to think he could swim to dry ground,
   If 'A very great Warman, Call'd Billy the Norman,'
Had not just at that moment sail'd by, outward bound.
   A shark of great size, With his great glassy eyes,
Sheer'd off as he came, and relinquish'd the prize;
So he pick'd up the lad,[1] swabb'd, and dry-rubb'd, and mopp'd
   him,
And, having no children, resolv'd to adopt him.
   Full many a year Did he hand, reef, and steer,
And by no means consider'd himself as small beer,
When old Norman at length died and left him his frigate,
With lots of pistoles in his coffer to rig it.

---

[1] An incident very like one in Jack Sheppard—
  A work some have lauded, and others have pepper'd—
  Where a Dutch pirate kidnaps, and tosses Thames Darrel
  Just so in the sea, and he's saved by a barrel,—
  On the coast, if I recollect rightly, it's flung whole,
  And the hero, half-drown'd, scrambles out of the bung-hole.

[It aint no sich thing!—the hero aint bung'd in no barrel at all.—He's
picked up by a Captain, just as Norman was afterwards.—PRINT. DEV.]
  * D 185

A sailor ne'er moans; So, consigning the bones
Of his friend to the locker of one Mr Jones,
For England he steers.—On the voyage it appears
That he rescued a maid from the Dey of Algiers;
And at length reached the Sussex coast, where, in a bay,
Not a great way from Brighton, most cosey-ly lay
His vessel at anchor, the very same day
That the Poet begins,—thus commencing his play:

ACT I

Giles Gaussen accosts old Sir Maurice de Beevor,
And puts the poor Knight in a deuce of a fever,
By saying the boy, whom he took out to please him,
Is come back a Captain on purpose to tease him.—
Sir Maurice, who gladly would see Mr Gaussen
Breaking stones on the highway, or sweeping a crossing,
Dissembles—observes, 'It's of no use to fret,'—
And hints he may find some more work for him yet;
Then calls at the castle, and tells Lady A.
That the boy they had ten years ago sent away
Is return'd a grown man, and, to come to the point,
Will put her son Percy's nose clean out of joint;
But adds, that herself she no longer need vex,
If she'll buy him (Sir Maurice) a farm near the Ex.
'Oh! take it,' she cries; 'but secure every document.'—
'A bargain,' says Maurice,—'including the stock you meant?'—

The Captain, meanwhile, With a lover-like smile,
And a fine cambric handkerchief, wipes off the tears
From Miss Violet's eyelash, and hushes her fears.
(That's the Lady he saved from the Dey of Algiers.)
Now arises a delicate point, and this is it—
The young Lady herself is but down on a visit.
She's perplexed; and, in fact,
Does not know how to act.
It's her very first visit—and then to begin
By asking a stranger—a gentleman, in—
One with moustaches too—and a tuft on his chin—
She 'really don't know— He had much better go,'—
Here the Countess steps in from behind, and says 'No!—
Fair sir, you are welcome. Do, pray, stop and dine—
You will take our pot-luck—and we've decentish wine.'
He bows, looks at Miss,—and he does not decline.

ACT II

After dinner, the Captain recounts, with much glee,
All he's heard, seen, and done since he first went to sea,
    All his perils and scrapes,
    And his hairbreadth escapes,
Talks of boa-constrictors, and lions, and apes,
And fierce 'Bengal Tigers,' like that which, you know,
If you've ever seen any respectable 'Show,'
'Carried off the unfortunate Mr Munro.'
Then, diverging a while, he adverts to the mystery
Which hangs, like a cloud, o'er his own private history—
How he ran off to sea—how they set him afloat
(Not a word, though, of barrel or bung-hole—*See Note*)
    —How he happen'd to meet
    With the Algerine fleet,
And forced them, by sheer dint of arms to retreat,
Thus saving his Violet—(One of his feet
Here just touch'd her toe, and she moved on her seat)—
    How his vessel was batter'd—
    In short, he so chatter'd,
Now lively, now serious, so ogled and flatter'd,
That the ladies much marvell'd a person should be able
To 'make himself,' both said, 'so very agreeable.'

Captain Norman's adventures were scarcely half done,
When Percy Lord Ashdale, her ladyship's son,
    In a terrible fume,   Bounces into the room,
And talks to his guest as you'd talk to your groom,
Claps his hand on his rapier, and swears he'll be through him—
The Captain does nothing at all but 'pooh! pooh!' him.
    Unable to smother   His hate of his brother,
He rails at his cousin, and blows up his mother.—
'Fie! fie!' says the first.—Says the latter, 'In sooth,
This is sharper by far than a keen serpent's tooth!'
(A remark, by the way, which King Lear had made years ago,
When he ask'd for his Knights, and his Daughter said 'Here's
    a go!')—
    This made Ashdale ashamed;
    But he must not be blamed
Too much for his warmth, for, like many young fellows he
Was apt to lose temper when tortur'd by jealousy.
    Still speaking quite gruff,   He goes off in a huff;
Lady A., who is now what some call 'up to snuff,'

    Straight determines to patch
    Up a clandestine match
Between the Sea-Captain she dreads like Old Scratch,
And Miss,—whom she does not think any great catch
For Ashdale; besides, he won't kick up such shindies
Were she once fairly married and off to the Indies.

ACT III

Miss Violet takes from the Countess her tone;
She agrees to meet Norman 'by moonlight alone,'
    And slip off to his bark,   'The night being dark,'
Though 'the moon,' the Sea-Captain says, rises in heaven
'One hour before midnight,' i.e. at eleven.
    From which speech I infer,—
    Though perhaps I may err—
That, though weatherwise, doubtless, 'midst surges and surf, he
When 'capering on shore' was by no means a Murphy.
He starts off, however, at sunset, to reach
An old chapel in ruins, that stands on the beach,
Where the Priest is to bring, as he's promised by letter, a
Paper to prove his name, 'birthright,' etc.
    Being rather too late, Gaussen, lying in wait,
Gives poor Father Onslow a knock on the pate,
But bolts, seeing Norman, before he has wrested
From the hand of the Priest, as Sir Maurice requested,
The marriage certificate duly attested.—
Norman kneels by the clergyman fainting and gory,
And begs he won't die till he's told him his story;
    The Father complies, Reopens his eyes,
And tells him all how and about it—and dies!

ACT IV

Norman, now call'd Le Mesnil, instructed of all,
Goes back, though it's getting quite late for a call,
Hangs his hat and his cloak on a peg in the hall,
And tells the proud Countess it's useless to smother
The fact any longer—he knows she's his Mother!
    His Pa's wedded Spouse,— She questions his $\nu o\hat{\upsilon}\varsigma$,
And threatens to have him turn'd out of the house.—
    He still perseveres, Till, in spite of her fears,
She admits he's the son she had cast off for years,
And he gives her the papers 'all blister'd with tears,'

When Ashdale, who chances his nose in to poke,
  Takes his hat and his cloak, Just as if in a joke,
Determined to put in his wheel a new spoke,
And slips off thus disguised, when he sees by the dial it
's time for the rendezvous fixed with Miss Violet.—
—Captain Norman, who, after all, feels rather sore
At his mother's reserve, vows to see her no more,
Rings the bell for the servant to open the door,
And leaves his Mamma in a fit on the floor.

ACT V

Now comes the catastrophe!—Ashdale, who's wrapped in
The cloak with the hat and the plume of the Captain,
Leads Violet down through the grounds to the chapel
Where Gaussen's conceal'd—he springs forward to grapple
The man he's erroneously led to suppose
Captain Norman himself by the cut of his clothes.
  In the midst of their strife, And just as the knife
Of the Pirate is raised to deprive him of life,
The Captain comes forward, drawn there by the squeals
Of the Lady, and, knocking Giles head over heels,
  Fractures his 'nob,' Saves the hangman a job,
And executes justice most strictly, the rather,
'Twas the spot where that rascal had murder'd his father.
  Then in comes the mother, Who, finding one brother
Had the instant before saved the life of the other,
  Explains the whole case. Ashdale puts a good face
On the matter; and, since he's obliged to give place,
Yields his coronet up with a pretty good grace;
Norman vows he won't have it—the kinsmen embrace,—
And the Captain, the first in this generous race,
  To remove every handle For gossip and scandal,
Sets the whole of the papers alight with the candle;
An arrangement takes place—on the very same night, all
Is settled and done, and the points the most vital
Are, N. takes the personals;—A., in requital,
Keeps the whole real property, Mansion, and Title.—
V. falls to the share of the Captain, and tries a
Sea-voyage, as a Bride, in the *Royal Eliza*.—
Both are pleased with the part they acquire as joint heirs,
And old Maurice Beevor is bundled downstairs!

MORAL

The public, perhaps, with the drama might quarrel
If deprived of all epilogue, prologue, and moral;
This may serve for all three then:—

'Young Ladies of property,
Let Lady A.'s history serve as a stopper t'ye;
Don't wed with low people beneath your degree,
And if you've a baby, don't send it to sea!

'Young Noblemen! shun everything like a brawl;
And be sure when you dine out, or go to a ball,
Don't take the best hat that you find in the hall,
And leave one in its stead that's worth nothing at all!

'Old Knights, don't give bribes!—above all, never urge a man
To steal people's things, or to stick an old Clergyman!

'And you, ye Sea-Captains! who've nothing to do
But to run round the world, fight, and drink till all's blue,
And tell us tough yarns, and then swear they are true,
Reflect, notwithstanding your seafaring life,
That you can't get on well long, without you've a wife;
So get one at once, treat her kindly and gently,
Write a nautical novel,—and send it to Bentley!'

MR PETERS'S STORY

THE BAGMAN'S DOG

'Stant littore Puppies!' [1]—VIRGIL.

IT was a litter, a litter of five,
Four are drown'd, and one left alive,
He was thought worthy alone to survive;
And the Bagman resolved upon bringing him up,
To eat of his bread, and to drink of his cup,
He was such a dear little cock-tail'd pup!

The Bagman taught him many a trick;
He would carry, and fetch, and run after a stick,

---

[1] A pun on 'stant litore puppes' ('the sterns rest upon the beach').

Could well understand   The word of command,
    And appear to doze   With a crust on his nose
Till the Bagman permissively waved his hand:
Then to throw up and catch it he never would fail,
As he sat up on end, on his little cock-tail.
Never was puppy so *bien instruit*,
Or possess'd of such natural talent as he;
    And as he grew older,   Every beholder
Agreed he grew handsomer, sleeker, and bolder.—
Time, however his wheels we may clog,
Wends steadily still with onward jog,
And the cock-tail'd puppy's a curly-tail'd dog!
    When, just at the time   He was reaching his prime,
And all thought he'd be turning out something sublime,
    One unlucky day,   How, no one could say,
Whether soft liaison induced him to stray,
Or some kidnapping vagabond coax'd him away,
    He was lost to the view,   Like the morning dew;—
He had been, and was not—that's all that they knew!
And the Bagman storm'd, and the Bagman swore
As never a Bagman had sworn before;
But storming or swearing but little avails
To recover lost dogs with great curly tails.—

In a large paved court, close by Billiter Square,
Stands a mansion, old, but in thorough repair,
The only thing strange, from the general air
Of its size and appearance, is how it got there;
In front is a short semicircular stair
    Of stone steps,—some half score,—
    Then you reach the ground floor,
With a shell-pattern'd architrave over the door.
It is spacious, and seems to be built on the plan
Of a Gentleman's house in the reign of Queen Anne;
    Which is odd, for, although,   As we very well know,
Under Tudors and Stuarts the City could show
Many Noblemen's seats above Bridge and below,
Yet that fashion soon after induced them to go
From St Michael, Cornhill, and St Mary-le-Bow,
To St James, and St George, and St Anne in Soho.—
Be this at it may,—at the date I assign
To my tale,—that's about Seventeen Sixty-Nine,—
This mansion, now rather upon the decline,
Had less dignified owners,—belonging, in fine,
To Turner, Dry, Weipersyde, Rogers, and Pyne—
A respectable House in the Manchester line.

There were a score   Of Bagmen, and more,
Who had travell'd full oft for the firm before;
But just at this period they wanted to send
Some person on whom they could safely depend—
A trustworthy body, half agent, half friend—
On some mercantile matter as far as Ostend;
And the person they pitch'd on was Anthony Blogg,
A grave, steady man, not addicted to grog,—
The Bagman, in short, who had lost this great dog.

'The Sea! the Sea! the open Sea!
That is the place where we all wish to be,
Rolling about on it merrily!'—
    So all sing and say   By night and by day,
In the boudoir, the street, at the concert, and play,
In a sort of coxcombical roundelay;—
You may roam through the City, transversely or straight,
From Whitechapel turnpike to Cumberland gate,
And every young Lady who thrums a guitar,
Ev'ry mustachio'd Shopman who smokes a cigar,
    With affected devotion,   Promulgates his notion,
Of being a 'Rover' and 'child of the Ocean'—
Whate'er their age, sex, or condition may be,
They all of them long for the 'Wide, Wide Sea'!
    But, however they dote,   Only send them afloat
In any craft bigger at all than a boat,
    Take them down to the Nore,
    And you'll see that before
The 'Wessel' they 'Woyage' in has made half her way
Between Shell-Ness Point and the pier at Herne Bay,
Let the wind meet the tide in the slightest degree,
They'll be all of them heartily sick of 'the Sea'!

I've stood in Margate, on a bridge of size
    Inferior far to that described by Byron,
Where 'palaces and pris'ns on each hand rise,'—
    —That too's a stone one, this is made of iron—
    And little donkey-boys your steps environ,
Each proffering for your choice his tiny hack,
    Vaunting its excellence; and, should you hire one,
For sixpence, will he urge, with frequent thwack,
The much-enduring beast to Buenos Aires—and back.

And there, on many a raw and gusty day,
    I've stood, and turn'd my gaze upon the pier,
And seen the crews, that did embark so gay
    That selfsame morn, now disembark so queer;

Then to myself I've sigh'd and said, 'Oh dear!
Who would believe yon sickly-looking man's a
   London Jack Tar,—a Cheapside Buccaneer!'—
But hold, my Muse!—for this terrific stanza
Is all too stiffly grand for our Extravaganza.

'So now we'll go up, up, up,
   And now we'll go down, down, down,
And now we'll go backwards and forwards,
   And now we'll go roun', roun', roun'.'—
—I hope you've sufficient discernment to see,
Gentle Reader, that here the discarding the *d*
Is a fault which you must not attribute to me;
Thus my Nurse cut it off when, 'with counterfeit glee,'
She sung, as she danced me about on her knee,
In the year of our Lord eighteen hundred and three:—
All I mean to say is, that the Muse is now free
From the self-imposed trammels put on by her betters,
And no longer like Filch, midst the felons and debtors
At Drury Lane, dances her hornpipe in fetters.
   Resuming her track,   At once she goes back
To our hero, the Bagman—Alas! and Alack!
   Poor Anthony Blogg   Is as sick as a dog,
Spite of sundry unwonted potations of grog,
By the time the Dutch packet is fairly at sea,
With the sands called the Goodwins a league on her lee.

And now, my good friends, I've a fine opportunity
To obfuscate you all by sea terms with impunity,
   And talking of 'caulking,'   And 'quarter deck walking,'
   'Fore and aft,'   And 'abaft,'
'Hookers,' 'barkeys,' and 'craft'
(At which Mr Poole has so wickedly laught),
Of binnacles,—bilboes,—the boom call'd the spanker,
The best bower cable,—the jib,—and sheet anchor;
Of lower-deck guns,—and of broadsides and chases,
Of taffrails and topsails, and splicing main-braces,
And 'Shiver my timbers!' and other odd phrases
Employ'd by old pilots with hard-featured faces;
Of the expletives seafaring Gentlemen use,
The allusions they make to the eyes of their crews;—
   How the Sailors, too, swear,
   How they cherish their hair,
And what very long pigtails a great many wear.—
But, Reader, I scorn it—the fact is, I fear,
To be candid, I can't make these matters so clear

As Marryat, or Cooper, or Captain Chamier,
Or Sir E. Lytton Bulwer, who brought up the rear
Of the 'Nauticals,' just at the end of the year
Eighteen thirty-nine—(how Time flies!—Oh dear!)—
With a well-written preface, to make it appear
That his play, the 'Sea Captain,' 's by no means small beer;
There!—'brought up the rear'—you see there's a mistake
Which none of the authors I've mentioned would make,
I ought to have said, that he 'sail'd in their wake.'—
So I'll merely observe, as the water grew rougher,
The more my poor hero continued to suffer,
Till the Sailors themselves cried, in pity, 'Poor Buffer!'
    Still rougher it grew,   And still harder it blew,
And the thunder kick'd up such a hullaballoo,
That even the Skipper began to look blue;
    While the crew, who were few,   Look'd very queer, too,
And seem'd not to know what exactly to do,
And they who'd the charge of them wrote in the logs
'Wind N.E.—blows a hurricane—rains cats and dogs.'
In short it soon grew to a tempest as rude as
That Shakespeare describes near the 'still vext Bermudas,' [1]
    When the winds, in their sport,
    Drove aside from its port
The King's ship, with the whole Neapolitan Court,
And swamp'd it to give 'the King's Son, Ferdinand,' a
Soft moment or two with the Lady Miranda,
While her Pa met the rest, and severely rebuked 'em
For unhandsomely doing him out of his Dukedom.
You don't want me, however, to paint you a Storm,
As so many have done, and in colours so warm;
Lord Byron, for instance, in manner facetious,
Mr Ainsworth more gravely,—see also Lucretius,
—A writer who gave me no trifling vexation
When a youngster at school on Dean Colet's foundation.—
    Suffice it to say   That the whole of that day,
And the next, and the next, they were scudding away
    Quite out of their course,   Propell'd by the force
Of those flatulent folks known in Classical story as
Aquilo, Libs, Notus, Auster, and Boreas,
    Driven quite at their mercy
    'Twixt Guernsey and Jersey,
Till at length they came bump on the rocks and the shallows,
In West longitude, One, fifty-seven, near St Maloes:
    There you'll not be surprised
    That the vessel capsized,

[1] See Appendix, page 108.

Or that Blogg, who had made, from intestine commotions,
His specifical gravity less than the Ocean's,
   Should go floating away,   Midst the surges and spray,
Like a cork in a gutter, which, swoln by a shower,
Runs down Holborn Hill about nine knots an hour.

You've seen, I've no doubt, at Bartholomew fair,
Gentle Reader,—that is, if you've ever been there,—
With their hands tied behind them, some two or three pair
Of boys round a bucket set up on a chair,
   Skipping, and dipping   Eyes, nose, chin, and lip in,
Their faces and hair with the water all dripping,
In an anxious attempt to catch hold of a pippin,
That bobs up and down in the water whenever
They touch it, as mocking the fruitless endeavour;
Exactly as Poets say,—how, though, they can't tell us,—
Old Nick's Nonpareils play at bob with poor Tantalus.
   Stay!—I'm not clear,   But I'm rather out here:
'Twas the water itself that slipp'd from him, I fear;
Faith, I can't recollect—and I haven't Lempriere.—
No matter,—poor Blogg went on ducking and bobbing,
Sneezing out the salt water, and gulping and sobbing,
Just as Clarence, in Shakespeare, describes all the qualms he
Experienced while dreaming they'd drown'd him in Malmsey.

'O Lord,' he thought, 'what pain it was to drown!'
   And saw great fishes with great goggling eyes,
Glaring as he was bobbing up and down,
   And looking as they thought him quite a prize;
When as he sank, and all was growing dark,
A something seized him with its jaws!—A shark?—

No such thing, Reader:—most opportunely for Blogg,
'Twas a very large, web-footed, curly-tail'd Dog!

I'm not much of a trav'ler, and really can't boast
That I know a great deal of the Brittany coast,
   But I've often heard say   That e'en to this day,
The people of Granville, St Maloes, and thereabout
Are a class that society doesn't much care about;
Men who gain their subsistence by contraband dealing,
And a mode of abstraction strict people call 'stealing';
Notwithstanding all which, they are civil of speech,
Above all to a stranger who comes within reach;
   And they were so to Blogg,   When the curly-tail'd dog
At last dragg'd him out, high and dry on the beach.

But we all have been told,   By the proverb of old,
By no means to think 'all that glitters is gold';
    And, in fact, some advance   That most people in France
Join the manners and airs of a *Maître de Danse*
To the morals—(as Johnson of Chesterfield said)—
Of an elderly Lady, in Babylon bred,
Much addicted to flirting, and dressing in red.—
    Be this as it might.   It embarrass'd Blogg quite
To find those about him so very polite.

A suspicious observer perhaps might have traced
The *petites soins*, tendered with so much good taste,
To the sight of an old-fashion'd pocket-book, placed
In a black leather belt well secured round his waist,
And a ring set with diamonds, his finger that graced,
So brilliant, no one could have guess'd they were paste.
    The group on the shore   Consisted of four;
You will wonder, perhaps, there were not a few more;
But the fact is they've not, in that part of the nation,
What Malthus would term a 'too dense population,'
Indeed the sole sign there of man's habitation
Was merely a single   Rude hut, in a dingle
That led away inland direct from the shingle,
Its sides clothed with underwood, gloomy and dark,
Some two hundred yards above high-water mark;
    And thither the party,   So cordial and hearty,
Viz. an old man, his wife, and two lads, made a start, he,
    The Bagman, proceeding,   With equal good breeding,
To express, in indifferent French, all he feels,
The great curly-tail'd Dog keeping close to his heels.—
They soon reach'd the hut, which seem's partly in ruin,
All the way bowing, chattering, shrugging, *Mon-Dieu*-ing,
Grimacing, and what sailors call *parley-vooing*.

Is it Paris, or Kitchener, Reader, exhorts
You, whenever your stomach's at all out of sorts,
To try, if you find richer viands won't stop in it,
A basin of good mutton broth with a chop in it?
(Such a basin and chop as I once heard a witty one
Call, at the Garrick, 'a c—d Committee one,'
An expression, I own, I do not think a pretty one.)
    However, it's clear   That, with sound table beer,
Such a mess as I speak of is very good cheer;
    Especially too   When a person's wet through,
And is hungry, and tired, and don't know what to do.
Now just such a mess of delicious hot pottage
Was smoking away when they enter'd the cottage,

And casting a truly delicious perfume
Through the whole of an ugly, old, ill-furnish'd room;
  'Hot, smoking hot,'   On the fire was a pot
Well replenish'd, but really I can't say with what;
For, famed as the French always are for ragouts,
No creature can tell what they put in their stews,
Whether bull-frogs, old gloves, or old wigs, or old shoes;
Notwithstanding, when offer'd I rarely refuse,
Any more than poor Blogg did, when, seeing the reeky
Repast placed before him, scarce able to speak, he
In ecstasy mutter'd 'By Jove, Cockey-leeky!'
  In an instant, as soon   As they gave him a spoon,
Every feeling and faculty bent on the gruel, he
No more blamed Fortune for treating him cruelly,
But fell tooth and nail on the soup and the *bouilli*.

Meanwhile that old man standing by,
Subducted his long coat-tails on high,
With his back to the fire, as if to dry
A part of his dress which the watery sky
Had visited rather inclemently.—
Blandly he smil'd, but still he look'd sly,
And a something sinister lurk'd in his eye.
Indeed, had you seen him his maritime dress in,
You'd have own'd his appearance was not prepossessing;
He'd a 'dreadnought' coat, and heavy sabots
With thick wooden soles turn'd up at the toes,
His nether man cased in a striped *quelque chose*,
And a hump on his back, and a great hook'd nose,
So that nine out of ten would be led to suppose
That the person before them was Punch in plain clothes.

Yet still, as I told you, he smiled on all present,
And did all that lay in his power to look pleasant.
  The old woman, too,   Made a mighty ado,
Helping her guest to a deal of the stew;
She fish'd up the meat, and she help'd him to that,
She help'd him to lean, and she help'd him to fat,
And it look'd like Hare—but it might have been Cat.
The little *garçons* too strove to express
Their sympathy towards the 'Child of distress'
With a great deal of juvenile French *politesse*;
  But the Bagman bluff   Continued to 'stuff'
Of the fat, and the lean, and the tender and tough,
Till they thought he would never cry 'Hold, enough!'
And the old woman's tones became far less agreeable,
Sounding like *peste!* and *sacre!* and *diable!*

I've seen an old saw, which is well worth repeating,
That says,
　'Good Catynge
Deserveth good Drynkynge.'
You'll find it so printed by Caxton or Wynkyn,
And a very good proverb it is to my thinking.
　Blogg thought so too;—　As he finish'd his stew,
His ear caught the sound of the word '*Morbleu!*'
Pronounced by the old woman under her breath.
Now, not knowing what she could mean by 'Blue Death!'
He conceiv'd she referr'd to a delicate brewing
Which is almost synonymous,—namely, 'Blue Ruin.'
So he pursed up his lip to a smile, and with glee,
In his cockneyfy'd accent, responded 'Oh, *Vee!*'
　　Which made her understand he
　　Was asking for brandy;
So she turn'd to the cupboard, and having some handy,
Produced, rightly deeming he would not object to it,
An orbicular bulb with a very long neck to it;
In fact you perceive her mistake was the same as his,
Each of them 'reasoning right from wrong premises';—
　—And here by the way,　Allow me to say,
Kind Reader, you sometimes permit me to stray—
'Tis strange the French prove, when they take to aspersing,
So inferior to us in the science of cursing:
　　Kick a Frenchman downstairs,
　　How absurdly he swears!
And how odd 'tis to hear him, when beat to a jelly,
Roar out, in a passion, 'Blue Death!' and 'Blue Belly!'

'To return to our sheep' from this little digression:—
Blogg's features assumed a complacent expression
As he emptied his glass, and she gave him a fresh one;
　Too little he heeded　How fast they succeeded.
Perhaps you or I might have done, though, as he did;
For when once Madam Fortune deals out her hard raps,
　It's amazing to think　How one 'cottons' to Drink!
At such times, of all things in nature, perhaps,
There's not one that is half so seducing as *Schnaps*.

Mr Blogg, besides being uncommonly dry,
Was, like most other Bagmen, remarkably shy,
　—'Did not like to deny'—
　'Felt obliged to comply'
Every time that she ask'd him to 'wet t'other eye';
For 'twas worthy remark that she spared not the stoup,
Though before she had seem'd so to grudge him the soup.

At length the fumes rose　To his brain; and his nose
Gave hints of a strong disposition to doze,
And a yearning to seek 'horizontal repose.'—
　　His queer-looking host,　Who, firm at his post,
During all the long meal had continued to toast
　　That garment 'twere rude to　Do more than allude to,
Perceived, from his breathing and nodding, the views
Of his guest were directed to 'taking a snooze':
So he caught up a lamp in his huge dirty paw,
With (as Blogg used to tell it) '*Mounseer, swivvy maw!*'
　　And 'marshall'd' him so　'The way he should go,'
Upstairs to an attic, large, gloomy, and low,
　　Without table or chair,　Or a movable there,
Save an old-fashion'd bedstead, much out of repair,
That stood at the end most remov'd from the stair.—
　　With a grin and a shrug　The host points to the rug,
Just as much as to say 'There!—I think you'll be snug!'
　　Puts the light on the floor,　Walks to the door,
Makes a formal Salaam, and is then seen no more;
When just as the ear lost the sound of his tread,
To the Bagman's surprise, and, at first to his dread,
The great curly-hair'd Dog crept from under the bed!—

—It's a very nice thing when a man's in a fright,
And thinks matters all wrong, to find matters all right;
As, for instance, when going home latish at night
Through the Churchyard, and seeing a thing all in white,
Which, of course, one is led to consider a Sprite,
　　To find that the Ghost　Is merely a post,
Or a miller, or chalky-faced donkey at most;
Or, when taking a walk as the evenings begin
To close, or, as some people call it, 'draw in,'
And some undefined form, 'looming large' through the haze,
Presents itself, right in your path, to your gaze,
　　Inducing a dread　Of a knock on the head,
Or a sever'd carotid, to find that instead
Of one of those ruffians who murder and fleece men,
It's your uncle, or one of the 'Rural Policemen';—
　　Then the blood flows again　Through artery and vein:
You're delighted with what just before gave you pain;
You laugh at your fears—and your friend in the fog
Meets a welcome as cordial as Anthony Blogg
Now bestow'd on *his* friend—the great curly-tail'd Dog.

For the Dog leap'd up, and his paws found a place
On each side his neck in a canine embrace,
And he lick'd Blogg's hands, and he lick'd his face,

And he waggled his tail as much as to say,
'Mr Blogg, we've forgather'd before to-day!'
And the Bagman saw, as he now sprang up,
    What, beyond all doubt,   He might have found out
Before, had he not been so eager to sup,
'Twas Sancho!—the Dog he had rear'd from a pup!—
The Dog who when sinking had seized his hair,—
The Dog who had saved and conducted him there,—
The Dog he had lost out of Billiter Square!!

    It's passing sweet,   An absolute treat
When friends, long sever'd by distance, meet,—
With what warmth and affection each other they greet!
Especially too, as we very well know,
If there seems any chance of a little *cadeau*,
A 'Present from Brighton,' or 'Token' to show,
In the shape of a work-box, ring, bracelet, or so,
That our friends don't forget us, although they may go
To Ramsgate, or Rome, or Fernando Po.
If some little advantage seems likely to start
From a fifty-pound note to a twopenny tart,
It's surprising to see how it softens the heart,
And you'll find those whose hopes from the other are strongest,
Use, in common, endearments the thickest and longest.
    But it was not so here;   For, although it is clear,
When abroad, and we have not a single friend near,
E'en a cur that will love us becomes very dear,
And the balance of interest 'twixt him and the Dog
Of course was inclining to Anthony Blogg,
    Yet he, first of all, ceased   To encourage the beast,
Perhaps thinking 'Enough is as good as a feast';
And besides, as we've said, being sleepy and mellow,
He grew tired of patting, and crying 'Poor fellow!'
So his smile by degrees harden'd into a frown,
And his 'That's a good dog!' into 'Down, Sancho, down!'

But nothing could stop his mute fav'rite's caressing,
Who, in fact, seem'd resolved to prevent his undressing,
Using paws, tail, and head,   As if he had said,
'Most beloved of masters, pray, don't go to bed;
You had much better sit up, and pat me instead!'
Nay, at last, when determined to take some repose,
Blogg threw himself down on the outside the clothes,
    Spite of all he could do,   The Dog jump'd up too,
And kept him awake with his very cold nose;

Scratching and whining,   And moaning and pining,
Till Blogg really believed he must have some design in
Thus breaking his rest; above all, when at length
The Dog scratch'd him off from the bed by sheer strength.

Extremely annoy'd by the 'tarnation whop,' as it
's call'd in Kentuck, on his head and its opposite,
    Blogg show'd fight;   When he saw, by the light
Of the flickering candle, that had not yet quite
Burnt down in the socket, though not over bright,
Certain dark-colour'd stains, as of blood newly spilt,
Reveal'd by the dog's having scratch'd off the quilt,—
Which hinted a story of horror and guilt!—
'Twas 'no mistake,'—   He was 'wide awake'
In an instant; for, when only decently drunk,
Nothing sobers a man so completely as 'funk.'

    And hark!—what's that?—   They have got into chat
In the kitchen below—what the deuce are they at?—
There's the ugly old Fisherman scolding his wife—
And she!—by the Pope! she's whetting a knife!—
    At each twist   Of her wrist,
    And her great mutton fist,
The edge of the weapon sounds shriller and louder!—
    The fierce kitchen fire   Had not made Blogg perspire
Half so much, or a dose of the best James's powder.—
It ceases—all's silent!—and now, I declare
There's somebody crawls up that rickety stair.

The horrid old ruffian comes, cat-like, creeping;—
He opens the door just sufficient to peep in,
And sees, as he fancies, the Bagman sleeping!
For Blogg, when he'd once ascertain'd that there was some
'Precious mischief' on foot, had resolv'd to play ''Possum';—
    Down he went, legs and head,   Flat on the bed,
Apparently sleeping as sound as the dead;
While, though none who look'd at him would think such a thing,
Every nerve in his frame was braced up for a spring.
    Then, just as the villain   Crept, stealthily still, in,
And you'd not have insur'd his guest's life for a shilling,
As the knife gleam'd on high, bright and sharp as a razor,
Blogg, starting upright, 'tipped' the fellow 'a facer';—
—Down went man and weapon.—Of all sorts of blows,
From what Mr Jackson reports, I suppose
There are few that surpass a flush hit on the nose.

Now, had I the pen of old Ossian or Homer
(Though each of these names some pronounce a misnomer,
   And say the first person
   Was call'd James M'Pherson,
While, as to the second, they stoutly declare
He was no one knows who, and born no one knows where),
Or had I the quill of Pierce Egan, a writer
Acknowledged the best theoretical fighter
   For the last twenty years,   By the lively young Peers,
Who, doffing their coronets, collars, and ermine, treat
Boxers to 'Max,' at the One Tun in Jermyn Street;—
—I say, could I borrow these Gentlemen's Muses,
More skill'd than my meek one in 'fibbings' and bruises,
   I'd describe now to you   As 'prime a Set-to,'
And 'regular turn-up,' as ever you knew;
Not inferior in 'bottom' to aught you have read of,
Since Cribb, years ago, half knock'd Molyneux' head off.
But my dainty Urania says, 'Such things are shocking!'
   Lace mittens she loves,   Detesting 'The Gloves';
And turning, with air most disdainfully mocking,
From Melpomene's buskin, adopts silk stocking.

So, as far as I can see,   I must leave you to 'fancy'
The thumps, and the bumps, and the ups and the downs,
And the taps, and the slaps, and the raps on the crowns,
That pass'd 'twixt the Husband, Wife, Bagman, and Dog,
As Blogg roll'd over them, and they roll'd over Blogg;
   While what's called 'The Claret'
   Flew over the garret:
   Merely stating the fact,   As each other they whack'd,
The Dog his old master most gallantly back'd;
Making both the *garçons*, who came running in, sheer off,
With 'Hippolyte's' thumb, and 'Alphonse's' left ear off;
   Next, making a stoop on   The buffeting group on
The floor, rent in tatters the old woman's *jupon*;
Then the old man turn'd up, and a fresh bite of Sancho's
Tore out the whole seat of his striped Calimancoes.—
   Really, which way   This desperate fray
Might have ended at last, I'm not able to say,
The dog keeping thus the assassins at bay:
But a few fresh arrivals decided the day;
   For bounce went the door,   In came half a score
Of the passengers, sailors, and one or two more
Who had aided the party in gaining the shore!

It's a great many years ago—mine then were few—
Since I spent a short time in the old *Courageux*;

I think that they say   She had been, in her day,
A First-rate,—but was then what they term a *Rasée*,—
And they took me on board in the Downs where she lay
(Captain Wilkinson held the command, by the way).
In her I pick'd up, on that single occasion,
The little I know that concerns Navigation,
And obtained, *inter alia*, some vague information
Of a practice which often, in cases of robbing,
Is adopted on shipboard—I think it's called 'Cobbing.'
How it's managed exactly I really can't say,
But I think that a Boot-jack is brought into play—
That is, if I'm right:—it exceeds my ability
   To tell how 'tis done;   But the system is one
Of which Sancho's exploit would increase the facility.
And, from all I can learn, I'd much rather be robb'd
Of the little I have in my purse, than be 'cobb'd';—
   That's mere matter of taste:
   But the Frenchman was placed—
I mean the old scoundrel whose actions we've traced—
In such a position, that, on this unmasking,
His consent was the last thing the men thought of asking.
   The old woman, too,   Was obliged to go through,
With her boys, the rough discipline used by the crew,
Who, before they let one of the set see the back of them,
'Cobb'd' the whole party,—ay, 'every man Jack of them.'

MORAL

And now, Gentle Reader, before that I say
Farewell for the present, and wish you good day,
Attend to the moral I draw from my lay!

It ever you travel, like Anthony Blogg,
Be wary of strangers!—don't take too much grog!—
And don't fall asleep, if you should, like a hog!—
Above all—carry with you a curly-tail'd Dog!

Lastly, don't act like Blogg, who, I say it with blushing,
Sold Sancho next month for two guineas at Flushing:
But still on these words of the Bard keep a fix'd eye,
   INGRATUM SI DIXERIS, OMNIA DIXTI!!!

L'ENVOYE

I felt so disgusted with Blogg, from sheer shame of him,
I never once thought to inquire what became of him;
If *you* want to know, Reader, the way, I opine,
   To achieve your design,—
    Mind, it's no wish of mine,—
Is,—(a penny will do't)—by addressing a line
To Turner, Dry, Weipersyde, Rogers, and Pyne.

APPENDIX [1]

SINCE penning this stanza, a learn'd Antiquary
Has put my poor Muse in no trifling quandary,
By writing an essay to prove that he knows a
   Spot which, in truth, is   The *real* 'Bermoothes,'
In the Mediterranean,—now called Lampedosa;
—For proofs, having made, as he farther alleges, stir,
An entry was found in the old Parish Register,
The which at his instance the excellent Vicar ex-
tracted: viz. 'Caliban, base son of Sycorax.'
   —He had rather, by half,
    Have found Prospero's 'Staff';
But 'twas useless to dig, for the want of a pick or axe.—
Colonel Pasley, however, 'tis everywhere said,
Now he's blown up the old Royal George at Spithead,
And the great cliff at Dover, of which we've all read,
Takes his whole apparatus, and goes out to look
And see if he can't try and blow up 'the Book.'
—Gentle Reader, farewell!—If I add one more line,
'He'll be, in all likelihood, blowing up *mine*!'

[1] See page 98.

SECOND SERIES

To Richard Bentley, Esq.

My Dear Sir,

You tell me that a 'generous and enlightened Public' has given a favourable reception to those extracts from our family papers, which, at your suggestion, were laid before it some two years since;—and you hint, with all possible delicacy, that a second volume might not be altogether unacceptable at a period of the year when 'auld warld stories' are more especially in request.— With all my heart,—the old oak chest is not yet empty; in addition to which, I have recently laid my hand upon a long MS. correspondence of my great-uncle, Sir Peregrine Ingoldsby, a cadet of the family, who somehow contrived to attract the notice of George the Second, and received from his 'honour-giving hand' the accolade of knighthood. To this last-named source I am indebted for several of the accompanying histories, while my inestimable friend Simpkinson has bent all the powers of his mighty mind to the task. From Father John's stores I have drawn largely. Our 'Honourable' friend Sucklethumbkin —by the way, he has been beating our covers lately, when he shot a woodcock, and one of the Governor's pointers—gives a graphic account of the Operatic 'row' in which he was heretofore so conspicuous; while even Mrs Barney Maguire (*née Mademoiselle Pauline*), whose horror of Mrs Botherby's cap has no jot diminished, furnishes me with the opening Legend of the series from the *historiettes* of her own *belle France*.

Why will you not run down to Tappington this Christmas?— We have been rather busy of late in carrying into execution the enclosure of Swingfield Minnis under the auspices of my Lord Radnor, and Her Majesty's visit to the neighbourhood has kept us quite alive: the Prince in one of his rides pulled up at the end of the avenue, and, as A—— told Sucklethumbkin, was much taken with the picturesque appearance of our old gable-ends. Unluckily we were all at Canterbury that morning, or proud indeed should we have been to offer his Royal Highness the humble hospitalities of the Hall—and then—fancy Mrs Botherby's —'My Gracious!' By the way, the old lady tells me you left

your night-cap here on your last visit; it is laid up in lavender for
you;—come and reclaim it.   The Yule log will burn bright as
ever in the cedar room.   Bin No. 6 is still one liquid ruby—the
old October yet smiles like mantling amber, in utter disdain of
that vile concoction of camomile which you so pseudonymously
dignify with the title of 'Bitter Ale.'   Make a start, then:—
pitch printers' ink to old Harry,—and come and spend a fortnight with

Yours, till the crack of doom,

THOMAS INGOLDSBY.

Tappington Everard,
    16th Dec. 1842.

THE BLACK MOUSQUETAIRE

A LEGEND OF FRANCE

CANTO I

FRANÇOIS XAVIER AUGUSTE was a gay Mousquetaire,
The Pride of the Camp, the delight of the Fair:
He'd a mien so *distingué*, and so *debonnaire*,
And shrugg'd with a grace so *recherché* and rare,
And he twirl'd his moustache with so charming an air,
—His moustaches I should say, because he'd a pair,—
And, in short, show'd so much of the true *savoir faire*,
All the ladies in Paris were wont to declare,
    That could anyone draw
    Them from Dian's strict law,
Into what Mrs Ramsbottom calls a 'Fox Paw,'
It would be François Xavier Auguste de St Foix.

Now, I'm sorry to say,   At that time of day,
The Court of Versailles was a little too gay;
The Courtiers were all much addicted to Play,
To Bordeaux, Chambertin, Frontignac, St Peray,
    Lafitte, Chateau Margaux,   And Sillery (a cargo
On which John Bull sensibly (?) lays an embargo),
    While Louis Quatorze   Kept about him, in scores,
What the Noblesse, in courtesy, term'd his 'Jane Shores'
—They were call'd by a much coarser name out of doors—
    This, we all must admit, in   A King's not befitting!
For such courses, when followed by persons of quality,
Are apt to detract on the score of morality.

François Xavier Auguste acted much like the rest of them,
Dress'd, drank, and fought, and *chassée*'d with the best of them;
    Took his *œil de perdrix*   Till he scarcely could see,
He would then sally out in the streets for 'a spree';
    His rapier he'd draw,   Pink a *Bourgeois*
(A word which the English translate 'Johnny Raw'),
For your thorough French Courtier, whenever the fit he's in,
Thinks it prime fun to astonish a citizen;
And, perhaps it's no wonder that this kind of scrapes,
In a nation which Voltaire, in one of his japes,
Defines 'an amalgam of Tigers and Apes,'
Should be merely considered as 'Little Escapes.'
    But I'm sorry to add,   Things are almost as bad
A great deal nearer home, and that similar pranks
Amongst young men who move in the very first ranks,
Are by no means confined to the land of the Franks.
    Be this as it will,   In the general, still,
    Though blame him we must,   It is really but just
To our lively young friend, François Xavier Auguste,
    To say, that howe'er   Well known his faults were,
At his Bacchanal parties he always drank fair,
And, when gambling his worst, always play'd on the square,
So that, being much more of pigeon than rook, he
Lost large sums at faro (a game like 'Blind Hookey'),
    And continued to lose,   And to give I O U's,
Till he lost e'en the credit he had with the Jews;
And, a parallel if I may venture to draw
Between François Xavier Auguste de St Foix,
And his namesake, a still more distinguished François,
    Who wrote to his '*sœur*'[1]   From Pavia, '*Mon Cœur,
I have lost all I had in the world *fors l'honneur*.'
    So St Foix might have wrote   No dissimilar note,
'*Vive la bagatelle!—toujours gai—idem semper—*
I've lost all I had in the world but—my temper!'
    From the very beginning,   Indeed, of his sinning,
His air was so cheerful, his manner so winning,
That once he prevailed—or his friends coin the tale for him—
On the bailiff who 'nabbed' him, himself to 'go bail' for him.

---

[1] Mrs Ingoldsby, who is deeply read in Robertson, informs me that this is a
mistake; that the lady to whom this memorable *billet* was delivered by the
hands of Pennalosa, was the unfortunate monarch's mamma, and not his
sister.   I would gladly rectify the error, but then—what am I to do for a
rhyme?—On the whole, I fear I must content myself, like Talleyrand, with
admitting that 'it is worse than a fault—it's a blunder!' for which enormity,
—as honest old Pepys says when he records having kissed his cookmaid,—'I
humbly beg pardon of Heaven, and Mrs Ingoldsby!'

Well—we know in these cases
   Your 'Crabs' and 'Deuce Aces'
Are wont to promote frequent changes of places;
Town doctors, indeed, are most apt to declare
That there's nothing so good as the pure 'country air,'
Whenever exhaustion of person, or purse, in
An invalid cramps him, and sets him a-cursing:
A habit, I'm very much grieved at divulging,
François Xavier Auguste was too prone to indulge in.
   But what could be done?   It's clear as the sun,
That, though nothing's more easy than say 'Cut and run!'
Yet a Guardsman can't live without some sort of fun—
   E'en I or you,   If we'd nothing to do,
Should soon find ourselves looking remarkably blue.
   And, since no one denies   What's so plain to all eyes,
It won't, I am sure, create any surprise
That reflections like these half reduced to despair
François Xavier Auguste, the gay Black Mousquetaire.

   Patience par force!   He *considered*, of course,
But in vain—he could hit on no sort of resource—
   Love?—Liquor?—Law?—Loo?
   They would each of them do,
There's excitement enough in all four, but in none he
Could hope to get on *sans l'argent*—i.e. money.
Love?—no;—ladies like little *cadeaux* from a suitor.
Liquor?—no,—that won't do, when reduced to 'the Pewter.'—
   Then Law?—'tis the same;   It's a very fine game,
But the fees and delays of 'the Courts' are a shame,
As Lord Brougham says himself—who's a very great name,
Though the TIMES made it clear he was perfectly lost in his
Classic attempt at translating Demosthenes,
   And don't know his 'particles.'—
   Who wrote the articles,
Showing his Greek up so, is not known very well;
Many thought Barnes, others Mitchell,—some Merivale;
   But it's scarce worth debate,   Because from the date
Of my tale one conclusion we safely may draw,
Viz.: 'twas not François Xavier Auguste de St Foix!

   Loo?—no;—that he had tried;
   'Twas, in fact, his weak side,
But required more than any purse well supplied.
'Love?—Liquor?—Law?—Loo?   No! 'tis all the same story.
Stay! I have it—*Ma foi!* (that's 'Odd's Bobs!') there is GLORY!
   Away with dull care!   *Vive le Roi! Vive la Guerre!*
Peste!   I'd almost forgot I'm a Black Mousquetaire!

When a man is like me,   *Sans six sous, sans souci,*
A bankrupt in purse,   And in character worse,
With a shocking bad hat, and his credit at Zero,
What on earth can he hope to become,—but a Hero?
    What a famous thought this is!   I'll go as Ulysses
Of old did—like him I'll see manners, and know countries;[1]
Cut Paris,—and gaming,—and throats in the Low Countries.'

So said, and so done—he arranged his affairs,
And was off like a shot to his Black Mousquetaires.

    Now it happen'd just then   That Field-Marshal Turenne
Was a good deal in want of 'some active young men,'
    To fill up the gaps   Which, through sundry mishaps,
Had been made in his ranks by a certain 'Great Condé,'
A General unrivall'd—at least in his own day—
    Whose valour was such,   That he did not care much
If he fought with the French,—or the Spaniards,—or Dutch,—
A fact which has stamped him a rather 'Cool hand,'
Being nearly related to *Louis le Grand.*
It had been all the same had that King been his brother;
He fought sometimes with one, and sometimes with another;
    For war, so exciting,   He took such delight in,
He did not care whom he fought, so he *was* fighting.
And, as I've just said, had amused himself then
By tickling the tail of Field-Marshal Turenne;
Since which, the Field-Marshal's most pressing concern
Was to tickle some other Chief's tail in his turn.

What a fine thing a battle is!—not one of those
Which one saw at the late Mr Andrew Ducrow's,
Where a dozen of scene-shifters, drawn up in rows,
Would a dozen more scene-shifters boldly oppose,
    Taking great care their blows
    Did not injure their foes,
And alike, save in colour and cut of their clothes,
Which were varied, to give more effect to 'Tableaux,'
    While Stickney the Great
    Flung the gauntlet to Fate,
And made us all tremble, so gallantly did he come
On to encounter bold General Widdicombe—
But a real, good fight, like Pultowa, or Lützen
Which Gustavus the great ended all his disputes in),
Or that which Suwarrow engaged without boots in,

----

[1] Qui mores hominum multorum vidit et urbes.
        Who viewed men's manners, Londons, Yorks, and Derbys.
    E 185

Or Dettingen, Fontenoy, Blenheim, or Minden,
Or the one Mr Campbell describes, Hohenlinden,
 Where 'the sun was low,'
 The ground all over snow,
And dark as mid-winter the swift Iser's flow,—
Till its colour was alter'd by General Moreau;
While the big drum was heard in the dead of the night,
Which rattled the Bard out of bed in a fright,
And he ran up the steeple to look at the fight.
 'Twas in just such another one
  (Names only bother one—
Dutch ones, indeed, are sufficient to smother one)
In the Netherlands somewhere—I cannot say where—
 Suffice it that there *La Fortune de guerre*
Gave a cast of her calling to our Mousquetaire,
One fine morning, in short, François Xavier Auguste,
After making some scores of his foes 'bite the dust,'
Got a mouthful himself of the very same crust;
And though, as the Bard says, 'No law is more just
Than for *Necis artifices*,'—so they call'd fiery
Soldados at Rome,—'*arte suâ perire*,'
 Yet Fate did not draw This poetical law
To its fullest extent in the case of St Foix.
His Good Genius most probably found out some flaw,
 And diverted the shot From some deadlier spot
To a bone which, I think, to the best of my memory, 's
Call'd by Professional men the '*os femoris*';
And the ball being one of those named from its shape.
And some fancied resemblance it bears to the grape,
 St Foix went down, With a groan and a frown,
And a hole in his small-clothes the size of a crown.—
 —Stagger'd a bit By this 'palpable hit,'
He turn'd on his face, and went off in a fit!

Yes!—a Battle's a very fine thing while you're fighting,
These same Ups-and-Downs are so very exciting.

 But a sombre sight is a Battle-field
  To the sad survivor's sorrowing eye,
 Where those, who scorn'd to fly or yield
  In one promiscuous carnage lie;
   When the cannon's roar Is heard no more,
 And the thick dun smoke has roll'd away,
 And the victor comes for a last survey
 Of the well-fought field of yesterday!

No triumphs flush that haughty brow,—
　No proud exulting look is there,—
His eagle glance is humbled now,
　As, earthward bent, in anxious care
It seeks the form whose stalwart pride
But yester-morn was by his side!

And there it lies!—on yonder bank
　Of corses, which themselves had breath
But yester-morn—now cold and dank,
　With other dews than those of death!
Powerless as it had ne'er been born
The hand that clasp'd his—yester-morn!

And there are widows wand'ring there,
　That roam the blood-besprinkled plain,
And listen in their dumb despair
　For sounds they ne'er may hear again!
One word, however faint and low,—
Ay, e'en a groan,—were music now!

And this is Glory!—Fame!—
　　　　　　　　　But, pshaw!
　Miss Muse, you're growing sentimental;
Besides, such things *we* never saw;
　In fact, they're merely Continental.
And then your Ladyship forgets
Some widows came for epaulettes.

So go back to your canter; for one, I declare,
Is now fumbling about our capsized Mousquetaire,
　A beetle-brow'd hag,　With a knife and a bag,
And an old tatter'd bonnet which, thrown back, discloses
The ginger complexion, and one of those noses
Peculiar to females named Levy and Moses,
Such as nervous folks still, when they come in their way, shun,
Old vixen-faced tramps of the Hebrew persuasion.

You remember, I trust,　François Xavier Auguste,
Had uncommon fine limbs, and a very fine bust.
Now there's something—I cannot tell what it may be—
About good-looking gentlemen turn'd twenty-three,
Above all when laid up with a wound in the knee,
Which affects female hearts, in no common degree,
With emotions in which many feelings combine,
Very easy to fancy, though hard to define;

Ugly or pretty,   Stupid or witty,
Young or old, they experience, in country or city,
What's clearly not Love—yet it's warmer than Pity—
And some such a feeling, no doubt, 'tis that stays
The hand you may see that old Jezebel raise,
    Arm'd with the blade,   So oft used in her trade,
The horrible calling e'en now she is plying,
Despoiling the dead, and dispatching the dying!
For these 'nimble Conveyancers,' after such battles,
Regarding as *treasure trove* all goods and chattels,
Think nought, in 'perusing and settling' the titles,
So safe as six inches of steel in the vitals.

    Now don't make a joke of   That feeling I spoke of;
For, as sure as you're born, that same feeling,—whate'er
It may be,—saves the life of the young Mousquetaire!
The knife, that was levell'd erstwhile at his throat,
Is employ'd now in ripping the lace from his coat,
And from what, I suppose, I must call his *culotte*;
    And his pockets, no doubt,   Being turned inside out,
That his *mouchoir* and gloves may be put 'up the spout'
(For of coin, you may well conceive, all she can do
Fails to ferret out even a single *écu*);
As a muscular Giant would handle an elf,
The virago at last lifts the soldier himself,
And, like a She-Samson, at length lays him down
In a hospital form'd in the neighbouring town!
    I am not very sure,   But I think 'twas Namur;
And there she now leaves him, expecting a cure.

CANTO II

I abominate physic—I care not who knows
That there's nothing on earth I detest like 'a dose'—
That yellowish-green-looking fluid, whose hue
I consider extremely unpleasant to view,
With its sickly appearance, that trenches so near
On what Homer defines the complexion of Fear;
    Χλωρὸν δέος, I mean,   A nasty pale green,
Though for want of some word that may better avail,
I presume, our translators have rendered it 'pale';
    For consider the cheeks
    Of those 'well-booted Greeks,'
Their Egyptian descent was a question of weeks;
Their complexion, of course, like a half-decayed leek's;
And you'll see in an instant the thing that I mean in it,
A Greek face in a funk had a good deal of green in it.

I repeat, I abominate physic; but then,
If folks *will* go campaigning about with such men
As the Great Prince de Condé, and Marshal Turenne,
     They may fairly expect   To be now and then check'd
By a bullet, or sabre cut.   Then their best solace is
Found, I admit, in green potions, and boluses;
     So, of course, I don't blame
     St Foix, wounded and lame,
If he swallowed a decent *quant. suff.* of the same;
Though I'm told, in such cases, it's not the French plan
To pour in their drastics as fast as they can,
The practice of many an English *Savan,*
     But to let off a man   With a little *ptisanne,*
And gently to chafe the *patella* (knee-pan).

'Oh, woman!' Sir Walter observes, 'when the brow
's wrung with pain, what a minist'ring Angel art thou!'
Thou'rt a 'minist'ring Angel' in no less degree,
I can boldly assert, when the pain's in the knee;
     And medical friction   Is, past contradiction,
Much better performed by a She than a He.
A fact which, indeed, comes within my own knowledge,
For I well recollect, when a youngster at College,
     And, therefore, can quote   A surgeon of note,
Mr Grosvenor of Oxford, who not only wrote
On the subject a very fine treatise, but, still as his
Patients came in, certain soft-handed Phyllises
Were at once set to work on their legs, arms, and backs,
And rubbed out their complaints in a couple of cracks.—
     Now, they say,   To this day,
     When sick people can't pay
On the Continent, many of this kind of nurses
Attend, without any demand on their purses;
And these females, some old, others still in their teens,
Some call 'Sisters of Charity,' others 'Beguines.'
They don't take the vows; but, half-Nun and half-Lay,
Attend you; and when you've got better, they say,
'You're exceedingly welcome!   There's nothing to pay.
     Our task is now done.   You are able to run,
We never take money; we cure you for fun!'
Then they drop you a curtsy, and wish you good day,
And go off to cure somebody else the same way.
—A great many of these, at the date of my tale,
In Namur walked the hospitals, workhouse, and jail.

     Among them was one,   A most sweet Demi-nun.
Her cheek pensive and pale; tresses bright as the Sun,—

Not carroty—no; though you'd fancy you saw burn
Such locks as the Greeks lov'd, which moderns call auburn.
These were partially seen through the veil which they wor
    all;
Her teeth were of pearl, and her lips were of coral;
Her eyelashes silken; her eyes, fine large blue ones,
Were sapphires (I don't call these similes new ones;
But, in metaphors, freely confess I've a leaning
To such, new or old, as convey best one's meaning).—
Then, for figure? In faith it was downright barbarity
    To muffle a form   Might an anchorite warm
In the fusty stuff gown of a *Sœur de la Charité*;
And no poet could fancy, no painter could draw
One more perfect in all points, more free from a flaw,
Than her's who now sits by the couch of St Foix,
    Chafing there,   With such care,
    And so dove-like an air,
His leg, till her delicate fingers are charr'd
With the Steer's opodeldoc, joint-oil, and goulard;
—Their Dutch appellations are really too hard
To be brought into verse by a transmarine Bard.—

    Now you'll see,   And agree,   I am certain, with me,
When a young man's laid up with a wound in his knee:
    And a Lady sits there,   On a rush-bottom'd chair,
To hand him the mixtures his doctors prepare,
And a bit of lump-sugar to make matters square;
Above all, when the Lady's remarkably fair,
And the wounded young man is a gay Mousquetaire,
It's a ticklish affair, you may swear, for the pair,
And may lead on to mischief before they're aware.

I really don't think, spite of what friends would call his
'*Penchant* for liaisons,' and graver men 'follies'
(For my own part, I think planting thorns on their pillows,
And leaving poor maidens to weep and wear willows,
Is not to be classed among mere peccadilloes),
His '*faults*,' I should say—I don't think François Xavier
Entertain'd any thoughts of improper behaviour
Tow'rds his nurse, or that once to induce her to sin he meant
While superintending his draughts and his liniment.
    But, as he grew stout,   And was getting about
Thoughts came into his head that had better been out;
While Cupid's an urchin   We know deserves birching,
He's so prone to delude folks, and leave them the lurch in.

'Twas doubtless his doing   That absolute ruin
Was the end of all poor dear Therèse's shampooing.—
'Tis a subject I don't like to dwell on: but such
Things will happen—ay, e'en 'mongst the phlegmatic Dutch.

'When Woman,' as Goldsmith declares, 'stoops to folly,
    And finds out too late that false man can betray,'
She is apt to look dismal, and grow 'melan-choly,'
    And, in short, to be anything rather than gay.

He goes on to remark that 'to punish her lover,
    Wring his bosom, and draw the tear into his eye,
There is but one method' which he can discover
    That's likely to answer—that one is 'to die'!

He's wrong—the wan and withering cheek;
    The thin lips, pale, and drawn apart;
The dim yet tearless eyes, that speak
    The misery of the breaking heart;

The wasted form, th' enfeebled tone
    That whispering mocks the pitying ear;
Th' imploring glances heavenward thrown,
    As heedless, helpless, hopeless here;

These wring the false one's heart enough,
    If 'made of penetrable stuff.'
    And poor Therèse   Thus pines and decays,
Till, stung with remorse, St Foix takes a post-chaise,
    With, for 'wheelers,' two bays,
    And, for 'leaders,' two greys,
And soon reaches France, by the help of relays,
Flying shabbily off from the sight of his victim,
And driving as fast as if Old Nick had kick'd him.

    She, poor sinner   Grows thinner and thinner,
Leaves off eating breakfast, and luncheon, and dinner,
Till you'd really suppose she could have nothing in her.—
One evening—'twas just as the clock struck eleven—
They saw she'd been sinking fast ever since seven,—
She breath'd one deep sigh, threw one look up to Heaven,
    And all was o'er!—   Poor Therèse was no more—
She was gone!—the last breath that she managed to draw
Escaped in one half-utter'd word—'twas 'St Foix!'

Who can fly from himself?   Bitter cares, when you feel 'em,
Are not cured by travel—as Horace says, '*Coelum*
Non animum mutant qui currunt trans mare!'
It's climate, not mind, that by roaming men vary—
Remorse for temptation to which you have yielded, is
A shadow you can't sell as Peter Schlemil did his;
It haunts you for ever—in bed and at board,—
    Ay, e'en in your dreams.
    And you can't find, it seems,
Any proof that a guilty man ever yet snored!
It is much if he slumbers at all, which but few,
—François Xavier Auguste was an instance—can do.
    Indeed, from the time   He committed the crime
Which cut off poor Sister Thérèse in her prime,
He was not the same man that he had been—his plan
Was quite changed—in wild freaks he no more led the van;
    He'd scarce sleep a wink in
    A week; but sit thinking,
    From company shrinking—
    He quite gave up drinking.
At the mess-table, too, where now seldom he came,
Fish, *fricassée, fricandeau, potage,* or game,
Dindon aux truffes, or *turbot à la crème,*
No!—he still shook his head,—it was always the same,
Still he never complained that the cook was to blame!
'Twas his appetite fail'd him—no matter how rare
And *recherché* the dish, how delicious the fare,—
What he used to like best he no longer could bear;
    But he'd there sit and stare   With an air of despair:
    Took no care, but would wear
    Boots that wanted repair;
Such a shirt too! you'd think he'd no linen to spare.
He omitted to shave;—he neglected his hair,
And looked more like a Guy than a gay Mousquetaire.

One thing, above all, most excited remark:
In the evening he seldom sat long after dark.
Not that then, as of yore, he'd go out for 'a lark'
    With his friends; but when they,
    After taking *café*
Would have broiled bones and kidneys brought in on a tray,
—Which I own I consider a very good way,
If a man's not dyspeptic, to wind up the day—
No persuasion on earth could induce him to stay;
But he'd take up his candlestick, just nod his head
By way of 'Good evening!' and walk off to bed.

Yet even when there he seem'd no better off,
For he'd wheeze, and he'd sneeze, and he'd hem! and he'd
  cough;
  And they'd hear him all night,
  Sometimes, sobbing outright,
While his valet, who often endeavour'd to peep,
Declared that 'his master was never asleep!
But would sigh, and would groan, slap his forehead, and weep;
  That about ten o'clock His door he would lock,
And then never would open it, let who would knock!—
  He had heard him,' he said,
  'Sometimes jump out of bed,
And talk as if speaking to one who was dead!
  He'd groan and he'd moan, In so piteous a tone,
Begging someone or other to let him alone,
That it really would soften the heart of a stone
To hear him exclaim so, and call upon Heaven;
Then—The bother began always *just at eleven*!'

François Xavier Auguste, as I've told you before,
I believe, was a popular man in his corps,
  And his comrades, not one Of whom knew of the Nun
Now began to consult what was best to be done.
  Count Cordon Bleu And the Sieur de la Roue
Confess'd they did *not* know at all what to do:
But the Chevalier Hippolyte Hector Achille
Alphonso Stanislaus Émile de Grandville
  Made a fervent appeal To the zeal they must feel
For their friend, so distinguished an officer, 's weal.
'The first thing,' he said, 'was to find out the matter
That bored their poor friend so, and caused all this clatter—
  Mort de ma vie!' —Here he took some rapee—
'Be the cause what it may, he shall tell it to me!'—
He was right, sure enough—in a couple of days
He worms out the whole story of Sister Thérèse,
Now entomb'd, poor dear soul! in some Dutch *Père la Chaise.*
—'But the worst thing of all,' François Xavier declares,
'Is, whenever I've taken my candle upstairs,
There's Thérèse sitting there—upon one of those chairs!
  Such a frown, too, she wears, And so frightfully glares
That I'm really prevented from saying my pray'rs,
While an odour,—the very reverse of perfume,—
More like rhubarb or senna,—pervades the whole room.

  Hector Achille Stanislaus Émile,
When he heard him talk so felt an odd sort of feel;
Not that *he* cared for Ghosts—he was far too genteel;
  * E 185

Still a queerish sensation came on when he saw
   Him, whom, for fun,   They'd, by way of a pun
On his person and principles, nicknamed *Sans Foi,*
   —A man whom they had, you see,
   Mark'd as a Sadducee,—
In his horns, all at once, so completely to draw,
And to talk of a Ghost with such manifest awe!—
It excited the Chevalier Grandville's surprise;
He shrugg'd up his shoulders, he turn'd up his eyes,
And he thought with himself that he could not do less
Than lay the whole matter before the whole Mess.

   Repetition's detestable;—   So, as you're best able,
Paint to your self the effect at the Mess-table—
   How the bold Brigadiers   Prick'd up their ears,
And received the account, some with fears, some with sneers:
   How the Sieur de la Roue   Said to Count Cordon Bleu,
'*Ma foi—c'est bien drôle*—Monseigneur, what say you?'—
   How Count Cordon Bleu
   Declared he 'thought so too';—
How the Colonel affirmed that 'the case was quite new';—
   How the Captains and Majors   Began to lay wagers
How far the Ghost part of the story was true;—
How, at last, when asked, 'What was the best thing to do?'
Everybody was silent,—for nobody knew!—
And how, in the end, they said, 'No one could deal
With the matter so well, from his prudence and zeal,
As the Gentleman who was the first to reveal
This strange story—viz. Hippolyte Hector Achille
Alphonse Stanislaus Émile de Grandville!'

I need scarcely relate   The plans, little and great,
Which came into the Chevalier Hippolyte's pate
To rescue his friend from his terrible foes,
Those mischievous Imps, whom the world, I suppose,
From extravagant notions respecting their hue
Has strangely agreed to denominate 'Blue,'
Inasmuch as his schemes were of no more avail
Than those he had, early in life, found to fail,
When he strove to lay salt on some little bird's tail.
   In vain did he try   With strong waters to ply
His friend, on the ground that he never could spy
Such a thing as a Ghost, with a drop in his eye;
St Foix never would drink now unless he was dry;
Besides, what the vulgar call 'sucking the monkey'
Has much less effect on a man when he's funky.

In vain did he strive to detain him at table
Till his 'dark hour' was over—he never was able,
　　Save once, when at Mess,　With that sort of address
Which the British call 'Humbug,' and Frenchmen '*Finesse*'
(It's 'Blarney' in Irish—I don't know the Scotch),
He fell to admiring his friend's English watch.[1]
　　He examined the face,　And the back of the case,
And the young Lady's portrait there, done on enamel, he
'Saw by the likeness was one of the family';
　　Cried '*Superbe!—Magnifique!*'
　　(With his tongue in his cheek)—
Then he open'd the case, just to take a peep in it, and
Seized the occasion to pop back the minute-hand.
With a demi-*congé*, and a shrug, and grin, he
Returns the bijou and—*c'est une affaire finie*—
'I've done him,' thinks he, 'now I'll wager a guinea!'

　　It happen'd that day　They were all very gay,
'Twas the *Grand Monarque*'s birthday—that is, 'twas St Louis's,
Which in Catholic countries, of course, they would view as his—
　　So when Hippolyte saw　Him about to withdraw,
He cried, 'Come—that won't do, my fine fellow, St Foix,—
Give us five minutes longer and drink *Vive le Roi*.'

　　François Xavier Auguste,　Without any mistrust
Of the trick that was play'd, drew his watch from his fob,
Just glanced at the hour, then agreed to 'hob-nob,'
　　Fill'd a bumper, and rose
　　With '*Messieurs*, I propose'—
He paused—his blanch'd lips fail'd to utter the toast!
'Twas *eleven*!—he thought it half past ten at most—
Ev'ry limb, nerve, and muscle grew stiff as a post,—
　　His jaw dropp'd—his eyes
　　Swell'd to twice their own size—
And he stood as a pointer would stand—at a Ghost!
—Then shriek'd, as he fell on the floor like a stone.
'Ah! Sister Thérèse! now—do let me alone!'

It's amazing by sheer perseverance what men do,—
As waters wear stone by the '*Saepe cadendo*,'
If they stick to Lord Somebody's motto, '*Agendo!*'
Was it not Robert Bruce?—I declare I've forgot,
But I think it was Robert—you'll find it in Scott—
Who, when cursing Dame Fortune, was taught by a Spider,
'She's sure to come round, if you will but abide her.'

---

[1] 'Tompion's, I presume?'—FARQUHAR.

Then another great Rob.
Called 'White-headed Bob,'
Whom I once saw receive such a thump on the 'nob'
From a fist which might almost an elephant brain,
That I really believed, at the first, he was slain,
For he lay like a log on his back on the plain,
Till a gentleman present, accustomed to *train*,
Drew out a small lancet, and open'd a vein
Just below his left eye, which relieving the pain,
He stood up, like a trump, with an air of disdain,
    While his 'backer' was fain,
    —For he could not refrain—
(He was dress'd in pea-green, with a pin and gold chain,
And I think I heard somebody call him 'Squire Hayne')
To whisper *ten words* one should always retain,
—TAKE A SUCK AT THE LEMON, AND AT HIM AGAIN!!!'—
A hint ne'er surpassed, though thus spoken at random,
Since Teucer's apostrophe—*Nil desperandum*!
—Grandville acted on it, and order'd his Tandem.

He had heard St Foix say,   That no very great way
From Namur was a snug little town call'd Grandpré,
Near which, a few miles from the banks of the Maese,
Dwelt a pretty twin-sister of poor dear Thérèse,
Of the same age, of course, the same father, same mother,
And as like to Thérèse as one pea to another;
    She liv'd with her Mamma,   Having lost her Papa,
Late of contraband *schnaps* an unlicensed distiller,
And her name was Des Moulins (in English, Miss Miller).

Now, though Hippolyte Hector
Could hardly expect her
To feel much regard for her sister's 'protector,'
When she'd seen him so shamefully leave and neglect her;
    Still, he very well knew   In this world there are few
But are ready much Christian forgiveness to shew,
For other folk's wrongs—if well paid so to do—
And he'd seen to what acts '*Res augustae*' compel beaux
And belles, whose affairs have once got out at elbows,
With the magic effect of a handful of crowns
Upon people whose pockets boast nothing but 'browns';
    A few francs well applied
    He'd no doubt would decide
Miss Agnes Des Moulins to jump up and ride
As far as headquarters, next day, by his side;
For the distance was nothing, to speak by comparison,
To the town where the Mousquetaires now lay in garrison;

Then he thought, by the aid
Of a veil, and gown made
Like those worn by the lady his friend had betray'd,
They might dress up Miss Agnes so like to the Shade,
Which he fancied he saw, of that poor injured maid,
Come each night, with her pale face, his guilt to upbraid;
That if once introduced to his room thus array'd,
And then unmask'd as soon as she'd long enough stay'd,
'Twould be no very difficult task to persuade
Him the whole was a scurvy trick, cleverly play'd,
Out of spite and revenge, by a mischievous jade!

With respect to the scheme—though I do not call that a gem—
Still I've known soldiers adopt a worse stratagem,
And that, too, among the decided approvers
Of General Sir David Dundas's 'Manœuvres.'
   There's a proverb, however,
   I've always thought clever,
Which my Grandmother never was tired of repeating,
'The proof of the Pudding is found in the eating!'
We shall see, in the sequel, how Hector Achille
Had mix'd up the suet and plums for *his* meal.

The night had set in;—'twas a dark and a gloomy one;—
Off went St Foix to his chamber; a roomy one,
   Five storeys high,   The first floor from the sky,
And lofty enough to afford great facility
For playing a game, with the youthful nobility
   Of 'crack corps' a deal in
   Request, when they're feeling,
In dull country quarters, ennui on them stealing;
   A wet wafer's applied   To a sixpence's side,
Then it's spun with the thumb up to stick on the ceiling;
Intellectual amusement, which custom allows old troops,—
I've seen it here practised at home by our Household troops.
   He'd a table, and bed,
   And three chairs; and all's said.—
A bachelor's barrack, where'er you discern it, you're
Sure to find not overburthen'd with furniture.

François Xavier Auguste lock'd and bolted his door
With just the same caution he'd practised before;
   Little he knew   That the Count Cordon Bleu,
With Hector Achille, and the Sieur de la Roue,
Had been up there before him, and drawn ev'ry screw!

And now comes the moment—the watches and clocks
All point to *eleven*!—the bolts and the locks
Give way—and the party turn out their bag-fox!—
   With step noiseless and light,   Though half in a fright,
'A cup in her left hand, a draught in her right,'
In her robe long and black, and her veil long and white,
Ma'amselle Agnes des Moulins walks in as a Sprite!—
   She approaches the bed   With the same silent tread
Just as though she had been at least half a year dead!
Then seating herself on the 'rush-bottom'd chair,'
Throws a cold stony glance on the Black Mousquetaire.

If you 're one of the 'play-going public,' kind reader,
And not a Moravian or rigid Seceder,
   You 've seen Mr Kean,   I mean in that scene
Of Macbeth,—by some thought the crack one of the piece,
Which has been so well painted by Mr M'Clise,—
When he wants, after having stood up to say grace,[1]
To sit down to his haggis, and can't find a place;
   You remember his stare
   At the high-back'd arm-chair,
Where the Ghost sits that nobody else knows is there,
And how, after saying 'What man dares I dare!'
He proceeds to declare   He should not so much care
If it came in the shape of a 'tiger' or 'bear,'
But he don't like its shaking its long gory hair!
While the obstinate Ghost, as determined to brave him,
   With a horrible grin,   Sits, and cocks up his chin,
Just as though he was asking the tyrant to shave him.
   And Lenox and Rosse   Seem quite at a loss
If they ought to go on with their sheep's head and sauce;
And Lady Macbeth looks uncommonly cross,
   And says in a huff   It 's all 'Proper stuff!'—
All this you 'll have seen, Reader, often enough;
So, perhaps 'twill assist you in forming some notion
Of what must have been François Xavier's emotion,
   If you fancy what troubled   Macbeth to be *doubled*
And, instead of *one* Banquo to stare in his face
Without 'speculation,' suppose he 'd *a brace*!

I wish I 'd poor Fuseli's pencil, who ne'er I believe was exceeded in painting the terrible,
   Or that of Sir Joshua   Reynolds, who was so a-
droit in depicting it—*vide* his piece
Descriptive of Cardinal Beaufort's decease,

              [1] 'May good digestion wait on appetite,
                And health on both.'—MACBETH.

Where that prelate is lying   Decidedly dying,
   With the King and his suite,
   Standing just at his feet,
And his hands, as Dame Quickly says, fumbling the sheet;
While, close at his ear, with the air of a scorner,
'Busy, meddling,' Old Nick's grinning up in the corner.
But painting's an art I confess I am raw in,
The fact is, I never took lessons in drawing:
   Had I done so, instead   Of the lines you have read,
I'd have giv'n you a sketch should have fill'd you with dread
François Xavier Auguste squatting up in his bed,
   His hands widely spread,   His complexion like lead,
Ev'ry hair that he has standing up on his head,
As when, Agnes des Moulins first catching his view,
Now right, and now left, rapid glances he threw,
Then shriek'd with a wild and unearthly halloo,
         Mon Dieu! v'la deux!!
      BY THE POPE THERE ARE TWO!!!'

He fell back—one long aspiration he drew.
   In flew De la Roue,   And Count Cordon Bleu,
Pommade, Pomme-de-terre, and the rest of their crew.
He stirr'd not,—he spoke not,—he none of them knew!
   And Achille cried 'Odzooks!   I fear by his looks,
Our friend, François Xavier, has popp'd off the hooks!'

'Twas too true!   *Malheureux!!*
It was done!—he had ended his earthly career,—
He had gone off at once with a flea in his ear;
—The Black Mousquetaire was as dead as Small-beer!!

L'Envoye

A moral more in point I scarce could hope
Than this, from Mr Alexander Pope.

If ever chance should bring some Cornet gay,
And pious Maid,—as, possibly, it may,—
From Knightsbridge Barracks, and the shades serene
Of Clapham Rise, as far as Kensal Green;
O'er some pale marble when they join their heads
To kiss the falling tears each other sheds;
Oh! may they pause!—and think, in silent awe,
He, that he reads the words, '*Ci gît St Foix!*'—
She, that the tombstone which her eye surveys
Bears this sad line,—'*Hic jacet Sœur Therèse!*'—

Then shall they sigh, and weep, and murmuring say,
'Oh! may we never play such tricks as they!'—
And if at such a time some Bard there be,
Some sober Bard, addicted much to tea
And sentimental song—like Ingoldsby—
If such there be—who sings and sips so well,
Let him this sad, this tender story tell!
Warn'd by the tale, the gentle pair shall boast,
'I've 'scaped the Broken Heart!'—'and I the Ghost!'

SIR RUPERT THE FEARLESS

A Legend of Germany

Sir Rupert the Fearless, a gallant young knight,
Was equally ready to tipple or fight,
   Crack a crown, or a bottle,   Cut sirloin, or throttle;
In brief, or as Hume says, 'to sum up the tottle,'
Unstain'd by dishonour, unsullied by fear,
All his neighbours pronounced him a *preux chevalier*.
Despite these perfections, corporeal and mental,
He had one slight defect, viz. a rather lean rental;
Besides, as 'tis own'd there are spots in the sun,
So it must be confessed that Sir Rupert had one;
   Being rather unthinking,   He'd scarce sleep a wink in
A night, but addict himself sadly to drinking,
   And, what moralists say   Is as naughty—to play,
To *Rouge et Noir*, Hazard, Short Whist, Écarté;
Till these and a few less defensible fancies
Brought the Knight to the end of his slender finances.

When at length through his boozing,
   And tenants refusing
Their rents, swearing 'times were so bad they were losing,'
   His steward said, 'O, sir,   It's some time ago, sir,
Since aught through my hands reach'd the baker or grocer,
And the tradesmen in general are grown great complainers,'
Sir Rupert the brave thus addressed his retainers:

'My friends, since the stock   Of my father's old hock
Is out, with the Kürchwasser, Barsac, Moselle,
And we're fairly reduced to the pump and the well,
   I presume to suggest,   We shall all find it best
For each to shake hands with his friends ere he goes,
Mount his horse, if he has one, and—follow his nose;

As to me, I opine,   Left *sans* money or wine,
My best way is to throw myself into the Rhine,
Where pitying travellers may sigh, as they cross over,
"Though he lived a *roué*, yet he died a philosopher."'

The Knight, having bow'd out his friends thus politely,
Got into his skiff, the full moon shining brightly,
    By the light of whose beam,
    He soon spied on the stream
A dame, whose complexion was fair as new cream,
    Pretty pink silken hose   Cover'd ankles and toes,
In other respects she was scanty of clothes;
For, so says tradition, both written and oral,
Her *one* garment was loop'd up with bunches of coral.
Full sweetly she sang to a sparkling guitar,
With silver cords stretch'd over Derbyshire spar,
    And she smiled on the Knight,
    Who, amazed at the sight,
Soon found his astonishment merged in delight;
    But the stream by degrees
    Now rose up to her knees,
Till at length it invaded her very chemise,
While the heavenly strain, as the wave seemed to swallow her,
And slowly she sank, sounded fainter and hollower;
    —Jumping up in his boat,   And discarding his coat,
'Here goes,' cried Sir Rupert, 'by jingo I'll follow her!'
Then into the water he plunged with a souse
That was heard quite distinctly by those in the house.

Down, down, forty fathom and more from the brink,
Sir Ruper the Fearless continues to sink,
    And, as downward he goes,
    Still the cold water flows
Through his ears, and his eyes, and his mouth, and his nose,
Till the rum and the brandy he'd swallow'd since lunch
Wanted nothing but lemon to fill him with punch;
Some minutes elapsed since he enter'd the flood,
Ere his heels touch'd the bottom, and stuck in the mud.

    But oh! what a sight   Met the eyes of the Knight,
When he stood in the depth of the stream bolt upright!—
    A grand stalactite hall,   Like the cave of Fingal,
Rose above and about him;—great fishes and small
Came thronging around him, regardless of danger,
And seemed all agog for a peep at the stranger.

Their figures and forms to describe, language fails—
They'd such very odd heads, and such very odd tails;
Of their genus or species a sample to gain,
You would ransack all Hungerford market in vain;
    E'en the famed Mr Myers
    Would scarcely find buyers,
Though hundreds of passengers doubtless would stop
To stare, were such monsters expos'd in his shop.

But little reck'd Rupert these queer-looking brutes,
    Or the efts and the newts   That crawled up his boots,
For a sight, beyond any of which I've made mention,
In a moment completely absorb'd his attention.
A huge crystal bath, which, with water far clearer
Than George Robins' filters, or Thorpe's (which are dearer),
    Have ever distill'd,   To the summit was fill'd,
Lay stretch'd out before him,—and every nerve thrill'd
    As scores of young women
    Were diving and swimming,
Till the vision a perfect quandary put him in;—
All slightly accoutred in gauzes and lawns,
They came floating about him like so many prawns.

Sir Rupert, who (barring the few peccadilloes
Alluded to) ere he leapt into the billows
Possess'd irreproachable morals, began
To feel rather queer, as a modest young man;
When forth stepp'd a dame, whom he recognized soon
As the one he had seen by the light of the moon,
And lisp'd, while a soft smile attended each sentence,
'Sir Rupert, I'm happy to make your acquaintance;
    My name is Lurline,   And the ladies you've seen,
All do me the honour to call me their Queen;
I'm delighted to see you, sir, down in the Rhine here,
And hope you can make it convenient to dine here.'

    The Knight blush'd, and bowed,
    As he ogled the crowd
Of subaqueous beauties, then answer'd aloud:
'Ma'am, you do me much honour,—I cannot express
The delight I shall feel—if you'll pardon my dress—
May I venture to say, when a gentleman jumps
In the river at midnight for want of "the dumps,"
He rarely puts on his knee-breeches and pumps;
If I could but have guess'd—what I sensibly feel—
Your politeness—I'd not have come *en dishabille*,
But have put on my *silk* tights in lieu of my *steel*.'

Quoth the lady, 'Dear sir, no apologies, pray,
You will take our "pot-luck" in the family way;
   We can give you a dish   Of some decentish fish,
And our water's thought fairish; but here in the Rhine,
I can't say we pique ourselves much on our wine.'

The Knight made a bow more profound than before,
When a Dory-faced page oped the dining-room door,
   And said, bending his knee,   '*Madame, on a servi!*'
Rupert tender'd his arm, led Lurline to her place,
And a fat little Mer-man stood up and said grace.

What boots it to tell of the viands, or how she
Apologiz'd much for their plain water-souchy,
   Want of Harvey's, and Cross's,
   And Burgess's sauces?
Or how Rupert, on his side, protested, by Jove, he
Preferr'd his fish plain, without soy or anchovy,
   Suffice it the meal   Boasted trout, perch, and eel,
Besides some remarkably fine salmon peel.
The Knight, sooth to say, thought much less of the fishes
Than of what they were served on, the massive gold dishes;
While his eye, as it glanced now and then on the girls,
Was caught by their persons much less than their pearls,
And a thought came across him and caused him to muse,
   'If I could but get hold   Of some of that gold,
I might manage to pay off my rascally Jews!'

When dinner was done, at a sign to the lasses,
The table was clear'd, and they put on fresh glasses;
   Then the lady addressed   Her redoubtable guest
Much as Dido, of old, did the pious Eneas,
'Dear sir, what induced you to come down and see us?'—
Rupert gave her a glance most bewitchingly tender,
Loll'd back in his chair, put his toes on the fender,
   And told her outright   How that he, a young Knight,
Had never been last at a feast or a fight;
   But that keeping good cheer   Every day in the year,
And drinking neat wines all the same as small-beer,
   Had exhausted his rent,   And, his money all spent,
How he borrow'd large sums at two hundred per cent;
   How they follow'd—and then,
   The once civillest of men,
Messrs Howard and Gibbs, made him bitterly rue it he
'd ever raised money by way of annuity;
And, his mortgages being about to foreclose,
How he jump'd in the river to finish his woes!

Lurline was affected, and own'd, with a tear,
That a story so mournful had ne'er met her ear;
    Rupert, hearing her sigh,   Look'd uncommonly sly,
And said, with some emphasis, 'Ah! miss, had I
        A few pounds of those metals
        You waste here on kettles,
        Then, Lord once again   Of my spacious domain,
A free Count of the Empire once more I might reign,
    With Lurline at my side,   My adorable bride
(For the parson should come, and the knot should be tied);
No couple so happy on earth should be seen
As Sir Rupert the brave and his charming Lurline;
Not that money's my object—No, hang it! I scorn it—
And as for my rank—but that *you*'d so adorn it—
    I'd abandon it all   To remain your true thrall,
And, instead of "the *Great*," be call'd "Rupert the *Small*";
—To gain but your smiles, were I Sardanapalus,
I'd descend from my throne, and be boots at an ale-house.' [1]

    Lurline hung her head,   Turned pale, and then red,
Growing faint at this sudden proposal to wed,
As though his abruptness, in 'popping the question'
So soon after dinner, disturb'd her digestion.
    Then, averting her eye,   With a lover-like sigh,
'You are welcome,' she murmur'd, in tones most bewitching,
'To every utensil I have in my kitchen!'
    Upstarted the Knight,   Half mad with delight,
        Round her finely-form'd waist
        He immediately placed
One arm, which the lady most closely embraced,
Of her lily-white fingers the other made capture,
And he press'd his adored to his bosom with rapture.
'And, oh!' he exclaim'd, 'let them go catch my skiff, I
'll be home in a twinkling, and back in a jiffy,
Nor one moment procrastinate longer my journey
Than to put up the banns and kick out the attorney.'

One kiss to her lip, and one squeeze to her hand,
And Sir Rupert already was half-way to land,
    For a sour-visaged Triton,
    With features would frighten
Old Nick, caught him up in one hand, though no light one,
Sprang up through the waves, popp'd him into his funny,
Which some others already had half-fill'd with money;

---

[1] 'Sardanapalus' and 'Boots,' the *Zenith* and *Nadir* of human society.

In fact, 'twas so heavily laden with ore
And pearls, 'twas a mercy he got it to shore;
    But Sir Rupert was strong,   And, while pulling along,
Still he heard, faintly sounding, the water-nymphs' song.

LAY OF THE NAIADS

'Away! away! to the mountain's brow,
    Where the castle is darkly frowning;
And the vassals, all in goodly row,
    Weep for their lord a-drowning!
Away! away! to the steward's room,
    Where law with its wig and robe is;
Throw us out John Doe and Richard Roe,
    And sweetly we'll tickle their tobies!'

The unearthly voices scarce had ceased their yelling,
When Ruper reach'd his old baronial dwelling.

    What rejoicing was there!
    How the vassals did stare!
The old housekeeper put a clean shirt down to air,
    For she saw by her lamp
    That her master's was damp,
And she fear'd he'd catch cold, and lumbago and cramp;
But, scorning what she did,   The Knight never heeded
Wet jacket or trousers, nor thought of repining,
Since their pockets had got such a delicate lining.
    But oh! what dismay   Fill'd the tribe of *Ca Sa,*
When they found he'd the cash, and intended to pay!
Away went '*cognovits,*' 'bills,' 'bonds,' and 'escheats,'—
Rupert clear'd off all scores, and took proper receipts.

    Now no more he sends out
    For pots of brown stout
Or *schnaps*, but resolves to do henceforth without,
Abjure from this hour all excess and ebriety,
Enrol himself one of a Temp'rance Society,
    All riot eschew,   Begin life anew,
And new-cushion and hassock the family pew!
Nay, to strengthen him more in his new mode of life
He boldly determines to take him a wife.

Now, many would think that the Knight, from a nice sense
Of honour, should put Lurline's name in the licence,
And that, for a man of his breeding and quality,
    To break faith and troth.   Confirm'd by an oath,
Is not quite consistent with rigid morality;

But whether the nymph was forgot, or he thought her
From her essence scarce wife, but at best wife-and-water,
   And declined as unsuited, A bride so diluted—
   Be this as it may, He, I'm sorry to say
(For, all things considered, I own 'twas a rum thing),
Made proposals in form to Miss *Una Von*—something
(Her name has escaped me), sole heiress, and niece
To a highly respectable Justice of Peace.

'Thrice happy's the wooing That's not long a-doing!'
So much time is saved in the billing and cooing—
The ring is now bought, the white favours, and gloves,
And all the *et cetera* which crown people's loves;
A magnificent bride-cake comes home from the baker,
And lastly appears, from the German Long Acre,
That shaft which the sharpest in all Cupid's quiver is,
A plum-colour'd coach, and rich Pompadour liveries.

'Twas a comely sight To behold the Knight,
With his beautiful bride, dress'd all in white,
And the bridesmaids fair with their long lace veils,
As they all walk'd up to the altar rails,
While nice little boys, the incense dispensers,
March'd in front with white surplices, bands, and gilt censers.

With a gracious air, and a smiling look,
Mess John had open'd his awful book,
And had read so far as to ask if to wed he meant?
And if 'he knew any just cause or impediment?'
When from base to turret the castle shook!!!
Then came a sound of a mighty rain
Dashing against each storeyed pane,
The wind blew loud, And a coal-black cloud
O'ershadowed the church, and the party, and crowd;
How it could happen they could not divine
The morning had been so remarkably fine!

Still the darkness increased, till it reach'd such a pass
That the sextoness hasten'd to turn on the gas;
   But harder it pour'd, And the thunder roar'd,
As if heaven and earth were coming together;
None ever had witness'd such terrible weather.
   Now louder it crash'd, And the lightning flash'd,
    Exciting the fears Of the sweet little dears
In the veils, as it danced on the brass chandeliers;
The parson ran off, though a stout-hearted Saxon,
When he found that a flash had set fire to his caxon.

Though all the rest trembled, as might be expected,
Sir Rupert was perfectly cool and collected,
    And endeavoured to cheer   His bride, in her ear
Whisp'ring tenderly, 'Pray don't be frighten'd, my dear;
Should it even set fire to the castle, and burn it, you're
Amply insured, both for buildings and furniture.'
    But now, from without   A trustworthy scout
    Rush'd hurriedly in,   Wet through to the skin,
Informing his master 'the river was rising,
And flooding the grounds in a way quite surprising,'

He'd no time to say more,   For already the roar
Of the waters was heard as they reach'd the church door,
While, high on the first wave that roll'd in, was seen,
Riding proudly, the form of the angry Lurline;
And all might observe, by her glance fierce and stormy,
She was stung by the *spretae injuria formae.*

What she said to the Knight, what she said to the bride,
What she said to the ladies who stood by her side,
What she said to the nice little boys in white clothes,
Oh, nobody mentions,—for nobody knows;
For the roof tumbled in, and the walls tumbled out,
And the folks tumbled down, all confusion and rout,
    The rain kept on pouring,
    The flood kept on roaring,
The billows and water-nymphs roll'd more and more in;
    Ere the close of the day
    All was clean washed away—
One only survived who could hand down the news,
A little old woman that open'd the pews;
    She was borne off, but stuck,
    By the greatest good luck.
In an oak-tree, and there she hung, crying and screaming,
And saw all the rest swallow'd up the wild stream in;
    In vain all the week,   Did the fishermen seek
For the bodies, and poke in each cranny and creek;
    In vain was their search
    After ought in the church,
They caught nothing but weeds, and perhaps a few perch;
    The Humane Society   Tried a variety
Of methods, and brought down, to drag for the wreck, tackles,
But they only fish'd up the clerk's tortoise-shell spectacles.

MORAL

This tale has a moral   Ye youths, oh, beware
Of liquor, and how you run after the fair!
Shun playing at *shorts*—avoid quarrels and jars—
And don't take to smoking those nasty cigars—
—Let no run of bad luck, or despair for some Jewess-eyed
Damsel, induce you to contemplate suicide!
Don't sit up much later than ten or eleven!—
Be up in the morning by half after seven!
Keep from flirting—nor risk, warned by Rupert's miscarriage,
An action for breach of a promise of marriage;—
    Don't fancy old fishes!   Don't prig silver dishes!
And to sum up the whole, in the shortest phrase I know,
BEWARE OF THE RHINE, AND TAKE CARE OF THE RHINO!

THE MERCHANT OF VENICE

A LEGEND OF ITALY

'. . . Of the Merchant of Venice there are two 4to editions in 1600, one by Heyes and the other by Roberts.   The Duke of Devonshire and Lord Francis Egerton have copies of the edition by Heyes, and *they vary importantly*.

'. . . It must be acknowledged that *this* is a very easy and happy emendation, which does not admit of a moment's doubt or dispute.

'. . . Readers in general are not all aware of the *nonsense* they have in many cases been accustomed to receive as the genuine text of Shakespeare!'

REASONS FOR A NEW EDITION OF SHAKESPEARE'S WORKS, by J. PAYNE COLLIER.

I BELIEVE there are few   But have heard of a Jew,
    Named Shylock, of Venice, as errant a 'Screw'
In money transactions, as ever you knew;
An exorbitant miser, who never yet lent
A ducat at less than three hundred per cent,
Insomuch that the veriest spendthrift in Venice,
Who'd take no more care of his pounds than his pennies,
When press'd for a loan, at the very first sight
Of his terms, would back out, and take refuge in *Flight*.
It is not my purpose to pause and inquire
If he might not, in managing thus to retire,
Jump out of the frying-pan into the fire;
Suffice it, that folks would have nothing to do,
Who could possibly help it, with Shylock the Jew.

But, however discreetly one cuts and contrives,
We've been most of us taught, in the course of our lives,
That 'Needs must when the Elderly Gentleman drives!'
  In proof of this rule,   A thoughtless young fool,
Bassanio, a Lord of the Tomnoddy school,
Who, by showing at Operas, Balls, Plays, and Court,
A 'swelling' (Payne Collier would read 'swilling') 'port,'
And inviting his friends to dine, breakfast, and sup,
Had shrunk his 'weak means,' and was 'stump'd' and 'hard up,'
  Took occasion to send   To his very good friend
Antonio, a merchant whose wealth had no end,
And who'd often before had the kindness to lend
Him large sums, on his note, which he'd managed to spend.

  'Antonio,' said he,   'Now listen to me:
I've just hit on a scheme which, I think, you'll agree,
All matters considered, is no bad design,
And which, if it succeeds, will suit your book and mine.
In the first place, you know all the money I've got,
Time and often, from you has been long gone to pot,
And in making those loans you have made a bad shot;
Now do as the boys do when, shooting at sparrows
And tomtits, they chance to lose one of their arrows,
—Shoot another the same way—I'll watch well its track,
And, turtle to tripe, I'll bring both of them back!—
  So list to my plan,   And do what you can
To attend to and second it, that's a good man!

'There's a Lady, young, handsome beyond all compare, at
A place they call Belmont, whom, when I was there, at
The suppers and parties my friend Lord Mountferrat
Was giving last season, we all used to stare at.
Then, as to her wealth, her Solicitor told mine,
Besides vast estates, a pearl-fishery, and gold mine,
  Her iron strong box   Seems bursting its locks,
It's stuffed so with shares in "Grand Junctions" and "Docks,"
Not to speak of the money she's got in the Stocks,
    French, Dutch, and Brazilian,
    Columbian, and Chilian,
In English Exchequer-bills full half a million,
Not "kites," manufactured to cheat and inveigle,
But the right sort of "flimsy," all sign'd by Monteagle.
Then I know not how much in Canal-shares and Railways,
And more speculations I need not detail, ways
Of vesting which, if not so safe as some think 'em,
Contribute a deal to improving one's income;

In short, she's a Mint!—   Now I say, deuce is in't
If, with all my experience, I can't take a hint,
And her "eye's speechless messages," plainer than print
At the time that I told you of, know from a squint.

     In short, my dear Tony,   My crusty old crony,
Do stump up three thousand once more as a loan—I
Am sure of my game—though, of course, there are brutes,
Of all sorts and sizes, preferring their suits
To her you may call the Italian Miss Coutts,
Yet Portia—she's named from that daughter of Cato's—
Is not to be snapp'd up like little potatoes,

     And I have not a doubt   I shall rout every lout
Ere you 'll whisper Jack Robinson—cut them all out—
Surmount every barrier,   Carry her, marry her!
—Then hey! my old Tony, when once fairly noosed,
For her Three-and-a-half per Cents—New and Reduced!

With a wink of his eye   His friend made reply
In his jocular manner, sly, caustic, and dry,
'Still the same boy, Bassanio—never say "die"!
—Well—I hardly know how I shall do 't, but I 'll try,—
Don't suppose my affairs are at all in a hash,
But the fact is, at present I 'm quite out of cash;
The bulk of my property, merged in rich cargoes, is
Tossing about, as you know, in my Argosies,
Tending, of course, my resources to cripple,—I
've one bound to England,—another to Tripoli—
Cyprus—Masulipatam—and Bombay;
     A sixth, by the way,   I consign'd t' other day,
To Sir Richard M'Gregor, Cacique of Poyais,
A country where silver's as common as clay.

     Meanwhile, till they tack,   And come, some of them, back,
What with Custom-house duties, and bills falling due,
My account with Jones Loyd and Co. looks rather blue:
While, as for the 'ready,' I 'm like a Church mouse,—
I really don't think there 's five pounds in the house.

     But, no matter for that,   Let me just get my hat,
And my new silk umbrella that stands on the mat,
And we 'll go forth at once to the market—we two,—
And try what my credit in Venice can do;
I stand well on 'Change, and, when all 's said and done, I
Don't doubt I shall get it for love or for money.'

They were going to go,   When, lo! down below,
In the street, they heard somebody crying, 'Old Clo'!'
—'By the Pope, there 's the man for our purpose!—I knew
We should not have to search long.   Salanio, run you,

—Salarino,—quick!—haste! ere he get out of view,
And call in that scoundrel, old Shylock the Jew!'
    With a pack,   Like a sack
Of old clothes, at his back,
And three hats on his head, Shylock came in a crack,
Saying, 'Rest you fair, Signior Antonio! vat, pray,
Might your vorship be pleashed for to vant in ma vay?'

—'Why, Shylock, although,   As you very well know,
I am what they call 'warm,'—pay my way as I go,
And, as to myself, neither borrow nor lend,
I can break through a rule, to oblige an old friend;
And that's the case now—Lord Bassanio would raise
Some three thousand ducats—well,—knowing your ways,
And that nought's to be got from you, say what one will,
Unless you've a couple of names to the bill,
    Why, for once, I'll put mine to it,
    Yea, seal and sign to it—
Now, then, old Sinner, let's hear what you'll say
As to "doing" a bill at three months from to-day?
Three thousand gold ducats, mind—all in good bags
Of hard money—no sealing-wax, slippers, or rags?'

'—Vell, ma tear,' says the Jew,
  'I'll see vat I can do!
But Mishter Antonio, hark you, 'tish funny
You say to me, "Shylock, ma tear, ve'd have money!"
    Ven you very well knows
    How you shpit on ma clothes,
And use naughty vords—call me Dog—and avouch
Dat I put too much int'resht py half in ma pouch,
And vhile I, like de resht of ma tribe, shrug and crouch,
You find fault mit ma pargains, and say I'm a Smouch.
  —Vell!—no matters, ma tear,—   Von vord in your ear!
I'd be friends mit you bote—and to make dat appear,
Vy, I'll find you de monies as soon as you vill,
Only von littel joke musht be put in de pill;—
    Ma tear, you musht say,   If on such and such day
Such sum, or such sums, you shall fail to repay,
I shall cut vere I like, as de pargain is proke,
A fair pound of your flesh—chest by vay of a joke.'

So novel a clause   Caused Bassanio to pause;
But Antonio, like most of those sage 'Johnny Raws'
    Who care not three straws   About Lawyers or Laws,
And think cheaply of 'Old Father Antic,' because
They have never experienced a gripe from his claws,

'Pooh pooh'd' the whole thing.—'Let the Smouch have his way—
   Why, what care I, pray,   For his penalty?—Nay,
It's a forfeit he'd never expect me to pay;
   And, come what come may,   I hardly need say
My ships will be back a full month ere the day.'
So, anxious to see his friend off on his journey,
And thinking the whole but a paltry concern, he
   Affixed with all speed   His name to a deed,
Duly stamp'd and drawn up by a sharp Jew attorney.
Thus again furnished forth, Lord Bassanio, instead
Of squandering the cash, after giving one spread,
With fiddling and masques at the Saracen's Head,
   In the morning 'made play,'
   And, without more delay,
Started off in the steam-boat for Belmont next day.
   But scarcely had he   From the harbour got free,
And left the Lagunes for the broad open sea,
Ere the 'Change and Rialto both rung with the news
That he'd carried off more than mere cash from the Jew's.

   Though Shylock was old,   And, if rolling in gold,
Was as ugly a dog as you'd wish to behold,
For few in his tribe 'mongst their Levis and Moseses,
Sported so Jewish an eye, beard, and nose as his,
Still, whate'er the opinions of Horace and some be,
Your *aquilae* generate *some*times *Columbae*.[1]
Like Jephthah, as Hamlet says, he'd 'one fair daughter,'
And every gallant, who caught sight of her, thought her
A jewel—a gem of the very first water;
   A great many sought her,   Till one at last caught her,
And, upsetting all that the Rabbis had taught her,
To feelings so truly reciprocal brought her,
   That the very same night   Bassanio thought right
To give all his old friends that farewell 'invite,'
And while Shylock was gone there to feed out of spite,
On 'wings made by a tailor' the damsel took flight.

   By these 'wings' I'd express   A grey duffle dress,
With brass badge and muffin cap, made, as by rule,
For an upper class boy in the National School.
Jessy ransack'd the house, popped her breeks on, and when so
Disguised, bolted off with her beau—one Lorenzo,
An 'Unthrift,' who lost not a moment in whisking
   Her into the boat,   And was fairly afloat
Ere her Pa had got rid of the smell of the griskin.

       [1] 'Nec imbellem feroces
        Progenerant aquilae columbam.'
       ('Nor do fierce eagles bring forth the peaceful dove.')—HORACE.

Next day, while old Shylock was making a racket,
And threatening how well he'd dust every man's jacket
Who'd helped her in getting aboard of the packet,
Bassanio at Belmont was capering and prancing,
And bowing, and scraping, and singing, and dancing,
Making eyes at Miss Portia, and doing his best
To perform the polite, and to cut out the rest;
And, if left to herself, he, no doubt, had succeeded,
For none of them waltz'd so genteelly as he did;
   But an obstacle lay,   Of some weight, in his way,
The defunct Mr P., who was now turned to clay,
Had been an odd man, and, though all for the best he meant
Left but a queer sort of 'Last will and testament,'—
   Bequeathing her hand,   With her houses and land,
Etc., from motives one don't understand,
As she rev'renced his memory, and valued his blessing,
To him who should turn out the best hand at guessing!

   Like a good girl, she did   Just what she was bid;
In one of three caskets her picture she hid,
And clapped a conundrum a-top of each lid.
A couple of Princes, a black and a white one,
Tried first, but they both failed in choosing the right one;
Another from Naples, who shoed his own horses;
A French Lord, whose graces might vie with Count
    D'Orsay's;—
A young English Baron;—a Scotch Peer his neighbour:—
A dull drunken Saxon, all moustache and sabre;—
As followed, and all had their pains for their labour.
Bassanio came last—happy man be his dole!
Put his conjuring cap on,—considered the whole,—
   The gold put aside as   Mere 'hard food for Midas,'
   The silver bade trudge   As a 'pale common drudge';
Then choosing the little lead box in the middle,
Came plump on the picture, and found out the riddle.

Now you're not such a goose as to think, I dare say,
Gentle Reader, that all this was done in a day,
   Any more than the dome   Of St Peter's at Rome
Was built in the same space of time; and, in fact,
   Whilst Bassanio was doing   His billing and cooing,
Three months had gone by ere he reach'd the fifth act;
Meanwhile, that unfortunate bill became due,
Which his Lordship had almost forgot, to the Jew,
   And Antonio grew   In a deuce of a stew,
For he could not cash up, spite of all he could do
(The bitter old Israelite would not renew),

What with contrary winds, storms, and wrecks, and embargoes,
his
Funds were all stopped, or gone down in his argosies,
None of the set having come into port,
And Shylock's attorney was moving the Court
For the forfeit supposed to be set down in sport.

   The serious news   Of this step of the Jew's,
And his fix'd resolution all terms to refuse,
Gave the newly-made Bridegroom a fit of 'the Blues,'
Especially, too, as it came from the pen
Of his poor friend himself on the wedding-day,—then,
When the Parson had scarce shut his book up, and when
The Clerk was yet uttering the final Amen.
'Dear Friend,' it continued, 'all's up with me—I
Have nothing on earth now to do but to die!
And, as death clears all scores, you're no longer my debtor;
   I should take it as kind
   Could you come—never mind—
If your love don't persuade you, why—don't let this letter!'
I hardly need say this was scarcely read o'er
   Ere a post-chaise and four
   Was brought round to the door,
And Bassanio, though, doubtless, he thought it a bore,
Gave his Lady one kiss, and then started at score.
   But scarce in his flight   Had he got out of sight,
Ere Portia, addressing a groom, said, 'My lad, you a
Journey must take on the instant to Padua;
Find out there Bellario, a doctor of Laws,
Who, like Follett, is never left out of a cause,
   And give him this note,   Which I've hastily wrote,
Take the papers he'll give you—then push for the ferry
Below, where I'll meet you—you'll do't in a wherry,
If you can't find a boat on the Brenta with sails to it—
—Stay!—bring his gown too, and wig with three tails to it.'

Giovanni (that's Jack)   Brought out his hack,
Made a bow to his mistress, then jump'd on its back,
Put his hand to his hat, and was off in a crack.
The Signora soon follow'd herself, taking as her
Own escort Nerissa her maid, and Balthazar.

'The Court is prepared, the Lawyers are met,
   The Judges all ranged, a terrible show!'
As Captain Macheath says,—and when one's in debt,
   The sight's as unpleasant a one as I know,

Yet still not so bad after all, I suppose,
As if, when one cannot discharge what one owes,
They should bid people cut off one's toes or one's nose;
    Yet here, a worse fate,   Stands Antonio, of late
A merchant, might vie e'en with Princes in state,
With his waistcoat unbutton'd, prepared for the knife,
Which, in taking a pound of flesh must take his life;
—On the other side Shylock, his bag on the floor,
And three shocking bad hats on his head, as before,
    Imperturbable stands,   As he waits their commands,
With his scales and his great *sniker-snee* in his hands;
—Between them, equipt in a wig, gown, and bands,
With a very smooth face, a young dandified Lawyer,
Whose air, ne'ertheless, speaks him quite a top-sawyer,
    Though his hopes are but feeble,   Does his *possible*
To make the hard Hebrew to mercy incline,
And in lieu of his three thousand ducats take nine,
Which Bassanio, for reasons we well may divine,
Shows in so many bags all drawn up in a line.
But vain are all efforts to soften him—still
    He points to the bond   He so often has conn'd,
And says in plain terms he'll be shot if he will.

So the dandified Lawyer, with talking grown hoarse,
Says, 'I *can* say no more—let the law take its course.'

Just fancy the gleam of the eye of the Jew,
As he sharpen'd his knife on the sole of his shoe
    From the toe to the heel,   And grasping the steel,
With a business-like air was beginning to feel
Whereabouts he should cut, as a butcher would veal,
When the dandified Judge puts a spoke in his wheel.
    'Stay, Shylock,' says he,
    'Here's one thing—you see
This bond of yours gives you here no jot of blood!
—The words are "A pound of flesh,"—that's clear as mud—
Slice away, then, old fellow—but mind!—if you spill
One drop of his claret that's not in your bill,
I'll hang you like Haman!—by Jingo I will!'

    When apprised of this flaw,   You never yet saw
Such an awfully marked elongation of jaw
As in Shylock, who cried, 'Plesh ma heart! ish that law?'—
    —Off went his three hats,
    And he look'd as the cats
Do, whenever a mouse has escaped from their claw.

'—Ish't the law?'—why the thing won't admit of a query—
  'No doubt of the fact,   Only look at the act;
Acto quinto, cap : tertio, Dogi Falieri—
Nay, if, rather than cut, you'd relinquish the debt,
The Law, Master Shy, has a hold on you yet.
See Foscari's "Statutes at large"—"If a Stranger
A Citizen's life shall, with malice, endanger,
The whole of his property, little or great,
Shall go, on conviction, one half to the State,
And one to the person pursued by his hate;
  And not to create   Any further debate,
The Doge, if he pleases, may cut off his pate."
So down on your marrowbones, Jew, and ask mercy!
Defendant and Plaintiff are now *wisy wersy*.'

What need to declare   How pleased they all were
At so joyful an end to so sad an affair?
Or Bassanio's delight at the turn things had taken,
His friend having saved, to the letter, his bacon?
How Shylock got shaved, and turn'd Christian, though late,
To save a life-int'rest in half his estate?—
How the dandified Lawyer, who'd managed the thing,
Would not take any fee for his pains but a ring
Which Mrs Bassanio had giv'n to her spouse,
With injunctions to keep it, on leaving the house?—
  How when he, and the spark
  Who appeared as his clerk,
Had thrown off their wigs, and their gowns, and their jetty coats,
There stood Nerissa and Portia in petticoats?—
How they pouted and flouted, and acted the cruel,
Because Lord Bassanio had not kept his jewel?—
  How they scolded and broke out,
  Till, having their joke out,
They kissed, and were friends, and, all blessing and blessed,
  Drove home by the light   Of a moonshiny night,
Like the one in which Troilus, the brave Trojan knight,
Sat astride on a wall, and sigh'd after his Cressid?—

All this, if 'twere meet,   I'd go on to repeat,
But a story spun out so's by no means a treat,
So, I'll merely relate what, in spite of the pains
I have taken to rummage among his remains,
No edition of Shakespeare, I've met with, contains;
But, if the account which I've heard be the true one,
We shall have it, no doubt, before long, in a new one.

In an MS., then, sold   For its full weight in gold,
And knock'd down to my friend, Lord Tomnoddy, I'm told
It's recorded that Jessy, coquettish and vain,
Gave her husband, Lorenzo, a good deal of pain;
Being mildly rebuked, she levanted again,
Ran away with a Scotchman, and, crossing the main,
Became known by the name of the 'Flower of Dumblane.'

That Antonio, whose piety caused, as we've seen,
Him to spit upon every old Jew's gaberdine,
    And whose goodness to paint   All colours were faint,
Acquired the well-merited prefix of 'Saint,'
And the Doge, his admirer, of honour the fount,
Having given him a patent, and made him a Count,
He went over to England, got nat'raliz'd there,
And espous'd a rich heiress in Hanover Square.
That Shylock came with him, no longer a Jew,
But converted, I think may be possibly true,
But that Walpole, as these self-same papers aver,
By changing the *y* in his name into *er*,
Should allow him a fictitious surname to dish up,
And in Seventeen-twenty-eight made him a Bishop,
I cannot believe—but shall still think them two men
Till some Sage proves the fact 'with his usual acumen.'

MORAL

From this tale of the Bard   It's uncommonly hard
If an Editor can't draw a moral.—'Tis clear,
Then,—In ev'ry young wife-seeking Bachelor's ear
A maxim, 'bove all other stories, this one drums,
'PITCH GREEK TO OLD HARRY, AND STICK TO CONUNDRUMS!!'

To new-married Ladies this lesson it teaches,
'You're "no that far wrong" in assuming the breeches!'

Monied men upon 'Change, and rich Merchants in schools
To look well to assets—nor play with edge-tools!

Last of all, this remarkable History shows men,
What caution they need when they deal with old-clothesmen!
    So bid John and Mary   To mind and be wary,
And never let one of them come down the are'!

THE AUTO-DA-FÉ

A Legend of Spain

CANTO I

WITH a moody air, from morn till noon,
King Ferdinand paces the royal saloon;
   From morn till eve   He does nothing but grieve;
Sighing and sobbings his midriff heave,
And he wipes his eyes with his ermined sleeve,
And he presses his feverish hand to his brow,
And he frowns, and he looks I can't tell you how:
   And the Spanish Grandees   In their degrees,
   Are whispering about in twos and in threes,
   And there is not a man of them seems at his ease,
But they gaze on the monarch, as watching what he does,
With their very long whiskers, and longer Toledos.
Don Gaspar, Don Gusman, Don Juan, Don Diego,
Don Gomez, Don Pedro, Don Blas, Don Rodrigo,
Don Jerome, Don Giacomo join Don Alphonso
   In making inquiries   Of grave Don Ramirez,
The Chamberlain, what it is makes him take on so;
A Monarch so great that the soundest opinions
Maintain the sun can't set throughout his dominions;
   But grave Don Ramirez   In guessing no nigher is
Than the other grave Dons who propound these inquiries;
When, pausing at length, as beginning to tire, his
Majesty beckons, with stately civility,
   To Señor Don Lewis   Condé d'Aranjuez,
Who in birth, wealth, and consequence second to few is.
And Señor Don Manuel, Count de Pacheco,
A lineal descendant from King Pharaoh Neco,
Both Knights of the Golden Fleece, highborn Hidalgos,
With whom e'en the King himself quite as a 'pal' goes.

'Don Lewis,' says he,   'Just listen to me:
And you, Count Pacheco,—I think that we three
On matters of state, for the most part agree,—
   Now you both of you know   That some six years ago,
Being then, for a King, no indifferent Beau,
At the altar I took, like my forbears of old,
   The Peninsula's paragon,   Fair Blanche of Aragon
For better, for worse, and to have and to hold—

And you're fully aware,   When the matter took air,
How they shouted, and fired the great guns in the Square,
Cried "*Viva!*" and rung all the bells in the steeple,
    And all that sort of thing   The mob do when a King
Brings a Queen-Consort home for the good of his people.

    'Well!—six years and a day   Have flitted away
Since that blessed event, yet I'm sorry to say—
In fact it's the principal cause of my pain—
I don't see any signs of an Infant of Spain!—
    Now I want to ask you,   Cavaliers true,
And Counsellors sage—what the deuce shall I do?—
The State—don't you see?—hey?—an heir to the throne—
Every monarch—you know—should have one of his own—
Disputed succession—hey?—terrible Go!—
Hum!—hey?—Old fellows—you see!—don't you know?'—

    Now, Reader, dear,   If you've ever been near
Enough to a Court to encounter a Peer
When his principal tenant's gone off in arrear,
And his brewer has sent in a long bill for beer,
And his butcher and baker, with faces austere,
    Ask him to clear   Off, for furnish'd good cheer,
Bills, they say, 'have been standing for more than a year,'
And the tailor and shoemaker also appear
    With their 'little account'   Of 'trifling amount,'
For Wellingtons, waistcoats, pea-jackets, and—gear
Which to name in society's thought rather queer,—
While Drummond's chief clerk, with his pen in his ear,
And a kind of a sneer, says, 'We've no effects here!'
    —Or if ever you've seen   An Alderman, keen
    After turtle, peep into a silver tureen,
In search of the fat call'd *par excellence* 'green,'
When there's none of the meat left—not even the lean!—
—Or if ever you've witness'd the face of a sailor
Return'd from a voyage, and escaped from a gale, or
Poeticè 'Boreas,' that 'blustering railer,'
To find that his wife, when he hastens to 'hail' her,
Has just run away with his cash—and a tailor—
If one of these cases you've ever surveyed,
    You'll, without my aid,   To yourself have portray'd
The beautiful mystification display'd,
And the puzzled expression of manner and air
Exhibited now by the dignified pair,
When thus unexpectedly ask'd to declare
Their opinions as Counsellors, several and joint,
On so delicate, grave, and important a point.

Señor Don Lewis   Condé d'Aranjuez
At length forced a smile 'twixt the prim and the grim,
And look'd at Pacheco—Pacheco at him—
Then, making a rev'rence, and dropping his eyes,
Cough'd, hemm'd, and deliver'd himself in this wise:

'My Liege!—unaccustom'd as I am to speaking
In public—an art I'm remarkably weak in—
I feel I should be—quite unworthy the name
Of a man and a Spaniard—and highly to blame,
    Were there not in my breast
    What—can't be exprest,—
And can therefore,—your Majesty—only be guess'd—
—What I mean to say is—since your Majesty deigns
To ask my advice on your welfare—and Spain's,—
And on that of your Majesty's Bride—that is, Wife—
It's the—as I may say—proudest day of my life!
But as to the point—on a subject so nice
It's a delicate matter to give one's advice,
    Especially too,   When one don't clearly view
The best mode of proceeding,—or know what to do;
My decided opinion, however, is this,
And I fearlessly say that you can't do amiss,
    If with all that fine tact   Both to think and to act,
In which all know your Majesty so much excels—
You are graciously pleased to—ask somebody else!'

Here the noble Grandee   Made that sort of congée,
Which, as Hill used to say, 'I once *happen'd to see*'
The great Indian conjuror, Ramo Samee,
Make, while swallowing what all thought a regular choker,
Viz. a small sword as long and as stiff as a poker.
    Then the Count de Pacheco,
    Whose turn 'twas to speak, o-
-mitting all preface, exclaim'd with devotion,
'Sire, I beg leave to second Don Lewis's motion!'

Now a Monarch of Spain   Of course could not deign
To expostulate, argue, or, much less, complain
Of an answer thus giv'n, or to ask them again;
So he merely observ'd, with an air of disdain,
'Well, Gentlemen,—since you both shrink from the task
Of advising your Sovereign—pray, whom shall I ask?'

Each felt the rub,   And in Spain not a Sub,
Much less an Hidalgo, can stomach a snub,

So the noses of these   Castilian Grandees
Rise at once in an angle of several degrees,
Till the under-lip's almost becoming the upper,
Each perceptibly grows, too, more stiff in the crupper,
  Their right hands rest   On the left side the breast,
While the hilts of their swords, by their left hands depressed,
Make the ends of their scabbards to cock up behind,
Till they're quite horizontal instead of inclined,
And Don Lewis, with scarce an attempt to disguise
The disgust he experiences, gravely replies,
'Sire, ask the Archbishop—his Grace of Toledo!—
He understands these things much better than we do!'
  —*Pauca Verba!*—enough,
  Each turns off in a huff,
This twirling his moustache, that fingering his ruff,
Like a blue-bottle fly on a rather large scale,
With a rather large corking-pin stuck through his tail.

King Ferdinand paces the royal saloon,
With a moody brow, and he looks like a 'Spoon,'
And all the Court Nobles who form the ring,
Have a spoony appearance, of course, like the King,
All of them eyeing King Ferdinand
As he goes up and down, with his watch in his hand,
Which he claps to his ear as he walks to and fro,—
'What is it can make the Archbishop so slow?'
Hark!—at last there's a sound in the courtyard below,
Where the Beefeaters all are drawn up in a row,—
I would say the 'Guards,' for in Spain they're in chief eaters
Of omelettes and garlic, and can't be called Beefeaters;
  In fact, of the few   Individuals I knew
Who ever had happened to travel in Spain
There has scarce been a person who did not complain
Of their cookery and dishes as all bad in grain,
And no one I'm sure will deny it who's tried a
Vile compound they have that's called *Olla podrida*.

(This, by the bye,   's a mere rhyme to the eye,
For in Spanish the *i* is pronounced like an *e*,
And they've not quite our mode of pronouncing the *d*.
In Castille, for instance, it's giv'n through the teeth,
And what we call Ma*drid* they sound more like Ma*dreeth*,)
Of course you will see in a moment they've no men
That at all correspond with our Beefeating Yeomen;
So call them 'Walloons,' or whatever you please,
By their rattles and slaps they're not 'standing at ease,'

But, beyond all disputing,   Engaged in saluting
Some very great person among the Grandees;—
Here a Gentleman Usher walks in and declares,
'His Grace the Archbishop's a-coming upstairs!'

The Most Reverend Don Garcilasso Quevedo
    Was just at this time, as he   Now held the Primacy
(Always attached to the See of Toledo),
A man of great worship *Officii virtute*
Versed in all that pertains to a Counsellor's duty,
    Well skill'd to combine   Civil law with divine;
As a statesman, inferior to none in that line;
    As an orator, too,   He was equalled by few;
Uniting, in short, in tongue, head-piece, and pen,
The very great powers of three very great men,
Talleyrand,—who will never drive down Piccadilly more
To the Traveller's Club-House!—Charles Phillips—and
    Phillimore.
    Not only at home   But even at Rome
There was not a Prelate among them could cope
With the Primate of Spain in the eyes of the Pope
(The Conclave was full, and they'd not a spare hat, or he
'd long since been Cardinal, Legate *à latere*,
A dignity fairly his due, without flattery,
So much he excited among all beholders
    Their marvel to see   At his age—thirty-three—
Such a very old head on such very young shoulders).
No wonder the King, then, in this his distress,
Should send for so sage an adviser express,
    Who, you'll readily guess   Could not do less
Than start off at once, without stopping to dress,
In his haste to get Majesty out of a mess.

His grace the Archbishop comes up the back way,
Set apart for such Nobles as have the *entrée*,
Viz. Grandees of the first class, both cleric and lay;
Walks up to the monarch, and makes him a bow,
As a dignified clergyman always knows how,
Then replaces the mitre at once on his brow;
    For, in Spain, recollect,   As a mark of respect
To the Crown, if a Grandee uncovers, it's quite
As a matter of option, and not one of right;
A thing not conceded by *our* royal Masters,
Who always make Noblemen take off their 'castors,'
    Except the heirs male   Of John Lord Kinsale,
A stalwart old Baron, who, acting as Henchman
To one of our early Kings, kill'd a big Frenchman;

A feat which his Majesty deigning to smile on,
Allow'd him thenceforward to stand with his 'tile' on;
And all his successors have kept the same privilege
Down from those barbarous times to our civil age.

Returning his bow with a slight demi-bob,
And replacing the watch in his hand in his fob,
'My Lord,' said the King, 'here's a rather tough job,
    Which it seems, of a sort is   To puzzle our *Cortes*.
And since it has quite flabbergasted that Diet, I
Look to your Grace with no little anxiety
    Concerning a point   Which has quite out of joint
Put us all with respect to the good of society:—
    Your Grace is aware   That we've not got an Heir;
Now, it seems, one and all, they don't stick to declare
That of all our advisers there is not in Spain one
Can tell, like your Grace, the best way to obtain one;
So put your considering cap on—we're curious
To learn your receipt for a Prince of Asturias.'

    One without the nice tact
    Of his Grace would have backed
Out at once, as the Noblemen did,—and, in fact,
He was, at the first, rather posed how to act—
    One moment—no more!—   Bowing then, as before,
He said, 'Sire, 'twere superfluous for me to acquaint
The "Most Catholic King" in the world, that a Saint
    Is the usual resource   In these cases,—of course
Of their influence your Majesty well knows the force;
If I may be, therefore, allow'd to suggest
The plan which occurs to my mind as the best,
    Your Majesty may go   At once to St Jago,
Whom, as Spain's patron Saint, I pick out from the rest;
    If your Majesty looks   Into Guthrie, or Brooks,
In all the approved Geographical books,
You will find Compostella laid down in the maps
Some two hundred and sev'nty miles off; and, perhaps,
In a case so important, you may not decline
A pedestrian excursion to visit his shrine;
    And, Sire, should you choose
    To put peas in your shoes,
The Saint, as a Gentleman, can't well refuse
So distinguish'd a Pilgrim,—especially when he
Considers the boon will not cost him one penny!'

His speech ended, his Grace bow'd, and put on his mitre
As tight as before, and perhaps a thought tighter.

'Pooh! pooh!' says the King,
  'I shall do no such thing!
It's nonsense,—Old fellow—you see—no use talking—
The peas set apart, I abominate walking—
Such a deuced way off, too—hey?—walk there—what me?
Pooh!—it's no Go, Old fellow!—you know—don't you see?'

'Well, Sire,' with much sweetness the Prelate replied,
'If your Majesty don't like to walk—you can ride!
    And then, if you please,   In lieu of the peas,
A small portion of horse-hair, cut fine, we'll insert,
As a substitute, under your Majesty's shirt;
Then a rope round your collar instead of a laced band,—
A few nettles tuck'd into your Majesty's waistband,—
Asafoetida mix'd with your bouquet and civet,
I'll warrant you'll find yourself right as a trivet!'

    'Pooh! pooh! I tell you,'
    Quoth the King, 'It won't do!'
A cold perspiration began to bedew
His Majesty's cheek, and he grew in a stew,
When Jozé de Humez, the King's privy-purse-keeper
(Many folks thought it could scarce have a worse keeper),
Came to the rescue, and said with a smile,
'Sire, your Majesty *can't* go—'twould take a long while,
And you won't post it under TWO SHILLINGS A MILE!!
    Twenty-seven pounds ten   To get there—and then
Twenty-seven pounds ten more to get back agen!!!
Sire, the *tottle's* enormous—you ought to be King
Of Golconda as well as the Indies, to fling
Such a vast sum away upon any such thing!'

    At this second rebuff   The Archbishop look'd gruff,
And his eye glanced on Humez as if he'd say 'Stuff!'
But seeing the King seem'd himself in a huff,
He changed his demeanour, and grew smooth enough;
Then taking his chin 'twixt his finger and thumb,
As a help to reflection, gave vent to a 'Hum!'
'Twas the pause of an instant—his eye assumed fast
That expression which says, 'Come, I've got it at last!'

'There's one plan,' he resumed, 'which, with all due respect to
Your Majesty, no one, I think, can object to—
—Since your Majesty don't like the peas in the shoe—or to
Travel—what say you to burning a Jew or two?—
    Of all cookeries, most   The Saints love a roast!
And a Jew's, of all others, the best dish to toast;

And then for a Cook   We have not far to look—
Father Dominic's self, Sire, your own Grand Inquisitor,
Luckily now at your Court is a visitor;
Of his Rev'rence's functions there is not one weightier
Than Heretic-burning—in fact, 'tis his *métier*.
    Besides Alguazils   Who still follow his heels,
He has always Familiars enough at his beck at home,
To pick you up Hebrews enough for a hecatomb!
And depend on it, Sire, such a glorious specific
Would make every Queen throughout Europe prolific!'

    Says the King, 'That'll do!
    Pooh! pooh!—burn a Jew?
Burn half a score Jews—burn a dozen—burn two—
    Your Grace, it's a match   Burn all you can catch,
Men, women, and children—Pooh! pooh! great and small—
Old clothes—slippers—sealing-wax—Pooh! burn them all.
    For once we'll be gay,   A Grand *Auto-da-fé*
Is much better fun than a ball or a play!'

So the warrant was made out without more delay,
Drawn, seal'd, and delivered, and
                              (Signed)
                              YO EL RE!

CANTO II

THERE is not a nation in Europe but labours
To toady itself, and to humbug its neighbours—
'Earth has no such folks—no folks such a city,
So great, or so grand, or so fine, or so pretty,'
    Said Louis Quatorze,   'As this Paris of ours!'
—Mr Daniel O'Connell exclaims, 'By the Pow'rs
Ould Ireland's on all hands admitted to be
The first flow'r of the earth, and first *Gim* of the sea!'—
—Mr Bull will inform you that Neptune,—a lad he,
With more of affection than rev'rence styles 'Daddy,'—
    Did not scruple to 'say   To Freedom one day,'
That if ever he changed his aquatics for dry land,
His home should be Mr B,'s 'Tight little Island.'—
He adds, too, that he,   The said Mr B.,
Of all possible Frenchmen can fight any three;
That, with no greater odds, he knows well how to treat them,
To meet them, defeat them, and beat them, and eat them.—
    * F 185

—In Italy, too, 'tis the same to the letter;
   There each Lazzarone   Will cry to his crony,
'See Naples, then die [1] and the sooner the better!'
The Portuguese say, as a well understood thing,
'Who has not seen Lisbon [2] has not seen a good thing!'—
While an old Spanish proverb runs glibly as under,
   'QUIEN NO HA VISTO SEVILLA
   NO HA VISTO MARAVILLA!'
'He who ne'er has viewed Seville has ne'er viewed a Wonder!'
And from all I can learn this is no such great blunder.
   In fact, from the river,   The famed Guadalquiver,
Where many a knight's had cold steel through his liver,[3]
The prospect *is* grand.   The *Iglesia Mayor*
Has a splendid effect on the opposite shore,
With its lofty *Giralda*, while two or three score
Of magnificent structures around, perhaps more,
As our Irish friends have it, are there 'to the fore';
   Then the old Alcazar,   More ancient by far,
As some say, while some call it one of the palaces
Built in twelve hundred and odd by Abdalasis,
With its horse-shoe shaped arches of Arabesque tracery,
Which the architect seems to have studied to place awry,
   Saracenic and rich;
   And more buildings, 'the which,'
As old Lilly, in whom I've been looking a bit o' late,
Says, 'You'd be bored should I now recapitulate'; [4]
   In brief, then, the view   Is so fine and so new,
It would make you exclaim, 'twould so forcibly strike ye,
If a Frenchman, '*Superbe!*'—If an Englishman 'Crikey!!'

Yes! thou *art* 'WONDERFUL!'—but oh,
   'Tis sad to think, 'mid scenes so bright
As thine, fair Seville, sounds of woe,
   And shrieks of pain, and wild affright,
And soul-wrung groans of deep despair,
And blood, and death should mingle there!

---

[1] 'Vedi Napoli e poi mori!'
[2] 'Quem naõ tem visto Lisboa
   Naõ tem visto cousa boa.'
[3] 'Rio verde, Rio verde, etc.'
  'Glassy water, glassy water,
     Down whose current clear and strong,
  Chiefs, confused in mutual slaughter,
     Moor and Christian, roll along.'—OLD SPANISH ROMANCE.
[4] 'Cum multis aliis quae nunc perscribere longum est.'
                        PROPRIA QUAEMA RIBUS.

Yes! thou art 'WONDERFUL!'—the flames
  That on thy towers reflected shine,
While earth's proud Lords and high-born Dames
  Descendants of a mighty line,
With cold unalter'd looks are by
To gaze, with an unpitying eye,
On wretches in their agony.

All speak thee 'WONDERFUL'—the phrase
Befits thee well—the fearful blaze
Of yon piled faggots' lurid light,
Where writhing victims mock the sight,—
The scorch'd limb shrivelling in its chains,—
The hot blood parch'd in *living* veins,—
The crackling nerve—the fearful knell
Rung out by that remorseless bell,—
Those shouts from human fiends that swell.—
That withering scream—that frantic yell,—
All Seville,—all too truly tell
Thou *art* a 'MARVEL'—and a Hell!
God!—that the worm whom thou has made
Should thus his brother worm invade!
Count deeds like these good service done,
And deem THINE eye looks smiling on!!

Yet there at his ease, with his whole Court around him,
King Ferdinand sits 'in his GLORY'—confound him!—
  Leaning back in his chair, With a satisfied air,
And enjoying the bother, the smoke, and the smother,
With one knee cocked carelessly over the other;
  His pouncet-box goes To and fro at his nose,
As somewhat misliking the smell of old clothes,
And seeming to hint, by this action emphatic,
That Jews, e'en when roasted, are not aromatic;
  There, too, fair Ladies From Xeres, and Cadiz,
Catalinas, and Julias, and fair Iñesillas.
In splendid lace-veils and becoming mantillas;
Elviras, Antonias, and Claras, and Floras,
And dark-eyed Jacinthas, and soft Isidoras,
Are crowding the 'boxes,' and looking on coolly as
Though 'twas but one of their common *tertulias*,
Partaking, as usual, of wafers and ices,
Snow-water, and melons cut out into slices,
And chocolate,—furnished at coffee-house prices;
  While many a suitor, And gay coadjutor
In the eating-and-drinking line, scorns to be neuter;
One, being perhaps just return'd with his tutor

From travel in England, is tempting his '*future*'
With a luxury neat as imported, 'The Pewter,'
And charming the dear Violantes and Iñeses
With a three-corner'd Sandwich, and *soupçon* of 'Guinness's';
While another, from Paris but newly come back,
Hints 'the least taste in life' of the best cogniac.

 Such ogling and eyeing, In short, and such sighing,
And such complimenting (one must not say l—g),
Of smart Cavaliers with each other still vying,
 Mix'd up with the crying, And groans of the dying,
All hissing, and spitting, and broiling and frying,
Form a scene, which, although there can be no denying
To a *bon Catholique* it may prove edifying,
I doubt if a Protestant, smart Beau, or merry Belle
Might not shrink from it as somewhat too terrible.
It's a question with me if you ever survey'd a
More stern-looking mortal than old Torquemada,
Renown'd Father Dominic, famous for twisting dom-
-estic and foreign necks all over Christendom;
 Morescoes or Jews, Not a penny to choose,
If a dog of a heretic dared to refuse
A glass of old port, or a slice from a griskin,
The good Padre soon would so set him a frisking,
That I would not, for—more than I'll say—be in his skin.
'Twas just the same thing with his own race and nation,
And Christian Dissenters of every persuasion,
 Muggletonian, or Quaker, Or Jumper, or Shaker,
No matter with whom in opinion partaker,
George Whitfield, John Bunyan, or Thomas Gat-acre,
They'd no better chance than a Bonze or a Fakir;
If a woman, it skill'd not—if she did not deem as he
Bade her to deem touching Papal supremacy,
 By the Pope, but he'd make her!
 From error awake her,
Or else—pop her into an oven and bake her!
No one, in short, ever came half so near as he
Did, to the full extirpation of heresy;
And if, in the times of which now I am treating,
There had been such a thing as a 'Manchester Meeting,'
'Pretty pork' he'd have made 'Moderator' and 'Minister,'
Had he but caught them on his side Cape Finisterre;—
Pye Smith, and the rest of them once in his bonfire, hence-
-forth you'd have heard little more of the 'CONFERENCE.'
And—there on the opposite side of the ring,
He, too, sits 'in his GLORY,' confronting the King,
With his cast-iron countenance frowning austerely,
That matched with his *en bon point* body but queerly,

For, though grim his visage, his person was pursy,
   Belying the rumour Of fat folks' good-humour;
Above waves his banner of 'Justice and Mercy,'
Below and around stand a terrible band ad-
-ding much to the scene,—viz. The '*Holy Hermandad*,'
That's 'Brotherhood,'—each looking grave as a Grand-dad.
   Within the arena Before them is seen a
Strange, odd-looking group, each one dress'd in a garment
Not 'dandified' clearly, as certainly 'varment,'
Being all over vipers and snakes, and stuck thick
With multiplied silhouette profiles of NICK;
   And a cap of the same, All devils and flame,
Extinguisher-shaped, much like Salisbury Spire,
Except that the latter's of course somewhat higher;
   A long yellow pinafore
   Hangs down, each chin afore,
On which, ere the wearer had donn'd it, a man drew
The Scotch badge, a Saltire, or Cross of St Andrew;
Though I fairly confess I am quite at a loss
To guess why they should choose that particular cross,
   Or to make clear to you What the Scotch had to do
At all with the business in hand,—though it's true
That the vestment aforesaid, perhaps, from its hue,
Viz. *yellow*, in juxtaposition with *blue*
(A tinge of which latter tint could but accrue
On the faces of wretches, of course, in a stew
As to what their tormentors were going to do),
Might make people fancy, who no better knew,
They were somehow connected with Jeffrey's Review;
   Especially too As it's certain that few
Things would make Father Dominic blither or happier
Than to catch hold of *it*, or its Chef, Macvey Napier.—
No matter for that—my description to crown,
All the flames and the devils were turn'd upside down
On this habit, facetiously term'd *San Benito*,
   Much like the dress suit Of some nondescript brute
From the show-van of Wombwell (not George), or Polito.

   And thrice happy they,[1] Dress'd out in this way
To appear with *éclat* at the *Auto-da-fé*,
Thrice happy indeed whom the good luck might fall to
Of devils tail upward, and '*Fuego revolto*,'
   For, only see there, In the midst of the Square,
Where, perch'd up on poles six feet high in the air,

---

[1] 'O fortunati nimium sua si bona nôrint!' ('Thrice happy they, if they knew their blessings').—VIRGIL.

Sit, chained to the stake, some two, three, or four pair
Of wretches, whose eyes, nose, complexion, and hair
Their Jewish descent but too plainly declare,
Each clothed in a garment more frightful by far, a
Smock-frock sort of gaberdine, call'd a *Samarra*,
With three times the number of devils upon it,—
A proportion observed on the sugar-loaf'd bonnet,
With this farther distinction—of mischief a proof—
That every fiend Jack stands upright on his hoof!
  While the pictured flames, spread
  Over body and head,
Are three times as crooked, and three times as red!
All, too, pointing upwards, as much as to say,
'Here's the real *bonne bouche* of the Auto-da-fé!'

Torquemada, meanwhile, With his cold, cruel smile,
Sits looking on calmly, and watching the pile,
As his hooded 'Familiars' (their names, as some tell, come
From their being so much more 'familiar' than 'welcome'),
  Have, by this time, begun To be 'poking their fun,'
And their firebrands, as if they were so many posies
  Of lilies and roses, Up to the noses
Of Lazarus Levi, and Money Ben Moses;
While similar treatment is forcing out hollow moans
From Aby Ben Lasco, and Ikey Ben Solomons,
Whose beards—this a black, that inclining to grizzle—
Are smoking, and curling, and all in a fizzle;
The King, at the same time, his Dons and his visitors,
Sit, sporting smiles, like the Holy Inquisitors,———

Enough!—no more!— Thank Heaven, 'tis o'er!
The tragedy's done! and we now draw a veil
O'er a scene which makes outraged humanity quail;
The last fire's exhausted, and spent like a rocket,
The last wretched Hebrew's burnt down in his socket;
The Barriers are open, and all, saints and sinners,
King, Court, Lords, and Commons, gone home to their dinners,
  With a pleasing emotion Produced by the notion
Of having exhibited so much devotion,
All chuckling to think how the Saints are delighted
At having seen so many '*Smouches*' ignited:—
  All, save Privy-purse Humez, Who sconced in his room is,
And, Cocker in hand, in his leather-backed chair,
Is puzzling to find out how much the 'affair'
(By deep calculations, the which I can't follow), cost,—
The *tottle*, in short, *of the whole* of the Holocaust.

Perhaps you may think it a rather odd thing,
That, while talking so much of the Court and the King,
   In describing the scene
   Through which we've just been,
I've not said one syllable as to the Queen;
Especially, too, as her Majesty's 'Whereabouts,'
All things considered, might well be thought thereabouts;
The fact was, however, although little known,
Sa Magestad had hit on a plan of her own,
And suspecting, perhaps, that an *Auto* alone
Might fail in securing this 'Heir to the throne,'
   Had made up her mind, Although well inclined
Towards galas and shows of no matter what kind,
   For once to retire, And bribe the Saints higher
Then merely by sitting and seeing a fire,—
A sight, after all, she did not much admire;
   So she locked herself up, Without platter or cup,
In her Oriel, resolved not to take bite or sup,
Not so much as her matin-draught (our 'early purl'),
Nor put on her jewels, nor e'en let the girl,
Who help'd her to dress, take her hair out of curl,
But to pass the whole morning in telling her beads,
And in reading the lives of the Saints, and their deeds,
And in vowing to visit, without shoes or sandals,
Their shrines, with unlimited orders for candles,
Holy water, and Masses of Mozart's, and Handel's.[1]
And many a *Pater*, and *Ave*, and *Credo*
Did She, and her Father Confessor, Quevedo
(The clever Archbishop, you know, of Toledo),
Who came, as before, at a very short warning,
Get through, without doubt, in the course of that morning;
   Shut up, as they were. With nobody there
To at all interfere with so pious a pair;
And the Saints must have been stony-hearted indeed,
If they had not allow'd all these pains to succeed.
Nay, it's not clear to me but their very ability
   Might, Spain throughout,
   Have been brought into doubt,
Had the Royal bed still remain'd curs'd with sterility;
St Jago, however, who always is jealous
In Spanish affairs, as their best authors tell us,
   And who, if he saw Anything like a flaw

---

[1] 'That his, is, She *would* have order'd them—but none are known, I fear, as
  For Handel never wrote a Mass—and so She'd David Perez's—
    Bow! wow! wow? Fol, lol, etc.'
                 (POSTHUMOUS NOTE BY THE GHOST OF JAMES SMITH, ESQ.

In Spain's welfare, would soon sing 'Old Rose, burn the
    bellows!'
Set matters to rights like a King of good fellows;
   By his interference,   Three-fourths of a year hence,
There was nothing but capering, dancing, and singing,
Cachucas, Boleros, and bells set a ringing,
    In both the Castilles,   Triple-bob-major peals,
Rope-dancing, and tumbling, and somerset-flinging,
    Seguidillas, Fandangos,   While ev'ry gun bang goes;
And all the way through, from Gibraltar to Biscay,
Figueras and Sherry made all the Dons frisky
(Save Moore's 'Blakes and O'Donnells,' who stick to the
    whisky);
    All the day long   The dance and the song
Continue the general joy to prolong;
And even long after the close of the day
You can hear little else but 'Hip! hip! hip! hurray!'
The Escurial, however, is not quite so gay,
For, whether the Saint had not perfectly heard
The petition the Queen and Archbishop preferr'd,—
Or whether his head, from his not being used
To an *Auto-da-fé*, was a little confused,—
Or whether the King, in the smoke and the smother,
Got bother'd, and so made some blunder or other,
    I am sure I can't say;   All I know is, that day
There must have been *some* mistake!—that I'm afraid is,
    Only too clear,   Inasmuch as the dear
Royal Twins—though fine babies,—proved both little LADIES!!

MORAL

Reader!—Not knowing what your 'persuasion' may be,
Mahometan, Jewish, or even Parsee,
Take a little advice which may serve for all three!

First—'When you're at *Rome*, do as Rome does!' and note all
    her
Ways—drink what She drinks! and don't turn Tea-totaler!
   Is Spain, *raison de plus*,   You must do as they do,
Inasmuch as they're all there 'at sixes or sevens,'
    Just, as you know,   They were, some years ago,
In the days of Don Carlos and Brigadier Evans;
Don't be nice, then—but take what they've got in their shops,
Whether griskins, or sausages, ham, or pork-chops!

Next—avoid Fancy-trousers!—their colours and shapes
Sometimes, as you see, may lead folks into scrapes!

For myself, I confess I've but small taste in dress,
My opinion is, therefore, worth nothing—or less—
But some friends I've consulted,—much given to watch one's
    Apparel—do say It's by far the best way,
And the safest, to do as Lord Brougham does—buy Scotch ones!
I might now volunteer some advice to a King,—
Let Whigs say what they will, I shall do no such thing,
But copy my betters, and never begin
Until, like Sir Robert, 'I'm duly CALLED IN!'

THE INGOLDSBY PENANCE!

A LEGEND OF PALESTINE—AND WEST KENT

'I'll devise thee brave punishments for him!'—SHAKESPEARE.

FYTTE I

OUT and spake Sir Ingoldsby Bray,
A stalwart knight, I ween, was he,
    'Come east, come west, Come lance in rest,
Come falchion in hand, I'll tickle the best
Of all the Soldan's Chivalrie!'

Oh, they came west, and they came east,
Twenty-four Emirs and Sheiks at the least,
    And they hammer'd away At Sir Ingoldsby Bray,
Fall back, fall edge, cut, thrust, and point,—
But he topp'd off head, and he lopp'd off joint;

    Twenty and three, Of high degree,
Lay stark and stiff on the crimson'd lea,
All—all save one—and he ran up a tree!
'Now count them, my Squire, now count them and see!'
    'Twenty and three! Twenty and three!—
All of them Nobles of high degree:
There they be lying on Ascalon lea!'

Out and spake Sir Ingoldsby Bray,
    'What news? what news? come, tell to me!
What news? what news, thou little Foot-page?—
I've been whacking the foe till it seems an age
    Since I was in Ingoldsby Hall so free!
What news? what news from Ingoldsby Hall?
Come tell me now, thou Page so small!'

'Oh, Hawk and Hound Are safe and sound,
Beast in byre, and Steed in stall;
   And the Watch-dog's bark, As soon as it's dark,
Bays wakeful guard around Ingoldsby Hall!'

  —'I care not a pound For Hawk or for Hound,
For Steed in stall, or for Watch-dog's bay:
   Fain would I hear Of my dainty dear;
How fares Dame Alice, my Lady gay?'—
Sir Ingoldsby Bray, he said in his rage,
'What news? what news! thou naughty Foot-page!'—

That little Foot-page full low crouch'd he,
And he doff'd his cap, and he bended his knee,
'Now lithe and listen, Sir Bray, to me:
Lady Alice sits lonely in bower and hall,
Her sighs they rise, and her tears they fall.
   She sits alone And she makes her moan;
   Dance and song She considers quite wrong;
   Feast and revel Mere snares of the devil;
She mendeth her hose, and she crieth 'Alack!
When will Sir Ingoldsby Bray come back?"'

'Thou liest! thou liest, thou naughty Foot-page,
Full loud dost thou lie, false Page, to me!
   There, in thy breast, 'Neath thy silken vest,
What scroll is that, false Page, I see?'

Sir Ingoldsby Bray in his rage drew near,
That little Foot-page he blench'd with fear;

'Now where may the Prior of Abingdon lie?
King Richard's confessor, I ween, is he,
   And tidings rare To him do I bear,
And news of price from his rich Ab-bee!'

'Now nay, now nay, thou naughty Page!
No learned clerk, I trow, am I,
   But well, I ween, May there be seen
Dame Alice's hand with half an eye;
Now nay, now nay, thou naughty Page,
From Abingdon Abbey comes not thy news;
   Although no clerk, Well may I mark
The particular turn of her P's and Q's!'

Sir Ingoldsby Bray, in his fury and rage,
By the back of the neck takes that little Foot-page;

The scroll he seizes,　The page he squeezes,
And buffets,—and pinches his nose till he sneezes;—
Then he cuts with his dagger the silken threads
Which they used in those days 'stead of little Queen's-heads.

When the contents of the scroll met his view,
Sir Ingoldsby Bray in a passion grew,
　　Backward he drew　His mailed shoe,
And he kicked that naughty Foot-page, that he flew
Like a cloth-yard shaft from a bended yew,
I may not say whither—I never knew.

　'Now count the slain　Upon Ascalon plain,—
Go count them, my Squire, go count them again!'

　'Twenty and three!　There they be,
Stiff and stark on that crimson'd lea!—
　　Twenty and three?——　——Stay—let me see!
Stretched in his gore　There lieth one more!
By the Pope's triple crown there are twenty and *four*!
Twenty-four trunks, I ween, are there,
But their heads and their limbs are nobody knows where!
Ay, twenty-four corses, I rede, there be,
Though one got away, and ran up a tree!'

　'Look nigher, look nigher,　My trusty Squire!'—
　'One is the corse of a barefooted Friar!!'

Out and spake Sir Ingoldsby Bray,
　'A boon, a boon, King Richard,' quoth he,
　　'Now Heav'n thee save,　A boon I crave,
A boon, Sir King, on my bended knee;
　　A year and a day　Have I been away,
King Richard, from Ingoldsby Hall so free;
Dame Alice, she sits there in lonely guise,
And she makes her moan, and she sobs and she sighs,
And tears like raindrops fall from her eyes,
And she darneth her hose, and she crieth, "Alack!
Oh, when will Sir Ingoldsby Bray come back?"
A boon, a boon, my Liege,' quoth he,
'Fair Ingoldsby Hall I fain would see!'

　'Rise up, rise up, Sir Ingoldsby Bray,'
King Richard said right graciously,
　　'Of all in my host　That I love the most,
I love none better, Sir Bray, than thee!

　'Rise up, rise up, thou hast thy boon;
But—mind you make haste, and come back again soon!'

FYTTE II

Pope Gregory sits in St Peter's chair,
  Pontiff proud, I ween, is he,
    And a belted Knight In armour dight,
Is begging a boon on his bended knee,
With signs of grief and sounds of woe,
Featly he kisseth his Holiness' toe.
'Now pardon, Holy Father, I crave,
  O Holy Father, pardon and grace!
    In my fury and rage A little Foot-page
I have left, I fear me, in evil case:
  A scroll of shame From a faithless dame
Did that naughty Foot-page to a paramour bear;
  I gave him a "lick" With a stick, And a kick,
That sent him—I can't tell your Holiness where
Had he as many necks as hairs,
He had broken them all down those perilous stairs!'

'Rise up, rise up, Sir Ingoldsby Bray,
  Rise up, rise up, I say to thee;
    A soldier, I trow, Of the Cross art thou;
Rise up, rise up from thy bended knee!
Ill it beseems that soldier true
Of holy Church should vainly sue:—
—Foot-pages, they are by no means rare,
  A thriftless crew, I ween, be they,
    Well mote we spare A Page—or a pair,
For the matter of that—Sir Ingoldsby Bray,
  But stout and true Soldiers, like you,
Grow scarcer and scarcer every day!—
  Be prayers for the dead Duly read,
Let a mass be sung, and a *pater* be said;
So may your qualms of conscience cease,
And the little Foot-page shall rest in peace!'

'—Now pardon, Holy Father, I crave.
  O Holy Father, pardon and grace!
    Dame Alice, my wife, The bane of my life,
I have left, I fear me, in evil case!
A scroll of shame in my rage I tore,
Which that caitiff Page to a paramour bore;
'Twere bootless to tell how I storm'd and swore;
Alack! alack! too surely I knew
The turn of each P, and the tail of each Q
And away to Ingoldsby Hall I flew!

Dame Alice I found,—She sank on the ground,—
I twisted her neck till I twisted it round!
With a jibe and jeer, and mock, and scoff,
I twisted it on—till I twisted it off!—
All the King's Doctors and all the King's Men
Can't put fair Alice's head on agen!'

'Well-a-day! well-a-day!   Sir Ingoldsby Bray,
Why really—I hardly know what to say:—
Foul sin, I trow, a fair Ladye to slay,
Because she's perhaps been a little too gay.—
—Monk must chaunt and Nun must pray;
For each mass they sing, and each pray'r they say,
    For a year, and a day,   Sir Ingoldsby Bray
A fair rose-noble must duly pay!
So may his qualms of conscience cease,
And the soul of Dame Alice may rest in peace!'

'Now pardon, Holy Father, I crave,
    O Holy Father, pardon and grace!
        No power could save   That paramour knave,
I left him, I wot, in evil case!
        There, 'midst the slain   Upon Ascalon plain,
Unburied, I trow, doth his body remain,
His legs lie here, and his arms lie there,
And his head lies—I can't tell your Holiness where!'

'Now out and alas! Sir Ingoldsby Bray,
Foul sin it were, thou doughty Knight,
    To hack and to hew   A champion true
Of holy Church in such pitiful plight!
Foul sin her warriors so to slay,
When they're scarcer and scarcer every day!—
    A chauntry fair,   And of Monks a pair,
To pray for his soul for ever and aye,
Thou must duly endow, Sir Ingoldsby Bray,
And fourteen marks by the year must thou pay
    For plenty of lights   To burn there o' nights—
None of your rascally '*dips*'—but sound,
Round, ten-penny moulds of four to the pound;—
And a shirt of the roughest and coarsest hair
For a year and a day, Sir Ingoldsby, wear!—
So may your qualms of conscience cease,
And the soul of the Soldier shall rest in peace!'

'Now nay, Holy Father, now nay, now nay!
Less penance may serve!' quoth Sir Ingoldsby Bray.
'No champion free of the Cross was he;
No belted Baron of high degree;
   No Knight nor Squire   Did there expire;
He was, I trow, but a bare-footed Friar!
And the Abbot of Abingdon long may wait
With his monks around him, and early and late
May look from loop-hole, and turret, and gate,
—He hath lost his Prior—his Prior his pate!'

'Now Thunder and turf!' Pope Gregory said,
And his hair raised his triple crown right off his head—
'Now Thunder and turf! and out and alas!
A horrible thing has come to pass!
What! cut off the head of a reverend Prior,
And say he was "*only* (!!!) a bare-footed Friar!"—
   "What Baron or Squire,   Or Knight of the shire
Is half so good as a holy Friar?"
   O, turpissime!   *Vir nequissime!*
Sceleratissime!—quissime!—issime!
Never, I trow, have the *Servi servorum*
   Had before 'em   Such a breach of decorum,
Such a gross violation of *morum bonorum*,
And won't have again *saecula saeculorum!*—
   Come hither to me,   My Cardinals three,
   My Bishops *in partibus*,   Masters *in Artibus*,
   Hither to me, A.B. and D.D.
   Doctors and Proctors of every degree!
Go fetch me a book!—go fetch me a bell
As big as a dustman's!—and a candle as well—
I'll send him—*where* good manners won't let me tell!'

—'Pardon and grace!—now pardon and grace!'
—Sir Ingoldsby Bray fell flat on his face—
   '*Meâ culpâ!*—in sooth I'm in pitiful case.
   Peccavi! peccavi!—I've done very wrong!
But my heart it is stout, and my arm it is strong,
And I'll fight for Holy Church all the day long;
And the Ingoldsby lands are broad and fair,
And they're here, and they're there, and I can't tell you where,
And Holy Church shall come in for her share!'

Pope Gregory paused, and he sat himself down,
And he somewhat relaxed his terrible frown,
And his Cardinals three they pick'd up his crown.

'Now, if it be so that you own you've been wrong,
And your heart is so stout, and your arm is so strong,
And you really will fight like a trump all day long;—
If the Ingoldsby lands do lie here and there,
And Holy Church shall come in for her share,—
    Why, my Cardinals three,   You'll agree   With me,
That it gives a new turn to the whole affair,
And I think that the Penitent need not despair!
—If it be so, as you seem to say,
Rise up, rise up, Sir Ingoldsby Bray!

'An Abbey so fair Sir Bray shall found,
Whose innermost wall's encircling bound
Shall take in a couple of acres of ground;
And there in that Abbey all the year round,
A full choir of monks, and a full choir of nuns,
Shall live upon cabbage and hot-cross buns;
    And Sir Ingoldsby Bray,   Without delay,
    Shall hie him again   To Ascalon plain,
And gather the bones of the foully slain:
And shall place said bones, with all possible care,
In an elegant shrine in his abbey so fair;
    And plenty of lights   Shall be there o' nights;
None of your rascally 'dips,' but sound,
Best superfine wax-wicks, four to the pound;
    And Monk and Nun   Shall pray, each one,
For the soul of the Prior of Abingdon!
And Sir Ingoldsby Bray, so bold and so brave,
Never shall wash himself, comb, or shave,
    Nor adorn his body,   Nor drink gin-toddy,
    Nor indulge in a pipe,—   But shall dine upon tripe
And blackberries gathered before they are ripe,
And for ever abhor, renounce, and abjure
Rum, hollands, and brandy, wine, punch, and liqueur!

    (Sir Ingoldsby Bray   Here gave way
To a feeling which prompted a word profane,
But he swallow's it down, by an effort, again,
And his Holiness luckily fancied his gulp a
Mere repetition of O, meâ culpâ!)

'Thrice three times upon Candlemas-day,
Between Vespers and Compline, Sir Ingoldsby Bray
Shall run round the Abbey, as best he may,
    Subjecting his back   To thump and to thwack,
Well and truly laid on by a bare-footed Friar,
With a stout cat o' ninetails of whip-cord and wire;

And nor he, nor his heir   Shall take, use, or bear
  Any more from this day,   The surname of Bray,
As being dishonour'd, but all issue male he has
Shall, with himself, go henceforth by an alias!
So his qualms of conscience at length may cease,
And Page, Dame, and Prior shall rest in peace!'

Sir Ingoldsby (now no longer Bray)
Is off like a shot away and away,
  Over the brine   To far Palestine,
To rummage and hunt over Ascalon plain
For the unburied bones of his victim slain.

'Look out, my Squire,   Look higher and nigher,
Look out for the corpse of a bare-footed Friar!
And pick up the arms, and the legs, of the dead,
And pick up his body, and pick up his head!'

FYTTE III

Ingoldsby Abbey is fair to see,
It hath manors a dozen, and royalties three,
With right of free-warren (whatever that be);
Rich pastures in front, and green woods in the rear,
All in full leaf at the right time of year;
About Christmas or so, they fall into the sear,
And the prospect, of course, becomes rather more drear:
But it's really delightful in spring-time,—and near
The great gate Father Thames rolls sun-bright and clear.
Cobham woods to the right,—on the opposite shore
Laindon Hills in the distance, ten miles off or more;
Then you've Milton and Gravesend behind,—and before
You can see almost all the way down to the Nore.[1]
  So charming a spot,   It's rarely one's lot
To see, and when seen it's as rarely forgot.

Yes, Ingoldsby Abbey is fair to see,
And its Monks and its Nuns are fifty and three,
And there they all stand each in their degree,

---

[1] Alas! one might almost say that of this sacred, and once splendid, edifice, *periêrunt etiam ruinae.* An elderly gentleman, however, of ecclesiastical cut, who oscillates between the Garrick Club and the Falcon in Gravesend, and is said by the host to be a 'foreigneering Bishop,' does not scruple to identify the ruins still to be seen by the side of the high Dover road, about a mile and a half below the town, with those of the haunted *Sacellum.* The general features of the landscape certainly correspond, and tradition, as certainly, countenances his conjecture.

Drawn up in the front of their sacred abode,
Two by two, in their regular mode,
While a funeral comes down the Rochester road.
Palmers twelve, from a foreign strand,
Cockle in hat, and staff in hand,
Come marching in pairs, a holy band!
Little boys twelve, dressed all in white,
Each with his brazen censer bright,
And singing away with all their might,
Follow the Palmers—a goodly sight;
   Next high in air   Twelve Yeomen bear
On their sturdy necks, with a good deal of care,
   A patent sarcophagus firmly rear'd,
   Of Spanish mahogany (not veneer'd),
   And behind walks a Knight with a very long beard.
     Close by his side   Is a Friar, supplied
With a stout cat o' ninetails of tough cowhide,
    While all sorts of queer men
    Bring up the rear—Men-
-at-arms, Nigger captives, and Bow-men, and Spear-men.

It boots not to tell   What you'll guess very well,
How some sang the requiem, some toll'd the bell;
   Suffice it to say,   'Twas on Candlemas-day
The procession I speak about reached the *Sacellum*;
   And in lieu of a supper   The Knight on his crupper
Received the first taste of the Father's flagellum;—
   That, as chronicles tell,   He continued to dwell
All the rest of his days in the Abbey he'd founded,
By the pious of both sexes ever surrounded,
And, partaking the fare of the Monks and the Nuns,
Ate the cabbage alone, without touching the buns;
—That year after year, having run round the Quad
With his back, as enjoin'd him, exposed to the rod,
Having not only kiss'd it, but bless'd it, and thank'd it, he
Died, as all thought, in the odour of sanctity,
When,—strange to relate! and you'll hardly believe
What I'm going to tell you,—next Candlemas Eve
The Monks and the Nuns in the dead of the night
Tumble, all of them, out of their beds in affright,
   Alarm'd by the bawls,   And the calls, and the squalls
Of someone who seem'd running all round the walls!

   Looking out, soon   By the light of the moon
There appears most distinctly to ev'ryone's view,
And making, as seems to them, all this ado,
The form of a Knight with a beard like a Jew,

As black as if steep'd in that 'Matchless!' of Hunt's,
And so bushy, it would not disgrace Mr Muntz;
A bare-footed Friar stands behind him, and shakes
A flagellum, whose lashes appear to be snakes;
While, more terrible still, the astounded beholders
Perceive the said Friar has NO HEAD ON HIS SHOULDERS,
   But is holding his pate.   In his left hand, out straight,
As if by a closer inspection to find
Where to get the best cut at his victim behind,
With the aid of a small 'bull's-eye lantern,'—as placed
By our own new Police,—in a belt round his waist.
   All gaze with surprise,   Scarce believing their eyes,
When the Knight makes a start like a race-horse, and flies
From his headless tormentor, repeating his cries,—
In vain,—for the Friar to his skirts closely sticks,
'Running after him,'—so said the Abbot,—'like Bricks!'

Thrice three times did the Phantom Knight
Course round the Abbey as best he might
Be-thwack'd and be-smack'd by the headless Sprite,
While his shrieks so piercing made all hearts thrill,—
Then a whoop and a halloo,—and all was still!

Ingoldsby Abbey has passed away,
   And at this time of day   One can hardly survey
Any traces or track, save a few ruins, grey
With age, and fast mouldering into decay,
Of the structure once built by Sir Ingoldsby Bray;
But still there are many folks living who say
That on every Candlemas eve, the Knight,
   Accoutred, and dight   In his armour bright,
With his thick black beard,—and the clerical Sprite,
With his head in his hand, and his lantern alight,
Run round the spot where the old Abbey stood,
And are seen in the neighbouring glebe-land and wood;
More especially still, if it's stormy and windy,
You may hear them for miles kicking up their wild shindy;
   And that once in a gale   Of wind, sleet, and hail,
They frighten'd the horses, and upset the mail.

   What 'tis breaks the rest   Of those souls unbless'd
Would now be a thing rather hard to be guess'd,
Though some say the Squire, on his death-bed, confess'd
That on Ascalon plain,   When the bones of the slain
Were collected that day, and packed up in a chest,
   Caulk'd, and made water-tight,
   By command of the Knight,

Though the legs and the arms they'd got all pretty right,
And the body itself in a decentish plight,
Yet the Friar's Pericranium was nowhere in sight;
So, to save themselves trouble, they pick'd up instead,
And popp'd on the shoulders a Saracen's Head!
Thus the Knight in the terms of his penance had fail'd,
And the Pope's absolution, of course, nought avail'd.

Now, though this might be, It don't seem to agree
With one thing which, I own, is a poser to me,—
I mean, as the miracles wrought at the shrine
Containing the bones brought from far Palestine
Were so great and notorious, 'tis hard to combine
This *fact* with the reason these people assign,
Or suppose that the head of the murder'd Divine
Could be aught but what Yankees would call 'genu-*ine*.'
'Tis a very nice question—but be't as it may,
The Ghost of Sir Ingoldsby (*ci-devant* Bray),
It is boldly affirm'd, by the folks great and small
About Milton, and Chalk, and around Cobham Hall,
Still on Candlemas-day haunts the old ruin'd wall,
And that many have seen him, and more heard him squall.
So I think, when the facts of the case you recall,
My inference, reader, you'll fairly forestall,
   Viz.: that, spite of the hope Held out by the Pope,
Sir Ingoldsby Bray was d—d after all!

MORAL

Foot-pages, and Servants of ev'ry degree,
In livery or out of it, listen to me!
See what comes of lying!—don't join in a league
To humbug your master, or aid in intrigue!

Ladies!—married and single, from this understand
How foolish it is to send letters by hand!
Don't stand for the sake of a penny,—but when you
   've a billet to send To a lover or friend,
Put it into the post, and don't cheat the revenue!

Reverend gentlemen!—you who are given to roam,
Don't keep up a soft correspondence at home!
But while you're abroad lead respectable lives;
Love your neighbours, and welcome,—but don't love their wives!
And, as bricklayers cry from the tiles and the leads
When they're shovelling the snow off, 'TAKE CARE OF YOUR HEADS!'

Knights!—whose hearts are so stout, and whose arms are so strong,
Learn,—to twist a wife's neck is decidedly wrong!

If your servants offend you, or give themselves airs,
Rebuke them—but mildly—don't kick them downstairs!
To 'Poor Richard's' homely old proverb attend,
'If you want matters well managed, *Go*!—if not, *Send*!'
A servant's too often a negligent elf;
—If it's business of consequence, Do IT YOURSELF!

The state of society seldom requires
People now to bring home with them unburied Friars,
But they sometimes do bring home an inmate for life;
Now—don't do that by proxy!—but choose your own wife!
For think how annoying 'twould be, when you're wed,
    To find in your bed,   On the pillow instead
Of the sweet face you look for—A SARACEN'S HEAD!

NETLEY ABBEY

A LEGEND OF HAMPSHIRE

I SAW thee, Netley, as the sun
Across the western wave
    Was sinking slow,   And a golden glow
To thy roofless towers he gave;
    And the ivy sheen,   With its mantle of green,
That wrapped thy walls around,
    Shone lovelily bright   In that glorious light,
And I felt 'twas holy ground.

Then I thought of the ancient time—
The days of thy Monks of old,—
When to Matin, and Vesper, and Compline chime,
    The loud Hosanna roll'd,
And, thy courts and 'long-drawn aisles' among
Swell'd the full tide of sacred song;
    And then a vision pass'd
    Across my mental eye; [1]
And silver shrines, and shaven crowns,
And delicate Ladies, in bombazeen gowns,
    And long white veils, went by,
    Stiff, and staid, and solemn, and sad,—
—But one, methought, wink'd at the Gardener-Lad!

Then came the Abbot, with mitre and ring,
And pastoral staff, and all that sort of thing,

[1] 'In my mind's eye, Horatio!'—HAMLET.

And a Monk with a book, and a Monk with a bell,
 And 'dear little souls,' In clean linen stoles,
 Swinging their censers, and making a smell.—
And see where the Choir-master walks in the rear,
 With front severe, And brow austere,
Now and then pinching a little boy's ear
When he chaunts the responses too late, or too soon,
Or his *Do, Re, Mi, Fa, Sol, La*'s not quite in tune.
 (Then, you know, They'd a 'movable *Do*,'
Not a fixed one as now—and of course never knew
How to set up a musical Hullabaloo.)
It was, in sooth, a comely sight,
And I welcom'd the vision with pure delight.

  But then 'a change came o'er'
  My spirit—a change of fear—
 That gorgeous scene I beheld no more,
 But deep beneath the basement floor
  A dungeon dark and drear!
And there was an ugly hole in the wall—
For an oven too big,—for a cellar too small!
 And mortar and bricks All ready to fix,
And I said, 'Here's a Nun has been playing some tricks!—
That horrible hole!—it seems to say,
"I'm a Grave that gapes for a living prey!"'
And my heart grew sick, and my brow grew sad—
And I thought of that wink at the Gardener-lad.
 Ah me! ah me! 'tis sad to think
 That Maiden's eye, which was made to wink,
 Should here be compelled to grow blear, and blink,
  Or be closed for aye In this kind of way,
 Shut out for ever from wholesome day,
 Wall'd up in a hole with never a chink,
 No light,—no air,—no victuals,—no drink!—
  And that Maiden's lip, Which was made to sip,
 Should here grow wither'd and dry as a chip!
 —That wandering glance and furtive kiss
 Exceedingly naughty, and wrong, I wis,
 Should yet be considered so much amiss
 As to call for a sentence severe as this!
 And I said to myself, as I heard with a sigh
 The poor lone victim's stifled cry,[1]

[1] About the middle of the last century a human skeleton was discovered in
a recess in the wall among the ruins of Netley.   On examination the bones
were pronounced to be those of a female.   *Teste* James Harrison, a youthful
but intelligent cab-driver of Southampton, who 'well remembers to have
heard his grandmother say that "Somebody told her so."'

'Well! I can't understand   How any man's hand
Could wall up that hole in a Christian land!—
    Why, a Mussulman Turk   Would recoil from the work,
And though, when his Ladies run after the fellows, he
Stands not on trifles, if madden'd by jealousy,
Its objects, I'm sure, would declare, could they speak,
In their Georgian, Circassian, or Turkish, or Greek,
"When all's said and done, far better it was for us,
    Tied back to back,   And sewn up in a sack,
To be pitched neck-and-heels from a boat in the Bosphorus!'
    —Oh! a Saint 'twould vex   To think that the sex
Should be treated no better than Combe's double X!
Sure someone might run to the Abbess, and tell her
A much better method of stocking her cellar.'

If ever on polluted walls
Heaven's red right arm in vengeance falls,—
If e'er its justice wraps in flame
The black abodes of sin and shame,
That justice, in its own good time,
Shall visit for so foul a crime,
Ope desolation's floodgate wide,
And blast thee, Netley, in thy pride!

Lo where it comes! the tempest lours,—
It bursts on thy devoted towers;
Ruthless Tudor's bloated form
Rides on the blast, and guides the storm;
I hear the sacrilegious cry,
'Down with the nests, and the rooks will fly!'

Down! down they come—a fearful fall—
Arch, and pillar, and roof-tree and all,
Stained pane, and sculptured stone,
There they lie on the greensward strown—
Mouldering walls remain alone!
    Shaven crown,   Bombazeen gown,
Mitre, and Crozier, and all are flown!

And yet, fair Netley, as I gaze
    Upon that grey and mouldering wall,
The glories of thy palmy days
    Its very stones recall!—
They 'come like shadows, so depart'—
I saw thee as thou wert—and art—

Sublime in ruin!—grand in woe!
  Lone refuge of the owl and bat;
No voice awakes thine echoes now!
    No sound—Good Gracious!—what was that?
      Was it the moan,   The parting groan
Of her who died forlorn and alone,
Embedded in mortar, and bricks, and stone?—
    —Full and clear   On my listening ear
It comes—again—near, and more near—
Why 'zooks! it's the popping of Ginger Beer!

      I rush to the door—   I tread the floor,
By Abbots and Abbesses trodden before,
In the good old chivalric days of yore,
    And what see I there?—   In a rush-bottom'd chair
A hag, surrounded by crockery-ware,
Vending, in cups, to the credulous throng,
A nasty decoction miscall'd 'Souchong,'—
And a squeaking fiddle and 'wry-necked fife'
Are screeching away, for the life!—for the life!—
Danced to by 'All the World and his wife.'
Tag, Rag, and Bobtail, are capering there,
Worse scene, I ween, than Bartlemy Fair!—
Two or three Chimney-sweeps, two or three Clowns,
Playing at 'pitch and toss,' sport their 'Browns,'
Two or three damsels, frank and free,
Are ogling, and smiling, and sipping Bohea.
Parties below, and parties above,
Some making tea, and some making love.

      Then the 'toot—toot—toot'
      Of that vile demi-flute,—
    The detestable din   Of that cracked violin,
And the odours of 'Stout,' and tobacco, and gin!
'—Dear me!' I exclaim'd, 'what a place to be in!'
And I said to the person who drove my 'shay'
(A very intelligent man, by the way),
'This, all things considered, is rather too gay!
It don't suit my humour,—so take me away!
Dancing! and drinking! cigar and song!
If not profanation, it's "coming it strong,"
And I really consider it all very wrong.—
—Pray, to whom does this property now belong?'—
  —He paused, and said,   Scratching his head,
'Why, I really *do* think he's a little to blame,
But I can't say I knows the Gentleman's name!'

'Well—well!' quoth I,   As I heaved a sigh,
And a tear-drop fell from my twinkling eye,
'My vastly good man, as I scarcely doubt
That some day or other you'll find it out,
    Should he come in your way,   Or ride in your "shay"
    (As perhaps he may),   Be so good as to say
That a Visitor, whom you drove over one day,
Was exceedingly angry, and very much scandalized,
Finding these beautiful ruins so Vandalized,
And thus of their owner to speak began,
    As he ordered you home in haste,
'NO DOUBT HE'S A VERY RESPECTABLE MAN,
    But—*I can't say much for his taste.*' [1]

FRAGMENT

A FEELING sad came o'er me as I trod the sacred ground [2]
Where Tudors and Plantagenets were lying all around:
I stepp'd with noiseless foot, as though the sound of mortal
    tread
Might burst the bands of the dreamless sleep that wraps the
    mighty dead!

The slanting ray of the evening sun shone through those cloisters
    pale,
With fitful light on regal vest, and warrior's sculptured mail;
As from the stained and storied pane it danced with quivering
    gleam,
Each cold and prostrate form below seem'd quickening in the
    beam.

Now, sinking low, no more was heard the organ's solemn swell,
And faint upon the listening ear the last Hosanna fell:
It died—and not a breath did stir; above each knightly stall,
Unmoved, the banner'd blazonry hung waveless as a pall.

I stood alone!—a living thing 'midst those that were no more—
I thought on ages past and gone—the glorious deeds of yore—
On Edward's sable panoply, on Cressy's tented plain,
The fatal roses twined at length—on great Eliza's reign.

---

[1] 'Adieu, Monsieur Gil Blas; je vous souhaite toutes sortes de prospérités,
avec un peu plus de goût!'—GIL BLAS.
[2] Westminster Abbey.

I thought on Naseby—Marston Moor—on Worc'ster's 'crown-
    ing fight'!
When on mine ear a sound there fell—it chill'd me with affright,
As thus in low, unearthly tones I heard a voice begin,
'—This here's the Cap of Giniral Monk!—Sir! please put
    summut in!'

Caetera desiderantur.

NELL COOK!!

A Legend of the 'Dark Entry'

THE KING'S SCHOLAR'S STORY

'From the "Brick Walk" branches off to the right a long narrow vaulted
passage, paved with flagstones, vulgarly known by the name of the "Dark
Entry." Its eastern extremity communicates with the cloisters, crypt, and,
by a private stair-case, with the interior of the Cathedral. On the west it
opens into the "Green-court," forming a communication between it and the
portion of the "Precinct" called the "Oaks."'

A WALK ROUND CANTERBURY, ETC.

Scene—A back parlour in Mr John Ingoldsby's house in the Precinct. A
blazing fire.—Mine Uncle is seated in a high-backed easy-chair, twirling his
thumbs, and contemplating his list shoe.—Little Tom, the 'King's Scholar,'
on a stool opposite.—Mrs John Ingoldsby at the table, busily employed in
manufacturing a cabbage-rose (cauliflower?) in many-coloured worsteds.
—Mine Uncle's meditations are interrupted by the French clock on the
mantelpiece.—He prologizeth with vivacity

'Hark! listen, Mrs Ingoldsby,—the clock is striking nine!
Give Master Tom another cake, and half a glass of wine,
And ring the bell for Jenny Smith, and bid her bring his coat
And a warm bandanna handkerchief to tie about his throat.

'And bid them go the nearest way, for Mr Birch has said
That nine o'clock's the hour he'll have his boarders all in bed;
And well we know when little boys their coming home delay,
They often seem to walk and sit uneasily next day!'

'—Nay, nay, dear Uncle Ingoldsby, now send me not, I pray,
Back by that Entry dark, for that you know's the nearest way;
I dread that Entry dark with Jane alone at such an hour,
It fears me quite—it's Friday night!—and then Nell Cook hath
    pow'r!'

G 185

'And who's Nell Cook, thou silly child?—and what's Nell
  Cook to thee?
That thou shouldst dread at night to tread with Jane that dark
  entrée?'
—'Nay, list and hear, mine Uncle dear! such fearsome things
  they tell
Of Nelly Cook, that few may brook at night to meet with Nell!'

'It was in bluff King Harry's days,—and Monks and Friars were
  then,
You know, dear Uncle Ingoldsby, a sort of Clergymen.
They'd coarse stuff gowns, and shaven crowns,—no shirts,—
  and no cravats;
And a cord was placed about their waist—they had no shovel
  hats!

'It was in bluff King Harry's days, while yet he went to shrift,
And long before he stamped and swore, and cut the Pope adrift;
There lived a portly Canon then, a sage and learned clerk;
He had, I trow, a goodly house, fast by that Entry dark!

'The Canon was a portly man—of Latin and of Greek,
And learned lore, he had good store,—yet health was on his
  cheek.
The Priory fare was scant and spare, the bread was made of rye,
The beer was weak, yet he was sleek—he had a merry eye.

'For though within the Priory the fare was scant and thin,
The Canon's house it stood without;—he kept good cheer
  within;
Unto the best he pressed each guest with free and jovial look,
And Ellen Bean ruled his cuisine.—He called her 'Nelly Cook!'

'For soups, and stews, and choice ragouts, Nell Cook was
  famous still;
She'd make them even of old shoes, she had such wond'rous
  skill:
Her manchets fine were quite divine, her cakes were nicely
  brown'd,
Her boil'd and roast, they were the boast of all the "Precinct"
  round;

'And Nelly was a comely lass, but calm and staid her air,
And earthward bent her modest look—yet she was passing fair;
And though her gown was russet brown, their heads grave
  people shook:
—They all agreed no Clerk had need of such a pretty Cook.

'One day—'twas on a Whitsun-Eve—there come a coach and
    four;—
It pass'd the 'Green-Court' gate, and stopp'd before the
    Canon's door;
The travel-stain on wheel and rein bespoke a weary way,—
Each panting steed relax'd its speed—out stepped a Lady gay.

'"Now welcome! welcome! dearest Niece,"—the Canon then
    did cry,
And to his breast the Lady pressed—he had a merry eye,—
"Now, welcome! welcome! dearest Niece! in sooth thou'rt
    welcome here,
'Tis many a day since we have met—how fares my Brother
    dear?"—

'"Now, thanks, my loving Uncle," that Lady gay replied;
"Gramercy for thy benison!"—then "Out, alas!" she sighed;
"My father dear he is not near; he seeks the Spanish Main;
He prays thee give me shelter here till he return again!"—

'"Now, welcome! welcome! dearest Niece; come lay thy mantle
    by!"
The Canon kissed her ruby lip—he had a merry eye,—
But Nelly Cook askew did look,—it came into her mind
They were a little less than "kin," and rather more than "kind."

'Three weeks are gone and over—full three weeks and a day,
Yet still within the Canon's house doth dwell that Lady gay;
On capons fine they daily dine, rich cates and sauces rare;
And they quaff good store of Bourdeaux wine,—so dainty is
    their fare.

'And fine upon the virginals is that gay Lady's touch,
And sweet her voice unto the lute, you'll scarce hear any such;
But is it "O Sanctissima!" she sighs in dulcet tone?
Or "Angels ever bright and fair"?—Ah, no!—it's "Bobbing
    Joan!"

'The Canon's house is lofty, and spacious to the view;
The Canon's cell is ordered well—yet Nelly looks askew;
The Lady's bower is in the tower,—yet Nelly shakes her head—
She hides the poker and the tongs in that gay Lady's bed?

'Six weeks were gone and over—full six weeks and a day,
Yet in that bed the poker and the tongs unheeded lay!
From which, I fear, it's pretty clear that Lady rest had none?
Or, if she slept in any bed—it was not in her own.

'But where that Lady pass'd her nights, I may not well divine,
Perhaps in pious orisons at good St Thomas' Shrine,
And for her father far away breathed tender vows and true—
It may be so—I cannot say—but Nelly look'd askew.

'And still at night, by fair moonlight, when all were lock'd in
     sleep,
She'd listen at the Canon's door,—she'd through the keyhole
     peep—
I know not what she heard or saw, but fury filled her eye—
—She bought some nasty Doctor's-stuff, and she put it in a pie!

'It was a glorious summer's eve—with beams of rosy red
The Sun went down—all Nature smiled—but Nelly shook her
     head!
Full softly to the balmy breeze rang out the Vesper bell—
—Upon the Canon's startled ear it sounded like a knell!

'"Now here's to thee, mine Uncle! a health I drink to thee!
Now pledge me back in Sherris sack, or a cup of Malvoisie!"—
The Canon sigh'd—but rousing, cried, "I answer to thy call,
And a Warden-pie's a dainty dish to mortify withal!"

'"Tis early dawn—the matin chime rings out for morning
     pray'r—
And Prior and Friar is in his stall—the Canon is not there!
Nor in the small Refect'ry hall, nor cloister'd walk is he—
All wonder—and the Sacristan says, "Lauk-a-daisey-me!"

'They've searched the aisles and Baptistry—they've searched
     above—around—
The "Sermon House"—the "Audit Room"—the Canon is not
     found.
They only find that pretty Cook concocting a ragout,
They ask her where her master is—but Nelly looks askew!

'They call for crowbars—"jemmies" is the modern name they
     bear—
They burst through lock, and bolt, and bar—but what a sight
     is there!—
The Canon's head lies on the bed—his Niece lies on the floor!
—They are as dead as any nail that is in any door!

'The livid spot is on his breast, the spot is on his back!
His portly form, no longer warm with life, is swoln and black!—
The livid spot is on her cheek, it's on her neck of snow,
And the Prior sighs, and sadly cries, "Well! here's a pretty Go!"

'All at the silent hour of night a bell is heard to toll,
A knell is rung, a requiem's sung as for a sinful soul,
And there's a grave within the Nave, it's dark, and deep, and
    wide,
And they bury there a Lady fair, and a Canon by her side!

'An Uncle—so 'tis whisper'd now throughout the sacred fane,—
And a Niece—whose father's far away upon the Spanish Main—
The Sacristan, he says no word that indicates a doubt,
But he puts his thumb unto his nose, and he spreads his fingers
    out!

'And where doth tarry Nelly Cook, that staid and comely
    lass?
Ay, where?—for ne'er from forth that door was Nelly known to
    pass.
Her coif, and gown of russet brown were lost unto the view,
And if you mention'd Nelly's name—the Monks all looked
    askew!

'There is a heavy paving-stone fast by the Canon's door,
Of granite grey, and it may weigh some half a ton or more,
And it is laid deep in the shade within that Entry dark,
Where sun or moonbeam never play'd, or e'en one starry spark.

'The heavy granite stone was moved that night, 'twas darkly
    said,
And the mortar round its sides next morn seem'd fresh and
    newly laid;
But what within the narrow vault beneath that stone doth lie,
Or if that there be vault, or no—I cannot tell—not I!

'But I've been told that moan and groan, and fearful wail and
    shriek
Came from beneath that paving-stone for nearly half a week—
For three long days and three long nights came forth those
    sounds of fear;
Then all was o'er—they never more fell on the listening ear.

'A hundred years were gone and past since last Nell Cook was
    seen,
When, worn by use that stone got loose, and they went and told
    the Dean.—
—Says the Dean, says he, 'My Masons three! now haste and
    fix it tight";
And the Masons three peep'd down to see, and they saw a fear-
    some sight.

'Beneath that heavy paving-stone a shocking hole they found—
It was not more than twelve feet deep, and barely twelve feet
      round;
—A fleshless, sapless skeleton lay in that horrid well!
But who the deuce 'twas put it there those Masons could not
      tell.

'And near this fleshless skeleton a pitcher small did lie,
And a mouldy piece of "kissing crust," as from a Warden-pie!
And Doctor Jones declared the bones were female bones and,
      "Zooks!
I should not be surprised," said he, "if these were Nelly
      Cook's!"

'It was in good Dean Bargrave's days, If I remember right,
Those fleshless bones beneath the stones these Masons brought
      to light;
And you may well in the "Dean's Chapelle" Dean Bargrave's
      portrait view,
"Who died one night," says old Tom Wright, "in sixteen
      forty-two!"

'And so two hundred years have passed since that these Masons
      three,
With curious looks, did set Nell Cook's unquiet spirit free;
That granite stone had kept her down till then—so some
      suppose,—
—Some spread their fingers out, and put their thumb unto their
      nose.

'But one thing's clear—that all the year on every Friday night,
Throughout that Entry dark doth roam Nell Cook's unquiet
      Sprite:
On Friday was that Warden-pie all by that Canon tried;
On Friday died he, and that tidy Lady by his side!

'And though two hundred years have flown, Nell Cook doth still
      pursue
Her weary walk, and they who cross her path the deed may rue;
Her fatal breath is fell as death! the Simoom's blast is not
More dire—(a wind in Africa that blows uncommon hot).

'But all unlike the Simoom's blast, her breath is deadly cold,
Delivering quivering, shivering shocks unto both young and old,
And whoso in that Entry dark doth feel that fatal breath,
He ever dies within the year some dire, untimely death!

'No matter who—no matter what condition, age, or sex,
But some "get shot," and some "get drown'd," and some "get"
broken necks;
Some "get run over" by a coach;—and one beyond the seas
"Got" scraped to death with oyster-shells among the Caribbees!

'Those Masons three, who set her free, fell first!—it is averred
That two were hang'd on Tyburn tree for murdering of the
third:
Charles Storey,[1] too, his friend who slew, had ne'er, if truth
they tell,
Been gibbeted on Chartham Downs, had they not met with
Nell!

'Then send me not, mine Uncle dear, oh! send me not, I pray,
Back through that Entry dark to-night, but round some other
way!
I will not be a truant boy, but good, and mind my book,
For Heaven forfend that ever I forgather with Nell Cook!'

The class was call'd at morning tide, and Master Tom was
there;
He look'd askew, and did eschew both stool, and bench, and
chair.
He did not talk, he did not walk, the tear was in his eye,—
He had not e'en that sad resource, to sit him down and cry.

Hence little boys may learn, when they from school go out to
dine,
They should not deal in rigmarole, but still be back by nine;
For if when they've their greatcoat on, they pause before they
part
To tell a long and prosy tale,—perchance their own may smart!

MORAL

—A few remarks to learned Clerks in country and in town—
Don't keep a pretty serving-maid, though clad in russet
brown!—
Don't let your Niece sing 'Bobbing Joan!'—don't with a merry
eye,
Hobnob in Sack and Malvoisie,—and don't eat too much pie!!

[1] In or about the year 1780, a worthy of this name cut the throat of a
journeyman paper-maker, was executed on Oaten Hill, and afterwards hung
in chains near the scene of his crime. It was to this place, as being the
extreme boundary of the City's jurisdiction, that the worthy Mayor with so
much naïveté wished to escort Archbishop M—— on one of his progresses,
when he begged to have the honour of 'attending his Grace *as far as the
Gallows.*'

And oh! beware that Entry dark,—especially at night,—
And don't go there with Jenny Smith all by the pale moon-
light!—
So bless the Queen and her Royal Weans,—and the Prince
whose hand she took,—
And bless us all, both great and small,—and keep us from Nell
Cook!

NURSERY REMINISCENCES

I REMEMBER, I remember,
  When I was a little Boy,
One fine morning in September
  Uncle brought me home a toy.

I remember how he patted
  Both my cheeks in kindliest mood;
'Then,' said he, 'you little Fat-head,
  There's a top because you're good!'

Grandmama—a shrewd observer—
  I remember gazed upon
My new top, and said with fervour,
  'Oh! how kind of Uncle John!'

While Mama, my form caressing,—
  In her eye the tear-drop stood,
Read me this fine moral lesson,
  'See what comes of being good!'

I remember, I remember,
  On a wet and windy day,
One cold morning in December,
  I stole out and went to play;

I remember Billy Hawkins
  Came, and with his pewter squirt
Squibb'd my pantaloons and stockings
  Till they were all over dirt!

To my mother for protection
  I ran, quaking every limb:
—She exclaimed, with fond affection,
  'Gracious Goodness! look at *him*!'—

Pa cried, when he saw my garment,
   —'Twas a newly purchased dress—
'Oh! you nasty little *Warment*,
   How came you in such a mess?'

Then he caught me by the collar,
   —Cruel only to be kind—
And to my exceeding dolour,
   Gave me—several slaps behind.

Grandmama, while yet I smarted,
   As she saw my evil plight,
Said—'twas rather stony-hearted—
   'Little rascal! *sarve* him right!'

I remember, I remember,
   From that sad and solemn day,
Never more in dark December
   Did I venture out to play.

And the moral, which they taught, I
   Well remember; thus they said—
'Little Boys, when they are naughty,
   Must be whipped and sent to bed!'

AUNT FANNY

A LEGEND OF A SHIRT

'Virginibus, Puerisque canto.'—HOR.
'Old Maids, and Bachelors I chaunt to!'—T. I.

I SING of a Shirt that *never was* new!
In the course of the year Eighteen hundred and two,
   Aunt Fanny began, Upon Grandmama's plan,
To make one for me, then her 'dear little man.'—
—At the epoch I speak about, I was between
   A man and a boy, A hobble-de-hoy,
A fat, little, punchy concern of sixteen,—
   Just beginning to flirt, And ogle,—so pert,
I'd been whipped every day had I had my desert,
—And Aunt Fan volunteer'd to make me a shirt!

I've said she *began* it,—   Some unlucky planet
No doubt interfered,—for, before she, and Janet
Completed the 'cutting-out,' 'hemming,' and 'stitching,'
A tall Irish footman appear'd in the kitchen;—
—This took off the maid,—   And, I'm sadly afraid,
My respected Aunt Fanny's attention, too, stray'd;
For, about the same period, a gay son of Mars,
Cornet Jones of the Tenth (then the Prince's) Hussars,
With his fine dark eyelashes,   And finer moustaches,
And the ostrich plume work'd on the corps' sabre-taches
(I say nought of the gold-and-red cord of the sashes,
Or the boots far above the Guards' vile spatterdashes)—
So eyed, and so sigh'd, and so lovingly tried
To engage her whole ear as he lounged by her side,
Looking down on the rest with such dignified pride,
      That she made up her mind
      She should certainly find
Cornet Jones at her feet, whisp'ring, 'Fan, be my bride!'—
—She had even resolved to say 'Yes' should he ask it,
—And I—and my Shirt—were both left in the basket.

      To her grief and dismay
      She discover'd one day
Cornet Jones of the tenth was a little too gay;
For, besides that she saw him—he could not say nay—
Wink at one of the actresses capering away
In a Spanish bolero, one night at the play,
She found he'd already a wife at Cambray;—
One at Paris,—a nymph of the *corps de ballet*;—
And a third down in Kent, at a place call'd Foot's Cray.
      He was 'viler than dirt!'—   Fanny vow'd to exert
All her powers to forget him,—and finish my Shirt.
      But, oh! lack-a-day!   How time slips away!—
Who'd have thought that while Cupid was playing these tricks,
Ten years had elapsed, and I'd turn'd twenty-six?—

      'I care not a whit,   —He's not grown a bit,'
Says my Aunt, 'it will still be a very good fit.'
      So Janet, and She.   Now about thirty-three
(The maid had been jilted by Mr Magee),
Each taking one end of 'the Shirt' on her knee,
Again began working with hearty good will,
'Felling the Seams,' and 'whipping the Frill,'—
For, twenty years since, though the Ruffle had vanish'd,
A Frill like a fan had by no means been banish'd;
People wore them at playhouses, parties, and churches,
Like overgrown fins of overgrown perches.—

Now, then, by these two thus laying their caps
Together, my 'Shirt' had been finish'd, perhaps,
But for one of those queer little three-corner'd straps,
Which the ladies call 'Side-bits,' that sever the 'Flaps';
    —Here unlucky Janet   Took her needle, and ran it
Right into her thumb, and cried loudly, 'Ads cuss it!
I've spoiled myself now by that 'ere nasty Gusset!'

    For a month to come   Poor dear Janet's thumb
Was in that sort of state vulgar people call 'Rum.'
    At the end of that time,   A youth, still in his prime,
The Doctor's fat Errand-boy,—just such a dolt as is
Kept to mix draughts, and spread plaisters and poultices,—
Who a bread-cataplasm each morning had carried her,
Sigh'd,—ogled,—proposed,—was accepted,—and married her!
    Much did Aunt Fan   Disapprove of the plan;—
She turn'd up her dear little snub at 'the Man.'
    She 'could not believe it'—
    'Could scarcely conceive it
Was possible—What! *such* a place!—and then leave it!—
And all for a "Shrimp" not as high as my hat—
A little contemptible "Shaver" like that!!
With a broad pancake face, and eyes buried in fat!'
    —For her part, 'She was sure
    She could never endure
A lad with a lisp, and a leg like a skewer.—
Such a name too!—('twas Potts!)—and so nasty a trade—
No, no,—she would much rather die an old maid!—
He a husband, indeed!—Well—mine, come what may come,
Shan't look like a blister, or smell of Guaiacum!'—
    But there!   She'd 'declare,   It was Janet's affair—
    —*Chacun à son goût*—   As she baked she might brew;
She could not prevent her—'twas no use in trying it—
Oh, no—she had made her own bed, and might lie in it.—
They "repent at leisure who marry at random."
No matter—*De gustibus non disputandum!*'

Consoling herself with this choice bit of Latin,
Aunt Fanny resignedly bought some white satin,
    And, as the Soubrette   Was a very great pet
After all,—she resolved to forgive and forget,
And sat down to make her a bridal rosette,
With magnificent bits of some white-looking metal
Stuck in, here and there, each forming a petal.—
—On such an occasion one couldn't feel hurt,
Of course, that she ceased to remember—my Shirt!

Ten years,—or nigh,—   Had again gone by,
When Fan, accidentally casting her eye
On a dirty old work-basket, hung up on high
In the store-closet where herbs were put by to dry,
Took it down to explore it—she didn't know why.—

Within, a pea-soup colour'd fragment she spied,
Of the hue of a November fog in Cheapside,
Or a bad piece of gingerbread spoilt in the baking.—
    —I still hear her cry,—   'I wish I may die
If here isn't Tom's Shirt, that's been so long a-making!
    My gracious me!   Well,—only to see!
I declare it's as yellow as yellow can be!
Why, it looks just as though't had been soak'd in green tea!
    Dear me!   *Did* you *ever*?—
    But come—'twill be clever
To bring matters round! so I'll do my endeavour—
"Better Late," says an excellent proverb, "than Never"!—
It *is* stain'd to be sure; but "grass-bleaching" will bring it
To rights "in a jiffy,"—We'll wash it, and wring it;
    Or stay,—"Hudson's Liquor"   Will do it still quicker,
And—' Here the new maid chimed in, 'Ma'am, Salt of Lemon
Will make it, in no time, quite fit for the Gemman!'—
So they 'set in the gathers,'—the large round the collar,
While those at the wrist-bands of course were much smaller,—
The button-holes now were at length 'overcast';
Then a button itself was sewn on—'twas the last!

        All's done!   All's won!   Never under the sun
Was Shirt so late finish'd—so early begun!—
    —The work would defy   The most critical eye.
It was 'bleach'd,'—it was wash'd,—it was hung out to dry,—
It was mark'd on the tail with a T, and an I!
        On the back of a chair   It   Was placed, just to air it,
In front of the fire.—'Tom to-morrow shall wear it!'—

—*O caeca mens hominum!*—Fanny, good soul,
Left her charge for one moment—but one—a vile coal
Bounced out from the grate, and set fire to the whole!

Had it been Doctor Arnott's new stove—not a grate;—
Had the coal been a 'Lord Mayor's coal,'—viz.: a slate;—
What a diff'rent tale had I had to relate!
And Aunt Fan—and my Shirt—been superior to Fate!—
    One moment—no more!   —Fan open'd the door!
The draught made the blaze ten times worse than before;
And Aunt Fanny sank down—in despair—on the floor!

You may fancy perhaps Agrippina's amazement,
When, looking one fine moonlight night from her casement,
   She saw, while thus gazing, All Rome a-blazing,
And, losing at once all restraint on her temper, or
Feelings, exclaimed, 'Hang that Scamp of an Emperor,
   Although he's my son!— —He thinks it prime fun,
No doubt!—While the flames are demolishing Rome,
There's my Nero a-fiddling, and singing "Sweet Home!"'
—Stay—I'm really not sure 'twas that lady who said
The words I've put down, as she stepp'd into bed,—
On reflection, I rather believe *she* was dead;
   But e'en when at College, I Fairly acknowledge, I
Never was very precise in Chronology;
So, if there's an error, pray set down as mine a
Mistake of no very great moment—in fine, a
Mere slip'—'twas some Pleb's wife, if not Agrippina.

You may fancy that warrior, so stern and so stony,
Whom thirty years since we all used to call BONEY,
When engaged in what he styled 'fulfilling his destinies,'
He led his rapscallions across the Borysthenes,
   And had made up his mind Snug quarters to find
In Moscow, against the catarrhs and the coughs
Which are apt to prevail 'mongst the 'Owskis' and 'Offs,'
   At a time of the year When your nose and your ear
Are by no means so safe there as people's are here,
Inasmuch as 'Jack Frost,' that most fearful of Bogles,
Makes folks leave their cartilage oft in their 'fogles.'
   You may fancy I say, That same BONEY's dismay,
   When Count Rostopchin
   At once made him drop chin,
And turn up his eyes, as his rapee he took,
With a sort of a *mort-da-me-vie* kind of look,
   On perceiving that 'Swing,'
   And 'all that sort of thing,'
Was at Work,—that he'd just lost the game without knowing
   it—
That the Kremlin was blazing—the Russians 'a going it,'—
Every plug in the place frozen hard as the ground,
And never a Turncock at all to be found!

You may fancy King Charles at some Court Fancy-Ball
   (The date we may fix In Sixteen sixty-six),
In the room built by Inigo Jones at Whitehall,
Whence his father, the Martyr,—(as such mourn'd by all
Who, in *his*, wept the Law's and the Monarchy's fall)—
Stepped out to exchange regal robes for a pall—

You may fancy King Charles, I say, stopping the brawl,[1]
As bursts on his sight the old church of St Paul,
By the light of its flames, now beginning to crawl
From basement to buttress, and topping its wall—
—You may fancy old Clarendon making a call,
And stating in cold, slow, monotonous drawl,
'Sire, from Pudding Lane's End, close by Fishmongers' Hall,
To Pye Corner, in Smithfield, there is not a stall
There, in market, or street,—not a house, great or small,
In which Knight wields his falchion, or Cobbler his awl,
But's on fire!!'—You may facy the general squall,
And bawl as they all call for wimple and shawl!—
—You may fancy all this—but I boldly assert
You *can't* fancy Aunt Fan—as she looked on MY SHIRT!!!

Was't Apelles! or Zeuxis?—I think 'twas Apelles,
That artist of old—I declare I can't tell his
Exact patronymic—I write and pronounce ill
These Classical names—whom some Grecian Town Council
Employ'd—I believe, by command of the Oracle,—
To produce them a splendid piece, purely historical,
    For adorning the wall   Of some fane, or Guildhall,
And who for his subject determined to try a
Large painting in oils of Miss Iphigenia
    At the moment her Sire,   By especial desire
Of 'that Spalpeen, O'Dysseus' (see Barney Maguire),
    Has resolved to devote   Her beautiful throat
To old Chalcas's knife, and her limbs to the fire;
—An act which we moderns by no means admire—
An off'ring, 'tis true, to Jove, Mars, or Apollo cost
No trifling sum in those days, if a holocaust,—
Still, although for economy we should condemn none,
In an ἄναξ ἀνδρῶν, like the great Agamemnon,
    To give up to slaughter   An elegant daughter,
After all the French, Music, and Dancing they'd taught her,
And Singing,—at Heaven knows how much a quarter,—
    In lieu of a Calf!—   It was too bad by half!
At a 'nigger'[2] so pitiful who would not laugh,
And turn up their noses at one who could find
No decenter method of 'Raising the Wind'?
    No doubt but he might,   Without any great *Flight*,
Have obtain'd it by what we call 'flying a kite,'

----

[1] Not a 'row,' but a dance—
    'The brave Lord Keeper led the *brawls*,
        The seals and maces danced before him.'—GRAY.
    And truly Sir Christopher danced to some tune.

[2] Hibernicè 'nigger,' *quasi* 'niggard.'   *Vide* B. Maguire *passim.*

Or on mortgage—or sure, if he couldn't so do it, he
Must have succeeded 'by way of annuity.'
   But there—it appears, His crocodile tears,
His 'Oh!s' and his 'Ah!s' his 'Oh Law!s' and 'Oh dear!s'
Were all thought sincere,—so in painting his Victim
The Artist was splendid—but could not depict *Him*.
   His features, and phiz awry Show'd so much misery,
   And so like a dragon he Look'd in his agony,
That the foil'd Painter buried—despairing to gain a
Good likeness—his face in a printed Bandanna.
—Such a veil is best thrown o'er one's face when one's hurt
By some grief which no power can repair or avert!—
—Such a veil I shall throw o'er Aunt Fan—and My Shirt!

MORAL

And now for some practical hints from the story
Of Aunt Fan's mishap, which I've thus laid before ye,
   For, if rather too gay, I can venture to say
A fine veil of morality is, in each lay
Of my primitive Muse, the distinguishing trait!
First of all—Don't put off till to-morrow what may,
Without inconvenience, be managed to-day!
That golden occasion we call 'Opportunity'
Rarely's neglected by man with impunity!
And the 'Future,' how brightly soe'er by Hope's dupe colour'd,
   Ne'er may afford You a lost chance restored,
Till both you, and YOUR SHIRT, are grown old and pea-soup-
    colour'd!

   I would also desire You to guard your attire,
Young Ladies,—and never go too near the fire!—
—Depend on't there's many a dear little Soul
Has found that a Spark is as bad as a coal,—
And 'in her best petticoat burnt a great hole!'

Last of all, gentle Reader, don't be too secure!—
Let seeming success never make you 'cock-sure!'
   But beware!—and take care,
   When all things look fair,
How you hang your Shirt over the back of your chair!—
   —'There's many a slip 'Twixt the cup and the lip!'
Be this excellent proverb, then, well understood,
And DON'T HALLOO BEFORE YOU'RE QUITE OUT OF THE WOOD!!!

MISADVENTURES AT MARGATE

A LEGEND OF JARVIS'S JETTY

MR SIMPKINSON *loquitur*

'TWAS in Margate last July, I walk'd upon the pier,
I saw a little vulgar Boy—I said, 'What make you here?—
The gloom upon your youthful cheek speaks anything but joy';
Again I said, 'What make you here, you little vulgar Boy?'

He frowned, that little vulgar Boy,—he deem'd I meant to scoff—
And when the little heart is big, a little 'sets it off';
He put his finger in his mouth, his little bosom rose,—
He had no little handkerchief to wipe his little nose!

'Hark! don't you hear, my little man?—it's striking Nine,' I said,
'An hour when all good little boys and girls should be in bed.
Run home and get your supper, else your Ma' will scold—Oh! fie!—
It's very wrong indeed for little boys to stand and cry!'

The tear-drop in his little eye again began to spring,
His bosom throbb'd with agony,—he cried like anything!
I stoop'd, and thus amidst his sobs I heard him murmur—'Ah!'
I haven't got no supper! and I haven't got no Ma'!!—

'My father, he is on the seas,—my mother's dead and gone!
And I am here, on this here pier, to roam the world alone;
I have not had this livelong day, one drop to cheer my heart,
Nor "*brown*" to buy a bit of bread with—let alone a tart!

'If there's a soul will give me food, or find me in employ,
By day or night, then blow me tight!' (he was a vulgar Boy);
'And, now I'm here, from this here pier it is my fixed intent
To jump, as Master Levi did from off the Monu-ment!'

'Cheer up! cheer up! my little man—cheer up!' I kindly said,
'You are a naughty boy to take such things into your head:
If you should jump from off the pier, you'd surely break your legs,
Perhaps your neck—then Bogey'd have you, sure as eggs are eggs!

Come home with me, my little man, come home with me and
    sup;
My landlady is Mrs Jones—we must not keep her up—
There's roast potatoes at the fire,—enough for me and you—
Come home, you little vulgar Boy—I lodge at Number 2.'

I took him home to Number 2, the house beside 'The Foy,'
I bade him wipe his dirty shoes,—that little vulgar Boy,—
And then I said to Mrs Jones, the kindest of her sex,
Pray be so good as go and fetch a pint of double X!'

But Mrs Jones was rather cross, she made a little noise,
She said she 'did not like to wait on little vulgar Boys.'
She with her apron wiped the plates, and, as she rubb'd the
    delf,
Said I might 'go to Jericho, and fetch my beer myself!'

I did not go to Jericho—I went to Mr Cobb—[1]
I changed a shilling—(which in town the people call 'a Bob')—
It was not so much for myself as for that vulgar child—
And I said, 'A pint of double X, and please to draw it mild!'

When I came back I gazed about—I gazed on stool and chair—
I could not see my little friend—because he was not there!
I peep'd beneath the table-cloth—beneath the sofa too—
I said, 'You little vulgar Boy! why, what's become of you?'

I could not see my table-spoons—I look'd, but could not see
The little fiddle-pattern'd ones I use when I'm at tea;
—I could not see my sugar-tongs—my silver watch—oh, dear!
I know 'twas on the mantelpiece when I went out for beer.

I could not see my mackintosh—it was not to be seen!—
Nor yet my best white beaver hat, broad-brimm'd and lined with
    green;
My carpet-bag—my cruet-stand, that holds my sauce and soy,—
My roast potatoes!—all are gone!—and so's that vulgar Boy!

I rang the bell for Mrs Jones, for she was down below,
'—Oh, Mrs Jones! what *do* you think?—ain't this a pretty go?—
—That horrid little vulgar Boy whom I brought here to-night,
—He's stolen my things and run away!!'—Says she, 'And
    sarve you right!!'

[1] QUI FACIT PER ALIUM FACIT PER SE—Deem not, gentle stranger, that Mr
Cobb is a petty dealer and chapman, as Mr Simpkinson would here seem to
imply. He is a *maker*, not a retailer of stingo,—and mighty pretty tipple he
makes.

Next morning I was up betimes—I sent the Crier round,
All with his bell and gold-laced hat, to say I'd give a pound
To find that little vulgar Boy, who'd gone and used me so;
But when the Crier cried, 'O Yes!' the people cried, 'O No!'

I went to 'Jarvis' Landing-place,' the glory of the town,
There was a Common-sailor-man a-walking up and down,
I told my tale, he seem'd to think I'd not been treated well,
And call'd me 'Poor old Buffer!'—what that means I cannot
    tell.

That Sailor-man, he said he'd seen that morning on the shore,
A son of—something—'twas a name I'd never heard before,
A little 'gallows-looking chap'—dear me! what could he mean?
With a 'carpet-swab' and 'muckingtogs,' and a hat turned up
    with green.

He spoke about his 'precious eyes,' and said he'd seen him
    'sheer,'
—It's very odd that Sailor-men should talk so very queer—
And then he hitched his trousers up, as is, I'm told, their use,
—It's very odd that Sailor-men should wear those things so
    loose.

I did not understand him well, but think he meant to say
He'd seen that little vulgar Boy, that morning, swim away
In Captain Large's *Royal George*, about an hour before,
And they were now, as he supposed, 'some*wheres*' about the
    Nore.

A landsman said, 'I *twig* the chap—he's been upon the Mill—
And 'cause he *gammons* so the *flats*, ve calls him Veeping Bill!'
He said he'd 'done me werry brown,' and nicely '*stow'd the
    swag*,'
—That's French, I fancy, for a hat—or else a carpet-bag.

I went and told the constable my property to track;
He asked me if 'I did not wish that I might get it back?'
I answered, 'To be sure I do!—it's what I'm come about.'
He smiled and said, 'Sir, does your mother know that you are
    out?'

Not knowing what to do, I thought I'd hasten back to town,
And beg our own Lord Mayor to catch the Boy who'd 'done me
    brown.'
His Lordship very kindly said he'd try and find him out
But he 'rather thought that there were several vulgar boys about.'

He sent for Mr Whithair then, and I described 'the swag,'
My mackintosh, my sugar-tongs, my spoons, and carpet-bag;
He promised that the New Police should all their powers
    employ;
But never to this hour have I beheld that vulgar Boy!

MORAL

Remember, then, what when a boy I've heard my Grandma'
    tell,
'BE WARN'D IN TIME BY OTHERS' HARM, AND YOU SHALL DO FULL
    WELL?'
Don't link yourself with vulgar folks, who've got no fixed abode,
Tell lies, use naughty words, and say they 'wish they may be
    blow'd!'

Don't take too much of double X!—and don't at night go out
To fetch your beer yourself, but make the pot-boy bring your
    stout!
And when you go to Margate next, just stop, and ring the bell,
Give my respects to Mrs Jones, and say I'm pretty well!

THE SMUGGLER'S LEAP

A LEGEND OF THANET

'Near this hamlet (Acol) is a long-disused chalk-pit of formidable depth,
known by the name of "The Smuggler's leap." The tradition of the parish
runs, that a riding-officer from Sandwich, called Anthony Gill, lost his life
here in the early part of the present (last) century, while in pursuit of a
smuggler. A fog coming on, both parties went over the precipice. The
smuggler's horse *only*, it is said, was found crushed beneath its rider. The
spot has, of course, been haunted ever since.'

See *Supplement to Lewis's History of Thanet, by the Rev. Samuel
Pegge, A.M., Vicar of Gomeriham.* W. Bristow, Canterbury, 1796, p. 127.

> THE fire-flash shines from Reculver cliff,
> And the answering light burns blue in the skiff,
>   And there they stand   That smuggling band,
> Some in the water, and some on the sand,
> Ready those contraband goods to land;
> The night is dark, they are silent and still,
> —At the head of the party is Smuggler Bill!

'Now lower away! come, lower away!
We must be far ere the dawn of the day.
If Exciseman Gill should get scent of the prey,
And should come, and should catch us here, what would he say?
Come, lower away, lads—once on the hill,
We'll laugh, ho! ho! at Exciseman Gill!'

The cargo's lower'd from the dark skiff's side,
And the tow-line drags the tubs through the tide,
   No flick nor flam, But your real Schiedam.
'Now mount, my merry men, mount and ride!'
Three on the crupper and one before,
And the led-horse laden with five tubs more;
   But the rich point-lace, In the oilskin case
Of proof to guard its contents from ill,
'The prime of the swag,' is with Smuggler Bill!

Merrily now, in a goodly row,
Away, and away, those smugglers go,
And they laugh at Exciseman Gill, ho! ho!
   When out from the turn Of the road to Herne,
Comes Gill, wide awake to the whole concern!
Exciseman Gill, in all his pride,
With his Custom-house officers all at his side;
—They were called Custom-house officers then;
There were no such things as 'Preventive men.'

   Sauve qui peut! That lawless crew,
Away, and away, and away they flew!
Some dropping one tub, some dropping two:—
Some gallop this way, and some gallop that,
Through Fordwich Level—o'er Sandwich Flat,
Some fly that way, and some fly this,
Like a covey of birds when the sportsmen miss;
   These in their hurry Make for Sturry,
With Custom-house officers close in their rear,
Down Rushbourne Lane, and so by Westbere,
   None of them stopping, But shooting and popping,
And many a Custom-house bullet goes slap
Through many a three-gallon tub like a tap,
   And the gin spirts out, And squirts all about,
And many a heart grew sad that day
That so much good liquor was thrown away.

   Sauve qui peut! That lawless crew,
Away, and away, and away they flew!

Some seek Whitstable—some Grove Ferry,
Spurring and whipping like madmen—very—
'For the life! for the life! they ride! they ride!
And the Custom-house officers all divide,
And they gallop on after them far and wide!
All, all, save one—Exciseman Gill,—
He sticks to the skirts of Smuggler Bill!

Smuggler Bill is six feet high,
He has curling locks, and a roving eye,
He has a tongue, and he has a smile
Train'd the female heart to beguile,
And there is not a farmer's wife in the Isle,
    From St Nicholas quite   To the Foreland Light,
But that eye, and that tongue, and that smile will wheedle her
To have done with the Grocer, and make *him* her Tea-dealer:
There is not a farmer there but he still
Buys gin and tobacco from Smuggler Bill.

Smuggler Bill rides gallant and gay
On his dapple-grey mare, away, and away
And he pats her neck, and he seems to say
Follow who will, ride after who may,
    In sooth he had need   Fodder his steed,
In lieu of Lent-corn, with a Quicksilver feed;
—Nor oats, nor beans, nor the best of old hay,
Will make him a match for my own dapple-grey!
Ho! ho!—ho! ho!' says Smuggler Bill—
He draws out his flask, and he sips his fill,
And he laughs 'Ho! ho!' at Exciseman Gill.

Down Chistlett Lane, so free and so fleet
Rides Smuggler Bill, and away to Up-street;—
    Sarre Bridge is won—   Bill thinks it fun;
Ho! ho! the old tub-gauging son of a gun—
His wind will be thick, and his breeks be thin,
Ere a race like this he may hope to win!'

    Away, away   Goes the fleet dapple-grey,
Fresh as the breeze, and free as the wind,
And Exciseman Gill lags far behind.
I would give my soul,' quoth Exciseman Gill,
For a nag that would catch that Smuggler Bill!—
No matter for blood, no matter for bone,
No matter for colour, bay, brown, or roan,
    So I had but one!'—   A voice cried 'Done!'

'Ay, dun,' said Exciseman Gill—and he spied
A custom-house officer close by his side,
On a high-trotting horse with a dun-coloured hide.—
'*Devil take me*,' again quoth Exciseman Gill,
'If I had but that horse, I'd have Smuggler Bill!'

From his using such shocking expressions, it's plain
That Exciseman Gill was rather profane.
   He was, it is true,   As bad as a Jew,
A sad old scoundrel as ever you knew,
And he rode in his stirrups sixteen stone two.
—He'd just utter'd the words which I've mentioned to you,
When his horse, coming slap on his knees with him, threw
Him head over heels, and away he flew,
And Exciseman Gill was bruised black and blue.

   When he arose,   His hands and his clothes
Were as filthy as could be,—he'd pitch'd on his nose,
And roll'd over and over again in the mud,
And his nose and his chin were all covered with blood;
Yet he scream'd with passion, 'I'd rather *grill*
Than not come up with that Smuggler Bill!'

—'Mount! Mount!' quoth the Custom-house officer, 'get
On the back of my Dun, you'll bother him yet.
Your words are plain, though they're somewhat rough,
"Done and Done" between gentlemen's always enough!—
I'll lend you a lift—there—you're up on him—so,—
He's a rum one to look at—*a devil to go*!'
   Exciseman Gill   Dash'd up the hill,
And mark'd not, so eager was he in pursuit,
The queer Custom-house officer's queer-looking boot.

Smuggler Bill rides on amain,
He slacks not girth—and he draws not rein,
Yet the dapple-grey mare bounds on in vain,
For nearer now—and he hears it plain—
Sounds the tramp of a horse—''Tis the Gauger again!'
   Smuggler Bill   Dashes round by the mill
That stands near the road upon Monkton Hill,—
'Now speed,—now speed,   My dapple-grey steed,
Thou ever, my dapple, wert good at need!
O'er Monkton Mead, and through Minster Level,
We'll baffle him yet, be he gauger or devil!
   For Manston Cave, away! away!
Now speed thee, now speed thee, my good dapple-grey!
It shall never be said that Smuggler Bill
Was run down like a hare by Exciseman Gill!'

Manston Cave was Bill's abode;
A mile to the north of the Ramsgate Road
  (Of late they say   It's been taken away,
That is, levell'd, and filled up with chalk and clay,
By a gentleman there of the name of Day),
Thither he urges his good dapple-grey;
    And the dapple-grey steed,   Still good at need,
Though her chest it pants, and her flanks they bleed,
Dashes along at the top of her speed;
But nearer and nearer Exciseman Gill
Cries, 'Yield thee! now yield thee, thou Smuggler Bill!'

Smuggler Bill, he looks behind,
And he sees a Dun horse come swift as the wind,
And his nostrils smoke, and his eyes they blaze
Like a couple of lamps on a yellow post-chaise!
    Every shoe he has got   Appears red hot!
And sparks round his ears snap, crackle, and play,
And his tail cocks up in a very odd way,
Every hair in his mane seems a porcupine's quill,
And there on his back sits Exciseman Gill,
Crying 'Yield thee! now yield thee, thou Smuggler Bill!'

Smuggler Bill from his holster drew
A large horse-pistol, of which he had two,
    Made by Nock;   He pull'd back the cock
As far as he could to the back of the lock;
The trigger he touch'd, and the welkin rang
To the sound of the weapon, it made such a bang;
Smuggler Bill he ne'er miss'd his aim,
The shot told true on the Dun—but there came
From the hole where it enter'd,—not blood,—but flame!
  —He changed his plan,   And fired at the man;
But his second horse-pistol flashed in the pan!
And Exciseman Gill, with a hearty good will,
Made a grab at the collar of Smuggler Bill.

The dapple-grey mare made a desperate bound
When that queer Dun horse on her flank she found,
Alack! and alas! on what dangerous ground!
It's enough to make one's flesh to creep
To stand on that fearful verge, and peep
Down the rugged sides so dreadfully steep,
Where the chalk-hole yawns full sixty feet deep,
O'er which that steed took that desperate leap!

It was so dark then under the trees,
No horse in the world could tell chalk from cheese—
Down they went—o'er that terrible fall,—
Horses, Exciseman, Smuggler, and all!!

Below were found   Next day on the ground,
By an elderly Gentleman walking his round
(I wouldn't have seen such a sight for a pound),
All smash'd and dash'd, three mangled corses,
Two of them human,—the third was a horse's,—
That good dapple-grey,—and Exciseman Gill
Yet grasping the collar of Smuggler Bill!

But where was the Dun? that terrible Dun?—
From that terrible night he was seen by none!—
There are some people think, though I am not one,
That part of the story all nonsense and fun,
    But the country-folks there,   One and all, declare,
When the 'Crowner's 'Quest' came to sit on the pair
They heard a loud Horse-laugh up in the air!—
    —If in one of the trips   Of the steam-boat *Eclipse*
You should go down to Margate to look at the ships,
Or to take what the bathing-room people call 'Dips,'
    You may hear old folks talk
    Of that quarry of chalk;
Or go over—it's rather too far for a walk,
But a three-shilling drive will give you a peep
At that fearful chalk-pit—so awfully deep,
Which is call'd to this moment 'The Smuggler's Leap'!

Nay more, I am told, on a moonshiny night,
If you're 'plucky,' and not over-subject to fright,
And go and look over that chalk-pit white,
    You may see, if you will,   The Ghost of Old Gill
Grappling the Ghost of Smuggler Bill,
And the Ghost of the dapple-grey lying between 'em.—
I'm told so—I can't say I know one who's seen 'em!

MORAL

And now, gentle Reader, one word ere we part,
Just take a friend's counsel, and lay it to heart.
Imprimis, don't smuggle!—if, bent to please Beauty,
You *must* buy French lace,—purchase what has paid duty!
Don't use naughty words, in the next place,—and ne'er in
Your language adopt a bad habit of swearing!

Never say 'Devil take me!'—
    Or, 'shake me!'—or, 'bake me!'
Or such-like expressions.—Remember Old Nick
To take folks at their word is remarkably quick.
Another sound maxim I'd wish you to keep,
Is, 'Mind what you're after, and—Look ere you Leap'!

Above all, to my last gravest caution attend—
NEVER BORROW A HORSE YOU DON'T KNOW OF A FRIEND!!!

𝕭𝕷𝕺𝖀𝕯𝕴𝕰 𝕵𝕬𝕮𝕶𝕰 𝕺𝕱 𝕾𝕳𝕽𝕰𝖂𝕾𝕭𝕰𝕽𝕽𝕴𝕰

THE SHROPSHIRE BLUEBEARD

A LEGEND OF 'THE PROUD SALOPIANS'

'*Hisce ferè temporibus, in agro Salopiensi, Quidam cui nomen Johannes,* 𝕷𝖊 𝕾𝖆𝖓𝖌𝖑𝖆𝖚𝖓𝖙 *deinde nuncupatus, uxores quamplurimas ducit, enecat et (ita referunt) manducat; ossa solùm cani mirae magnitudinis relinquens. Túm demúm in flagrante delicto, vel "manu rubrâ," ut dicunt Jurisconsulti, deprensus, carnifice vix opprimitur.*'[1]—RADULPHUS DE DICETO.

OH! why doth thine eye gleam so bright,
                              𝕭𝖑𝖔𝖚𝖉𝖎𝖊 𝕵𝖆𝖈𝖐𝖊?
Oh! why doth thine eye gleam so bright?—
    The Mother's at home,   The Maid may not roam,
She never will meet thee to-night!
                              By the light
Of the moon—it's impossible—quite!

Yet thine eye is still brilliant and bright,
                              𝕭𝖑𝖔𝖚𝖉𝖎𝖊 𝕵𝖆𝖈𝖐𝖊!
It gleams with a fiendish delight—
    '"Tis done—   She is won!   Nothing under the sun
Can loose the charm'd ring, though it's slight!
                              Ho! ho!
It fits so remarkably tight!'

The wire is as thin as a thread,
                              𝕭𝖑𝖔𝖚𝖉𝖎𝖊 𝕵𝖆𝖈𝖐𝖊!
The wire is as thin as a thread!—

[1] 'About this time, in the Shropshire country, a man named John, afterwards called the "Bloody," married a great many wives, murdered and (so it is said) devoured them, leaving only the bones to a dog of marvellous size. Caught at last in the very act of committing the crime, or as lawyers say, "red-handed," he was with difficulty overpowered by the executioner.'

'Though slight be the chain,   Again might and main
Cannot rend it in twain—She is wed!

                            She is wed!

She is **mine,** be she living or dead!

                            Haw! haw!!'

Nay, laugh not, I pray thee, so loud,

                            𝔅loudie 𝔍acke!

Oh! laugh not so loud and so clear!
   Though sweet is thy smile   The heart to beguile,
Yet thy laugh is quite shocking to hear,

                            O dear!

It make the blood curdle with fear!

The Maiden is gone by the glen,

                            𝔅loudie 𝔍acke!

She is gone by the glen and the wood—
   It's a very odd thing   She should wear such a ring,
While her tresses are bound with a snood.

                            By the rood!

It's a thing that's not well understood!

The Maiden is stately and tall,

                            𝔅loudie 𝔍acke!

And stately she walks in her pride;
   But the Young Mary-Anne   Runs as fast as she can,
To o'ertake her, and walk by her side:

                         Though she chide—

She deems not her sister a bride!

But the Maiden is gone by the glen,

                            𝔅loudie 𝔍acke!

Mary-Anne she is gone by the lea;
   She o'ertakes not her sister,
   It's clear she has miss'd her,
And cannot think where she can be!

                          Dear me!

'Ho! ho!—We shall see—we shall see!'

Mary-Anne is gone over the lea,

                            𝔅loudie 𝔍acke!

Mary-Anne, she is come to the Tower;
   But it makes her heart quail,   For it looks like a jail,
A deal more than a fair Lady's bower,

                            So sour

Its ugly grey walls seem to lour.

For the Barbican's massy and high,

𝔅𝔩𝔬𝔲𝔡𝔦𝔢 𝔍𝔞𝔠𝔨𝔢!

And the oak-door is heavy and brown,
  And with iron it's plated   And machicolated,
To pour boiling oil and lead down;

How you'd frown

Should a ladle-full fall on your crown!

The rock that it stands on is steep,

𝔅𝔩𝔬𝔲𝔡𝔦𝔢 𝔍𝔞𝔠𝔨𝔢!

To gain it one's forced for to creep;
  The Portcullis is strong,   And the Drawbridge is long,
And the water runs all round the Keep;

At a peep

You can see that the Moat's very deep!

The Drawbridge is long, but it's down,

𝔅𝔩𝔬𝔲𝔡𝔦𝔢 𝔍𝔞𝔠𝔨𝔢!

And the Portcullis hangs in the air;
  And no Warder is near   With his horn and his spear,
To give notice when people come there.—

I declare

Mary-Anne has run into the square!

The oak-door is heavy and brown,

𝔅𝔩𝔬𝔲𝔡𝔦𝔢 𝔍𝔞𝔠𝔨𝔢!

But the oak-door is standing ajar,
  And no one is there   To say, 'Pray take a chair,
You seem tired, Miss, with running so far—

So you are—

With grown people you're scarce on a par!'

But the young Mary-Anne is *not* tired,

𝔅𝔩𝔬𝔲𝔡𝔦𝔢 𝔍𝔞𝔠𝔨𝔢!

She roams o'er your Tower by herself;
  She runs through, very soon,   Each boudoir and saloon,
And examines each closet and shelf,

Your pelf,

All your plate, and your china—and delf.

She looks at your Arras so fine,

𝔅𝔩𝔬𝔲𝔡𝔦𝔢 𝔍𝔞𝔠𝔨𝔢!

So rich, all description it mocks;
  And she now and then pauses   To gaze at the vases,
Your pictures, and or-molu clocks;

Every box,

Every cupboard, and drawer she unlocks.

She looks at the paintings so rare,

Bloudie Jacke!

That adorn every wall in your house;
  Your *impayable* pieces, Your Paul Veroneses,
Your Rembrandts, your Guidos, and Dows,

                      Moreland's Cows,

Claude's Landscapes,—and Landseer's Bow-wows.

She looks at your Statues so fine,

Bloudie Jacke!

And mighty great notice she takes
  Of your Niobe crying, Your Mirmillo dying,
Your Hercules strangling the snakes,—

                    How he shakes

The nasty great things as he wakes!

Your Laocoön, his serpents and boys,

Bloudie Jacke!

She views with some little dismay;
  A copy of that I can See in the Vatican
Unless the Pope's sent it away,

                    As they say,

In the *Globe*, he intended last May.[1]

There's your Belvidere Phoebus, with which,

Bloudie Jacke!

Mr Milman says none other vies.
  (His lines on Apollo Beat all the rest hollow,
And gained him the Newdigate prize.)

                    How the eyes

Seem watching the shaft as it flies!

There's a room full of satins and silks,

Bloudie Jacke!

There's a room full of velvets and lace,
  There are drawers full of rings,
  And a thousand fine things,
And a splendid gold watch with a case

                    O'er its face,

Is in every room in the place.

There are forty fine rooms on a floor,

Bloudie Jacke!

And every room fit for a Ball,

[1] 'The Pope is said—this fact is hardly credible—to have sold the Laocoön and the Apollo Belvidere to the Emperor of Russia for nine million of francs. —GLOBE AND TRAVELLER.

It's so gorgeous and rich,   With so lofty a pitch,
And so long, and so broad, and so tall;
Yes, all,
Save the last one—and that's very small!

It boasts not stool, table, or chair,
𝔅loudie 𝔍acke!
But *one* Cabinet, costly and grand,
   Which has little gold figures   Of little gold Niggers,
With fishing-rods stuck in each hand.—
It's japann'd,
And it's placed on a splendid buhl stand.

Its hinges and clasps are of gold,
𝔅loudie 𝔍acke!
And of gold are its keyhole and key,
   And the drawers within   Have each a gold pin,
And they're number'd with 1, 2, and 3,
You may see
All the figures in gold filigree!

Number 1's full of emeralds green,
𝔅loudie 𝔍acke!
Number 2's full of diamonds and pearl;
   But what does she see   In drawer Number 3
That makes all her senses to whirl,
Poor Girl!
And each lock of her hair to uncurl?—

Wedding Fingers are sweet pretty things,
𝔅loudie 𝔍acke!
To salute them one eagerly strives,
   When one kneels to 'propose'—
   It's another *quelque chose*
When cut off at the knuckles with knives
From our wives,
They are tied up in bunches of fives.

Yet there they lie, one, two, three, four!
𝔅loudie 𝔍acke!
There lie they, five, six, seven, eight!
   And by them, in rows   Lie eight little Great-Toes,
To match in size, colour, and weight!
From their state,
It would seem they'd been sever'd of late.

Beside them are eight Wedding-rings,

Bloudie Jacke!

And the gold is as thin as a thread—
  'Ho! ho!—She is mine—
  This will make up the Nine!'—
Dear me! who those shocking words said?—

—She fled

To hide herself under the bed.

But, alas! there's no bed in the room,

Bloudie Jacke!

And she peeps from the window on high;
  Only fancy her fright   And the terrible sight
Down below, which at once meets her eye!

'Oh My!!'

She half utter'd,—but stifled her cry.

For she saw it was You and your Man,

Bloudie Jacke!

And she heard your unpleasant 'Haw! haw!'
  While her sister, stone dead,   By the hair of her head,
O'er the bridge you were trying to draw,

As she saw—

A thing quite contra-ry to law!

Your man has got hold of her heels,

Bloudie Jacke!

Bloudie Jacke! you've got hold of her hair!
  But nor *Jacke* nor his Man
  Can see young Mary-Anne,
She has hid herself under the stair,

And there

Is a horrid great Dog, I declare!

His eyeballs are bloodshot and blear,

Bloudie Jacke!

He's a sad ugly cur for a pet;
  He seems of the breed   Of that 'Billy,' indeed,
Who used to kill rats for a bet;

—I forget

How many one morning he ate.

He has skulls, ribs, and vertebrae there,

Bloudie Jacke!

And thigh-bones;—and, though it's so dim,
  Yet it's plain to be seen
  He has pick'd them quite clean,—

She expects to be torn limb from limb,
                              So grim
He looks at her—and she looks at him!

She has given him a bun and a roll,
                              𝔅𝔩𝔬𝔲𝔡𝔦𝔢 𝔍𝔞𝔠𝔨𝔢!
She has given him a roll and a bun,
   And a Shrewsbury cake,   Of 𝔓𝔞𝔦𝔩𝔦𝔫'𝔰 [1] own make,
Which she happened to take ere her run
                              She begun—
She'd been used to a luncheon at One.

It's 'a pretty particular Fix,'
                              𝔅𝔩𝔬𝔲𝔡𝔦𝔢 𝔍𝔞𝔠𝔨𝔢!
—Above,—there's the Maiden that's dead;
   Below—growling at her—
   There's that Cannibal Cur,
Who at present is munching her bread,
                              Instead
Of her leg,—or her arm,—or her head.

It's 'a pretty particular Fix,'
                              𝔅𝔩𝔬𝔲𝔡𝔦𝔢 𝔍𝔞𝔠𝔨𝔢!
She is caught like a mouse in a trap;—
   Stay! there's something, I think,
   That has slipp'd through a chink,
And fall'n, by a singular hap,
                              Slap,
Into poor little Mary-Anne's lap!

It's a very fine little gold ring,
                              𝔅𝔩𝔬𝔲𝔡𝔦𝔢 𝔍𝔞𝔠𝔨𝔢!
Yet, though slight, it's remarkably stout,
   But it's made a sad stain,   Which will always remain
On her frock—for Blood will not wash out;
                              I doubt
Salts of Lemon won't bring it about!

She has grasp'd that gold ring in her hand,
                              𝔅𝔩𝔬𝔲𝔡𝔦𝔢 𝔍𝔞𝔠𝔨𝔢!
In an instant she stands on the floor,
   She makes but one bound   O'er the back of the hound,
And a hop, skip, and jump to the door,
                              And she's o'er
The drawbridge she traversed before!

[1] Oh, Pailin! Prince of cake-compounders! the mouth liquefies at thy very
name—but there!

Her hair's floating loose in the breeze,
                                    𝔅𝔩𝔬𝔲𝔡𝔦𝔢 𝔍𝔞𝔠𝔨𝔢!

For gone is her 'bonnet of blue.'
   —Now the Barbican's past!—   Her legs 'go it' as fast
As two drumsticks a-beating tattoo,
                                    As they do

At Réveille, Parade, or Review!

She has run into Shrewsbury town,
                                    𝔅𝔩𝔬𝔲𝔡𝔦𝔢 𝔍𝔞𝔠𝔨𝔢!
She has called out the Beadle and May'r,
   And the Justice of Peace,   And the Rural Police,
Till 'Battle Field' swarms like a Fair,—
                                    And see there!—

E'en the Parson's beginning to swear!!

There's a pretty to-do in your Tower,
                                    𝔅𝔩𝔬𝔲𝔡𝔦𝔢 𝔍𝔞𝔠𝔨𝔢!

In your Tower there's a pretty to-do!
   All the people of Shrewsbury
   Playing old gooseberry
With your choice bits of taste and virtu;
                                    Each bijou

Is upset in their search after you!

They are playing the deuce with your things,
                                    𝔅𝔩𝔬𝔲𝔡𝔦𝔢 𝔍𝔞𝔠𝔨𝔢!
There's your Cupid is broken in two,
   And so to, between us, is   Each of your Venuses.
The 'Antique' ones you bought of the Jew,
                                    And the new

One, George Robins swears came from St Cloud.

The CALLIPYGE's injured behind,
                                    𝔅𝔩𝔬𝔲𝔡𝔦𝔢 𝔍𝔞𝔠𝔨𝔢!

The DE MEDICI's injured before;
   And the ANADYOMENE   's injured in so many
Places, I think there's a score,
                                    If not more,

Of her fingers and toes on the floor

They are hunting you upstairs and down,
                                    𝔅𝔩𝔬𝔲𝔡𝔦𝔢 𝔍𝔞𝔠𝔨𝔢!

Every person to pass is forbid,

While they turn out the closets
  And all their deposits—
'There's the dust-hole—come lift up the lid!'
                              So they did—
But they could not find where you were hid!

Ah! Ah!—they will have you at last,
                              Bloudie Jacke!
The chimneys to search they begin;—
  They have found you at last!—
  There you are, sticking fast,
With your knees doubled up to your chin,
                              Though you're thin!
—Dear me! what a mess you are in!—

What a terrible pickle you're in,
                              Bloudie Jacke!
Why, your face is as black as your hat!
  Your fine Holland shirt   Is all over dirt!
And so is your point-lace cravat!
                              What a Flat
To seek such an asylum as that—

They can scarcely help laughing, I vow,
                              Bloudie Jacke!
In the midst of their turmoil and strife;
  You're not fit to be seen!   —You look like Mr Kean
In the play, where he murders his wife!—
                              On my life
You ought to be scraped with a knife!

They have pull'd you down flat on your back,
                              Bloudie Jacke!
They have pull'd you down flat on your back!
  And they smack, and they thwack,
  Till your 'funny bones' crack,
As if you were stretched on the rack,
                              At each thwack!—
Good lack! what a savage attack!

They call for the Parliament Man,
                              Bloudie Jacke!
And the Hangman, the matter to clinch,
  And they call for the Judge,
  But others cry 'Fudge!—
H ¹⁸⁵

Don't budge Mr Calcraft,[1] an inch!

       Mr Lynch![2]

Will do very well at a pinch!'

It is useless to scuffle and cuff,

      𝕭𝖑𝖔𝖚𝖉𝖎𝖊 𝕵𝖆𝖈𝖐𝖊!

It is useless to struggle and bite!
 And to kick and to scratch!
  You have met with your match,
And the Shrewsbury Boys hold you tight,

        Despite

Your determined attempts 'to show fight.'

They are pulling you all sorts of ways,

     𝕭𝖑𝖔𝖚𝖉𝖎𝖊 𝕵𝖆𝖈𝖐𝖊!

They are twisting your right leg Nor-West,
 And your left leg due South,
  And your knee's in your mouth,
And your head is poked down on your breast,

        And it's pressed,

I protest, almost into your chest!

They have pulled off your arms and your legs,

     𝕭𝖑𝖔𝖚𝖉𝖎𝖊 𝕵𝖆𝖈𝖐𝖊!

As the naughty boys serve the blue flies;
 And they've torn from their sockets,
  And put in their pockets
Your fingers and thumbs for a prize!

       And your eyes

A Doctor has bottled—from Guy's.[3]

---

[1] Jehan de Ketche acted as Provost Marshal to the army of William the Conqueror, and received from that monarch a grant of the dignity of Heredi-tary Grand Functionary of England, together with a croft or 'parcel of land,' known by the name of 𝕺𝖑𝖉 𝕭𝖆𝖎𝖑𝖎𝖊, co. Middx., to be held by him, and the heirs general of his body, in Grand Serjeantry, by the yearly presentation of 'ane hempen cravatte.' After remaining for several generations in the same name, the office passed, by marriage of the heiress, into the ancient family of the Kirbys, and thence again to that of Callcraft (1st Eliz. 1558).—Abhorson Callcraft, Esq. of Saffron Hill, co. Middx., the present repre-sentative of the Ketches, exercised his 'function' on a very recent occasion, and claimed and was allowed the fee of 13½d. under the ancient grant as 𝕳𝖆𝖓𝖌𝖒𝖆𝖓'𝖘 𝕸𝖆𝖌𝖊𝖘.

ARMS.—1st and 4th, Quarterly, Argent and Sable; in the first quarter a Gibbet of the second, noosed proper, *Callcraft*. 2nd, Sable, three Nightcaps Argent, tufted Gules, 2 and 1, *Ketche*. 3rd, Or, a Nosegay *fleurant*, *Kirby*.

SUPPORTERS.—*Dexter:* a Sheriff in his pride, robed Gules, chained and collared Or.—*Sinister*: An Ordinary displayed proper, wigged and banded Argent, nosed Gules.

MOTTO.—SIC ITUR AD ASTRA!

[2] The American Justinian, Compiler of the 'Yankee Pandects.'

[3] A similar appropriation is said to have been made, by an eminent practi-tioner, of those of the late Monsieur Courvoisier.

Your trunk, thus dismember'd and torn,

Bloudie Jacke!

They hew, and they hack, and they chop;
  And, to finish the whole,   They stick up a pole
In the place that's still called the '*Wylde Coppe*,'

And they pop

Your grim gory head on the top!

They have buried the fingers and toes,

Bloudie Jacke!

Of the victims so lately your prey.
  From those fingers and eight toes   Sprang early potatoes,
'*Ladyes' Fyngers*' they're called to this day;

—So they say,—

And you usually dig them in May.

What became of the dear little girl?

Bloudie Jacke!

What became of the young Mary-Anne?
  Why, I'm sadly afraid   That she died an Old Maid,
For she fancied that every Young Man

Had a plan

To trepan her like 'poor Sister Fan!'

So they say she is now leading apes,

Bloudie Jacke!

And mends Bachelors' small-clothes below;
  The story is old,   And has often been told,
But I cannot believe it is so—

No! No!

Depend on't the tale is 'No Go!'

MORAL

And now for the moral I'd fain,

Bloudie Jacke!

That young Ladies should draw from my pen,—
  It's 'Don't take these flights   Upon moon-shiny nights,
With gay, *harum-scarum* young men,

Down a glen!—

You really can't trust one in ten!'

Let them think of your terrible Tower,

Bloudie Jacke!

And don't let them liberties take,
  Whether Maidens or Spouses,   In Bachelors' houses;
Or, some time or another, they'll make

A Mistake!

And lose—more than a *Shrewsberrie Cake*!!

THE BABES IN THE WOOD; OR THE NORFOLK TRAGEDY

AN OLD SONG TO A NEW TUNE

WHEN we were all little and good,—
  A long time ago, I'm afraid, Miss
We were told of the Babes in the Wood
  By their false, cruel Uncle betray'd, Miss;
Their Pa was a Squire, or a Knight;
  In Norfolk I think his estate lay—
That is, if I recollect right,
  For I've not read the history lately.[1]

  Rum ti, etc.

Their Pa and their Ma being seized
  With a tiresome complaint, which in some seasons,
People are apt to be seized
  With, who're not on their guard against plum-seasons,
Their medical man shook his head
  As he could not get well to the root of it;
And the Babes stood on each side the bed,
  While their Uncle, he stood at the foot of it.

'Oh, Brother!' their Ma whisper'd, faint
  And low, for breath seeming to labour, 'Who'd
Think that this horrid complaint,
  That's been going about in the neighbourhood,
Thus should attack me,—nay, more,
  My poor husband besides,—and so fall on him!
Bringing us so near to Death's door
  That we can't avoid making a call on him!

'Now think, 'tis your Sister invokes
  Your aid, and the last word she says is,
Be kind to those dear little folks
  When our toes are turned up to the daisies!—
By the servants don't let them be snubb'd,—
  —Let Jane have her fruit and her custard,—
And mind Johnny's chilblains are rubb'd
  Well with Whitehead's best essence of mustard.

---

[1] See Bloomfield's *History of the County of Norfolk*, in which all the particulars of this lamentable history are (or ought to be) fully detailed, together with the names of the parties, and an elaborate pedigree of the family.

'You know they'll be pretty well off in
   Respect to what's called "worldly gear,"
For John, when his Pa's in his coffin,
   Comes into three hundred a year;
And Jane's to have five hundred pound
   On her marriage paid down, ev'ry penny,
So you'll own a worse match might be found,
   Any day in the week, than our Jenny!'

Here the Uncle pretended to cry,
   And, like an old thorough-paced rogue, he
Put his handkerchief up to his eye,
   And devoted himself to Old Bogey
If he did not make matters all right,
   And said, should he covet their riches,
He 'wished the old Gentleman might
   Fly away with him, body and breeches!'

No sooner, however, were they
   Put to bed with a spade by the sexton,
Than he carried the darlings away
   Out of that parish into the next one,
Giving out he should take them to town,
   And select the best school in the nation,
That John might not grow up a clown,
   But receive a genteel education.

'Greek and Latin old twaddle I call!'
   Says he, 'While his mind's ductile and plastic,
I'll place him at Dotheboys Hall,
   Where he'll learn all that's new and gymnastic.
While Jane, as, when girls have the dumps,
   Fortune-hunters, by scores, to entrap 'em rise,
Shall go to those worthy old frumps,
   The two Misses Tickler of Clapham Rise!'

Having thought on the How and the When
   To get rid of his nephew and niece,
He sent for two ill-looking men,
   And he gave them five guineas apiece.—
Says he, 'Each of you take up a child
   On the crupper, and when you have trotted
Some miles through that wood lone and wild,
   Take your knife out, and cut its carotid!'—

'Done' and 'done' is pronounced on each side,
    While the poor little dears are delighted
To think they a-cock-horse shall ride,
    And are not in the least degree frighted;
They say their 'Ta! Ta!' as they start,
    And they prattle so nice on their journey,
That the rogues themselves wish to their heart
    They could finish the job by attorney.

Nay, one was so taken aback
    By seeing such spirit and life in them,
That he fairly exclaim'd, 'I say, Jack,
    I'm blowed if I *can* put a knife in them!'—
'Pooh!' says his pal, 'you great dunce!
    You've pouched the good gentleman's money,
So out with your whinger at once,
    And scrag Jane, while I spifflicate Johnny!'

He refused, and harsh language ensued,
    Which ended at length in a duel,
When he that was mildest in mood
    Gave the truculent rascal his gruel;
The Babes quake with hunger and fear,
    While the ruffian his dead comrade, Jack, buries;
Then he cries, 'Loves, amuse yourselves here
    With the hips, and the haws, and the blackberries!

'I'll be back in a couple of shakes;
    So don't, dears, be quivering and quaking:
I'm going to get you some cakes,
    And a nice butter'd roll that's a-baking!'
He rode off with a tear in his eye,
    Which ran down his rough cheek, and wet it,
As he said to himself with a sigh,
    'Pretty souls!—don't they wish they may get it!!'

From that moment the Babes ne'er caught sight
    Of the wretch who thus wrought their undoing,
But passed all that day and that night
    In wandering about and 'boo-hoo'-ing.
The night proved cold, dreary, and dark,
    So that, worn out with sighings and sobbings,
Next morn they were found stiff and stark,
    And stone-dead, by two little Cock-Robins.

These two little birds it sore grieves
    To see what so cruel a dodge I call,—
They cover the bodies with leaves,
    An interment quite ornithological;
It might more expensive have been,
    But I doubt, though I've not been to see 'em,
If among those in all Kensal Green
    You could find a more neat Mausoleum.

Now, whatever your rogues may suppose,
    Conscience always makes restless their pillows,
And Justice, though blind, has a nose
    That sniffs out all conceal'd peccadilloes.
The wicked old Uncle, they say,
    In spite of his riot and revel,
Was hippish and qualmish all day,
    And dreamt all night long of the d—l.

He grew gouty, dyspeptic, and sour,
    And his brow, once so smooth and so placid,
Fresh wrinkles acquired every hour,
    And whatever he swallow'd turn'd acid.
The neighbours thought all was not right,
    Scarcely one with him ventured to parley,
And Captain Swing came in the night,
    And burnt all his beans and his barley.

There was hardly a day but some fox
    Ran away with his geese and his ganders;
His wheat had the mildew, his flocks
    Took the rot, and his horses the glanders;
His daughters drank rum in their tea,
    His son, who had gone for a sailor,
Went down in a steamer at sea,
    And his wife ran away with a tailor!

It was clear he lay under a curse,
    None would hold with him any communion;
Every day matters grew worse and worse,
    Till they ended at length in the Union;
While his man being caught in some fact
    (The particular crime I've forgotten),
When he came to be hanged for the act,
    Split, and told the whole story to Cotton.

Understanding the matter was blown,
    His employer became apprehensive
Of what, when 'twas more fully known,
    Might ensue—he grew thoughtful and pensive;
He purchased some sugar-of-lead,
    Took it home, popp'd it into his porridge,
Ate it up, and then took to his bed,
    And so died in the workhouse at Norwich.

MORAL

Ponder well now, dear Parents, each word
    That I've wrote, and when Sirius rages
In the dog-days, don't be so absurd
    As to blow yourself out with Greengages!
Of stone-fruits in general be shy,
    And reflect it's a fact beyond question
That Grapes, when they're spelt with an *i*,
    Promote anything else but digestion.—

—When you set about making your will,
    Which is commonly done when a body's ill,
Mind, and word it with caution and skill,
    And avoid, if you can, any codicil!
When once you've appointed an heir
    To the fortune you've made, or obtained, ere
You leave a reversion, beware
    Whom you place in contingent remainder!

Executors, Guardians, and all
    Who have children to mind, don't ill-treat them,
Nor think that, because they are small
    And weak, you may beat them, and cheat them!
Remember that 'ill-gotten goods
    Never thrive'; their possession's but cursory;
So never turn out in the woods
    Little folks you should keep in the nursery.

Be sure he who does such base things
    Will ne'er stifle Conscience's clamour;
His 'riches will make themselves wings,'
    And his property come to the hammer!
Then He,—and not those he bereaves,—
    Will have most cause for sighings and sobbings,
When he finds *himself* smother'd with leaves
    (Of fat catalogues) heaped up by Robins!

THE DEAD DRUMMER

A Legend of Salisbury Plain

Oh, Salisbury Plain is bleak and bare,—
At least so I've heard many people declare,
For I fairly confess I never was there;—
  Not a shrub nor a tree,   Nor a bush can you see;
No hedges, no ditches, no gates, no stiles,
Much less a house, or a cottage for miles;—
—It's a very sad thing to be caught in the rain
When night's coming on upon Salisbury Plain.

  Now, I'd have you to know   That, a great while ago,
The best part of a century, may be, or so,
Across this same plain, so dull and so dreary,
A couple of Travellers, wayworn and weary,
    Were making their way;
    Their profession, you'd say,
At a single glance did not admit of a query;
The pump-handled pig-tail, and whiskers, worn then,
With scarce an exception by seafaring men,
The jacket,—the loose trousers 'bows'd up together'—all
Guiltless of braces, as those of Charles Wetherall,—
The pigeon-toed step, and the rollicking motion,
Bespoke them two genuine sons of the Ocean,
And show'd in a moment their real char*á*cters,
(The accent's so placed on this word by our Jack Tars.)

The one in advance was sturdy and strong,
With arms uncommonly bony and long,
    And his Guernsey shirt   Was all pitch and dirt,
Which sailors don't think inconvenient or wrong.
    He was very broad-breasted,   And very deep-chested;
His sinewy frame correspond with the rest did,
Except as to height, for he could not be more
At the most, you would say, than some five feet four,
And if measured, perhaps had been found a thought lower.
Dame Nature, in fact,—whom some person or other,
—A Poet,—has call'd 'a capricious stepmother,'—
    You saw, when beside him,
    Had somehow denied him
In longitude what she had granted in latitude,
    A trifling defect   You'd the sooner detect
From his having contracted a stoop in his attitude.
  * H 185

Square-built and broad-shoulder'd, good-humoured and gay,
With his collar and countenance open as day,
The latter—'twas mark'd with smallpox, by the way,—
Had a sort of expression goodwill to bespeak;
He'd a smile in his eye, and a quid in his cheek!
And, in short, notwithstanding his failure in height,
He was just such a man as you'd say, at first sight,
You would much rather dine, or shake hands, with than fight!

The other, his friend and companion, was taller
By five or six inches, at least, than the smaller;—
 From his air and his mien It was plain to be seen,
 That he was, or had been, A something between
The real 'Jack Tar' and the 'Jolly Marine.'
For, though he would give an occasional hitch,
Sailor-like to his 'slops,' there was something, the which,
On the whole savoured more of the pipe-clay than pitch.—

Such were now the two men who appeared on the hill,
Harry Waters the tall one, the short 'Spanking Bill.'

 To be caught in the rain, I repeat it again,
Is extremely unpleasant on Salisbury Plain;
And when with a good soaking shower there are blended
Blue lightnings and thunder, the matter's not mended;
 Such was the case In this wild dreary place,
On the day that I'm speaking of now, when the brace
Of trav'llers alluded to quickened their pace,
Till a good steady walk became more like a race,
To get quit of the tempest which held them in chase.

 Louder, and louder Than mortal gunpowder,
The heav'nly artill'ry kept crashing and roaring,
The lightning kept flashing, the rain too kept pouring,
 While they, helter-skelter, In vain sought for shelter
From, what I have heard term'd, 'a regular pelter';
 But the deuce of a screen Could be anywhere seen,
Or an object except that on one of the rises,
 An old way-post show'd Where the Lavington road
Branch'd off to the left from the one to Devizes;
And thither the footsteps of Waters seem'd tending,
Though a doubt might exist of the course he was bending,
To a landsman, at least, who, wherever he goes,
Is content, for the most part, to follow his nose;—
 While Harry kept 'backing
 And filling'—and 'tacking,'—

Two nautical terms which, I'll wager a guinea, are
    Meant to imply What you, Reader, and I
Would call going zigzag, and not rectilinear.

But here, once for all, let me beg you'll excuse
All mistakes I may make in the words sailors use
    'Mongst themselves, on a cruise,
    Or ashore with the Jews,
Or in making their court to their Polls and their Sues,
Or addressing those slop-selling females afloat—women
Known in our navy as oddly-named boat-women.
The fact is, I can't say I'm vers'd in the school
So ably conducted by Marryat and Poole
(See the last-mentioned gentleman's *Admiral's Daughter*,
    The grand *vade mecum* For all who to sea come,
And get, the first time in their lives, in blue water);
Of course in the use of sea terms you'll not wonder
If I now and then should fall into some blunder,
For which Captain Chamier, or Mr T. P. Cooke
Would call me a 'Lubber,' and 'Son of a Sea-cook.'

To return to our muttons—This mode of progression
At length upon Spanking Bill made some impression.
    —'Hillo, messmate, what cheer?
    How queer you *do* steer!'
Cried Bill, whose short legs kept him still in the rear.
'Why, what's in the wind, Bo?—what is it you fear?'
For he saw in a moment that something was frightening
His shipmate much more than the thunder and lightning.

—'Fear?' stammer'd out Waters, 'why, HIM!—don't you see
What faces that Drummer-boy's making at me!—
    —How he dodges me so Wherever I go?—
What is it he wants with me, Bill,—do you know?'

—'What Drummer-boy, Harry?' cries Bill, in surprise
(With a brief explanation, that ended in 'eyes'),
'What Drummer-boy, Waters?—the coast is all clear,
We haven't got never no Drummer-boy here!'

—'Why, there!—don't you see How he's following me?
Now this way, now that way, and won't let me be!
    Keep him off, Bill—look here—
    Don't let him come near!
Only see how the blood-drops his features besmear!
What, the dead come to life again!—Bless me!—Oh dear!'

Bill remarked in reply, 'This is all very queer—
What, a Drummer-boy—bloody, too—eh!—well, I never—
I can't see no Drummer-boy here whatsumdever!'
'Not see him!—why there;—look!—he's close by the post—
Hark!—hark!—how he drums at me now!—he's a Ghost!'

'A what?' return'd Bill,—at that moment a flash
More than commonly awful preceded a crash
Like what's call'd in Kentucky 'an Almighty Smash.'—
And down Harry Waters went plump on his knees,
While the sound, though prolong'd, died away by degrees;
In its last sinking echoes, however, were some
Which, Bill could not help thinking, resembled a drum!

     'Hollo! Waters!—I says,' Quoth he in amaze,
'Why, I never see'd *nuffin* in all my born days
     Half so queer   As this here,
     And I'm not very clear
But that one of us two has good reason for fear—
You to jaw about drummers, with nobody near us!—
I must say as how that I thinks it's mysterus.'

'Oh, mercy!' roared Waters, 'do keep him off, Bill,
And, Andrew, forgive!—I'll confess all!—I will!
     I'll make a clean breast,   And as for the rest,
You may do with me just what the lawyers think best;
But haunt me not thus!—let these visitings cease,
And, your vengeance accomplish'd, Boy, leave me in peace!'
—Harry paused for a moment,—then turning to Bill,
Who stood with his mouth open, steady and still,
Began 'spinning' what nauticals term 'a tough yarn,'
Viz.: his tale of what Bill call'd 'this precious *consarn*.'

          'It was in such a hour as this,
               On such a wild and wint'ry day,
          The forked lightning seemed to hiss,
               As now, athwart our lonely way,
          When first these dubious paths I tried—
          Yon livid form was by my side!—

          'Not livid then—the ruddy glow
               Of life, and youth, and health it bore!
          And bloodless was that gory brow,
               And cheerful was the smile it wore,
          And mildly then those eyes did shine—
          —Those eyes which now are blasting mine!!

'They beamed with confidence and love
   Upon my face,—and Andrew Brand
Had sooner fear'd yon frighten'd dove
   Than harm from Gervase Matcham's hand!
—I am no Harry Waters—men
Did call me Gervase Matcham then.

'And Matcham, though a humble name,
   Was stainless as the feathery flake
From Heaven, whose virgin whiteness came
   Upon the newly-frozen lake;
Commander, comrade, all began
To laud the Soldier,—like the Man.

'Nay, muse not, William, I have said
   I was a soldier—staunch and true
As any he above whose head
   Old England's lion banner flew;
And, duty done,—her claims apart,—
'Twas said I had a kindly heart.

'And years roll'd on,—and with them came
   Promotion—Corporal—Sergeant—all
In turn—I kept mine honest fame—
   Our Colonel's self,—whom men did call
The veriest Martinet—ev'n he,
Though cold to most, was kind to me!—

'One morn—oh! may that morning stand
   Accursed in the rolls of fate
Till latest time!—there came command
   To carry forth a charge of weight
To a detachment far away,—
—It was their regimental pay!—

'And who so fit for such a task
   As trusty Matcham, true and tried,
Who spurn'd the inebriating flask,
   With honour for his constant guide?—
On Matcham fell their choice—and HE,—
"Young Drum,"—should bear him company!

'And grateful was that sound to hear,
   For he was full of life and joy,
The mess-room pet—to each one dear,
   Was that kind, gay, light-hearted boy.
—The veriest churl in all our band
Had aye a smile for Andrew Brand.—

'—Nay, glare not as I name thy name!
   That threat'ning hand, that fearful brow
Relax—avert that glance of flame!
   Thou seest I do thy bidding now!
Vex'd Spirit, rest!—'twill soon be o'er,—
Thy blood shall cry to Heav'n no more!

'Enough—we journey'd on—the walk
Was long,—and dull and dark the day,—
And still young Andrew's cheerful talk
   And merry laugh beguiled the way;
Noon came—a sheltering bank was there,—
We paused our frugal meal to share.

'Then 'twas, with cautious hand, I sought
   To prove my charge secure,—and drew
The packet from my vest, and brought
   The glittering mischief forth to view,
And Andrew cried,—No! 'twas not He!—
It was THE TEMPTER spoke to me!

'But it was Andrew's laughing voice
   That sounded in my tingling ear,
"Now, Gervase Matcham, at thy choice,"
   It seem'd to say, "are gawds and gear,
And all that wealth can buy or bring,
Ease,—wassail,—worship,—everything!

'"No tedious drill, no long parade,
   No bugle call at early dawn;—
For guard-room bench, or barrack bed,
   The downy couch, the sheets of lawn,
And I thy Page,—thy steps to tend,
Thy sworn companion,—servant,—friend!"

—'He ceased—that is, I heard no more,
   Though other words pass'd idly by,
And Andrew chatter'd as before,
   And laugh'd—I mark'd him not—not I.
"'*Tis at thy choice!*" that sound alone
Rang in mine ear—voice else was none.

'I could not eat—the untasted flask
   Mock'd my parch'd lip,—I passed it by.
"What ails thee, man?" he seem'd to ask.—
   I *felt*, but could not *meet* his eye,—
"'*Tis at thy choice!*" —it sounded yet,—
A sound I never may forget.

—'"Haste! haste! the day draws on," I cried,
  "And, Andrew, thou hast far to go!"—
"*Hast far to go!*" the Fiend replied
  Within me,—'twas *not* Andrew—no!
'Twas Andrew's voice no more—'twas HE
Whose then I was, and aye must be!

—'On, on we went;—the dreary plain
  Was all around us—we were *Here*!
Then came the storm,—the lightning,—rain,—
  No earthly living thing was near,
Save one wild Raven on the wing,
—If that, indeed, were earthly thing!

'I heard its hoarse and screaming voice
  High hovering o'er my frenzied head,
"'*Tis, Gervase Matcham, at thy choice!*
  But he—the Boy!" methought it said.
—Nay, Andrew, check that vengeful frown,—
I lov'd thee when I struck thee down!

''Twas done!—the deed that damns me—done
  I know not how—I never knew;
And *Here* I stood—but not alone,—
  The prostrate Boy my madness slew,
Was by my side—limb, feature, name,
'Twas HE!!—another—yet the same!

'Away! away! in frantic haste
  Throughout that livelong night I flew—
Away! away!—across the waste,—
  I know not how—I never knew—
My mind was one wild blank—and I
Had but one thought,—one hope—to fly!

'And still the lightning ploughed the ground,
  The thunder roared—and there would come
Amidst its loudest bursts a sound,
  Familiar once—it was—A DRUM!—
Then came the morn,—and light,—and then
Streets,—houses,—spires,—the hum of men.

'And Ocean roll'd before me—fain
  Would I have whelm'd me in its tide,
At once beneath the billowy main
  My shame, my guilt, my crime to hide;
But HE was there!—HE cross'd my track,—
I dared not pass—HE waved me back!

'And then rude hands detained me—sure.
    Justice had grasp'd her victim—no!
Though powerless, hopeless, bound, secure,
    A captive thrall, it was not so;
They cry, "The Frenchman's on the wave!"
The press was hot—and I a slave.

'They dragg'd me o'er the vessel's side;
    The world of waters roll'd below;
The gallant ship, in all her pride
    Of dreadful beauty, sought her foe;
—Thou saw'st me, William, in the strife—
Alack! I bore a charmed life;

'In vain the bullets round me fly,
    In vain mine eager breast I bare;
Death shuns the wretch who longs to die,
    And every sword falls edgeless there!
Still HE is near!—and seems to cry,
"Not *here*, nor *thus*, may Matcham die!"—

'Thou saw'st me, on that fearful day,
    When, fruitless all attempts to save,
Our pinnace foundering in the bay,
    The boat's-crew met a watery grave,—
All, all—save ONE—the ravenous sea
    That swallow'd all—rejected ME!

'And now, when fifteen suns have each
    Fulfilled in turn its circling year,
Thrown back again on England's beach,
    Our bark paid off—HE drives me *Here*!
I could not die in flood or fight—
    HE drives me HERE!!'—
                        'And sarve you right!

'What! bilk your Commander!—desart—and then rob!
And go scuttling a poor little Drummer-boy's nob!
Why, my precious eyes! what a bloodthirsty swab!—
    There's old Davy Jones, Who cracks sailor's bones
For his jaw-work would never, I'm sure, s'elp me Bob,
Have come for to go for to do sich a job!
Hark ye, Waters,—or Matcham—whichever's your purser-
    name,—
—T'other, your own, is, I'm sartain, the worser name,—
Twelve years have we lived on like brother and brother!—
Now—your course lays one way, and mine lays another!'

'No, William, it may not be so;
   Blood calls for blood!—'tis Heaven's decree!
And thou with me this night must go,
   And give me to the gallows-tree!
Ha!—see—HE smiles—HE points the way!
On, William, on! no more delay!'

Now Bill,—so the story, as told to me, goes,
And who, as his last speech sufficiently shows,
Was a 'regular trump,'—did not like to 'turn Nose'!
But then came a thunder-clap louder than any
Of those that preceded, though they were so many;
And hark!—as its rumblings subside in a hum
What sound mingles too?—'By the hokey—A DRUM!!'

I remember I once heard my Grandfather say,
That some sixty years since he was going that way,
   When they show'd him the spot
   Where the gibbet—was not—
On which Matcham's corse had been hung up to rot!
It had fall'n down—but how long before, he'd forgot;
And they told him, I think, at the Bear in Devizes,
The town where the Sessions are held—or the 'Sizes,
   That Matcham confess'd,   And made a clean breast
To the May'r; but that, after he'd had a night's rest,
And the storm had subsided, he 'pooh-pooh'd' his friend,
Swearing all was a lie from beginning to end;
   Said 'he'd only been drunk—
   That his spirits had sunk
At the thunder—the storm put him into a funk,—
That, in fact, he had nothing at all on his conscience,
And found out, in short, he'd been talking great nonsense.'—

   But now one Mr Jones   Comes forth and depones
That, fifteen years since, he had heard certain groans
On his way to Stone Henge (to examine the stones
Described in a work of the late Sir John Soane's),
   That he'd followed the moans,
   And led by their tones,
Found a Raven a-picking a Drummer-boy's bones!—
   —Then the Colonel wrote word
   From the King's Forty-third,
That the story was certainly true which they'd heard,
For, that one of their drummers, and one Sergeant Matcham,
Had 'brushed with the dibs,' and they never could catch 'em.

So Justice was sure, though a long time she'd lagg'd,
And the Sergeant, in spite of his 'Gammon,' got 'scragg'd';
  And people averr'd   That an ugly black bird,
The Raven, 'twas hinted, of whom we have heard,
Though the story, I own, appears rather absurd,
Was seen (Gervase Matcham not being interr'd),
To roost all that night on the murderer's gibbet;
An odd thing, if so, and it may be a fib—it,
However, 's a thing Nature's laws don't prohibit.
—Next morning, they add, that 'black gentleman' flies out,
Having picked Matcham's nose off, and gobbled his eyes out!

MORAL

Avis au Voyageur

Imprimis.

    If you contemplate walking o'er Salisbury Plain,
    Consult Mr Murphy, or Moore, and refrain
From selecting a day when it's likely to rain!

2°

    When trav'lling, don't 'flash'
    Your notes or your cash
Before other people—it's foolish and rash!

3°

    At dinner be cautious, and note well your party;—
    There's little to dread where the appetite's hearty,—
But mind and look well to your purse and your throttle
When you see a man shirking, and passing his bottle!

4°

    If you chance to be needy,
    Your coat and hat seedy,
In war-time especially, never go out,
When you've reason to think there's a press-gang about!

5°

    Don't chatter, nor tell people all that you think,
    Nor blab secrets,—especially when you're in drink,—
But keep your own counsel in all that you do!
    —Or a Counsel may, some day or other, keep you.

6°

    Discard superstition!—and don't take a post,
If you happen to see one at night, for a Ghost!
    —Last of all, if by choice, or convenience, you're led,
To cut a man's throat, or demolish his head,
Don't do't in a thunderstorm—wait for the summer!
And mind, above all things, the MAN'S NOT A DRUMMER!!

A ROW IN AN OMNIBUS (BOX)

A LEGEND OF THE HAYMARKET

'Omnibus hoc vitium cantoribus.' [1]—HOR.

DOL-DRUM the Manager sits in his chair,
With a gloomy brow and dissatisfied air,
And he says as he slaps his hands on his knee,
'I'll have nothing to do with Fiddle-de-dee!'

—'But Fiddle-de-dee sings clear and loud,
And his trills and his quavers astonish the crowd;
  Such a singer as he   You'll nowhere see;
They'll all be screaming for Fiddle-de-dee!'

—'Though Fiddle-de-dee sings loud and clear,
And his tones are sweet, yet his terms are dear!
  The "glove won't fit!"   The deuce a bit.
I shall give an engagement to Fal-de-ral-tit!'

The Prompter bow'd, and he went to his stall,
And the green-baize rose at the Prompter's call,
And Fal-de-ral-tit sang fol-de-rol-lol;
  But, scarce had he done   When a row begun,
Such a noise was never heard under the sun.

  'Fiddle-de-dee!—   —Where is he?
He's the *Artiste* whom we all want to see!—
  Dol-drum!—Dol-drum!—   Bid the Manager come!
It's a scandalous thing to exact such a sum
For boxes and gallery, stalls and pit,
And then fob us off with a Fal-de-ral-tit!—
  Deuce a bit!   We'll never submit!
Vive Fiddle-de-dee! *à bas* Fal-de-ral-tit!'

Dol-drum the Manager rose from his chair,
With a gloomy brow and dissatisfied air;
  But he smooth'd his brow,   As he well knew how,
And he walk'd on, and made a most elegant bow,
And he paused, and he smiled, and advanced to the lights,
In his opera-hat, and his opera-tights;
'Ladies and Gentlemen,' then said he,
'Pray what may you please to want with me?'

[1] All singers have this fault.'

'Fiddle-de-dee!—   Fiddle-de-dee!'
Folks of all sorts and of every degree,
Snob, and Snip, and haughty Grandee,
Duchesses, Countesses, fresh from their tea,
And Shopmen, who'd only come there for a spree,
Halloo'd, and hooted, and roar'd with glee
    'Fiddle-de-dee!—   —None but He!—
Subscribe to his terms, whatever they be!—
Agree, agree, or you'll very soon see
In a brace of shakes we'll get up an O.P.!'

Dol-drum the Manager, full of care,
With a gloomy brow and dissatisfied air,
    Looks distressed,   And he bows his best,
And he puts his right hand on the side of his breast,
    And he says,—says he, 'We *can't* agree;
His terms are a vast deal too high for me.—
There's the rent, and the rates, and the sesses, and taxes—
I can't afford Fiddle-de-dee what he *axes*.
    If you'll only permit   Fal-de-ral-tit——'
The 'Generous Public' cried, 'Deuce a bit!

    'Dol-drum!—Dol-drum!—   We'll none of us come.
It's "No Go!"—it's "Gammon!"—it's "all a Hum":—
    You're a miserly Jew!—   "Cock-a-doodle-do!"
He *don't* ask too much, as you know—so you do—
It's a shame—it's a sin—it's really too bad—
You ought to be 'shamed of yourself—so you had!'

Dol-drum the Manager never before
In his lifetime had heard such a wild uproar.
Dol-drum the Manager turn'd to flee;
    But he says—says he, '*Mort de ma vie!*
I shall *nevare* engage vid dat Fiddle-de-dee!'
Then all the gentlefolks flew in a rage,
And they jump'd from the Omnibus on to the Stage,
Lords, Squires, and Knights, they came down to the lights,
In their opera-hats, and their opera-tights.
    Ma'am'selle Cherrytoes   Shook to her very toes,
She couldn't hop on, so hopped off on her merry toes.
And the 'evening concluded' with 'Three times three!'
'Hip!—hip!—hurrah! for Fiddle-de-dee!'

Dol-drum the Manager, full of care,
With a troubled brow and dissatisfied air,

Saddest of men,   Sat down, and then
Took from his table a Perryan pen,
And he wrote to the *News*,
How MacFuze, and Tregooze,
Lord Tomnoddy, Sir Carnaby Jenks of the Blues,
And the whole of their tail, and the separate crews
Of the Tags and the Rags, and the No-one-knows-whos,
Had combined Monsieur Fal-de-ral-tit to abuse,
    And make Dol-drum agree   With Fiddle-de-dee,
Who was not a bit better singer than he.
—Dol-drum declared 'he never could see,
For the life of him, yet, why Fiddle-de-dee,
    Who, in B flat, or C,   Or whatever the key,
Could never at any time get below G,
Should expect a fee the same in degree
As the great Burlybumbo who sings double D.'
Then slily he added a little N.B.
'If they'd have him in Paris he'd not come to me!'

    The Manager rings,   And the Prompter springs
To his side in a jiffy, and with him he brings
A set of those odd-looking envelope things,
Where Britannia (who seems to be crucified) flings
To her right and her left funny people with wings,
Amongst Elephants, Quakers, and Catabaw Kings;
    And a taper and wax,
    And small Queen's heads in packs,
Which, when notes are too big, you're to stick on their backs.
Dol-drum the Manager sealed with care
The letter and copies he'd written so fair,
And sat himself down with a satisfied air;
    Without delay   He sent them away,
In time to appear in 'our columns' next day!

Dol-drum the Manager, full of care,
Walk'd on to the stage with an anxious air,
And peep'd through the curtain to see who were there.
    There was MacFuze,   And Lieutenant Tregooze,
And there was Sir Carnaby Jenks of the Blues,
And the Tags, and the Rags, and the No-one-knows-whos;
And the green-baize rose at the Prompter's call,
And they all began to hoot, bellow, and bawl,
And cry 'Cock-a-doodle,' and scream, and squall
    'Dol-drum!—Dol-drum!   Bid the Manager come!'
    You'd have thought from the tones
    Of their hisses and groans,
They were bent upon breaking his (Opera) bones.

And Dol-drum comes, and he says—says he,
'Pray what may you please to want with me?'—
    'Fiddle-de-dee!—   Fiddle-de-dee!—
We'll have nobody give us *sol fa* but He!
For he's the *Artiste* whom we all want to see.'

—Manager Dol-drum says—says he—
(And he looks like an Owl in 'a hollow beech-tree')
    'Well, since I see   The thing must be,
I'll sign an agreement with Fiddle-de-dee!'
    Then Macfuze, and Tregooze,   And Jenks of the Blues,
And the Tags, and the Rags, and the No-one-knows-whos,
Extremely delighted to hear such good news,
Desist from their shrill 'Cock-a-doodle-doos.'
    '*Vive* Fiddle-de-dee!   Dol-drum, and He!
They are jolly good fellows as ever need be!
And so's Burlybumbo, who sings double D!
And whenever they sing, why, we'll all come and see!'

    So, after all   This terrible squall,
    Fiddle-de-dee   's at the top of the tree,
And Dol-drum and Fal-de-ral-tit sing small!
Now Fiddle-de-dee sings loud and clear
At I can't tell you how many thousands a year,
And Fal-de-ral-tit is considered 'Small Beer';
    And Ma'am'selle Cherrytoes   Sports her merry toes,
Dancing away to the fiddles and flutes,
In what the folks call a 'Lithuanian' in boots.

So here's an end to my one, two, and three;
And bless the Queen—and long live She!
And grant that there never again may be
Such a hullaballoo as we've happened to see
About nothing on earth but 'Fiddle-de-dee!'

THE LAY OF ST CUTHBERT; OR, THE DEVIL'S DINNER-PARTY

A LEGEND OF THE NORTH COUNTREE

'*Nobilis quidam, cui nomen* Monsr. Lescrop, Chivaler, *cum invitasset convivas, et, hora convivii jam instante et apparatu facto, spe frustratus esset, excusantibus se convivis cur non comparerent, prorupit iratus in haec verba: " Veniant igitur omnes daemones, si nullus hominum mecum esse potest!"*'

'*Quod cum fieret, et Dominus, et famuli, et ancillae, a domo properantes, forte obliti, infantem in cunis jacentem secum non auferunt. Daemones incipiunt comessari et vociferari, prospicereque per fenestras formis ursorum, luporum, felium, et monstrare pocula vino repleta. Ah, inquit pater, ubi infans meus? Vix cum haec dixisset, unus ex Daemonibus ulnis suis infantem ad fenestram gestat, etc.*'[1]—CHRONICON DE BOLTON.

IT's in Bolton Hall, and the Clock strikes One,
And the roast meat's brown, and the boil'd meat's done,
And the barbecu'd sucking-pig's crisp'd to a turn,
And the pancakes are fried, and beginning to burn;
    The fat stubble-goose Swims in gravy and juice
With the mustard and apple-sauce ready for use;
Fish, flesh, and fowl, and all of the best,
Want nothing but eating—they're all ready dressed.
But where is the Host, and where is the Guest?

Pantler and serving-man, henchman and page,
Stand sniffing the duck-stuffing (onion and sage),
    And the scullions and cooks, With fidgety looks,
Are grumbling, and mutt'ring, and scowling as black
As cooks always do when the dinner's put back;
For though the board's deckt, and the napery, fair
As the unsunn'd snowflake, is spread out with care,

---

[1] 'A noble named M. Lescrop, Chevalier, issued invitations to some guests, but when the hour of the party approached and preparations had been made, had his hopes disappointed, the guests making excuses for their failure to appear. Enraged, he burst out with these words: "Let all the demons come, then, if no man can be with me."
'When this happened the master and his servants, male and female, as they hurried from the house, omitted, perhaps through forgetfulness, to take with them the baby lying in its cradle. The demons began to revel and shout, peer through the windows in the form of bears, wolves, and cats, and display cups full of wine. "Ah," said the father, "where is my child?" He had scarcely spoken, when one of the demons carried the baby to the window in his arms.'

And the Dais is furnish'd with stool and with chair,
And plate of *orfèvrerie* costly and rare,
Apostle-spoons, salt-cellar, all are there,
　　And Mess John in his place,　With his rubicund face,
And his hands ready folded, prepared to say Grace,
Yet where is the Host?—and his convives—where?

The Scroope sits lonely in Bolton Hall,
And he watches the dial that hangs by the wall,
He watches the large hand, he watches the small,
　　And he fidgets, and looks　As cross as the cooks,
And he utters—a word which we'll soften to 'Zooks!'
As he cries, 'What on earth has become of them all?—
　　What can delay　De Vaux and De Saye?
What makes Sir Gilbert de Umfraville stay?
What's gone with Poyntz, and Sir Reginald Braye?
Why are Ralph Ufford and Marny away?
And De Nokes, and De Stiles, and Lord Marmaduke Grey?
　　And De Roe?　And De Doe?—
Poynings, and Vavasour—where be they?
Fitz-Walter, Fitz-Osbert, Fitz-Hugh, and Fitz-John,
And the Mandevilles, *père et filz* (father and son)?
Their cards said "Dinner precisely at One!"
　　There's nothing I hate, in　The world, like waiting!
It's a monstrous great bore, when a Gentleman feels
A good appetite, thus to be kept from his meals!'

It's in Bolton Hall, and the clock strikes Two!
And the scullions and cooks are themselves in 'a stew,'
And the kitchen-maids stand, and don't know what to do,
For the rich plum-puddings are bursting their bags,
And the mutton and turnips are boiling to rags,
　　And the fish is all spoil'd　And the butter's all oil'd,
And the soup'd got cold in the silver tureen,
And there's nothing, in short, that is fit to be seen!
While Sir Guy Le Scroope continues to fume,
And to fret by himself in the tapestried room,
　　And still fidgets, and looks　More cross than the cooks,
And repeats that bad word, which we've soften'd to 'Zooks!'

Two o'clock's come, and Two oclock's gone,
And the large and the small hands move steadily on,
　　Still nobody's there,　No De Roos, or De Clare,
To taste of the Scroope's most delicate fare,
Or to quaff off a health unto Bolton's Heir,
That nice little boy who sits there in his chair,

Some four years old, and a few months to spare,
With his laughing blue eyes, and his long curly hair,
Now sucking his thumb, and now munching his pear.

Again, Sir Guy the silence broke,
'It's hard upon Three!—it's just on the stroke!
Come, serve up the dinner!—A joke is a joke!'
Little he deems that Stephen de Hoaques,[1]
Who 'his fun,' as the Yankees say, everywhere 'pokes,'
And is always a great deal too fond of his jokes,
Has written a circular note to De Nokes,
And De Stiles, and De Roe, and the rest of the folks,
    One and all,   Gret and small,
Who were asked to the Hall,
To dine there, and sup, and wind up with a ball,
And had told all the party a great bouncing lie he
Cook'd up, that 'the fête was postponed *sine die*,
The dear little curly-wig'd heir of Le Scroope
Being taken alarmingly ill with the croup!'

    When the clock struck Three,
    And the Page on his knee
Said, 'An't please you, Sir Guy Le Scroope, *On a servi!*'
And the Knight found the banquet-hall empty and clear,
    With nobody near   To partake of his cheer,
He stamp'd, and he storm'd—then his language!—Oh dear!
'Twas awful to see, and 'twas awful to hear!
And he cried to the button-deck'd Page at his knee,
Who had told him so civilly '*On a servi*,'
'Ten thousand fiends seize them, wherever they be!
—The Devil take *them*! and the Devil take *thee*!
And the DEVIL MAY EAT UP THE DINNER FOR ME!!'

In a terrible fume   He bounced out of the room,
He bounced out of the house—and page, footman, and groom
Bounced after their master; for scarce had they heard
Of this left-handed Grace the last finishing word,
Ere the horn, at the gate of the Barbican tower,
Was blown with a loud twenty-trumpeter power,

[1] For a full account of this facetious '*Chivaler*,' see the late (oh! that we
should have to say 'late'!) Theodore Hook's *History of the Illustrious
Commononers of Great Britain*, as quoted in the Memoirs of John Bragg,
Esq., page 344 of the 75th volume of the Standard Novels.   In the third
volume of Sir Harris Nicholas's elaborate account of the Scrope and Grosvenor
controversy, commonly called the 'Scrope Roll,' a Stephen de Hoques, Ecuyer,
is described as giving his testimony on the Grosvenor side.—*Vide* page 247.

And in rush'd a troop
  Of strange guests!—such a group
As had ne'er before darkened the doors of the Scroope!

This looks like De Saye—yet—it is not De Saye—
And this is—no, 'tis not—Sir Reginald Braye—
This has somewhat the favour of Marmaduke Grey—
But stay!—*Where on earth did he get those long nails?*
Why, they're *claws!*—then, Good Gracious!—they've all of
    them *tails!*
That can't be De Vaux—why, his nose is a bill,
Or, I would say, a beak!—and he can't keep it still!—
Is that Poynings?—Oh Gemini!—look at his feet!!
Why, they're absolute *hoofs!*—is it gout or his corns
That have crumpled them up so?—by Jingo, he's *horns!*
Run! run!—There's Fitz-Walter, Fitz-Hugh, and Fitz-John,
And the Mandevilles, *père et fils* (father and son),
And Fitz-Osbert, and Ufford—*they've all got them on!*
  Then their great saucer eyes— It's the Father of lies
And his Imps—run! run! run!—they're all fiends in disguise,
Who've partly assumed, with more sombre complexions,
The forms of Sir Guy Le Scroope's friends and connections,
And He—at the top there—that grim-looking elf—
Run! run!—that's the 'muckle-horned Clootie' himself!

  And now what a din Without and within!
For the court-yard is full of them.—How they begin
To mop, and to mowe, and make faces, and grin!
    Cock their tails up together,
    Like cows in hot weather,
And butt at each other, all eating and drinking,
The viands and wine disappearing like winking.
  And then such a lot As together had got!
Master Cabbage, the steward, who'd made a machine
To calculate with, and count noses,—I ween
The cleverest thing of the kind ever seen,—
    Declared, when he'd made,
    By the said machine's aid,
Up, what's now called, the 'tottle' of those he survey'd,
There were just—how he proved it I cannot divine,—
Nine thousand, nine hundred, and ninety, and nine,
  Exclusive of Him, Who, giant in limb,
And black as the crow they denominate *Jim,*
With a tail like a bull, and a head like a bear,
Stands forth at the window,—and what holds he there,

Which he hugs with such care,
And pokes out in the air,
And grasps as its limbs from each other he'd tear?
  Oh! grief and despair! I vow and declare
It's Le Scroope's poor, dear, sweet, little, curly-wigg'd Heir!
Whom the nurse had forgot, and left there in his chair,
Alternately sucking his thumb and his pear!

  What words can express The dismay and distress
    Sir Guy, when he found what a terrible mess
His cursing and banning had now got him into?
That words, which to use are a shame and a sin too,
Had thus on their speaker recoiled, and his malison
Placed in the hands of the Devil's own 'pal' his son!—
  He sobb'd, and he sigh'd,
  And he scream'd and he cried,
And behaved like a man that is mad, or in liquor,—he
Tore his peaked beard, and he dashed off his 'Vicary,' [1]
  Stamped on the jasey As though he were crazy,
And staggering about just as if he were 'hazy,'
Exclaimed, 'Fifty pounds!' (a large sum in those times)
'To the person, whoever he may be, that climbs
To that window above there, *en ogive*, and painted,
And brings down my curly-wi'——' here Sir Guy fainted!

  With many a moan And many a groan,
What with tweaks of the nose, and some eau-de-Cologne,
He revived,—Reason once more remounted her throne,
Or rather the instinct of Nature,—'twere treason
To Her, in the Scroope's case, perhaps, to say Reason,—
But what saw he then?—Oh! my goodness! a sight
Enough to have banished his reason outright!

[1] A peruke so named from its inventor. Robert de Ros and Eudo Fitz-Vicari, who flourished in the eleventh century. The latter is noticed in the Battle Abbey roll, and is said to have curled William the Conqueror's hair when dressing for the battle of Hastings. Dugdale makes no mention of him, but Camden says, that Humfrey, one of his descendants, was summoned to Parliament, 26 Jan. 25 Edw. I (1927). It is doubtful, however, whether that writ can be deemed a regular writ of Summons to Parliament, for reasons amply detailed in the *Synopsis of the British Peerage*.—(Art. Fitz-John.) A writ was subsequently addressed to him as '*Humfry Fitz-Vicari, Chiv'*.' 8 Jan. 6 Edw. II (1313), and his descendants appear to have been regularly summoned as late as 5 and 6 of Philip and Mary, 1557–8. Soon after which Peter Fitz-Vicari dying, S. P. M. this Barony went into abeyance between his two daughters, Joan, married to Henry de Truefit, of Fullbottom, and Alice, wife of Roger Wigram, of Caxon Hall, in Wigton, co. Cumb. Esq., among whose representatives it is presumed to be still in abeyance.

In that broad banquet hall   The fiends, one and all,
Regardless of shriek, and of squeak, and of squall,
From one to another were tossing that small,
Pretty, curly-wigg'd boy, as if playing at ball:
Yet none of his friends or his vassals might dare
To fly to the rescue, or rush up the stair,
And bring down in safety his curly-wigg'd Heir!

Well a day!   Well a day!   All he can say
Is but just so much trouble and time thrown away;
Not a man can be tempted to join the *mêlée*,
E'en those words cabalistic, 'I promise to pay
Fifty pounds on demand,' have, for once, lost their sway,
   And there the Knight stands,   Wringing his hands
In his agony—when, on a sudden, one ray
Of hope darts through his midriff!—His Saint!—Oh, it's funny,
   And almost absurd,   That it never occurr'd!—
'Ay! the Scroope's Patron Saint!—he's the man for my money!
Saint—who is it?—really I'm sadly to blame,—
On my word I'm afraid,—I confess it with shame,—
That I've almost forgot the good Gentleman's name,—
Cut—let me see—Cutbeard?—no!—CUTHBERT!—egad
St Cuthbert of Bolton!—I'm right—he's the lad!
Oh! holy St Cuthbert, if forbears of mine—
Of myself I say little,—have knelt at your shrine,
And have lash'd their bare backs, and—no matter—with twine,
   Oh! list to the vow   Which I make to you now,
Only snatch my poor little boy out of the row
Which that Imp's kicking up with his fiendish bow-wow,
And his head like a bear, and his tail like a cow!
Bring him back here in safety!—perform but this task,
And I'll give!—Oh!—I'll give you whatever you ask!—
   There is not a shrine   In the County shall shine
With a brilliancy half so resplendent as thine,
Or have so many candles, or look half so fine!—
Haste, holy St Cuthbert, then,—hasten in pity!'—
   —Conceive his surprise   When a strange voice replies,
'It's a bargain!—but, mind, sir, THE BEST SPERMACETI!'—

Say, whose that voice?—whose that form by his side,
That old, old grey man, with his beard long and wide,
   In his coarse Palmer's weeds,
   And his cockle and beads?—
And, how did he come?—did he walk?—did he ride?—
Oh! none could determine,—oh! none could decide,—
The fact is, I don't believe anyone tried,
For while ev'ryone stared, with a dignified stride,

And without a word more,   He march'd on before,
Up a flight of stone steps, and so through the front door,
To the banqueting-hall, that was on the first floor,
While the fiendish assembly were making a rare
Little shuttlecock there of the curly-wigg'd Heir.—
—I wish, gentle Reader, that you could have seen
The pause that ensued when he stepp'd in between,
With his resolute air, and his dignified mien,
And said, in a tone most decided, though mild,
'Come!—I'll trouble you just to hand over that child!'

The Demoniac crowd   In an instant seem'd cowed;
Not one of the crew volunteer'd a reply,
All shrunk from the glance of that keen-flashing eye,
Save one horrid Humgruffin, who seem'd by his talk,
And the airs he assumed, to be Cock of the walk,
He quailed not before it, but saucily met it,
And as saucily said, 'Don't you wish you may get it?'

My goodness!—the look that the old Palmer gave!
And his frown!—'twas quite dreadful to witness—'Why, slave!
   You rascal!' quoth he, 'This language to ME!!
—At once, Mr Nicholas! down on your knee,
And hand me that curly-wigg'd boy!—I command it—
Come!—none of your nonsense!—you know I won't stand it.'

Old Nicholas trembled,—he shook in his shoes,
And seem'd half inclined, but afraid, to refuse.
   'Well, Cuthbert,' said he, 'If so it must be,
—For you've had your own way from the first time I knew ye;—
Take your curly-wigg'd brat, and much good may he do ye!
But I'll have in exchange—' here his eye flash'd with rage—
'That chap with the buttons—he *gave me* the Page!'

'Come, come,' the Saint answer'd, 'you very well know
The young man's no more his than your own to bestow—
Touch one button of his if you dare, Nick—no! no!
Cut your stick, sir—come, mizzle!—be off with you!—go!'—
   The Devil grew hot—'If I do I'll be shot!
An you come to that, Cuthbert, I'll tell you what's what;
He has *asked* us to *dine here*, and go we will not!
   Why, you Skinflint,—at least
   You may leave us the feast!
Here we've come all that way from our brimstone abode,
Ten million good leagues, Sir, as ever you strode,
And the deuce of a luncheon we've had on the road—

—"Go!"—"Mizzle!" indeed—Mr Saint, who are you,
I should like to know?—"Go!"—I'll be hang'd if I do!
He invited us all—we've a right here—it's known
That a Baron may do what he likes with his own—
Here, Asmodeus—a slice of that beef!—now the mustard!—
What have *you* got?—oh, apple-pie—try it with custard!'

The Saint made a pause—As uncertain, because
He knew Nick is pretty well 'up' in the laws,
And they *might* be on *his* side—and then, he'd such claws!
On the whole, it was better, he thought, to retire
With the curly-wigg'd boy he'd pick'd out of the fire,
And give up the victuals—to retrace his path,
And to compromise—(spite of the Member for Bath).
So to Old Nick's appeal,　As he turn'd on his heel,
He replied, 'Well, I'll leave you the mutton and veal,
And the soup *à al Reine*, and the sauce *Bechamel*.
As The Scroope *did* invite you to dinner, I feel
I can't well turn you out—'twould be hardly genteel—
But be moderate, pray,—and remember thus much,
Since you're treated as Gentlemen, show yourselves such,
　　And don't make it late,　But mind and go straight
Home to bed when you've finish'd—and don't steal the plate!
Nor wrench off the knocker—or bell from the gate.
Walk away, like respectable Devils, in peace,
And don't "lark" with the watch, or annoy the police!'

Having thus said his say,　That Palmer grey
Took up little Le Scroope, and walk'd coolly away,
While the Demons all set up a 'Hip! hip! hurray!'
Then fell, tooth and claw, on the victuals, as they
Had been guests at Guildhall upon Lord Mayor's day,
All scrambling and scuffling for what was before 'em,
No care for precedence or common decorum.
Few ate more hearty　Than Madame Astarte,
And Hecate,—considered the Belles of the party,
Between them was seated Leviathan, eager
To 'do the polite,' and take wine with Belphegor;
Here was *Morbleu* (a French devil), supping soup-meagre,
And there, munching leeks, Davy Jones of Tredegar
(A Welsh one), who'd left the domains of Ap Morgan,
To 'follow the sea,'—and next him Demogorgon,—
Then Pan with his pipes, and Fauns grinding the organ
To Mammon and Belial, and half a score dancers.
Who'd joined with Medusa to get up 'the Lancers';

—Here's Lucifer lying blind drunk with Scotch ale,
While Beëlzebub's tying huge knots in his tail.
There's Setebos, storming because Mephistopheles
   Gave him the lie,   Said he'd 'blacken his eye,'
And dash'd in his face a whole cup of hot coffee-lees;—
   Ramping, and roaring,   Hiccoughing, snoring,—
Never was seen such a riot before in
A gentleman's house, or such profligate revelling
At any soirée—where they don't let the Devil in.

   Hark!—as sure as fate   The clock's striking Eight!
(An hour which our ancestors called 'getting late')
When Nick, who by this time was rather elate,
Rose up and addressed them.
               ''Tis full time,' he said,
'For all elderly Devils to be in their bed;
For my own part I mean to be jogging, because
I don't find myself now quite so young as I was;
But, Gentlemen, ere I depart from my post,
I must call on you all for one bumper—the toast
Which I have to propose is,—OUR EXCELLENT HOST!
—Many thanks for his kind hospitality—may
   We also be able   To see at *our* table
Himself, and enjoy, in a family way,
His good company *downstairs* at no distant day!
   You'd, I'm sure, think me rude
   If I did not include
In the toast my young friend there, the curly-wigg'd Heir,
He's in very good hands, for you're all well aware
That St Cuthbert has taken him under his care;
   Though I must not say 'bless,'—
   —Why, you'll easily guess,—
May our Curly-wigg'd Friend's shadow never be less!'
Nick took off his heel-taps—bow'd—smiled—with an air
Most graciously grim,—and vacated the chair,—
   Of course the *élite*   Rose at once on their feet,
And followed their leader, and beat a retreat;
When a sky-larking imp took the President's seat,
And, requesting that each would replenish his cup,
Said, 'Where we have dined, my boys, there let us sup!'—
—It was three in the morning before they broke up!!!

   I scarcely need say   Sir Guy didn't delay
To fulfil his vow made to St Cuthbert, or pay
For the candles he'd promised, or make light as day
The shrine he assured him he'd render so gay.

In fact, when the votaries came there to pray,
All said there was nought to compare with it—nay,
    For fear that the Abbey   Might think he was shabby,
Four Brethren thenceforward, two cleric, two lay,
He ordained should take charge of a new-founded chantry,
With six marks apiece, and some claims on the pantry;
    In short, the whole County
    Declared, through his bounty,
The Abbey of Bolton exhibited fresh scenes
From any displayed since Sir William de Meschines,[1]
And Cecily Roumeli came to this nation
With William the Norman, and laid its foundation.

    For the rest, it is said,   And I know I have read
In some Chronicle—whose, has gone out of my head—
That, what with these candles, and other expenses,
Which no man would go to if quite in his senses,
    He reduced, and brought low   His property so,
That, at last, he'd not much of it left to bestow;
And that, many years after that terrible feast,
Sir Guy in the Abbey was living a Priest;
And there, in one thousand and—something,—deceased.
    (It's supposed by this trick
    He bamboozled Old Nick,
And slipped through his fingers remarkably 'slick'),
While, as to young Curly-wig,—dear little Soul,
Would you know more of him, you must look at 'The Roll,'
    Which records the dispute,   And the subsequent suit,
Commenced in 'Thirteen sev'nty-five,'—which took root
In Le Grosvenor's assuming the arms Le Scroope swore
That none but *his* ancestors, ever before,
In foray, joust, battle, or tournament wore,
To wit, '*On a Prussian-blue field a Bend Or*';
While the Grosvenor averred that *his* ancestors bore
The same, and Scroope lied like a—somebody tore
Off the simile,—so I can tell you no more,
Till some A double S shall the fragment restore.[2]

[1] *Vide* Dugdale's *Monasticon*, art. 'Prioratus de Bolton, in agro Eboracensi.'
[2] It is with the greatest satisfaction that I learn from Mr Simpkinson this consummation, so devoutly to be wished, is about to be realized, and that the remainder of this most interesting document, containing the whole of the defendant's evidence, will appear in the course of the ensuing summer, under the same auspices as the former portion. We shall look with eagerness for the identification of 'Curly-wig.'

MORAL

This Legend sound maxim exemplifies—e.g.—

1*mo.* Should anything tease you,
    Annoy, or displease you,
Remember what Lilly says, '*Animum rege!*' [1]
And as for that shocking bad habit of swearing,—
In all good society voted past bearing,—
Eschew it!—and leave it to dustmen and mobs,
Nor commit yourself much beyond 'Zooks!' or 'Ods-bobs!'

2*do.* When asked out to dine by a Person of Quality,
Mind, and observe the most strict punctuality!—
    For should you come late,
    And make dinner wait,
And the victuals get cold, you'll incur, sure as fate,
The Master's displeasure, the Mistress's hate—
And—though both may, perhaps, be too well bred to swear,
They heartily *wish* you—I need not say *Where*.

3*tio.* Look well to your Maidservants!—say you expect them
To see to the children, and not to neglect them!—
And if you're a widower, just throw a cursory
Glance in, at times, when you go near the Nursery!—
—Perhaps it's as well to keep children from plums
And from pears in the season,—and sucking their thumbs!

4*to.* To sum up the whole with a 'Saw' of much use,
Be *just,* and be *generous*—don't be *profuse!*—
Pay the debts that you owe,—keep your word to your friends,
But—DON'T SET YOUR CANDLES ALIGHT AT BOTH ENDS!!—

For of this be assured, if you 'go it' too fast,
    You'll be 'dish'd' like Sir Guy,
    And like him, perhaps, die
A poor, old, half-starved Country Parson at last.

---

[1] '*Animum rege! qui nisi paret, imperat*' ('Control the temper! which, if it does not obey, commands').—LILLY'S *Grammar*.

THE LAY OF ST ALOYS

A Legend of Blois

'*S. Heloïus in hâc urbe fuit episcopus, qui, defunctus, sepulturus est a fidelibus. Nocte autem sequenti, veniens quidam paganus lapidem, qui sarcophagum tegebat, revolvit, erectumque contra se corpus Sancti spoliare conatur. At ille, lacertis constrictum, ad se hominem fortiter amplexatur, et usque mane, populis spectantibus, tanquam constipatum loris, ita miserum brachiis detinebat. . . . Judex loci sepulchri violatorem jubet abstrahi, et legali poenae sententiâ condemnari; sed non laxabatur a Sancto. Tunc intelligens voluntatem defuncti, Judex, factâ de vitâ promissione, absolvit, deinde laxatur, et sic incolumis redditur: non vero fur demissus quin se vitam monastericam amplexurum spopondisset.*' [1]

GREG: TURONENS: DE GLORIÂ CONFESSORUM.

SAINT ALOYS
    Was the Bishop of Blois,
And a pitiful man was he,
    He grieved and he pined
    For the woes of mankind,
And of brutes in their degree.—
    He would rescue the rat
    From the claws of the cat,
And set the poor captive free;
    Though his cassock was swarming
    With all sorts of vermin,
He'd not take the life of a flea!—
    Kind, tender, forgiving
    To all things living,
From injury still he'd endeavour to screen 'em,
Fish, flesh, or fowl,—no difference between 'em—
    NIHIL PUTAVIT A SE ALIENUM.

[1] 'St Aloys was a bishop in this city who, when he died, was buried by his faithful followers. The following night, however, a pagan came, rolled back the stone which covered the grave, and setting the body of the saint upright before him tried to rob it. But the other, gripping him in his arms, strongly grappled the robber to him, and kept the wretch in his embrace, as though tightly bound with thongs, till morning, when he was seen by the people. .. The local judge commanded that the violator of the tomb should be taken away and condemned to the punishment the law prescribes; but the saint did not let him go. Then the judge, understanding the dead man's wish, promised the thief his life and acquitted him, whereupon he was released and given up unharmed; but the thief was not allowed to leave until he had pledged himself to embrace a monastic life.'

The Bishop of Blois was a holy man,—
    A holy man was he!
For Holy Church
He'd seek and he'd search
    As a Bishop in his degree.
From foe and from friend
He'd 'rap and he'd rend,'
    To augment her treasurie.
Nought would he give, and little he'd lend,
That Holy Church might have more to spend.—
Count Stephen [1] (of Blois) 'was a worthy Peer,
  His breeches cost him but a crown,
He held them sixpence all too dear.
  And so he call'd the Tailor lown.'
Had it been the Bishop instead of the Count.
And he'd overcharged him to half the amount,
  He had knock'd that Tailor down!—
  Not for himself!— He despised the pelf;
He dressed in sackcloth, he dined off delf;
And, when it was cold, in lieu of a surtout,
The good man would wrap himself up in his virtue.[2]
Alack! that a man so holy as he,
So frank and so free in his degree,
And so good and so kind, should mortal be!

Yet so it is—for loud and clear
From St Nicholas' tower, on the listening ear,
    With solemn swell, The deep-toned bell
  Flings to the gale a funeral knell;
    And hark!—at its sound, As a cunning old hound,
When he opens, at once causes all the young whelps
Of the cry to put in their less dignified yelps,
  So—the little bells all, No matter how small,
From the steeples both inside and outside the wall,
    With bell-metal throat Respond to the note,
And join the lament that a prelate so pious is
Forced thus to leave his disconsolate diocese,
  Or, as Blois' Lord May'r Is heard to declare,
'Should leave this here world for to go to that there.'

---

[1] *Teste* Messire Iago, a distinguished subaltern in the Venetian service, *circiter* A.D. 1580. His Biographer, Mr William Shakespeare, a contemporary writer of some note, makes him say '*King* Stephen,' inasmuch as the 'worthy peer' subsequently usurped the crown of England. The anachronism is a pardonable one.—MR SIMPKINSON OF BATH.

[2]   '————Meâ
    Virtute me involvo.'—HOR.

And see, the portals opening wide,
From the Abbey flows the living tide;—
    Forth from the doors   The torrent pours,
Acolytes, Monks, and Friars in scores,
This with his chasuble, that with his rosary,
This from his incense-pot turning his nose awry,
    Holy Father, and Holy Mother,
    Holy Sister, and Holy Brother,
    Holy Son, and Holy Daughter,
    Holy Wafer, and Holy Water;
        Everyone dressed   Like a guest in his best.
In the smartest of clothes they're permitted to wear,
Serge, sackcloth, and shirts of the same sort of hair
As now we make use of to stuff an arm-chair,
Or weave into gloves at three shillings a pair,
And employ for shampooing in cases rheumatic,—a
Special specific, I'm told, for Sciatica.

Through groined arch, and by cloister'd stone,
With mosses and ivy long o'ergrown,
    Slowly the throng   Come passing along,
With many a chaunt and solemn song,
Adapted for holidays, high-days, and Sundays,—
    Dies irae, and *De profundis*,
    Miserere, and *Domine dirige nos*,—
Such as, I hear, to a very slow tune are all,
Commonly chaunted by Monks at a funeral,
    To secure the defunct's repose,
And to give a broad hint to Old Nick, should the news
Of a prelate's decease bring him there on a cruise,
That he'd better be minding his P's and his Q's,
And not come too near,—since they can, if they choose,
Make him shake in his hoofs—as he does not wear shoes.

    Still on they go,   A goodly show,
With footsteps sure, though certainly slow,
Two by two, in a very long row;
    With feathers, and Mutes,   In mourning suits,
Undertaker's men walking in hat-bands and boots,—
Then comes the Crosier, all jewels and gold,
Borne by a lad about eighteen years old;
Next, on a black velvet cushion, the Mitre,
Borne by a younger boy, 'cause it is lighter.
    Eight Franciscans, sturdy and strong,
    Bear, in the midst, the good Bishop along;

Eight Franciscans, stout and tall,
    Walk at the corners, and hold up the pall;
    Eight more hold a canopy high over all,
With eight Trumpeters tooting the Dead March in Saul.—
Behind, as Chief Mourner, the Lord Abbot goes, his
Monks coming after him, all with posies,
And white pocket-handkerchiefs up at their noses,
Which they blow whenever his Lordship blows his—
        And oh! 'tis a comely sight to see
        How Lords and Ladies, of high degree,
        Vail, as they pass, upon bended knee,
While quite as polite are the Squires and the Knights,
In their helmets, and hauberks, and cast-iron tights.

    Ay, 'tis a comely sight to behold,
        As the company march
        Through the rounded arch
        Of that Cathedral old!—
Singers behind 'em, and singers before 'em,
All of them ranging in due decorum,
Around the inside of the *Sanctum Sanctorum,*
    While, brilliant and bright,   An unwonted light
(I forgot to premise this was all done at night)
The links, and the torches, and flambeaux shed
On the sculptured forms of the Mighty Dead,
That rest below, mostly buried in lead,
And above, recumbent in grim repose,
        With their mailed hose,
        And their dogs at their toes,
And little boys kneeling beneath them in rows,
Their hands join'd in pray'r, all in very long clothes,
With inscriptions on brass, begging each who survives,
As they some of them seem to have led so-so-lives,
To Praie for the Sowies of themselves and their wives.—
—The effect of the music, too, really was fine,
When they let the good prelate down into his shrine,
    And by old and young,   The '*Requiem*' was sung;
Nor vernacular French, but a classical tongue,
That is—Latin—I don't think they meddled with Greek—
In short, the whole thing produced—so to speak—
What in Blois they would call a *Coup d'œil magnifique!*

                Yet, surely, when the level ray
                    Of some mild eve's descending sun
                Lights on the village pastor, grey
                    In years ere ours had well begun—

As there—in simplest vestment clad,
   He speaks, beneath the churchyard tree,
In solemn tones—but yet not sad,—
   Of what Man is—what Man shall be!

And clustering round the grave, half hid
   By that same quiet churchyard yew,
The rustic mourners bend, to bid
   The dust they loved a last adieu—

—That ray, methinks, that rests so sheen
Upon each briar-bound hillock green,
So calm, so tranquil, so serene,
Gives to the eye a fairer scene,—
Speaks to the heart with holier breath
Than all this pageantry of Death.—

But *Chacun à son gout*—this is talking at random—
We all know '*De gustibus non disputandum!*'
So canter back, Muse, to the scene of your story,
   The Cathedral of Blois— Where the Sainted Aloys
Is by this time, you'll find, 'left alone in his glory,'
'In the dead of the night,' though with labour opprest,
Some 'mortals' disdain 'the calm blessings of rest';
Your cracksman, for instance, thinks night-time the best
To break open a door, or the lid of a chest;
And the gipsy who close round your premises prowls,
To ransack your hen-roost, and steal all your fowls,
Always sneaks out at night with the bats and the owls,
—So do Witches and Warlocks, Ghosts, Goblins, and Ghouls,
To say nothing at all of these troublesome 'Swells'
Who come from the playhouses, 'flash-kens,' and 'hells,'
To pull off people's knockers, and ring people's bells.

Well—'tis now the hour Ill things have power!
And all who, in Blois, entertain honest views,
Have long been in bed, and enjoying a snooze,—
   Nought is waking Save Mischief and Faking [1]
And a few who are sitting up brewing or baking,
When an ill-looking Infidel, sallow of hue,
Who stands in his slippers some six feet two

---

[1] 'Nix my dolly, pals, *Fake* away!'—words of deep and mysterious import
in the ancient language of Upper Egypt, and recently inscribed on the sacred
standard of Mehemet Ali. They are supposed to intimate, to the initiated in
the art of Abstraction, the absence of all human observation, and to suggest
the propriety of making the best use of their time—and fingers.

(A rather remarkable height for a Jew),
Creeps cautiously out of the churchwarden's pew,
Into which, during service, he'd managed to slide himself—
While all were intent on the anthem, and hide himself.

    From his lurking place,   With stealthy pace,
Through the 'long-drawn aisle' he begins to crawl.
As you see a cat walk on the top of a wall,
When it's stuck full of glass, and she thinks she shall fall.
    —He proceeds to feel   For his flint and steel,
(An invention on which we've improved a great deal
Of late years—the substitute best to rely on
's what Jones of the Strand calls his *Pyrogeneion*,)
    He strikes with dispatch!—his   Tinder catches!—
Now where is his candle?—and where are his matches?—
    'Tis done!—they are found!—
    He stands up, and looks round
By the light of a 'dip' of sixteen to the pound!
—What is it that now makes his nerves to quiver?—
His hand to shake—and his limbs to shiver?—
Fear?—Pooh!—it is only a touch of the liver,—
    All is silent—all is still—
It's 'gammon'—it's 'stuff!'—he may do what he will!
Carefully now he approaches the shrine,
In which, as I've mentioned before, about nine,
They had placed in such state the lamented Divine!
But not to worship—No!—No such thing!—
His aim is—TO 'PRIG' THE PASTORAL RING!!

    Fancy his fright,   When, with all his might
Having forced up the lid, which they'd not fastened quite,
Of the marble sarcophagus—'All in white'
The dead Bishop started up, bolt upright
On his hinder end,—and grasped him so tight,
    That the clutch of a kite,   Or a bull-dog's bite
When he's most provoked and in bitterest spite,
Mat well be conceived in comparison slight,
And having thus 'tackled' him—blew out his light!!

    Oh dear! Oh, dear!   The fright and the fear!—
        No one to hear!—nobody near!—
In the dead of the night!—at a bad time of year!—
A defunct Bishop squatting upright on his bier,
And shouting so loud, that the drum of his ear

He thought would have split as these awful words met it—
'AH, HA! MY GOOD FRIEND!—DON'T YOU WISH YOU MAY GET
 IT?'—
 Oh, dear! Oh, dear! 'Twas a night of fear!
—I should just like to know, if the boldest man here,
In his situation, would not have felt queer?

 The wretched man bawls,
  And he yells, and he squalls,
But there's nothing responds to his shrieks save the walls,
And the desk, and the pulpit, the pews, and the stalls.
 Held firmly at bay, Kick and plunge as he may,
His struggles are fruitless—he can't get away,
He really can't tell what to do or to say,
And being a Pagan, don't know how to pray;
Till, through the east window, a few streaks of grey
Announce the approach of the dawn of the day!

 Oh, a welcome sight Is the rosy light,
Which lovelily heralds a morning bright,
Above all to a wretch kept in durance all night
By a horrid dead gentleman holding him tight,—
Of all sorts of gins that a trespasser can trap,
The most disagreeable kind of a man trap!
 —Oh! welcome that bell's Matin chime, which tells
To one caught in this worst of all possible snares,
That the hour is arrived to begin Morning Prayer,
And the monks and the friars are coming downstairs!

 Conceive the surprise
  Of the Choir—how their eyes
Are distended to twice their original size,—
How some begin bless,—some anathematize,—
And all look on the thief as Old Nick in disguise.
While the mystified Abbot cries, 'Well!—I declare!—
—This is really a very mysterious affair!—
Bid the bandy-legg'd sexton go run for the May'r!'

 The May'r and his suite
  Are soon on their feet—
(His worship kept house in the very same street—).
 At once he awakes, 'His compliments' makes,
'He'll be up at the Church in a couple of shakes!'
Meanwhile the whole Convent is pulling and hauling,
 And bawling and squalling, And terribly mauling

The thief whose endeavour to follow his calling
Had thus brought him into a grasp so enthralling.—
   Now high, now low,   They drag 'to and fro,'—
Now this way, now that way they twist him but—No!—
The glazed eye of St Aloys distinctly says 'Poh!
You may pull as you please, I shall *not* let him go!'
Nay, more;—when his Worship at length came to say
He was perfectly ready to take him away,
And fat him to grace the next *Auto-da-fé*,
   Still closer he pressed   The poor wretch to his breast,
While a voice—though his jaws still together were jamm'd—
Was heard from his chest, 'If you do, I'll——' here slamm'd
The great door of the Church,—with so awful a sound
That the close of the good Bishop's sentence was drown'd!
      Out spake *Frère Jehan*. A pitiful man,
        Oh! a pitiful man was he!
       And he wept, and he pined
       For the sins of mankind,
        As a Friar in his degree.
'Remember, good gentlefolks,' so he began,
'Dear Aloys was always a pitiful man!—
   That voice from his chest   Has clearly expressed
He has pardoned the culprit—and as for the rest,
Before you shall burn him—he'll see you all blessed!'

The Monks, and the Abbot, the Sexton, and Clerk
Were exceedingly struck with the Friar's remark,
And the Judge, who himself was by no means a shark
Of a Lawyer, and who did not do things in the dark,
But still leaned (having once been himself a gay spark)
To the merciful side,—like the late Alan Park,—
   Agreed that, indeed,   The best way to succeed,
And by which this poor caitiff alone could be freed,
Would be to absolve him, and grant a free pardon,
On a certain condition, and that not a hard one,
Viz.—'That he, the said Infidel, straightway should ope
His mind to conviction, and worship the Pope,
And "ev'ry man Jack" in an amice or cope;—
   And that, to do so,   He should forthwith go
To Rome, and salute there His Holiness' toe;—
   And never again   Read Voltaire, or Tom Paine,
Or Percy Bysshe Shelley, or Lord Byron's *Cain*:—
His pilgrimage o'er, take St Francis's habit;—
If anything lay about, never to "nab" it;—
Or, at worst, if he *should* light on articles gone astray,
To be sure and deposit them safe in the Monast'ry!'
* I 185

The oath he took—   —As he kiss'd the book,
Nave, transept, and aisle with a thunder-clap shook!
The Bishop sank down with a satisfied look,
    And the Thief, releas'd   By the Saint deceas'd,
Fell into the arms of a neighbouring Priest!

    It skills not now   To tell you how
The transmogrified Pagan perform'd his vow;
    How he quitted his home,   Travell'd to Rome,
And went to St Peter's, and look'd at the Dome,
And obtain'd from the Pope an assurance of bliss,
And kiss'd—whatever he gave him to kiss—
Toe, relic, embroidery, naught came amiss;
    And how Pope Urban   Had the man's turban
Hung up in the Sistine chapel, by way
Of a relic—and how it hangs there to this day.—

    Suffice it to tell,   Which will do quite as well,
That the whole of the Convent the miracle saw,
And the Abbot's report was sufficient to draw
Ev'ry *bon Catholique* in *la belle France* to Blois,
Among others, the Monarch himself, François,
The Archbishop of Rheims, and his 'Pious Jack-daw,' [1]
And there was not a man in Church, Chapel, or Meeting-house,
Still less in Cabaret, Hotel, or Eating-house,
    But made an oration,   And said, 'In the nation
If ever a man deserved canonization,
It was the kind, pitiful, pious Aloys.'—
    So the Pope says,—says he,'   Then a Saint he shall be!'
So he made him a Saint,—and remitted the fee.

What became of the Pagan I really can't say;
    But I think I've been told,   When he'd enter'd their fold,
And was now a Franciscan some twenty days old,
He got up one fine morning before break of day,
Put the Pyx in his pocket—and then ran away.

MORAL

I think we may coax out a moral or two
From the facts which have lately come under our view.
First—Don't meddle with Saints!—for you'll find if you do,
They're what Scotch people call, 'kittle cattle to shoe!'
And when once they have managed to take you in tow,
It's a deuced hard matter to make them let go!

[1] *Vide* page 41.

Now to you, wicked Pagans!—who wander about,
Up and down Regent Street every night, 'on the scout,'—
Recollect the Police keep a sharpish look-out,
And, if once you're suspected, your skirts they will stick to,
Till they catch you at last *in flagrante delicto!*—
    Don't the inference draw   That because he of Blois
Suffer'd *one* to bilk 'Old father Antic the Law,'
That *our* May'rs and *our* Aldermen—and we've a City full—
Show themselves, at *our* Guildhall, quite so pitiful!

Lastly, as to the Pagan who play'd such a trick,
First assuming the tonsure, then cutting his stick,
There is but one thing which occurs to me—that
Is,—Don't give too much credit to people who 'rat'!
    —Never forget   Early habit's a net
Which entangles us all, more or less, in its mesh;
And 'What's bred in the bone won't come out of the flesh!'
We must all be aware Nature's prone to rebel, as
Old Juvenals tell us, *Naturam expellas,*
    Tamen usque recurret!   There's no making Her rat
So that all that I have on this head to advance
Is,—whatever they think of these matters in France,
There's a proverb, the truth of which each one allows here,
'YOU NEVER CAN MAKE A SILK PURSE OF A SOW'S EAR!'

THE LAY OF THE OLD WOMAN
CLOTHED IN GREY

A LEGEND OF DOVER

ONCE there lived, as I've heard people say,
An 'Old Woman clothed in grey,'
    So furrow'd with care,   So haggard her air,
In her eye such a wild supernatural stare,
    That all who espied her   Immediately shied her,
And strove to get out of her way.

This fearsome Old Woman was taken ill:
—She sent for the Doctor—he sent her a pill,
    And by way of a trial,   A two-shilling phial

Of green-looking fluid, like lava diluted,
To which I've profess'd an abhorrence most rooted,[1]
One of those draughts they so commonly send us,
Labell'd '*Haustus catharticus mane sumendus*';
   She made a wry face,   And, without saying Grace,
Toss'd it off like a dram—it improv'd not her case.
   —The Leech came again;   He now open'd a vein,
Still the little Old Woman continued in pain.
So her 'Medical Man,' although loth to distress her,
Conceived it high time that her Father Confessor
Should be sent for to shrive, and assoilzie, and bless her,
That she might not slip out of these troublesome scenes
'Unanneal'd and Unhouseled,'—whatever that means.[2]

   Growing afraid,   He calls to his aid
A bandy-legg'd neighbour, a '*Tailor by trade*,'[3]
   Tells him his fears,   Bids him lay by his shears,
His thimble, his goose, and his needle, and hie
With all possible speed to the Convent hard by,
   Requests him to say   That he begs they'll all pray
Viz.: The whole pious brotherhood, Cleric and Lay,
For the soul of an Old Woman clothed in grey,
Who was just at that time in a very bad way,
And he really believed couldn't last out the day;—
   And to state his desire   That some erudite Friar
Would run over at once, and examine, and try her;
   For he thought he would find
   There was 'something behind,'
A something that weigh'd on the Old Woman's mind,—
'In fact he was sure, from what fell from her tongue,
That this little Old Woman had done something wrong.'
—Then he wound up the whole with this hint to the man,
'Mind and pick out as holy a friar as you can!'

   Now I'd have you to know   That this story of woe,
Which I'm telling you, happen'd a long time ago;
I can't say exactly *how* long, nor, I own,
What particular monarch was then on the throne,

---

[1] *Vide* page 116.
[2] Alack for poor William Linley to settle the point! His elucidation of Macbeth's 'Hurlyburly' casts a halo around his memory. In him the world lost one of its kindliest Spirits, and the Garrick Club its acutest commentator.
[3] All who are familiar with the Police Reports, and other Records of our Courts of Justice, will recollect that every gentleman of this particular profession invariably thus describes himself, in contradistinction to the Bricklayer, whom he probably presumes to be indigenous, and to the Shoemaker, *born* a Snob.

But 'twas here in Old England: and all that one knows is,
It must have preceded the Wars of the Roses.[1]
    Inasmuch as the times   Described in these rhymes
Were as fruitful in virtues as ours are in crimes;
    And if 'mongst the Laity   Unseemly gaiety
Sometimes betray'd an occasional taint or two,
    At once all the Clerics   Went into hysterics,
While scarcely a convent but boasted its Saint or two;
So it must have been long ere the line of the Tudors,
    As since then the breed   Of Saints rarely indeed
With their dignified presence have darken'd our pew doors.
—Hence the late Mr Froude, and the live Dr Pusey
We moderns consider as each worth a Jew's eye;
Though Wiseman, and Dullman [2] combined against Newman,
With Doctors and Proctors, and say he's no true man.
—But this by the way.—The Convent I speak about
Had Saints in scores—they said Mass week and week about;
And the two now on duty were each, for their piety,
'Second to none' in that holy society,
    And well might have borne
    Those words which are worn
By our '*Nulli Secundus*' Club—poor dear lost muttons
Of Guardsmen—on Club days, inscribed on their buttons.—
    They would read, write, and speak
    Latin, Hebrew, and Greek,
A radish-bunch munch for a lunch,—or a leek;
    Though scoffers and boobies   Ascribe certain rubies
That garnished the nose of the good Father Hilary
To the overmuch use of Canary and Sillery,
—Some said spirituous compounds of viler distillery—
    Ah! little reck'd they   That with Friars, who say
Fifty *Paters* a night, and a hundred a day,
A very slight sustenance goes a great way—
Thus the consequence was that his colleague, Basilius
Won golden opinions, by looking more bilious,
From all who conceived strict monastical duty
By no means conducive to personal beauty;
And being more meagre, and thinner and paler,
He was snapped up at once by the bandy-legg'd Tailor.

[1] 'An antient and most pugnacious family,' says our Bath friend. 'One of their descendants, George Rose, Esq., late M.P. for Christchurch (an elderly gentleman now defunct), was equally celebrated for his vocal abilities and his wanton destruction of furniture when in a state of excitement.—'Sing, old Rose, and burn the bellows!' has grown into a proverb.

[2] The worthy Jesuit's polemical publisher.—I am not quite sure as to the orthography;—it's *idem sonans*, at all events.

The latter's concern   For a speedy return
Scarce left the Monk time to put on stouter sandals,
Or go round to his shrines, and snuff all his Saint's candles;
Still less had he leisure to change the hair-shirt he
Had worn the last twenty years—probably thirty,—
Which, not being wash'd all that time, had grown dirty.
   —It seems there's a sin in
   The wearing clean linen,
Which Friars must eschew at the very beginning,
Though it makes them look frowsy, and drowsy, and blowsy,
And—a rhyme modern etiquette never allows ye.—
   As for the rest   E'en if time had not pressed,
It didn't much matter how Basil was dressed,
Nor could there be any great need for adorning,
The Night being almost at odds with the Morning.

Oh! sweet and beautiful is Night,
   When the silver Moon is high,
And countless Stars, like clustering gems,
   Hang sparkling in the sky,
While the balmy breath of the summer breeze
   Comes whispering down the glen,
And one fond voice alone is heard—
   Oh! Night is lovely then!
But when that voice, in feeble moans
   Of sickness and of pain,
But mocks the anxious ear that strives
   To catch its sounds in vain,—
When silently we watch the bed,
   By the taper's flickering light,
Where all we love is fading fast—
   How terrible is Night!!

More terrible yet,   If you happen to get
By an old woman's bedside, who, all her life long,
Has been what the vulgar call, 'coming it strong'
In all sorts of ways that are naughty and wrong.—

As Confessions are sacred, it's not very facile
To ascertain what the old hag said to Basil;
   But whatever she said,   It fill'd him with dread,
And made all his hair stand on end on his head,—
No great feat to perform, inasmuch as said hair
Being clipp'd by the tonsure, his crown was left bare,
So of course Father Basil had little to spare;
   But the little he had
   Seem'd as though't had gone mad,

Each lock, as by action galvanic, uprears
In the two little tufts on the tops of his ears.—
  What the old woman said
  That so 'fill'd him with dread,'
We should never have known any more than the dead
If the bandy-legg'd Tailor, his errand thus sped,
Had gone quietly back to his needle and thread,
  As he ought; but instead, Curiosity led,—
A feeling we all deem extremely ill-bred,—
He contrived to secrete himself under the bed!
  —Not that he heard One half, or a third
Of what passed as the Monk and the Patient conferred,
But he here and there managed to pick up a word,
  Such as 'Knife,' And 'Life,'
And he thought she said 'Wife,'
And 'Money,' that source of all evil and strife; [1]
Then he plainly distinguished the words 'Gore,' and 'Gash,'
Whence he deem'd—and I don't think his inference rash—
She had cut someone's throat for the sake of his cash!

  Intermix'd with her moans,
  And her sighs, and her groans,
Enough to have melted the hearts of the stones,
Came at intervals Basil's sweet, soft silver tones,
For somehow it happened—I can't tell you why—
The good Friar's indignation,—at first rather high,—
To judge from the language he used in reply,
Ere the Old Woman ceased, had a good deal gone by;
And he gently addressed her in accents of honey,
'Daughter, don't you despair!—WHAT'S BECOME OF
    THE MONEY?'

In one just at Death's door it was really absurd
To see how her eye lighted up at that word—
Indeed there's not one in the language that I know
(Save its synonyms 'Spanish,' 'Blunt,' 'Stumpy,' and 'Rhino')
  Which acts so direct, And with so much effect
On the human sensorium, or makes one erect
One's ears so, as soon as the sound we detect—
  It's a question with me Which of the three,
Father Basil himself, though a grave S. T. P.
(Such as he have, you see, the degree of D.D.)
Or the eavesdropping, bandy-legg'd Tailor,—or She
Caught it quickest—however, traditions agree
That the Old Woman perked up as brisk as a bee,—

---

[1] 'Effodiuntur Opes Irritamenta Malorum.'
LILLY's *Grammar*

'Twas the last quivering flare of the taper,—the fire
It so often emits when about to expire!
Her excitement began the same instant to flag,
She sank back, and whisper'd 'Safe!—Safe! in the Bag!!'

Now I would not by any means have you suppose
That the good Father Basil was just one of those
    Who entertain views   We're so apt to abuse,
As neither befitting Turks, Christians, nor Jews,
    Who haunt deathbed scenes,   By underhand means
To toady or tease people out of a legacy,—
For few folk, indeed, had such good right to beg as he,
Since Rome, in her pure Apostolical beauty,
Not only permits, but enjoins, as a duty,
    Her sons to take care   That, let who will be heir,
The Pontiff shall not be chous'd out of his share,
Nor stand any such mangling of chattels and goods,
As, they say, was the case with the late Jemmy Wood's;
Her Conclaves, and Councils, and Synods, in short, main
-tain principles adverse to statutes of Mortmain;
    Besides, you'll discern   It at once, when you learn
That Basil had something to give in return,
Since it rested with him to say how she would burn,
Nay, as to her ill-gotten wealth, should she turn it all
To uses he named, he could say, 'You shan't burn at all,
    Or nothing to signify,   Not what you'd dignify
So much as even to call it a roast,
But a mere little singeing, or scorching at most,—
What many would think not unpleasantly warm,—
Just to keep up appearance—mere matter of form.'
    All this in her ear—He declared, but I fear
That her senses were wand'ring—she seem'd not to hear,
Or, at least understand,—for mere unmeaning talk her
Parch'd lips babbled now,—such as 'Hookey!'—and 'Walker!'
—She expired, with her last breath expressing a doubt
If 'his Mother were fully aware he was out?'

Now it seems there's a place they call Purgat'ry—so
I must write it, my verse not admitting the O—
But as for the venue, I vow I'm perplexed
To say if it's in this world, or if in the next—
Or whether in both—for 'tis very well known
That St Patrick, at least, has got one of his own,
In a 'tight little Island' that stands in a Lake
Call'd 'Lough-dearg'—that's 'The Red Lake,' unless I
    mistake,—

In Fermanagh—or Antrim—or Donegal—which
   I declare I can't tell,   But I know very well
It's in latitude 54, nearly their pitch
(At Tappington, now, I could look in the Gazetteer,
But I'm out on a visit, and nobody has it here).
   There are some, I'm aware   Who don't stick to declare
There's 'no differ' at all 'twixt 'this here' and 'that there,'
That it's all the same place, but the Saint reserves his entry
From the separate use of the 'finest of pisentry,'
   And that his is no more   Than a mere private door
For the *rez-de-chaussée*,—as some call the ground floor,—
To the one which the Pope had found out long before.
   But no matter—lay   The locale where you may;
—And where it is no one exactly can say—
There's one thing, at least, which is known very well,
That it acts as a Tap-room to Satan's Hotel.
   'Entertainment' there's worse
   Both for 'Man and for Horse';
   For broiling the souls
   They use Lord Mayor's coals;—
Then the sulphur's inferior, and boils up much slower
Than the fine fruity brimstone they give you down lower,
   It's by no means so strong—
   Mere sloe-leaves to Souchong;
The 'prokers' are not half so hot, or so long,
By an inch or two, either in handle or prong;
The Vipers and Snakes are less sharp in the tooth,
And the Nondescript Monsters not near so uncouth;—
In short, it's a place the good Pope, its creator,
Made for what's called by Cockneys a 'Minor The-átre.'
Better suited, of course, for a 'minor performer,'
Than the 'House,' that's so much better lighted and warmer,
Below, in that queer place which nobody mentions,—
   —You don't understand where,
   I don't question—down there,
Where, in lieu of wood blocks, and such modern inventions,
The Paving Commissioners use 'Good Intentions,'
Materials which here would be thought on by few men,
With so many founts of Asphaltic bitumen
At hand, at the same time to pave and illumine.

   To go on with my story,   This same Purga-tory
(There! I've got in the O, to my Muse's great glory)
Is close lock'd, and the Pope keeps the keys of it—that I can
Boldly affirm—in his desk in the Vatican;
   —Not those of St Peter—
   Those of which I now treat, are

A bunch by themselves, and much smaller and neater—
And so cleverly made, Mr Chubb could not frame a
Key better contrived for its purpose—nor Bramah.
    Now it seems that by these   Most miraculous keys
Not only the Pope, but his 'clargy,' with ease
Can let people in and out, just as they please;
And—provided you 'make it all right' about fees,
There is not a friar, Dr Wiseman will own, of them,
But can always contrive to obtain a short loan of them;
    And Basil, no doubt,   Had brought matters about,
If the little old woman would but have 'spoke out,'
So far as to get for her one of those tickets,
Or passes, which clear both the great gates and wickets;
    So that after a grill,   Or short turn on the Mill,
And with no worse a singeing, to purge her iniquity,
Than a Freemason gets in the 'Lodge of Antiquity,'
        She'd have rubb'd off old scores,
        Popp'd out of doors,
And sheer'd off at once for a happier port,
Like a whitewash'd Insolvent that's 'gone through the Court.'

    But Basil was one   Who was not to be *done*
By anyone, either in earnest or fun;—
The cunning old beads-telling son of a gun,
In all bargains, unless he'd his *quid* for his *quo,*
Would shake his bald pate, and pronounce it 'No Go.'
    So, unless you're a dunce,   You'll see clearly, at once,
When you come to consider the facts of the case, he
Of course never gave her his *Vade in pace*;
And the consequence was, when the last mortal throe
Released her pale Ghost from these regions of woe,
The little Old Woman had nowhere to go!

    For, what could she do?   She very well knew
If she went to the gates I have mention'd to you,
Without Basil's, or some other passport to show,
The Cheque-takers never would let her go through;
While, as to *the other place*, e'en had she tried it,
And really had wished it, as much as she shied it
(For no one who knows what it is can abide it),
Had she knock'd at the portal with ne'er so much din,
Though she died in, what folks at Rome call, 'Mortal sin,'
Yet Old Nick, for the life of him, daren't take her in,
As she'd not been turn'd formally out of 'the pale';—
So much the bare name of the Pope made him quail,
In the times that I speak of, his courage would fail

Of Rome's vassals the lowest and worst to assail,
Or e'en touch with so much as the end of his tail;
   Though, now he's grown older,
   They say he's much bolder,
And his Holiness not only gets the 'cold shoulder,'
But Nick rumps him completely, and don't seem to care a
Dump—that's the word—for his triple tiara.

   Well—what shall she do?—
   What's the course to pursue?—
'Try St Peter?—the step is a bold one to take;
For the Saint is, there can't be a doubt, "wide awake";
   But then there's a quaint Old Proverb says, "Faint
Heart ne'er won fair Lady," then how win a Saint?—
   I've a great mind to try— One can but apply;
If things come to the worst, why he can but deny—
   The sky's rather high To be sure—but, now I
That cumbersome carcass of clay have laid by,
I am just in the "order" which some folks—though why
I am sure I can't tell you—would call "Apple-pie."
   Then "never say die!" It won't do to be shy,
So I'll tuck up my shroud, and—here goes for a fly!'—
—So said and so done—she was off like a shot,
And kept on the whole way at a pretty smart trot.

   When she drew so near That the Saint could see her,
In a moment he frown'd, and began to look queer,
And scarce would allow her to make her case clear,
Ere he pursed up his mouth 'twixt a sneer and a jeer,
With 'It's all very well—but you do not lodge here!'—
   Then, calling her everything but 'My dear!'
He applied his great toe with some force *au derrière*,
And dismissed her at once with a flea in her ear.

   'Alas! poor Ghost!' It's a doubt which is most
To be pitied—one doom'd to fry, broil, boil, and roast,—
Or one bandied about thus from pillar to post,—
To be 'all abroad'—to be 'stump'd' not to know where
   To go—so disgraced As not to be 'placed,'
Or, as Crocky would say to Jem Bland, 'To be Nowhere.'—
   However that be, The *affaire* was *finie*,
And the poor wretch rejected by all, as you see!

Mr Oliver Goldsmith observes—not the Jew—
That the 'Hare whom the hounds and the huntsmen pursue,'
Having no other sort of asylum in view,

'Returns back again to the place whence she flew,'—
A fact which experience has proved to be true.—
Mr Gray,—in opinion with whom Johnson clashes,—
Declares that our 'wonted fires live in our ashes.' [1]—
These motives combined, perhaps, brought back the hag,
The first to her mansion, the last to her bag,
When only conceive her dismay and surprise,
As a Ghost how she open'd her cold stony eyes,
When there,—on the spot where she'd hid her 'supplies,'—
In an underground cellar of very small size,
    Working hard with a spade,   All at once she survey'd
That confounded old bandy-legged 'Tailor by trade.'

    Fancy the tone   Of the half moan, half groan,
Which burst from the breast of the Ghost of the crone!
As she stood there,—a figure 'twixt moonshine and stone,—
Only fancy the glare in her eyeballs that shone!
Although, as Macbeth says, 'they'd no speculation,'
    While she uttered that word,   Which American Bird
Or James Fenimore Cooper, would render, 'Tarnation!!'
    At the noise which she made
    Down went the spade!—
And up jump'd the bandy-legg'd 'Tailor by trade'
(Who had shrewdly conjectured, from something that fell, her
Deposit was somewhere concealed in the cellar);
    Turning round at a sound   So extremely profound,
The moment her shadowy form met his view
He gave vent to a sort of lengthen'd 'Bo-o—ho-o!'—
With a countenance Keeley alone could put on,
Made one grasshopper spring to the door—and was gone!
    Erupit! Evasit!
    As at Rome they would phrase it—
His flight was so swift, the eye scarcely could trace it,
Though elderly, bandy-legg'd, meagre, and sickly,
I doubt if the Ghost could have vanish'd more quickly;—
He reach'd his own shop, and then fell into fits,
And it's said never rightly recover'd his wits,
While the chuckling old Hag takes his place, and there sits!

    I'll venture to say,   She'd sat there to this day,
Brooding over what Cobbett calls 'vile yellow clay,'
Like a Vulture, or other obscene bird of prey,
O'er the nest-full of eggs she has managed to lay,

---

[1] 'E'en in our ashes live their wonted fires!'—GRAY.

'A position at which Experience revolts, Credulity hesitates, and even Fancy stares!'—JOHNSON.

If, as legends relate, and I think we may trust 'em, her
Stars had not brought her another guess customer—
   'Twas Basil himself!— Come to look for her pelf:
But not, like the tailor, to dig, delve, and grovel,
And grub in the cellar with pickaxe and shovel;
   Full well he knew Such tools would not do,—
Far other the weapons he brought into play,
Viz. a Wax-taper 'hallow'd on Candlemas-day,'
   To light to her ducats,— Holy Water, two buckets
(Made with salt—half a peck to four gallons—which brews a
Strong triple X 'strike,'—see Jacobus de Chusa).
   With these, too, he took His bell and his book—
Not a nerve ever trembled,—his hand never shook
As he boldly march'd up where she sat in her nook,
Glow'ring round with that wild indescribable look,
Which *Some* may have read of, perchance, in 'Nell Cook,' [1]
All, in *Martha the Gipsy* by Theodore Hook.

And now, for the reason I gave you before,
Of what passed then and there I can tell you no more,
As no Tailor was near with his ear at the door;
   But I've always been told, With respect to the gold,
For which she her 'jewel eternal' had sold,
   That the old Harridan, Who, no doubt, knew her man,
Made some compromise—hit upon some sort of plan,
By which Friar and Ghost were both equally pinn'd—
Heaven only knows how the 'Agreement' got wind;—
   But its purport was this, That the things done amiss
By the Hag should not hinder her ultimate bliss;
   Provided—'*Imprimis*, The cash from this time is
The Church's—impounded for good pious uses—
—Father B. shall dispose of it just as he chooses,
   And act as trustee— In the meantime, that She,
The said Ghostess,—or Ghost,—as the matter may be,
From "impediment," "hindrance," and "let" shall be free,
To sleep in her grave, or wander, as he,
The said Friar, with said Ghost may hereafter agree.—
   Moreover—The whole Of the said cash, or "cole,"
Shall be spent for the good of said Old Woman's soul!

'It is farther agreed—while said cash is so spending,
Said Ghost shall be fully absolv'd from attending,
   And shall quiet remain In the grave, her domain,
To have, and enjoy, and uphold, and maintain,

---

[1] See page 177.

Without molestation, or trouble, or pain,
Hindrance, let, or impediment, (over again)
From Old Nick, or from anyone else of his train,
Whether Pow'r,—Domination,—or Princedom,—or Throne,[1]
Or by what name soever the same may be known,
Howsoe'er called by Poets, or styled by Divines,—
Himself,—his executors, heirs, and assigns.

'Provided that,—nevertheless,—notwithstanding
All herein contained,—if whoever's a hand in
Dispensing said cash,—or said "cole,"—shall dare venture
To misapply money, note, bill, or debenture
To uses not named in this present Indenture,
Then that such sum, or sums, shall revert, and come home again
Back to said Ghost,—who thenceforward shall roam again
Until such time, or times, as the said Ghost produces
Some good man and true, who no longer refuses
To put sum, or sums, aforesaid, to said uses;
Which duly performed, the said Ghost shall have rest,
The full term of her natural death, of the best,
In full consideration of this, her bequest,
In manner and form aforesaid,—as expressed:—
In witness whereof, we, the parties aforesaid,
Hereunto set our hands and our seals—and no more said,
Being all that these presents intend to express,
Whereas—notwithstanding—and nevertheless.—

'Sign'd, sealed, and deliver'd, this 20th of May,
Anno Domini, blank (though I've mentioned the day),
(Signed)
         BASIL.
             OLD WOMAN (late) CLOTHED IN GREY.'

Basil now, I am told,   Walking off with the gold,
Went and straight got the document duly enroll'd,
And left the testatrix to mildew and mould
In her sepulchre, cosy, cool,—not to say cold.
But somehow—though how I can hardly divine,—
   A runlet of fine   Rich Malvoisie wine
Found its way to the Convent that night before nine,
With custards, and 'flawns' and a 'fayre florentine,'
Peach, apricot, nectarine, melon, and pine;—
And some half a score Nuns of the rule Bridgetine,
Abbess and all, were invited to dine
At a very late hour,—that is after Compline.—

---

[1] Thrones! Dominations! Princedoms! Virtues! Powers!

—Father Hilary's rubies began soon to shine
With fresh lustre, as though newly dug from the mine;
  Through all the next year, Indeed, 'twould appear
That the Convent was much better off, as to cheer,
Even Basil himself, as I very much fear,
No longer addicted himself to small beer;
  His complexion grew clear, While in front and in rear
He enlarged so, his shape seem'd approaching a sphere.

No wonder at all, then, one cold winter's night,
That a servant girl going downstairs with a light
To the cellar we've spoken of, saw, with affright,
An Old Woman, astride on a barrel, invite
Her to take, in a manner extremely polite,
With her left hand, a bag, she had got in her right;—
For tradition asserts that the Old Woman's purse
Had come back to her *scarcely one penny the worse*!

  The girl, as they say, Ran screaming away,
Quite scared by the Old Woman clothed in grey;
But there came down a Knight, at no distant a day,
  Sprightly and gay As the bird on the spray,
One Sir Rufus Mountfardington, Lord of Foot's-cray,
Whose estate, not unlike those of most of our 'Swell' beaux.
Was, what's, by a metaphor, term'd 'out at elbows';
And the fact was, said Knight was now merely delay'd
From crossing the water to join the Crusade
For converting the Pagans with bill, bow, and blade,
By the want of a little pecuniary aid
To buy arms and horses, the tools of his trade,
And enable his troop to appear on parade;—
  The unquiet Shade Thought Sir Rufus, 'tis said,
Just the man for her money,—she readily paid
For the articles named, and with pleasure convey'd
To his hands every farthing she ever had made;
  But alas! I'm afraid Most unwisely she laid
Out her cash—the *beaux yeux* of a Saracen maid
(Truth compels me to say a most pestilent jade)
Converted the gallant converter—betray'd
Him to do everything which a Knight could degrade,
—E'en to worship Mahound!—She required—He obey'd,—
The consequence was, all the money was wasted
On Infidel pleasures he should not have tasted;
So that, after a very short respite, the Hag
Was seen down in her cellar again with her bag.

Don't fancy, dear Reader, I mean to go on
Seriatim through so many ages by-gone,
   And to bore you with names
   Of the Squires, and the Dames,
Who have managed, at times, to get hold of the sack,
But spent the cash so that it always came back;
   The list is too long To be giv'n in my song,—
There are reasons beside would perhaps make it wrong;
I shall merely observe, in those orthodox days,
When Mary set Smithfield all o'er in a blaze,
   And show'd herself very se- -vere against heresy,
While many a wretch scorned to flinch, or to scream, as he
Burnt for denying the Papal supremacy,
   Bishop Bonner the bag got,
   And all thought the Hag got
Releas'd, as he spent all in fuel and faggot.—
   But somehow—though how I can't tell you, I vow—
I suppose by mismanagement—ere the next reign
The Spectre had got all her money again.—

   The last time, I'm told, That the Old Woman's gold
Was obtained,—as before,—for the asking,—'twas had
By a Mr O—Something—from Ballinafad;
And the whole of it, so 'tis reported, was sent
To John Wright's, in account for the Catholic Rent,
And thus—like a great deal more money—'it went'!
   So 'tis said at Maynooth, But I can't think it's truth;
Though I know it was boldly asserted last season,
Still I can *not* believe it; and that for this reason,
It's certain *the cash has got back to its owner!*—
—Now no part of the Rent to do *so* e'er was known,—or,
In any shape, ever come home to the donor.
GENTLE READER!—you must know the proverb, I think—
'To a blind horse a Nod is as good as a Wink!'
   Which some learned Chap, In a square College cap,
Perhaps would translate by the words '*Verbum Sap!*'

   —Now, should it so chance
   That you're going to France
In the course of next Spring, as you probably may,
   Do pull up, and stay, Pray, If but for a day,
At Dover, through which you must pass on your way,
At the York,—or the Ship,—where, as all people say,
You'll get good wine yourself, and your horses good hay,
Perhaps, my good friend, you may find it will *pay*,
And you cannot lose much by so short a delay.

First DINE!—you can do That on joint or ragout—
Then say to the waiter,—'I'm just passing through,—
Pray,—where can I find out the old *Maison Dieu*?'—
He'll show you the street—(the French call it a *Rue*,
But you won't have to give here a *petit écu*).

Well,—when you've got there,—never mind how you're
    taunted,—
Ask boldly, 'Pray, which is the house here that's haunted?'
—I'd tell you myself, but I can't recollect
The proprietor's name; but he's one of that sect
Who call themselves 'Friends,' and whom others call
    'Quakers,'—
You'll be sure to find out if you ask at the Baker's.—
    Then go down, with a light, To the cellar at night!
And as soon as you see her don't be in a fright!
    But ask the old Hag, At once, for the bag!—
If you find that she's shy, or your senses would dazzle,
Say, 'Ma'am, I insist!—in the name of St Basil!'
    If she gives it you, seize It, and—do as you please—
But there is not a person I've ask'd but agrees,
You should spend—part at least—for the Old Woman's ease!
—For the rest—if it *must* go back some day—why—let it!—
Meanwhile, if you're poor, and in love, or in debt, it
May do you some good, and—
        I WISH YOU MAY GET IT!!!

RAISING THE DEVIL

A LEGEND OF CORNELIUS AGRIPPA

'AND hast thou nerve enough?' he said,
That grey Old Man above whose head
    Unnumber'd years had roll'd.—
'And hast thou nerve to view,' he cried,
'The incarnate Fiend that Heaven defied?—
    —Art thou indeed so bold?

'Say, canst thou, with unshrinking gaze,
Sustain rash youth, the withering blaze
    Of that unearthly eye,
That blasts where'er it lights,—the breath
That, like the Simoom, scatters death
    On all that yet *can* die!

—'Darest thou confront that fearful form,
That rides the whirlwind, and the storm,
　　In wild unholy revel?—
The terrors of that blasted brow,
Archangel's once,—though ruin'd now—
　　Ay,—dar'st thou face THE DEVIL?'—

'I dare!' the desperate Youth replied,
And placed him by that Old Man's side,
　　In fierce and frantic glee,
Unblenched his cheek, and firm his limb;
—No paltry juggling Fiend, but HIM!
　　—THE DEVIL!—I fain would see!—

'In all his Gorgon terrors clad,
His worst, his fellest shape!' the Lad
　　Rejoined in reckless tone.—
—'Have then thy wish!' Agrippa said,
And sigh'd, and shook his hoary head,
　　With many a bitter groan.

He drew the mystic circle's bound,
With skull and cross-bones fenc'd around;
He traced full many a sigil there;
He mutter'd many a backward pray'r,
　　That sounded like a curse—
'He comes!' he cried, with wild grimace,
'The fellest of Apollyon's race!'—
—Then in his startled pupil's face
　　He dash'd an EMPTY PURSE!!

SAINT MEDARD

A Legend of Afric

'*Heus tu! inquit Diabolus, hei mihi! fessis insuper humeris reponenda est sarcina; fer opem, quaeso!*

'*Le Diable a des vices;—c'est là ce qui le perd.—Il est gourmand.   Il eut dans cette minute-là l'idée de joindre l'âme de Medard aux autres âmes qu'il allait emporter.—Se rejeter en arrière, saisir de sa main droite son poignard, et en percer l'outre avec une violence, et une rapidité formidable,—c'est ce que fit Medard.—Le Diable poussa un grand cri.   Les âmes délivrés s'enfuirent par l'issue que le poignard venait de leur ouvrir, laissant dans l'outre leurs noirceurs, leurs crimes, et leurs méchancetés,' etc., etc.[1]*

In good King Dagobert's palmy days,
  When Saints were many, and sins were few,
    Old Nick, 'tis said,   Was sore bested
One evening,—and could not tell what to do.—

He had been East, and he had been West,
  And far had he journey'd o'er land and sea;
    For women and men   Were warier then,
And he could not catch one where now he'd catch three.

He had been North, and he had been South,
  From Zembla's shores unto far Peru,
    Ere he fill'd the sack   Which he bore on his back—
Saints were so many, and sins so few!

The way was long, and the day was hot;
  His wings were weary; his hoofs were sore;
    And scarce could he trail   His nerveless tail,
As it furrowed the sand on the Red Sea shore!

The day had been hot, and the way was long;
  —Hoof-sore, and weary, and faint was he;
    He lower'd his sack,   And the *heat of his back*
As he leaned on a palm-trunk blasted the tree!

[1] "'Hi, you!' said the Devil, "alas, I have to get the pack on my weary shoulders.   Please help me."

'The Devil has vices; that is what ruins him.   He is greedy.   He had at this moment the idea of putting Medard's soul with the other souls that he was going to carry off.   To fling himself backward, seize his dagger in his right hand, and pierce the sack with terrific force and speed, was Medard's action.   The Devil uttered a loud cry.   The rescued souls escaped by the hole that the dagger had just made for them, leaving in the sack their wickedness, their crimes, and their evil ways.'

He sat himself down in the palm-tree's shade,
  And he gaz'd, and he grinn'd in pure delight,
    As he peep'd inside   The buffalo's hide
He had sewn for a sack, and had cramm'd so tight.

For, though he'd 'gone over a good deal of ground,'
  And game had been scarce, he might well report
    That still he had got   A decentish lot,
And had had, on the whole, not a bad day's sport.

He had pick'd up in France a *Maître de Danse*,—
  A *Maîtresse en titre*,—two smart *Grisettes*,
    A Courtier at play,—   And an English *Roué*—
Who had bolted from home without paying his debts.

—He had caught in Great Britain a Scrivener's clerk,
  A Quaker,—a Baker,—a Doctor of Laws,—
    And a Jockey of York—But Paddy from Cork
'Desaved the ould divil,' and slipp'd through his claws!

In Moscow, a Boyar knouting his wife—
  A Corsair's crew, in the Isles of Greece—
    And, under the dome   Of St Peter's, at Rome,
He had snapp'd up a nice little Cardinal's Niece.—

He had bagg'd an Inquisitor fresh from Spain—
  A mendicant Friar—of Monks a score;
    A grave Don or two,   And a Portuguese Jew,
Whom he nabb'd while clipping a new Moidore.

And he said to himself, as he lick'd his lips,
  'Those nice little Dears! what a delicate roast!—
    Then, that fine fat Friar,   At a very quick fire,
Dress'd like a Woodcock, and serv'd on toast!'

—At the sight of titbits so toothsome and choice
  Never did mouth water more than Nick's;
    But,—alas! and alack!—   He had stuff'd his sack
So full that he found himself quite 'in a fix':

For, all he could do, or all he could say,
  When, a little recruited, he rose to go,
    Alas! and alack! he could *not* get the sack
Up again on his shoulders 'whether or no!'

Old Nick look'd East, old Nick look'd West,
   With many a stretch, and with many a strain,
      He bent till his back   Was ready to crack,
And he pull'd and he tugg'd,—but he tugg'd in vain.

Old Nick look'd North, old Nick look'd South;
   Weary was Nicholas, weak, and faint,—
      And he was aware   Of an old man there,
In Palmer's weeds, who look'd much like a Saint.

Nick eyed the Saint,—then he eyed the Sack—
   The greedy old glutton!—And thought, with a grin,
      —'Dear heart alive! If I could but contrive
To pop that elderly gentleman in!—

'For, were I to choose among all the ragouts
   The cuisine can exhibit—flesh, fowl, or fish,—
      To myself I can paint,   That a barbecued Saint
Would be for my palate the best side-dish!'

Now St Medard dwelt on the banks of the Nile,
   —In a Pyramis fast by the lone Red Sea.
      (We call it 'Semiramis,'   Why not say Pyramis!—
Why should we change the S into a D?)

St Medard, he was a holy man,
   A holy man I ween was he,
      And even by day,   When he went to pray,
He would light up a candle, that all might see!

He salaam'd to the East, he salaam'd to the West;—
   —Of the gravest cut, and the holiest brown
      Were his Palmer's weeds,   And he finger'd his beads
With the right side up, and the wrong side down.—

       (*Hiatus in MSS. valde deflendus.*)

St Medard dwelt on the banks of the Nile;—
   He had been living there years fourscore,—
      And now, 'taking the air,   And saying a pray'r,'
He was walking at eve on the Red Sea shore.

Little he deem'd—that Holy man!—
   Of old Nick's wiles, and his fraudful tricks,—
      When he was aware   Of a Stranger there,
Who seem'd to have got himself into a fix.

Deeply that Stranger groan'd and sigh'd,
That wayfaring Stranger, grisly and grey:—
'I can't raise my sack On my poor old back!—
Oh! lend me a lift, kind Gentleman, pray!—

'For I have been East, and I have been West,
Footsore, weary, and faint am I,
And, unless I get home Ere the Curfew bome,
Here in this desert I well may die!'

'Now Heav'n thee save!'—Nick winced at the words,
As ever he winces at words divine—
'Now Heav'n thee save!—
What strength I have,—
It's little, I wis,—shall be freely thine!

'For foul befall that Christian man
Who shall fail, in a fix—woe worth the while!—
His hand to lend To foe, or to friend,
Or to help a lame dog over a stile!'—

—St Medard hath boon'd himself for the task:
To hoist up the sack he doth well begin;
But the fardel feels Like a bag full of eels,
For the folks are all curling, and kicking within.—

St Medard paused—he began to 'smoke'—
For a Saint—if he isn't exactly a cat,—
Has a very good nose, As this world goes,
And not worse than his neighbour's for 'smelling a rat.'

The Saint look'd up, and the Saint look'd down;
He '*smelt* the rat,' and he '*smoked*' the trick;
When he came to view His comical shoe,
He saw in a moment his friend was Nick!

He whipp'd out his oyster-knife, broad and keen—
A Brummagem blade which he always bore,
To aid him to eat, By way of a treat,
The 'natives' he found on the Red Sea shore;—

He whipp'd out his Brummagem blade so keen,
And he made three slits in the Buffalo's hide,
And all its contents,
Through the rents, and the vents,
Came tumbling out,—and away they all hied!

Away went the Quaker,—away went the Baker,
   Away went the Friar—that fine fat Ghost,
     Whose marrow Old Nick Had intended to pick,
Dress'd like a Woodcock, and served on toast!

—Away went the nice little Cardinal's Niece,—
   And the pretty *Grisettes*,—and the Dons from Spain,—
     And the Corsair's Crew,
     And the coin-clipping Jew,—
And they scamper'd, like lamplighters, over the plain!—

Old Nick is a black-looking fellow at best,
   Ay, e'en when he's pleased; but never before
     Had he look'd *so* black As on seeing his sack
Thus cut into slits on the Red Sea shore.

You may fancy his rage, and his deep despair,
   When he saw himself thus befool'd by one
     Whom, in anger wild He profanely styled
'A stupid old snuff-colour'd Son of a gun!'

Then his supper—so nice!—that had cost him such pains—
   Such a hard day's work—now 'all on the go!'
     —'Twas beyond a joke, And enough to provoke
The mildest and best-temper'd Fiend below!

Nick snatch'd up one of those great big stones,
   Found in such numbers on Egypt's plains,
     And he hurl'd it straight At the Saint's bald pate,
To knock out 'the gruel he call'd his brains.'

Straight at his pate he hurl'd the weight,
   The crushing weight of that great big stone;—
     But St Medard Was remarkably hard
And solid about the parietal bone.

And though the whole weight of that great big stone
   Came straight on his pate, with a great big thump,
     It fail'd to graze The skin,—or to raise
On the tough epidermis a lump, or bump!—

As the hail bounds off from the penthouse slope,—
   As the cannon recoils when it sends its shot,—
     As the finger and thumb Of an old woman come
From the kettle she handles, and finds too hot;—

—Or, as you may see, in the Fleet, or the Bench,—
—Many folks do in the course of their lives,—
   The well-struck ball   Rebound from the wall,
When the Gentleman jail-birds are playing at 'fives':

All these,—and a thousand fine similes more,—
   Such as all have heard of, or seen, or read
     Recorded in print,   May give you a hint
How the stone bounced off from St Medard's head!

—And it curl'd, and it twirl'd, and it whirl'd in air,
   As this great big stone at a tangent flew!—
     —Just missing his crown,   It at last came down
Plump upon Nick's Orthopedical shoe!

Oh! what a yell and a screech were there!—
   How did he hop, skip, bellow, and roar!
     —'Oh dear! oh dear!'—
     You might hear him here,
Though we're such a way off from the Red Sea shore!

It smash'd his shin, and it smash'd his hoof,
   Notwithstanding his stout Orthopedical shoe;
     And this is the way   That, from that same day,
Old Nick became what the French call *Boiteux*!

Quakers, and Bakers, *Grisettes*, and Friars,
   And Cardinal's Nieces,—wherever ye be,
     St Medard bless;   You can scarcely do less
If you of your *corps* possess any *esprit*.—

And, mind and take care, yourselves,—and beware
   How you get in Nick's buffalo-bag!—if you do,
     I very much doubt   If you'll ever get out,
Now sins are so many, and Saints so few!!

MORAL

Gentle Reader, attend   To the voice of a friend!
And if ever you go to Herne Bay or Southend,
Or any gay Wat'ring-place outside the Nore,
Don't walk out at eve on the lone seashore!
—Unless you're too Saintly to care about Nick,
And are sure that your head is sufficiently thick!—

Learn not to be greedy!—and, when you've enough,
Don't be anxious your bags any tighter to stuff—
Recollect that good fortune too far you may push,
And, 'A BIRD IN THE HAND IS WORTH TWO IN THE BUSH!'
Then turn not each thought to increasing your store,
Nor look always like 'Oliver asking for more'!

Gourmandise is a vice—a sad failing, at least;—
So remember 'Enough is as good as a feast!'
And don't set your heart on 'stew'd,' 'fried,' 'boil'd,' or 'roast,'
Nor on delicate 'Woodcocks served up upon toast!'

Don't give people nicknames!—don't, even in fun,
Call any one 'snuff-coloured son of a gun!'
Nor fancy, because a man *nous* seems to lack,
That, whenever you please, you can 'give him the sack!'

Last of all, as you'd thrive, and still sleep in whole bones,
IF YOU'VE ANY GLASS WINDOWS, NEVER THROW STONES!!!

THIRD SERIES

THE LORD OF THOULOUSE

A Legend of Languedoc

'Veluti in speculum.' [1]

THEATRE ROYAL COV. GARD.

COUNT RAYMOND rules in Languedoc,
  O'er the champaign fair and wide,
With town and stronghold many a one,
Wash'd by the wave of the blue Garonne,
And from far Auvergne to Rousillon,
    And away to Narbonne,
    And the mouths of the Rhône;
And his Lyonnois silks and his Narbonne honey,
Bring in his lordship a great deal of money.

A thousand lances, stout and true,
Attend Count Raymond's call;
And Knights and Nobles, of high degree,
From Guienne, Provence, and Burgundy,
Before Count Raymond bend the knee,
    And vail to him one and all.

And Isabel of Arragon
  He weds, the pride of Spain,
You might not find so rich a prize,
A Dame so 'healthy, wealthy, and wise';
So pious withal—with such beautiful eyes—
So exactly the Venus de Medicis' size
  In all that wide domain.

    Then his cellar is stored   As well as his board,
With the choicest of all *La Belle France* can afford;
Chambertin, Château Margaux, La Rose, and Lafitte,
With Moet's Champagne, 'of the Comet year,' 'neat
As imported,'—'fine sparkling,'—and not over sweet;

---

[1] 'As in a glass.'

While his Chaplain, good man, when call'd in to say Grace,
Would groan, and put on an elongated face
At such turtle, such turbot, John Dory, and plaice;
Not without blushing, pronouncing a benison,
Worthy old soul! on such *very* fat venison,
  Sighing to think   Such victuals and drink
Are precisely the traps by which Satan makes men his own,
  And grieving o'er scores   Of huge barbecued Boars,
Which he thinks should not darken a Christian man's doors,
Though 'twas all very well Pagan Poets should rate 'em
As '*Animal propter convivia natum.*'

  He was right, I must say,   For at this time of day,
When we're not so precise, whether cleric or lay,
With respect to our food, as in time so *passé*,
We still find our Boars, whether grave ones or gay,
After dinner, at least, very much in the way
(We spell the word now with an E, not an A);
And as honest *Père Jacques* was inclined to spare diet, he
Gave this advice to all grades of society,
'Think less of pudding—and think more of piety.'

  As to his clothes,   Oh! nobody knows
What lots the Count had of cloaks, doublets, and hose,
  Pantoufles, with bows   Each as big as a rose,
And such shirts, with lace ruffles, such waistcoats, and those
Indescribable garments it is not thought right
To do more than whisper to *oreilles* polite.

Still in spite of his power, and in spite of his riches,
In spite of his dinners, his dress, and his——which is
The strangest of all things—in spite of his Wife,
The Count led a rather humdrum sort of life.
He grew tired, in fact, of mere eating and drinking,
Grew tired of flirting, and ogling, and winking
  At nursery maids   As they walk'd the Parades,
The Crescents, the Squares, and the fine Colonnades,
And the other gay places, which young ladies use
As their promenade through the good town of Thoulouse.

He was tired of hawking, and fishing, and hunting,
Of billiards, short-whist, chicken-hazard, and punting;
  Of popping at pheasants,   Quails, woodcocks, and—peasants:
  Of smoking, and joking,   And soaking, provoking
  Such headaches next day   As his fine St Peray,
Though the best of all Rhône wines can never repay,

Till weary of war, women, roast-goose, and glory,
With no great desire to be 'famous in story,'
    All the day long,   This was his song,
     'Oh, dear! what will become of us?
       Oh, dear! what shall we do?
    We shall die of blue devils if some of us
      Can't hit on something that's new!'

Meanwhile his sweet Countess, so pious and good,
Such pomps and such vanities stoutly eschew'd,
With all fermented liquors and high-seasoned food,
Devilled kidneys, and sweatbreads, and ducks and green peas;
Baked sucking-pig, goose, and all viands like these,
Hash'd calf's-head included, no longer could please,
A curry was sure to elicit a breeze,
So was ale, or a glass of Port wine after cheese,
    Indeed, anything strong,   As to tipple, was wrong;
She stuck to 'fine Hyson,' 'Bohea,' and 'Souchong,'
And similar imports direct from Hong Kong.
In vain does the family doctor exhort her
To take with her chop one poor half-pint of porter;
    No!—she alleges   She's taken the pledges!
    Determined to aid   In a gen'ral Crusade
Against publicans, vintners, and all of that trade,
And to bring in sherbet, ginger pop, lemonade,
Eau sucrée, and drinkables mild and home-made;
So she claims her friends' efforts, and vows to devote all hers
Solely to found 'The Thoulousian Teetotallers.'
    Large sums she employs   In dressing small boys
In long duffle jackets, and short corduroys,
And she boxes their ears when they make too much noise;
In short, she turns out a complete Lady Bountiful,
Filling with drugs and brown Holland the county full.

Now just at the time when our story commences,
    It seems that a case   Past the common took place,
To entail on her ladyship further expenses,
In greeting with honour befitting his station
The Prior of Arles, with a Temperance Legation,
Dispatched by Pope Urban, who seized this occasion
To aid in diluting that part of the nation,
    An excellent man,   One who stuck to his can
Of cold water 'without'—and he'd take such a lot of it;
    None of your sips   That just moisten the lips;
At one single draught he'd toss off a whole pot of it,

No such bad thing   By the way, if they bring
It you iced, as at Verrey's, or fresh from the spring,
When the Dog Star compels folks in town to take wing,
Though I own even then I should see no great sin in it,
Were there three drops of Sir Felix's gin in it.

Well, leaving the lady to follow her pleasure,
And finish the pump with the Prior at leisure,
Let's go back to Raymond, still bored beyond measure,
    And harping away   On the same dismal lay,
        'Oh dear! what will become of us?
            Oh dear! what can we do?
        We shall die of blue devils if some of us
            Can't find out something that's new!'

At length in despair of obtaining his ends
By his own mother wit, he takes courage, and sends,
Like a sensible man as he is, for his friends,
Not his Lyndhursts or Eldons, or any such high sirs,
But only a few of his 'backstairs' advisers;
    'Come hither,' says he,   'My gallants so free,
My bold Rigmarole, and my brave Rigmaree,
And my grave Baron Proser, now listen to me!
You three can't but see I'm half dead with ennui.
    What's to be done?   I *must* have some fun,
And I will too, that's flat—ay, as sure as a gun.
So find me out "something new under the sun,"
Or I'll knock your three jobbernowls all into one;—
    You three   Agree!   Come, what shall it be?
    Resolve me—propound in three skips of a flea!'
Rigmarole gave a 'Ha!' Rigmaree gave a 'Hem!'
They look'd at Count Raymond—Count Raymond at them,
As much as to say, 'Have you *nihil ad rem*?'
    At length Baron Proser
    Responded, 'You know, sir,
That question's some time been a regular poser;
    Dear me!—Let me see,—   In the way of a "spree"
Something new?—Eh!—No!—Yes!——*No!*—'tis really no go,
    sir.'
    Says the Count, 'Rigmarole,   You're as jolly a soul,
On the whole, as King Cole, with his pipe and his bowl;
Come, I'm sure you'll devise something novel and droll.'—
In vain—Rigmarole with a look most profound,
With his hand to his heart and his eye to the ground,
Shakes his head as if nothing was there to be found.
    'I can only remark,   That as touching a "lark"
I'm as much as your Highness can be, in the dark;

I can hit on no novelty—none, on my life,
Unless, peradventure you'd "tea" with your wife!'
   Quoth Raymond, 'Enough!
   Nonsense!—humbug!—fudge!—stuff!
Rigmarole, you're an ass,—you're a regular Muff!
Drink tea with her ladyship?—I?—not a bit of it!
Call you that fun?—faith I can't see the wit of it;
   Mort de ma vie! My dear Rigmaree,
You're the man, after all,—come, by way of a fee,
If you will but be bright, from the simple degree
Of a knight I'll create you at once a *Mar-quis*!
Put your conjuring cap on—consider and see,
If you can't beat that stupid old "Sumph" with his "tea"!'

   'That's the thing! that will do!
   Ay, marry, that's new!'
Cries Rigmaree, rubbing his hands, 'that will please—
My "*Conjuring cap*"—it's the thing;—it's "the cheese"!
It was only this morning I picked up the news;
Please your Highness a *Conjuror's* come to Thoulouse;
   I'll defy you to name us A man half so famous
For devildoms,—Sir, it's the great Nostradamus!
Cornelius Agrippa 'tis said went to school to him,
Gyngell's an ass, and old Faustus a fool to him,
Talk of Lilly, Albertus, Jack Dee!—pooh! all six
He'd soon put in a pretty particular fix;
Why, he'd beat at digesting a sword, or "Gun tricks"
The great Northern Wizard himself all to sticks!
   I should like to see you Try to *sauter le coup*
With this chap at short whist, or unlimited loo,
By the Pope you'd soon find it a regular "Do":
Why, he does as he likes with the cards,—when he's got 'em,
There's always an Ace or a King at the bottom;
Then for casting Nativities!—only you look
At the volume he's published,—that wonderful book!
In all France not another, to swear I dare venture, is
Like, by long chalks, his "Prophetical Centuries"—
Don't you remember how, early last summer, he
Warned the late King 'gainst the Tournament mummery?
Didn't his Majesty call it all flummery,
   Scorning The warning, And get the next morning
His poke in the eye from that clumsy Montgomery?
   Why, he'll tell you before You're well inside his door,
All your Highness may wish to be up to, and more!'

'Bravo!—capital!—come, let's disguise ourselves—quick!
—Fortune's sent him on purpose here, just in the nick;

We'll see if old Hocus will smell out the trick;
Let's start off at once—Rigmaree, you're a Brick!'
    The moon in gentle radiance shone
      O'er lowly roof and lordly bower,
      O'er holy pile and armed tower,
    And danced upon the blue Garonne:
    Through all that silver'd city fair,
    No sound disturbed the calm, cool air,
      Save the lover's sigh alone!
    Or where, perchance, some slumberer's nose
    Proclaim'd the depth of his repose,
    Provoking from connubial toes
      A hint—or elbow bone;
It might, with such trifling exceptions, be said,
That Thoulouse was as still as if Thoulouse were dead,
And her 'oldest inhabitant' buried in lead.

      But hark! a sound invades the ear,
      Of horses' hoofs advancing near!
      They gain the bridge—they pass—they're here!
        Side by side   Two strangers ride,
For the streets in Thoulouse are sufficiently wide,
That is I'm assured they are—not having tried.
  —See, now they stop   Near an odd-looking shop,
And they knock, and they ring, and they won't be denied.
    At length the command   Of some unseen hand
      Chains, and bolts, and bars obey,
      And the thick-ribbed oaken door, old and grey,
      In the pale moonlight gives, slowly, way.

They leave their steeds to a page's care,
Who comes mounted behind on a Flanders mare,
And they enter the house, that resolute pair,
With a blundering step but a dare-devil air,
And ascend a long, darksome, and rickety stair;
While, armed with a lamp that just helps you to see
How uncommonly dark a place can be,
The grimmest of lads with the grimmest of grins,
Says, 'Gentlemen, please to take care of your shins!
Who ventures this road need be firm on his pins!
Now turn to the left—now turn to the right—
Now a step—now stoop—now again upright—
Now turn once again, and directly before ye
's the door of the great Doctor's Labora-tory.'

    A word! a blow!   And in they go!
No time to prepare, or to get up a show,

Yet everything there they find quite *comme il faut*;
Such as queer-looking bottles and jars in a row,
Retorts, crucibles, such as all Conjurors stow
In the rooms they inhabit, huge bellows to blow
The fire burning blue with its sulphur and tow;
From the roof a huge crocodile hangs rather low,
With a tail such as that which, we all of us know,
Mr Waterton managed to tie in a bow;
Pickled snakes, potted lizards, in bottles and basins
Like those at Morel's, or at Fortnum and Mason's,
All articles found, you're aware without telling,
In every respectable Conjuror's dwelling.

Looking solemn and wise,   Without turning his eyes,
Or betraying the slightest degree of surprise,
In the midst sits the Doctor—his hair is white,
And his cheek is wan—but his glance is bright,
And his long black roquelaure, not over-tight,
Is marked with strange characters much, if not quite,
Like those on the bottles of green and blue light
Which you see in a chymist's shop-window at night.
His figure is tall and erect—rather spare about
Ribs,—and no wonder—such folks never care about
   Eating or drinking,   While reading and thinking,
Don't fatten—his age might be sixty or thereabout.

Raising his eye so grave and so sage,
From some manuscript work of a bygone age,
The seer very composedly turns down the page,
   Then shading his sight,   With his hand from the light,
Says, 'Well, Sirs, what would you at this time of night?
What brings you abroad these lone chambers to tread,
When all sober folks are at home and abed?'
   'Trav'lers we,   In our degree,
   All strange sights we fain would see,
   And hither we come in company;
We have far to go, and we come from far,
Through Spain and Portingale, France and Navarre;
   We have heard of your name,
   And your fame, and our aim,
Great Sir, is to witness, ere yet we depart
From Thoulouse, and to-morrow at cock-crow we start—
Your skill—we would fain crave a touch of your art!'

'Now naye, now naye—no trav'lers ye!
   Nobles ye be   Of high degree!

With half an eye that one may easily see,—
Count Raymond, your servant!—Yours, Lord Rigmaree!
I must call you so now since you're made a *Mar-quis*;
Faith, clever boys both, but you can't humbug me!
    No matter for that! I see what you'd be at—
    Well—pray no delay, For it's late, and ere day
I myself must be hundreds of miles on my way;
So tell me at once what you want with me—say!
    Shall I call up the dead
    From their mouldering bed?—
Shall I send you yourselves down to Hades instead?—
Shall I summon old Harry himself to this spot?'
—'Ten thousand thanks, No! we had much rather not.
    We really can't say That we're curious that way;
But, in brief, if you'll pardon the trouble we're giving,
We'd much rather take a sly peep at the living?
    Rigmaree, what say you, in This case, as to viewing
Our spouses, and just ascertain what they're doing?'
'Just what pleases your Highness—I don't care a *sous* in
The matter—but don't let old Nick and his crew in!'
—'Agreed!—pray proceed then, most sage Nostradamus,
And show us our *Wives*—I dare swear they won't shame us!'

A change comes o'er the Wizard's face,
And his solemn look by degrees gives place
To a half grave, half comical, kind of grimace.
    'For good or for ill, I work your will!
    Yours be the risk, and mine the skill;
    Blame not my art if unpleasant the pill!'

He takes from a shelf, and he pops on his head,
A square sort of cap, black, and turned up with red,
And desires not a syllable more may be said;
    He goes on to mutter, And stutter, and sputter
Hard words, such as no men but Wizards dare utter.
    'Dies mies!—Hocus pocus—
    Adsis Demon! non est jokus!
    Hi Cocolorum—don't provoke us!—
    Adesto! Presto! Put forth your best toe!'
And many more words, to repeat which would choke us,—
Such a sniff then of brimstone!—it did not last long,
Or they could not have borne it, the smell was so strong.

A mirror is near, So large and so clear,
If you priced such a one in a drawing-room here,
And was ask'd fifty pounds, you'd not say it was dear;
But a mist gather'd round at the words of the Seer,

Till at length, as the gloom,   Was subsiding, a room,
On its broad polish'd surface began to appear,
And the Count and his comrade saw plainly before 'em
The room Lady Isabel called her 'Sanctorum.'

    They start, well they might,   With surprise at the sight,
Methinks I hear some lady say, 'Serve 'em right!'
    For on one side the fire   Is seated the Prior,
At the opposite corner a fat little Friar;
By the side of each gentleman, easy and free,
Sits a lady, as close as close well may be,
She might almost as well have been perch'd on his knee.

    Dear me! dear me!   Why one's Isabel—she
On the opposite side's *La Marquise Rigmaree!*—
    To judge from the spread
    On the board, you'd have said
That the *partie quarrèe* had like aldermen fed,
And now from long flasks, with necks covered with lead,
They were helping themselves to champagne, white and red,
    Hobbing and nobbing,   And nodding and bobbing,
    With many a sip   Both from cup and from lip,
And with many a toast followed up by a 'Hip!—
    Hip!—hip!—huzzay!'   —The Count, by the way,
Though he sees all they're doing, can't hear what they say,
    Not withstanding both he   And *Mar-quis Rigmaree*
Are so vex'd and excited at what they can *see,*
That each utters a sad word beginning with D.

    That word once spoke,   The silence broke,
In an instant the vision is cover'd with smoke!
But enough has been seen.   'Horse! horse! and away!'
They have, neither, the least inclination to stay,
'Een to thank Nostradamus, or ask what's to pay.—
    They rush down the stair,
    How, they know not, nor care,
The next moment the Count is astride on his bay,
And my Lord Rigmaree on his mettlesome grey;
    They dash through the town,
    Now up, and now down,
And the stones rattle under their hoofs as they ride,
As if poor Thoulouse were as mad as Cheapside; [1]
    Through lane, alley, and street,
    Over all that they meet;
The Count leads the way on his courser so fleet,

---

[1] 'The stones did rattle underneath
    As if Cheapside were mad.'
        GILPIN'S TOUR IN MIDDLESEX AND HERTS.

My Lord Rigmaree close pursuing his beat.
With the Page in the rear to protect the retreat.
Where the bridge spans the river, so wide and so deep,
Their headlong career o'er the causeway they keep,
Upsetting the Watchman, two dogs, and a Sweep,
All the town population that was not asleep.
They at length reached the castle, just outside the town,
Where—in peace it was usual with Knights of renown—
The portcullis was up, and the drawbridge was down.
They dash by the sentinels—'*France et Thoulouse!*'
Ev'ry soldier (—they then wore cock'd hats and long queues,
Appendages banish'd from modern reviews),
His arquebus lower'd, and bow'd to his shoes;
While Count Raymond pushed on to his lady's boudoir—he
Had made up his mind to make one at her soirée.

   He rush'd to that door,   Where ever before
He had rapped with his knuckles, and 'tirled at the pin,'
Till he heard the soft sound of his Lady's 'Come in!'
But now, with a kick from his iron-heeled boot,
Which, applied to a brick wall, at once had gone through 't,
   He dash'd open the lock;   It gave way at the shock!
(—Dear ladies, don't think, in recording the fact,
That your bard's for one moment defending the act,
No—it is not a gentleman's—none but a low body—
No—could perform it)—and there he saw—NOBODY!!

   Nobody? —No!! Oh, ho!—Oh, ho!
There was not a table, there was not a chair
Of all that Count Raymond had ever seen there
(They'd maroon-leather bottoms well stuff'd with horse hair)
   That was out of its place!—There was not a trace
Of a party—there was not a dish or a plate—
No sign of a tablecloth—nothing to prate
Of a supper, symposium, or sitting up late;
There was not a spark of fire left in the grate,
It had all been poked out, and remained in that state.
   If there was not a fire,   Still less was there Friar,
Marquise, or long glasses, or Countess, or Prior,
And the Count, who rush'd in open-mouth'd, was struck dumb,
And could only ejaculate, 'Well, this *is* rum!'

He rang for the maids—had them into the room,
With the butler, the footman, the coachman, the groom.
He examined them all very strictly—but no!
Notwithstanding he cross- and re-questioned them so,
'Twas in vain—it was clearly a case of 'No go'!
   'Their Lady,' they said,   'Had gone early to bed,
Having rather complain'd of a cold in her head—

The stout little Friar, as round as an apple,
Had pass'd the whole night in a vigil in chapel,
While the Prior himself, as he'd usually done,
Had rung in the morning, at half after one,
For his jug of cold water and twopenny bun,
And been visible, since they were brought him, to none
  But,' the servants averr'd,
    'From the sounds that were heard
To proceed now and then from the father's *sacellum*,
    They thought he was purging
    His sins with a scourging,
And making good use of his knotted flagellum.'
    For Madame Rigmaree,   They all testified, she
Had gone up to her bedchamber soon after tea,
And they really supposed that there still she must be,
    Which her spouse, the *Mar-quis*,
    Found at once to agree
With the rest of their tale, when he ran up to see.

Alack for Count Raymond! he could not conceive
How the case really stood, or know *what* to believe;
Nor could Rigmaree settle to laugh or to grieve.
    There was clearly a hoax,
    But which of the folks
Had managed to make them the butt of their jokes,
Wife or Wizard, they both knew no more than Jack Nokes;
    That glass of the Wizard's
    Stuck much in their gizzards,
His cap, and his queer cloak all X's and Izzards;
Then they found, when they came to examine again,
Some slight falling off in the stock of champagne,
Small, but more than the butler could fairly explain.
However, since nothing could make the truth known,
Why,—they thought it was best to let matters alone.
    The Count in the garden   Begg'd Isabel's pardon
Next morning for waking her up in a fright,
By the racket he'd kicked up at that time of night;
And gave her his word he had ne'er misbehaved so,
Had he not come home as tipsy as David's sow.
Still, to give no occasion for family snarls,
The Friar was pack'd back to his convent at Arles,
    While as for the Prior,   At Raymond's desire,
The Pope raised his rev'rence a step or two higher,
And made him a Bishop *in partibus*—where
His see was I cannot exactly declare,
Or describe his cathedral, not having been there,

But I dare say you'll all be prepared for the news,
When I say 'twas a good many miles from Thoulouse,
Where the prelate, in order to set a good precedent,
Was enjoined, as a *sine quâ non*, to be resident.
     You will fancy with me,
     That Count Raymond was free,
For the rest of his life, from his former ennui;
Still it somehow occurr'd that as often as he
Chanced to look in the face of my Lord Rigmaree,
There was something or other—a trifling degree
Of constraint—or embarrassment—easy to see,
And which seem'd to be shared by the noble *Marq-uis*,
While the ladies—the queerest of all things by half in
My tale, never met from that hour without laughing!

MORAL

Good gentlemen all, who are subjects of Hymen,
Don't make new acquaintances rashly, but try men,
Avoid above all things your cunning (that's sly) men!
     Don't go out o' nights   To see conjuring sleights,
But shun all such people, delusion whose trade is;
Be wise!—stay at home and take tea with the ladies.

     If you *chance* to be out,   At a 'regular bout,'
And get too much of 'Abbot's Pale Ale' or 'Brown Stout,'
Don't be cross when you come home at night to your spouse,
Nor be noisy, nor kick up a dust in the house!

Be careful yourself, and admonish your sons,
To beware of all folks who love twopenny buns!
And don't introduce to your wife or your daughter
A sleek, meek, weak gent—who subsists on cold water!

THE WEDDING-DAY
Or, The Buccaneer's Curse

A Family Legend

It has a jocund sound
That gleeful Marriage chime,
  As from the old and ivied tower,
  It peals, at the early Matin hour,
  Its merry, merry round;
And the Spring is in its prime,
  And the Song-bird, on the spray,
Trills from his throat, in varied note,
  An emulative lay—
  It has a joyous sound!!
And the Vicar is there with his wig and his book,
And the Clerk with his grave, *quasi*-sanctified look,
And there stand the Village maids all with their posies,
Their lilies, and daffy-down-dillies, and roses,
  Dight in white,   A comely sight,
Fringing the path to the left and the right;
—From our nursery days we all of us know
Ne'er doth 'Our Ladye's garden grow'
So fair for a 'Grand Horticultural Show'
As when border'd with 'pretty maids all on a row.'
And the urchins are there, escap'd from the rule
Of that 'Limbo of Infants,' the National School,
  Whooping, and bawling,   And squalling, and calling,
  And crawling, and creeping,
  And jumping, and leaping,
Bo-peeping 'midst 'many a mouldering heap' in
Whose bosom their own 'rude forefathers' are sleeping;
—Young rascals!—instead of lamenting and weeping,
  Laughing and gay,   *A gorge deployée*—
Only now and then pausing—and checking their play,
To 'wonder what 'tis makes the gentlefolks stay,'
  Ah, well-a-day!   Little deem they,
Poor ignorant dears! the bells, ringing away,
  Are anything else   Than mere parish bells,
Or that each of them, should we go into its history,
Is but a 'Symbol' of some deeper mystery—
  That the clappers and ropes
  Are mere practical tropes
Of 'trumpets' and 'tongues,' and of 'preachers,' and popes,
Unless Clement the Fourth's worthy Chaplain, *Durand*, err,
See the '*Rationale*,' of that goosey-gander.

Gently! gently, Miss Muse!
Mind your P's and your Q's!
Don't be malapert—laugh, Miss, but never abuse!
Calling names, whether done to attack or to back a schism,
Is, Miss, believe me, a great piece of Jack-ass-ism,
    And as, on the whole,   You're a good-natured soul,
    You must never enact such a pitiful role.
No, no, Miss, pull up, and go back to your boys
In the churchyard, who're making this hubbub and noise—
But hush! there's an end to their romping and mumming,
For voices are heard—here's the company coming!

      And see!—the avenue gates unfold,
        And forth they pace, that bridal train,
      The grave, the gay, the young, the old,
        They cross the green and grassy lane,
Bridesman, Bridesmaid, Bridegroom, Bride,
Two by two, and side by side,
Uncles, and aunts, friends tried and prov'd,
And cousins, a great many times removed.
    A fairer or a gentler She,
    A lovelier Maid, in her degree,
    Man's eye might never hope to see,
    Than darling, bonnie Maud Ingoldsby,
    The flow'r of that goodly company;
While whispering low, with bated voice,
Close by her side, her heart's dear choice,
Walks Fredville's hope, young Valentine Boys.
    —But where, oh where,— Is Ingoldsby's heir?
Little Jack Ingoldsby?—where, oh where?
    Why, he's here,—and he's there,
    And he's everywhere—
    He's there, and he's here;
    In the front—in the rear,—
Now this side, now that side,—now far, and now near—
The Puck of the Party, the darling 'pet' boy,
Full of mischief, and fun, and good humour and joy;
With his laughing blue eye, and his cheek like a rose,
And his long curly locks, and his little snub nose;
In his tunic, and trousers, and cap—there he goes!
Now pinching the bridesmen,—now teasing his sister,
And telling the bridesmaids how 'Valentine kiss'd her';
The torment, the plague, the delight of them all,
See he's into the churchyard!—he's over the wall—
Gambolling, frolicking, capering away,
He's the first in the church, be the second who may!

'Tis o'er;—the holy rite is done,
The rite that 'incorporates two in one,'
—And now for the feasting, and frolic, and fun!
Spare we to tell of the smiling and sighing,
The shaking of hands, the embracing, and crying,
   The 'toot—toot—toot' Of the tabor and flute,
Of the white-wigg'd Vicar's prolonged salute,
Or of how the blithe 'College *Youths*,' rather old stagers,
Accustom'd, for years, to pull bell ropes for wagers—
Rang, faster than ever, their 'triple-bob-MAJORS'
   (So loud as to charm ye, At once and alarm ye;
—'*Symbolic*,' of course, of that rank in the army).

Spare we to tell of the fees and the dues
To the 'little old woman that open'd the pews,'
Of the largesse bestow'd on the Sexton and Clerk,
Of the four-year-old sheep roasted whole in the park,
   Of the laughing and joking,
   The quaffing and smoking,
And chaffing, and broaching—that is to say, poking
A hole in a mighty magnificent tub
Of what men, in our hemisphere, term 'Humming Bub,'
But which Gods,—who, it seems, use a different lingo
From mortals,—are wont to denominate 'Stingo.'

Spare we to tell of the Horse-collar grinning;
The Cheese! the reward of the ugly one winning;
Of the young ladies racing for Dutch body-linen,—
—The soapy-tail'd Sow,—a rich prize when you've caught
      her,—
Of little boys bobbing for pippins in water;
   The smacks and the whacks,
   And the jumpers in sacks,
These down on their noses and those on their backs;—
Nor skills it to speak of those darling old ditties,
Sung rarely in hamlets now—never in cities,
The 'King and the Miller,' the 'Bold Robin Hood,'
'Chevy Chase,' 'Gilderoy,' and the 'Babes in the Wood'!
  —You'll say that my taste Is sadly misplaced,
But I can't help confessing those simple old tunes,
The 'Auld Robin Grays,' and the 'Aileen Aroons,'
The 'Gramachree Mollys,' and the 'Sweet Bonny Doons,'
   Are dearer to me, In a tenfold degree,
Than a fine fantasia from over the sea;

And, for sweetness, compared with a Beethoven fugue, are
As 'best-refined loaf' to the coarsest 'brown sugar'; [1]
—Alack, for the Bard's want of Science! to which he owes
All this misliking of foreign *capriccios*!—
　　Not that he'd say　One word, by the way,
To disparage our new Idol, Monsieur Duprez—
But he grudges, he owns, his departed half-guinea,
Each Saturday night when, devoured by chagrin, he
Sits listening to singers whose names end in *ini*.

But enough of the rustics—let's leave them pursuing
Their out-of-door gambols, and just take a view in
The inside the Hall, and see what *they* are doing;
　　And first there's the Squire,　The hale, hearty Sire
Of the Bride,—with his coat-tails subducted and higher,
A thought, than they're commonly wont to aspire;
His back and his buckskins exposed to the fire;—
—Bright, bright are his buttons,—and bright is the hue
Of his squarely cut coat of fine Saxony blue;
And bright the shalloon of his little quilled queue;
　　White, white as 'Young England's,' the dimity vest
Which descends like an avalanche o'er his broad breast,
Till its further progression is put in arrest
By the portly projection that springs from his chest,
Overhanging the garment—that can't be expressed;
—White, white are his locks,—which, had Nature fair play,
Had appeared a clear brown, slightly sprinkled with grey;
But they're white as the peaks of Plinlimmon to-day,
Or Ben Nevis, his pate is *si bien poudré*!
Bright, bright are the boots that envelop his heels,
—Bright, bright is the gold chain suspending his seals,
And still brighter yet may the gazer descry
The Tear-drop that spangles the fond Father's eye
　　As it lights on the Bride—
　　His belov'd One—the pride
And delight of his heart,—sever'd now from his side;—
　　But brighter than all　Arresting its fall,
Is the smile, that rebukes it for spangling at all,
—A clear case, in short, of what old Poets tell, as
Blind Homer for instance, ἐν δάκρυσι γέλας.[2]

Then, there are the Bride and the Bridegroom, withdrawn
To the deep Gothic window that looks on the lawn,

---

[1] *Ad Amicum, Servientem ad legem*—
　　　　This rhyme, if, when scann'd by your critical ear, it
　　　　Is not *quite* legitimate, comes pretty near it.—T. I.
[2] 'Laughter in tears.'

Ensconced on a squab of maroon-coloured leather,
And talking—and *thinking*, no doubt—of the weather.

But here comes the party—Room! room for the guests!
In their Pompadour coats, and laced ruffles, and vests,
  —First, Sir Charles Grandison,   Baronet, and his Son,
Charles, the Mamma does not venture to 'show'—
  —Miss Byron, you know,   She was call'd long ago—
For that Lady, 'twas *said*, had been playing the d—l,
Last season, in town, with her old beau, Squire Greville,
Which very much shock'd, and chagrin'd, as may well be
Supposed, 'Doctor Bartlett,' and 'Good Uncle Selby.'
—Sir Charles, of course, could not give Greville his gruel, in
Order to prove his abhorrence of duelling,
Nor try for, deterr'd by the serious expense, a
Complete separation *a thoro et mensâ*,
So he 'kept a calm sough,' and, when asked to a party,
A dance, or a dinner, or tea and écarte,
He went with his son, and said, looking demurely,
He'd 'left her at home, as she found herself poorly.'
    Two Foreigners near, 'Of distinction,' appear;
A pair more illustrious you ne'er heard of, or saw,
Count Ferdinand Fathom,—Count Thaddeus of Warsaw,
All cover'd with glitt'ring bijouterie and hair—Poles,
Whom Lord Dudley Stuart calls 'Patriot,'—Hook 'Bare
        Poles';
Such rings, and such brooches, such studs, and such pins.
    'Twere hard to say which
    Were more gorgeous and rich,
Or more truly Mosaic, their chains or their chins!
Next Sir Roger de Coverley,—Mr Will Ramble,
With Dame Lismahago (*née* Tabitha Bramble),—
Mr Random and Spouse—Mrs Pamela Booby
(Whose nose was acquiring a tinge of the ruby,
And 'people *did say*'—but no matter for that. . . .
Folks were not then enlighten'd by good Father Mat)—
—Three friends from 'the Colonies' near them were seen,
The great Massachusetts man, General Muff Green,—
Mr Jonathan W. Doubikins,—men
'Influential *some*,'—and their 'smart' Uncle Ben;—
Rev. Abraham Adams (preferr'd to a stall),—
—Mr Jones and his Lady, from Allworthy Hall;
    —Our friend Tom, by the way,
    Had turn'd out rather gay
For a married man—certainly 'people *did say*,'
He was shrewdly suspected of using his wife ill,
And being as sly as his half-brother Blifil.—

(Miss Seagrim, 'tis well known, was now in high feather,
And 'people *did say*,' they'd been seen out together,—
A fact, the 'Boy Jones,' who, in our days, with malice
Aforethought, so often got into the Palace,
Would seem to confirm, as, 'tis whispered he owns, he's
The son of a natural son of Tom Jones's.)
Lady Bellaston, (*mem.* she had not been invited!)
Sir Peregrine Pickle, now recently knighted,—
All joyous, all happy, all looking delighted!
—It would bore you to death should I pause to describe,
Or enumerate, half of the elegant tribe
    Who filled the background,
    And among whom were found
The *élite* of the old County families round,
Such as Honeywood, Oxenden, Knatchbull, and Norton,
Matthew Robinson,[1] too, with his beard from Monk's Horton,
The Faggs, and Finch-Hattons, Tokes, Derings, and Deedses,
And Fairfax (who then called the castle of Leeds his);
    Esquires, Knights, and Lords,
    In bag-wigs and swords;
    And the troops, and the groups
    Of fine Ladies in hoops;
The pompons, the toupees, and the diamonds and feathers,
    The flowered-silk sacques
    Which they wore on their backs,—
—How?—sacques and pompons, with the Squire's boots and
    leathers?—
    Stay! stay!—I suspect,   Here's a trifling neglect
On your part, Madame Muse—though you're commonly accurate
As to costume, as brown Quaker, or black Curate,
    For once, I confess,   Here you're out as to dress;—
You've been fairly caught napping, which gives me distress,
For I can't but acknowledge it is not the thing,
Sir Roger de Coverley's laced suit to bring
Into contact with square-cut coats,—such as George Byng,
And poor dear Sir Francis appeared in, last spring.—
So, having for once been compelled to acknowledge, I
've made a small hole in our mutual chronology,
Canter on, Miss, without further apology,—
    Only don't make   Such another mistake,
Or you'll get in a scrape, of which I shall partake;—
Enough!—you are sorry for what you have done,
So dry your eyes, Miss, blow your nose, and go on!

---

[1] A worthy and eccentric country gentleman, afterwards the second Lord Rokeby, being cousin ('a great many times removed') and successor in the barony to Richard, Archbishop of Armagh, who first bore that title.—His beard was truly patriarchial.—Mr Muntz's—pooh!—

Well—the party are met, all radiant and gay,
And how ev'ry person is dress'd—we won't say;
Suffice it, they all come glad homage to pay
To our dear 'bonnie Maud,' on her own wedding-day,
To dance at her bridal, and help 'throw the stocking,'
—A practice that's now discontinued as shocking.

There's a breakfast, they know—   There always is so
On occasions like these, wheresoever you go.
Of course there are 'lots' of beef, potted and hung,
Prawns, lobsters, cold fowl, and cold ham, and cold tongue,
Hot tea, and hot coffee, hot rolls, and hot toast,
Cold pigeon-pie (rook?), and cold boil'd and cold roast,
Scotch marmalade, jellies, cold creams, colder ices—
Blancmange, which young Ladies say, so very nice is,—
Rock-melons in thick, pines in much thinner slices,—
Char, potted with clarified butter and spices,
Renewing an appetite long past its crisis—
Refined barley-sugar, in various devices,
Such as bridges, and baskets, and temples, and grottoes—
And nasty French lucifer snappers with mottoes.
—In short, all these gimcracks together were met
Which people of fashion tell Gunter to get
When they give a *grand déjeuner à la fourchette*—
(A phrase which, though French, in our language still lingers,
Intending a breakfast with forks and not fingers)
And see! what a mountainous bridecake!—a thing
By itself—with small pieces to pass through the ring!

Now as to the wines!—'Ay, the Wine?' cries the Squire,
Letting fall both his coat-tails,—which nearly take fire,—
   Rubbing his hands,   He calls out, as he stands,
To the serving-men waiting 'his Honour's' commands,
'The wine!—to be sure—here you, Harry—Bob—Dick—
The wine, don't you hear?—bring us lights—come, be quick!—
And a crowbar to knock down the mortar and brick—
   Say what they may,   'Fore George, we'll make way
Into old Roger Ingoldsby's cellar to-day;
And let loose his captives, imprison'd so long,
His flasks, and his casks, that he bricked up so strong!'—
—'Oh dear! oh dear! Squire Ingoldsby, bethink you what you
      do!'
Exclaims old Mrs Botherby,[1]—she is in *such* a stew!—

---

[1] Great grandmamma, by the father's side, to the excellent lady of the
same name who yet 'keeps the keys' at Tappington.

'Oh dear! oh dear! what do I hear?—full oft you've heard me
　　tell
Of the curse "Wild Roger" left upon whoe'er should break his
　　cell!

'Full five-and-twenty years are gone since Roger went away,
As I bethink me, too, it was upon this very day!
And I was then a comely dame, and you, a springald gay,
Were up and down to London town, at opera, ball, and play;
Your locks were nut-brown then, Squire—you grow a little
　　grey!

'"Wild Roger," so we call'd him then, your Grandsire's
　　　　youngest son,
　　He was in truth　　A wayward youth,
　　　　We fear'd him, every one.
In ev'rything he had his will, he would be stayed by none,
And when he did a naughty thing, he laugh'd and call'd it fun!
—One day his father chid him sore—I know not what he'd done,
　　But he scorn'd reproof;　　And from this roof
　　　　Away that night he run!

'Seven years were gone and over—"Wild Roger" came again,
He spoke of forays and of frays upon the Spanish Main;
And he had store of gold galore, and silks, and satins fine,
And flasks and casks of Malvoisie, and precious Gascon wine!
Rich booties he had brought, he said, across the western wave,
And came, in penitence and shame, now of his Sire to crave
Forgiveness and a welcome home—his Sire was in his grave!

'Your Father was a kindly man—he played a brother's part,
He press'd his brother to his breast—he had a kindly heart,
Fain would he have him tarry here, their common hearth to
　　share,
But Roger was the same man still,—he scorn'd his brother's
　　pray'r!
He call'd his crew,—away he flew, and on those foreign shores
Got kill'd in some outlandish place—they call it the Eyesores; [1]
　　But ere he went,　　And quitted Kent,
　　　　—I well recall the day,—
His flasks and casks of Gascon wine he safely "stow'd away";
Within the cellar's deepest nook, he safely stow'd them all,
And Mason Jones brought bricks and stones, and they built up
　　the wall.

[1] Azores?—Mrs Botherby's orthography, like that of her distinguished
contemporary Baron Duberly, was a 'little loose.'

'Oh! then it was a fearful thing to hear "Wild Roger's" ban!
Good gracious me! I never heard the like from mortal man;
"Here's that," quoth he, "shall serve me well when I return at
    last,
A batter'd hulk, to quaff and laugh at toils and dangers past;
Accurst be he, whoe'er he be, lays hand on gear of mine,
Till I come back again from sea, to broach my Gascon wine!"
And more he said, which filled with dread all those who listen'd
    there;
In sooth my very blood ran cold, it lifted up my hair
With very fear, to stand and hear "Wild Roger" curse and swear!!
He saw my fright, as well he might, but still he made his game,
He called me "Mother Bounce-about," my Gracious, what a
    name!
Nay more, "an old"—some "boat-woman"—I may not say for
    shame!—
Then, gentle Master, pause awhile, give heed to what I tell,
Nor break, on such a day as this, "Wild Roger's" secret cell!'

    'Pooh! pooh!' quoth the Squire,
    As he mov'd from the fire,
And bade the old Housekeeper quickly retire,
    'Pooh!—never tell me! Nonsense—fiddle-de-dee!
What?—wait Uncle Roger's return back from sea?—
    Why he may, as you say,
    Have been somewhat too gay,
And, no doubt, was a broth of a boy in his way;
But what's that to us, now, at this time of day?
    What if some quarrel With Dering or Darrell—
—I hardly know which, but I think it was Dering,—
Sent him back in a huff to his old privateering,
Or what his unfriends chose to call Buccaneering,
It's twenty years since, as we very well know,
He was knock'd on the head in a skirmish, and so
Why rake up "auld warld" tales of deeds long ago?—
—Foul befall him who would touch the deposit
Of living man, whether in cellar or closet!
    But since, as I've said, Knock'd on the head,
Uncle Roger has now been some twenty years dead.
    As for his wine, I'm his heir, and it's mine!
And I'd long ago work'd it well, but that I tarried
    For this very day—
    And I'm sure you'll all say
I was right—when my own darling Maud should get married!
So lights and a crowbar!—the only thing lies
On my conscience, at all, with respect to this prize,
Is some little compunction anent the Excise—

Come—you, Master Jack,
  Be the first, and bring back
Whate'er comes to hand—Claret, Burgundy, Sack—
Head the party, and mind that you're back in a crack!'

    Away go the clan,   With cup and with can,
Little Jack Ingoldsby leading the van;
Little reck they of the Buccaneer's ban:
Hope whispers, 'Perchance we'll fall in with strong beer too
    here!'
Blest thought! which sets them all grinning from ear to ear!

Through cellar one, through cellars two,
Through cellars three they past!
    And their way they took   To the farthest nook
Of cellar four—the last!—
Blithe and gay, they batter away,
  On this wedding-day of Maud's,
With all their might, to bring to light
  'Wild Roger's' 'Custom-house frauds'!
    And though stone and brick   Be never so thick,
When stoutly assailed, they are no bar
    To the powerful charm   Of a Yeoman's arm
When wielding a decentish crowbar!
Down comes brick, and down comes stone,
    One by one—   The job's half done!—

'Where is he?—now come—where's Master John?'—
—There's a breach in the wall three feet by two,
And little Jack Ingoldsby soon pops through!
Hark!—what sound's that?—a sob?—a sigh?—
The choking gasp of a stifled cry?—
    '—What can it be?—
    Let's see!—let's see!—
It *can't* be little Jack Ingoldsby?
    The candle—quick!'—
    Through stone and through brick
They poke in the light on a long split stick;
But ere he who holds it can wave it about,
He gasps, and he sneezes—the LIGHT GOES OUT!

Yet were there those, in after days,
Who said that pale light's flickering blaze,
For a moment, gleam'd on a dark Form there,
Seem'd as bodied of foul black air!—
—In Mariner's dress,—with cutlass braced
By buckle and broad black belt, to its waist,—

   —On a cock'd-hat, laced With gold, and placed
With a *degagée*, devil-may-care, kind of taste,
O'er a *balafré* brow by a scar defaced!—
That Form, they said, so foul and so black,
Grinn'd as it pointed at poor little Jack.—
—I know not, I, how the truth may be,
But the pent-up vapour, at length set free,
    Set them sneexing, And coughing, and wheezing,
    As, working its way To the regions of day,
It, at last, let a purer and healthier breeze in!

    Of their senses bereft, To the right and the left,
Those varlets so lately courageous and stout,
There they lay kicking and sprawling about,
Like Billingsgate fresh fish, unconscious of ice,
Or those which, the newspapers give us advice,
Mr Taylor, of Lombard-street, sells at half-price;
—Nearer the door, some half-dozen or more!
    Scramble away To the *rez de chaussée*
(As our Frenchified friend always calls his ground floor),
And they call, and they bawl, and they bellow and roar
For lights, vinegar, brandy, and fifty things more.
At length, after no little clamour and din,
The foul air let out, and the fresh air let in,
    They drag one and all Up into the hall,
Where a medical Quaker, the great Dr Lettsom,
Who's one of the party, 'bleeds, physics, and sweats 'em.'
    All?—all—save One— —'But He!—my Son?—
Merciful Heaven!—where—WHERE IS JOHN?'

        Within that cell, so dark and deep,
        Lies One, as in a tranquil sleep,
        A sight to make the sternest weep!—
        —That little heart is pulseless now,
        And cold that fair and open brow,
        And closed that eye that beam'd with joy
        And hope—'Oh, God!—my Boy!—my Boy!'

        Enough!—I may not,—dare not,—show
        The wretched Father's frantic woe,
        The Mother's tearless, speechless—No!
        I may not such a theme essay—
        Too bitter thoughts crowd in and stay
        My pen—sad memory will have way!
        Enough!—at once I close the lay,
        Of fair Maud's fatal Wedding-day!

It has a mournful sound,
    That single, solemn Bell!
As to the hills and woods around
    It flings its deep-toned knell;
That measured toll!—alone—apart,
It strikes upon the human heart!
—It has a mournful sound!—

MORAL

Come, come, Mrs Muse, we can't part in this way,
Or you'll leave me as dull as ditch-water all day.
Try and squeeze out a Moral or two from your lay!
And let us part cheerful, at least, if not gay!

First and foremost then, Gentlefolks, learn from my song,
Not to lock up your wine, or malt-liquor, too long!
        Though Port should have age,
        Yet I don't think it sage
To entomb it, as some of your connoisseurs do,
Till it's losing in flavour, and body, and hue;
—I question if keeping it does it much good
After ten years in bottle and three in the wood.

If any young man, though a snubb'd younger brother,
When told of his faults by his father and mother,
Runs restive, and goes off to sea in a huff,
Depend on't, my friends, that young man is a Muff!

        Next—ill-gotten gains   Are not worth the pains!—
They prosper with no one!—so whether cheroots,
Or Havanna cigars,—or French gloves, or French boots,—
Whatever you want, pay the duty! nor when you
Buy any such articles, cheat the revenue!

        And 'now to conclude,'—
        For it's high time I should,—
When you *do* rejoice, mind,—whatsoever you do,
That the hearts of the lowly rejoice with you too!—
        Don't grudge them their jigs,
        And their frolics and 'rigs,'
And don't interfere with their soapy-tail'd pigs;
Nor 'because thou art virtuous,' rail, and exhale
An anathema, breathing of vengeance and wail,
Upon every complexion less pale than sea-kail!
Nor dismiss the poor man to his pump and his pail,
With 'Drink *there*!—we'll have henceforth no more cakes and
        ale!!'

THE BLASPHEMER'S WARNING

A LAY OF ST ROMWOLD

'Mox Regina filium peperit a multis optatum et a Deo sanctificatum. Cumque Infans natus fuisset, statim clarâ voce, omnibus audientibus, clamavit "Christianus sum! Christianus sum! Christianus sum!" Ad hanc vocem Presbyteri duo, Widerinus et Edwoldus, dicentes Deo Gratias, et omnes qui aderant mirantes, coeperunt cantare Te Deum laudamus. Quo facto rogabat Infans cathecumenum a Widerino sacerdote fieri, et ab Edwoldo teneri ad praesignaculum fidei et Romwoldum vocari.' [1]—NOV. LEGEND. ANGL. IN VITA SCTI ROMUALDI.

IN Kent, we are told,   There was seated of old,
A handsome young gentleman, courteous and bold,
He'd an oaken strong-box, well-replenish'd with gold,
With broad lands, pasture, arable, woodland, and wold,
Not an acre of which had been mortgaged or sold;
He'd a Pleasaunce and Hall passing fair to behold,
He had beeves in the byre, he had flocks in the fold,
And was somewhere about five-and-twenty years old.
   His figure and face,   For beauty and grace,
To the best in the county had scorn'd to give place.
   Small marvel, then,   If, of women and men
Whom he chanced to foregather with, nine out of ten
Express'd themselves charm'd with Sir Alured Denne.

   From my earliest youth,
   I've been taught, as a truth,
A maxim which most will consider as sooth,
Though a few, peradventure, may think it uncouth;
There are three social duties, the whole of the swarm
In this great human hive of ours, ought to perform,
And that too as soon as conveniently may be;
   The first of the three—   Is, the planting a Tree!
The next, the producing a Book—then, a Baby!
(For my part, dear Reader, without any jesting, I
So far at least, have accomplished my destiny.)

---

[1] 'Soon the Queen brought forth a son that many had hoped for and who was blessed by God. When the child was born, at once with a clear voice, while all listened, he cried out: "I am a Christian! I am a Christian! I am a Christian!" At this utterance two priests, Widerinus and Edwoldus, said: "Thanks be to God," and all who were present, marvelling, began to sing "We praise thee, O God." When this was done the child asked to be made a catechumen by the priest Widerinus and to be baptized by Edwoldus and called Romwold.'

From the foremost, i.e.   The 'planting the Tree,'
The Knight may, perchance, have conceiv'd himself free,
Inasmuch as that, which way soever he looks,
Over park, mead, or upland, by streamlets and brooks,
His fine beeches and elms shelter thousands of rooks;
    In twelve eighty-two,   There would also accrue
Much latitude as to the article, Books;
But, if those we've disposed of, and need not recall,
Might, as duties, appear in comparison small,
One remain'd, there was no getting over at all,
—The providing a male Heir for Bonnington Hall;
Which, doubtless, induced the good Knight to decide,
As a matter of conscience, on taking a Bride.

It's a very fine thing, and delightful to see
Inclination and duty unite and agree,
    Because it's a case   That so rarely takes place;
In the instance before us, then, Alured Denne
Might well be esteem'd the most lucky of men,
    Inasmuch as hard by,   Indeed so very nigh,
That her chimneys, from his, you might almost descry,
Dwelt a Lady at whom he'd long cast a sheep's eye,
One whose character scandal itself could defy,
While her charms and accomplishments rank'd very high
    And who would not deny   A propitious reply,
But reflect back his blushes, and give sigh for sigh.
(A line that's not mine, but Tom Moore's, by-the-bye.)

There was many a gay and trim bachelor near,
Who felt sick at heart when the news met his ear,
That fair Edith Ingoldsby, she whom they all
The 'Rosebud of Tappington' ceased not to call,
    Was going to say,   'Honour, love, and obey'
To Sir Alured Denne, Knight, of Bonnington Hall,
That all other suitors were left in the lurch,
And the parties had even been 'out-asked' in church.
    For everyone says,   In those primitive days,
And I must own I think it redounds to their praise,
None dream'd of transferring a daughter or niece,
As a bride, by an 'unstamp'd agreement' or lease,
'Fore a Register's Clerk, or a Justice of Peace,
    While young ladies had fain   Single women remain,
And unwedded maids to the last 'crack of doom' stick,
Ere marry, by taking a jump o'er a broomstick.

So our bride and bridegroom agreed to appear
At holy St Romwold's, a Priory near,

Which a long while before, I can't say in what year,
Their forbears had join'd with the neighbours to rear,
And endow'd, some with bucks, some with beef, some with beer,
To comfort the friars, and make them good cheer.
  Adorning the building,   With carving and gilding,
And stone altars, fix'd to the chantries and fill'd in;
(Papistic in substance and form, and on this count
With Judge Herbert Jenner Fust justly at discount.
See *Cambridge Societas Camdeniensis*
V. *Faulkner, tert, prim. Januarii mensis,*
With 'Judgment reversed, costs of suit, and expenses');
All raised to St Romwold, with some reason styled
By Duke Humphrey's confessor,[1] 'a Wonderful Child,'
For ne'er yet was Saint, except him, upon earth
Who made his 'profession of faith' at his birth,
And when scarce a foot high, or six inches in girth,
Converted his 'Ma,' and contrived to amend a
Sad hole in the creed of his grandsire, King Penda.

  Of course to the shrine   Of so young a divine
Flow'd much holy water, and some little wine,
And when any young folks did to marriage incline,
The good friars were much in request, and not one
Was more 'sought unto' than the Sub-Prior, Mess John;
  To him, there and then,   Sir Alured Denne
Wrote a three-corner'd note with a small crow-quill pen,
To say what he wanted, and fix 'the time when,'
And, as it's well known that your people of quality
Pique themselves justly on strict punctuality,
Just as the clock struck the hour he'd nam'd in it,
The whole bridal party rode up to the minute.

Now whether it was that some rapturous dream,
Comprehending 'fat pullets and clouted cream,'
Had borne the good man, in his vision of bliss
Far off to some happier region than this—
Or whether his beads, 'gainst the fingers rebelling,
Took longer than usual that morning in telling;
Or whether, his conscience with knotted cord purging,
Mess John was indulging himself with a scourging,
In penance for killing some score of the fleas,
Which, infesting his hair-shirt, deprived him of ease,

[1] Honest John Capgrave, the veracious biographer of *English Saints,*
author, or rather compiler of the *Nova Legenda Angliae,* was chaplain to
Humphrey, 'the Good Duke' of Gloucester.   A beautiful edition of his
work was printed by Wynkyn de Worde.

Or whether a barrel of Faversham oysters,
Brought in, on the evening before, to the cloisters,
    Produced indigestion, Continues a question,
The particular case is not worth a debate;
For my purpose it's clearly sufficient to state
That whatever the reason, his rev'rence *was* late.
    And Sir Alured Denne, Not the meekest of men,
Began banning away at a deuce of a rate.

Now here, though I do it with infinite pain,
Gentle reader, I find I must pause to explain
    That there was—what, I own,
    I grieve to make known—
On the worthy Knight's character one single stain,
But for which, all his friends had borne witness, I'm sure,
He had been *sans reproche*, as he still was *sans peur*.
The fact is, that many distinguish'd commanders
'Swore terribly' (*teste* T. Shandy) 'in Flanders.'
Now into these parts our Knight chancing to go, countries
Named from this sad, vulgar custom, 'The *Low* Countries,'
Though on common occasions as courteous as daring,
Had pick'd up this shocking bad habit of swearing.
And if anything vex'd him, or matters went wrong,
Was given to what low folks call 'Coming it strong.'
Good, bad, or indifferent then, young or old,
He'd consign them, when once in a humour to scold,
To a place where they certainly would not take cold.
—Now if there are those, and I've some in my eye,
Who'd esteem this a crime of no very deep dye,
Let them read on—they'll find their mistake by and by.

    Near or far, Few people there are
But have heard, read, or sung about Young Lochinvar,
How in Netherby Chapel, 'at morning tide,'
The Priest and the Bridegroom stood waiting the Bride;
    How they waited, 'but ne'er A Bride was there.'
Still I don't find, on reading the ballad with care,
The bereaved Mr Graham proceeded to swear,
And yet to experience so serious a blight in
One's dearest affections, is somewhat exciting.
    'Tis manifest then That Sir Alured Denne
Had far less excuse for such bad language, when
It was only the Priest not the Bride who was missing—
He had fill'd up the interval better with kissing,

And 'twas really surprising, And not very wise in
A Knight to go on so anathematizing,
When the head and the front of the Clergyman's crime
Was but being a little behind as to time:—
　　Be that as it may, He swore so that day
At the reverend gentleman's ill-judged delay,
That not a bystander who heard what he said,
But listen'd to all his expressions with dread,
And felt all his hair stand on end on his head;
　　Nay, many folks there Did not stick to declare
The phenomenon was not confined to the hair,
For the little stone Saint who sat perched o'er the door,
St Romwold himself, as I told you before,
　　What will scarce be believed, Was plainly perceived
To shrug up his shoulders, as very much grieved,
　　And look down with a frown So remarkably brown,
That all saw he'd now quite a different face on
From that he received at the hands of the mason;
Nay, many averr'd he half rose in his niche,
When Sir Alured, always in metaphor rich,
Call'd his priest an 'old son of'—some animal—which,
Is not worth the inquiry—a hint's quite enough on
The subject—for more I refer you to Buffon.

　　It's supposed that the Knight
　　Himself saw the sight,
And it's likely he did, as he easily might,
For 'tis certain he paused in his wordy attack,
And, in nautical language, seem'd 'taken aback.'
　　In so much that when now
　　The 'prime cause of the row,'
Father John, in the chapel at last made his bow,
The Bridegroom elect was so mild and subdued,
None could ever suppose he'd been noisy and rude,
Or made use of the language to which I allude;
Fair Edith herself, while the knot was a tying,
Her bridesmaids around her, some sobbing, some sighing,
Some smiling, some blushing, half-laughing, half-crying,
Scarce made her responses in tones more complying
Than he who'd been raging and storming so recently,
All softness now, and behaving quite decently.
Many folks thought too the cold stony frown
Of the Saint up aloft from his niche looking down,
Brought the sexton and clerk each an extra half-crown,
When, the rite being over, the fees were all paid,
And the party remounting, the whole cavalcade
Prepared to ride home with no little parade.

In a climate so very unsettled as ours
It's as well to be cautious and guard against showers,
　　For though, about One,　You've a fine brilliant sun,
When your walk or your ride is but barely begun,
Yet long ere the hour-hand approaches the Two,
There is not in the whole sky one atom of blue,
But it 'rains cats and dogs,' and you're fairly wet through
Ere you know where to turn, what to say, or to do;
For which reason I've bought, to protect myself well, a
Good stout *Taglioni* and gingham umbrella.
But in Edward the First's days I very much fear,
　　Had a gay cavalier　Thought fit to appear
In any such 'toggery'—then 'twas term'd 'gear'—
He'd have met with a highly significant sneer,
Or a broad grin extending from ear unto ear
On the features of every soul he came near;
There was no taking refuge too then, as with us,
On a slip-sloppy day, in a cab or a bus;
　　As they rode through the woods
　　In their wimples and hoods,
Their only resource against sleet, hail, or rain
Was, as Spenser describes it, to 'pryck o'er the plaine,'
That is to clap spurs on, and ride helter-skelter
In search of some building or other for shelter.

　　Now it seems that the sky,　Which had been of a dye
As bright and as blue as your lady love's eye,
The season in fact being genial and dry,
　　Began to assume　An appearance of gloom
From the moment the Knight began fidget and fume,
Which deepen'd and deepen'd till all the horizon
Grew blacker than aught they had ever set eyes on,
And soon, from the far west the elements' rumbling
Increased, and kept pace with Sir Alured's grumbling,
　　Bright flashes between,　Blue, red, and green,
All livid and lurid began to be seen;
At length down it came—a whole deluge of rain,
A perfect Niagara, drenching the plain,
　　And up came the reek,　And down came the shriek
Of the winds like a steam-whistle starting a train;
And the tempest began so to roar and to pour,
That the Dennes and the Ingoldsby's, starting at score,
As they did from the porch of St Romwold's church door,
Had scarce gain'd a mile, or a mere trifle more,
　　Ere the whole of the crew
　　Were completely wet through:

They dash'd o'er the downs, and they dash'd through the vales,
They dash'd up the hills, and they dash'd down the dales,
As if elderly Nick was himself at their tails;
   The Bridegroom in vain   Attempts to restrain
The Bride's frighten'd palfrey by seizing the rein,
     When a flash and a crash,
     Which produced such a splash,
That a Yankee had called it 'an Almighty Smash,'
   Came down so complete   At his own-courser's feet,
That the rider, though famous for keeping his seat,
From its kickings and plungings, now under now upper,
Slipp'd out of his demi-pique over the crupper,
And fell from the back of his terrified cob
On what bards less refined than myself term his 'Nob.'
(To obtain a *genteel* rhyme's sometimes a tough job.)

Just so—for the nonce to enliven my song
With a classical simile cannot be wrong—
Just so—in such roads and in similar weather,
Tydides and Nestor were riding together,
When, so says old Homer, the King of the Sky,
The great 'Cloud-compeller,' his lightnings let fly,
And their horses both made such a desperate shy
   At this freak of old Zeus,
   That at once they broke loose,
Reins, traces, bits, breechings were all of no use;
If the Pylian Sage, without any delay,
Had not whipp'd them sharp round and away from the fray,
They'd have certainly upset his cabriolet.
And there'd been the—a name I won't mention—to pay.

Well, the Knight in a moment recover'd his seat,
Mr Widdicombe's mode of performing that feat
At Astley's could not be more neat or complete,
—It's recorded, indeed, by an eminent pen
Of our own days, that this *our* great Widdicombe, then
In the heyday of life, had afforded some ten
Or twelve lessons in riding to Alured Denne,—
   It is certain the Knight   Was so agile and light
That an instant sufficed him to set matters right,
Yet the Bride was by this time almost out of sight;
For her palfrey, a rare bit of blood, who could trace
Her descent from the 'pure old Caucasian race,'
   Sleek, slim, and bony, as   Mr Sidonia's
   Fine 'Arab Steed'   Of the very same breed,
Which that elegant gentleman rode so genteelly
—See *Coningsby* written by 'B. Disraeli'—

L 185

That palfrey, I say,   From this trifling delay
Had made what at sea's call'd a 'great deal of way.'
'More fleet than the roe-buck,' and free as the wind,
She had left the good company rather behind;
They whipp'd and they spurr'd, and they after her pressed,
Still Sir Alured's steed was 'by long chalks' the best
Of the party, and very soon distanced the rest;
But long ere e'en he had the fugitive near'd,
She dashed into the wood and at once disappear'd!
It's a 'fashious' affair when you're out on a ride,
—Ev'n supposing you're *not* in pursuit of a bride,
If you are it's more fashious, which can't be denied,—
And you come to a place where three cross-roads divide
Without any way-post, stuck up by the side
Of the road, to direct you and act as a guide,
With a road leading here, and a road leading there,
And a road leading no one exactly knows where.
   When Sir Alured came   In pursuit of the dame
To a fork of this kind,—a three-prong'd one—small blame
To his scholarship if in selecting his way
His respect for the Classics now led him astray;
But the rule, in a work I wont stop to describe is,
In medio semper tutissimus ibis,
So the Knight being forced of the three paths to enter one,
Dash'd, with these words on his lips, down the centre one.

Up and down hill,   Up and down hill,
Through brake and o'er briar he gallops on still
Aye banning, blaspheming, and cursing his fill
At his courser because he had given him a 'spill';
   Yet he did not gain ground
   On the palfrey, the sound,
On the contrary, made by the hoofs of the beast
Grew fainter, and fainter,—and fainter,—and—ceased!
Sir Alured burst through the dingle at last,
To a sort of a clearing, and there—he stuck fast;
For his steed, though a freer one ne'er had a shoe on,
Stood fix'd as the Governor's nag in *Don Juan,*
Or much like the statue that stands, cast in copper, a
Few yards south-east of the door of the Opera,
Save that Alured's horse had not got such a big tail,
While Alured wanted the cock'd hat and pig-tail.

Before him is seen   A diminutive Green
Scoop'd out from the covert—a thick leafy screen
Of wild foliage, trunks with broad branches between
Encircle it wholly, all radiant and sheen,

For the weather at once appear'd clear and serene,
And the sky up above was a bright mazarine,
Just as though no such thing as a tempest had been,
In short it was one of those sweet little places
In Egypt and Araby known as 'oases.'

There, under the shade   That was made by the glade,
The astonish'd Sir Alured sat and survey'd
A little low building of Bethersden stone,
With ivy and parasite creepers o'ergrown,
    A *Sacellum*, or cell   In which Chronicles tell
Saints and anchorites erst were accustomed to dwell;
A little round arch, on which, deeply indented,
The zigzaggy pattern by Saxons invented
Was cleverly chisell'd, and well represented,
    Surmounted a door   Some five feet by four
It might have been less or it might have been more,
In the primitive ages they made these things lower
Than we do in buildings that had but one floor.
    And these Chronicles say   When an anchorite grey
Wish'd to shut himself up and keep out of the way,
He was commonly wont in such low cells to stay,
And pray night and day on the *rez de chaussée*.

There, under the arch I've endeavoured to paint,
    With no little surprise,   And scarce trusting his eyes,
The Knight now saw standing that little Boy Saint!
    The one whom before   He'd seen over the door
Of the Priory shaking his head as he swore—
With mitre, and crozier, and rochet, and stole on,
The very self-same—or at least his Eidolon!
With a voice all unlike to the infantine squeak
You'd expect, that small Saint now address'd him to speak;
    In a bold, manly tone, he   Began, while his stony
Cold lips breath'd an odour quite Eau-de-Cologne-y;
In fact, from his christening, according to rumour, he
Beat Mr Brummell to sticks, in perfumery.[1]

'Sir Alured Denne!'   Said the Saint, 'be atten-
—tive!   Your ancestors, all most respectable men,

---

[1] '*In eodem autem prato in quo baptizatus Sanctus Romualdus nunquam gratissimus odor deficit; neque ibi herbae pallescunt, sed semper in viriditate permanentes magna nectaris suavitate redolent*' ('In that same meadow where St Romwold was baptized there was always a most pleasant fragrance; the plants there did not fade, but always kept green and were scented with the strong sweetness of nectar').—NOV. LEGEND. ANGL.

Have for some generations been vot'ries of mine;
They have bought me mould candles, and bow'd at my shrine,
They have made my monks presents of ven'son and wine,
With a right of free pasturage, too, for their swine,
    And, though you in this   Have been rather remiss,
Still I owe you a turn for the sake of "Lang Syne."
And I now come to tell you, your cursing and swearing
Have reach'd to a pitch that is really past bearing.
    'Twere a positive scandal.   In even a Vandal,
It ne'er should be done, save with bell, book, and candle:
And though I've now learn'd, as I've always suspected,
Your own education's been somewhat neglected;
Still, you're not such an uninformed pagan, I hope,
As not to know cursing belongs to the Pope!
And his Holiness feels, very properly, jealous
Of all such encroachments by paltry lay fellows.
    Now, take my advice,   Saints never speak twice,
So take it at once, as I once for all give it;
Go home! you'll find there all as right as a trivet,
But mind, and remember, if once you give way
To that shocking bad habit, I'm sorry to say,
I have heard you so sadly indulge in to-day,
As sure as you're born, on the very first trip
That you make—the first oath that proceeds from your lip,
    I'll soon make you rue it!—   I've said it—I'll do it!
"Forewarned is forearmed," you shan't say but you knew it;
Whate'er you hold dearest or nearest your heart,
I'LL TAKE IT AWAY, if I come in a cart!
I will, on my honour! you know it's absurd
To suppose that a Saint ever forfeits his word
For a pitiful Knight, or to please any such man—
I've said it! I'll do't—if I don't, I'm a Dutchman!'—

He ceased—he was gone as he closed his harangue,
And someone inside shut the door with a bang!
    Sparkling with dew,   Each green herb anew
Its profusion of sweets round Sir Alured threw,
As pensive and thoughtful he slowly withdrew
(For the hoofs of his horse had got rid of their glue),
And the cud of reflection continued to chew
Till the gables of Bonnington Hall rose in view.
Little reck'd he what he smelt, what he saw,
    Brilliance of scenery,   Fragrance of greenery,
Fail'd in impressing his mental machinery;
Many an hour had elapsed, well I ween, ere he
Fairly was able distinction to draw
'Twixt the odour of garlic and *bouquet du Roi*.

Merrily, merrily sounds the horn,
 And cheerily ring the bells;
  For the race is run, The goal is won,
The little lost mutton is happily found,
The Lady of Bonnington's safe and sound
  In the Hall where her new Lord dwells!
Hard had they ridden, that company gay,
After fair Edith, away and away:
This had slipp'd back o'er his courser's rump,
That had gone over his ears with a plump,
But the Lady herself had stuck on like a trump,
 Till her panting steed Relax'd her speed,
And feeling, no doubt, as a gentleman feels
When he's once shown a bailiff a fair pair of heels,
Stopp'd of herself, as it's very well known
Horses will do, when they're thoroughly blown,
And thus the whole group had forgathered again,
Just as the sunshine succeeded the rain.

Oh, now the joy, and the frolicking, rollicking
 Doings indulged in by one and by all!
Gaiety seized on the most melancholic in
 All the broad lands around Bonnington Hall.
  All sorts of revelry, All sorts of devilry,
   All play at 'High Jinks' and keep up the ball.
Days, weeks, and months, it is really astonishing,
 When one's so happy, how Time flies away;
Meanwhile the Bridegroom requires no admonishing
 As to what pass'd on his own wedding day;
  Never since then Had Sir Alured Denne
Let a word fall from his lip or his pen
That began with a D, or left off with an N!

Once, and once only, when put in a rage,
By a careless young rascal he'd hired as a Page,
 All buttons and brass, Who in handling a glass
 Of spiced hippocras, throws It all over his clothes,
And spoils his best pourpoint, and smartest trunk hose,
While stretching his hand out to take it and quaff it (he
'd given a rose noble a yard for the taffety),
Then, and then only, came into his head
A very sad word that began with a Z,
   But he check'd his complaint,
   He remember'd the Saint,
In the nick—Lady Denne was beginning to faint—
That sight on his mouth acted quite as a bung,
Like Mahomet's coffin, the shocking word hung
Half-way 'twixt the root and the tip of his tongue.

Many a year   Of mirth and good cheer
Flew over their heads, to each other more dear
Every day, they were quoted by peasant and peer
As the rarest examples of love ever known,
Since the days of *Le Chivalier D'Arbie* and *Joanne*,
Who in Bonnington chancel lie sculptured in stone.

Well—it happen'd at last,   After certain years past,
That an embassy came to our court from afar—
From the Grand-duke of Muscovy—now call'd the Czar,
And the Spindleshank'd Monarch, determined to do
All the grace that he could to a Nobleman, who
Had sail'd all that way from a country which few
In our England had heard of, and nobody knew,
With a hat like a muff, and a beard like a Jew,
Our arsenals, buildings, and dock-yards to view,
And to say how desirous   His Prince Wladimirus
Had long been with mutual regard to inspire us,
And how he regretted he was not much nigher us,
With other fine things,   Such as Kings say to Kings
When each tries to humbug his dear Royal Brother, in
Hopes by such 'gammon' to take one another in—
King Longshanks, I say,   Being now on his way
Bound for France, where the rebels had kept him at bay
Was living in clover   At this time at Dover
I' the castle there, waiting a tide to go over.

He had summon'd, I can't tell you how many men,
Knights, nobles, and squires to the wars of Guienne,
And among these of course was Sir Alured Denne,
Who, acting like most   Of the knights in the host,
Whose residence was not too far from the coast,
Had brought his wife with him, delaying their parting,
Fond souls, till the very last moment of starting.
Of course, with such lots of lords, ladies, and knights,
In their *Saracenettes*,[1] and their bright chain-mail tights,
All accustom'd to galas, grand doings, and sights,
A matter like this was at once put to rights;
'Twould have been a strange thing,
If so polish'd a king,
With his board of Green Cloth, and Lord Steward's department,
Couldn't teach an Ambassador what the word 'smart' meant.
A banquet was order'd at once for a score,
Or more, of the corps that had just come on shore,
And the King, though he thought it 'a bit of a bore,'

[1] This silk, of great repute among our ancestors, had been brought home,
a few years before, by Edward, from the Holy Land.

Ask'd all the *élite*   Of his levee to meet
The illustrious Strangers and share in the treat;
For the Boyar himself, the Queen graciously made him her
Beau for the day, from respect to Duke Wladimir.
(Queer as this name may appear in the spelling,
    You won't find it trouble you,   Sound but the W
Like the first L in Llan, Lloyd, and Llewellyn!)

Fancy the fuss and the fidgety looks
Of Robert de Burghersh, the constables, cooks;
    For of course the cuisine   Of the King and the Queen
Was behind them at London, or Windsor, or Sheen,
Or wherever the Court ere it started had been,
    And it's really no jest,   When a troublesome guest
Looks in at a time when you're busy and pressed,
Just going to fight, or to ride, or to rest,
And expects a good lunch when you've none ready dressed.
    The servants no doubt   Were much put to the rout
By this very extempore sort of set out,
But they wisely fell back upon poor Richard's plan,
'When you can't what you would, you must do what you can!'
So they ransack'd the country, folds, pigsties, and pens,
For the sheep and the porkers, the cocks and the hens;
'Twas said a Tom-cat of Sir Alured Denne's,
    A fine tabby-grey,   Disappear'd on that day,
And whatever became of him no one could say;
    They brought all the food   That ever they cou'd,
Fish, flesh, and fowl, with sea-coal and dry wood,
To his Majesty's *Dapifer*, Eudo (or Ude),
They lighted the town up, sat ringing the bells,
And borrow'd the waiters from all the hotels.
A bright thought, moreover, came into the head
Of *Dapifer* Eudo, who'd some little dread,
As he said, for the thorough success of his spread.
So he said to himself, 'What a thing it would be
    Could I have here with me   Some one two or three
Of their outlandish scullions from over the sea!
It's a hundred to one if the Suite or their Chief
Understand our plum-puddings, and barons of beef;
But with five minutes' chat with their cooks or their valets
We'd soon dish up something to tickle their palates!'
With this happy conceit for improving the Mess,
Pooh-poohing expense, he dispatch'd an express
In a wagon and four on the instant to Deal,
Who dash'd down the hill without locking the wheel,
And, by means which I guess but decline to reveal,

Seduced from the Downs, where at anchor their vessel rode,
Lumpoff Icywitz, serf to a former Count Nesselrode,
  A cook of some fame, Who invented the same
Cold pudding that still bears the family name.
This accomplish'd, the Chef's peace of mind was restor'd,
And in due time a banquet was placed on the board
'In the very best style,' which implies in a word
'All the dainties the season' (and king) 'could afford.'
        There were snipes, there were rails,
        There were woodcocks and quails,
There were peacocks served up in their pride (that is tails),
  Fricandeau, fricassees, Ducks and green peas,
Cotelettes à l'Indienne, and chops *à la Soubise*
(Which last you may call 'onion sauce' if you please),
    There were barbecu'd pigs
    Stuff'd with raisins and figs,
Omelettes and haricots, stews and ragouts,
And pork griskins, which Jews still refuse and abuse.
Then the wines—round the circle how swiftly they went!
Canary, Sack, Malaga, Malvoisie, Tent;
Old Hock from the Rhine, wine remarkably fine,
Of the Charlemagne vintage of seven ninety-nine,—
Five cent'ries in bottle had made it divine!
The rich juice of Rousillon, Gascoygne, Bordeaux,
  Marasquin, Curaçoa, Kirchen Wasser, Noyeau,
And Gin which the company voted 'No Go';
  The guests all hobnobbing, And bowing and bobbing;
Some prefer white wine, while others more value red,
  Few, a choice few, Of more orthodox *goût*,
Stick to 'old crusted port,' among whom was Sir Alured;
Never indeed at a banquet before
Had that gallant commander enjoy'd himself more.

Then came 'sweets'—served in silver were tartlets and pies—in
     glass
Jellies composed of punch, calves' feet, and isinglass,
Creams, and whipped-syllabubs, some hot, some cool,
Blancmange, and quince-custards, and gooseberry fool.
And now from the good taste which reigns it's confesed
In a gentleman's, that is an Englishman's, breast,
And makes him polite to a stranger and guest,
      They soon play'd the deuce
      With a large Charlotte Russe;
More than one of the party dispatched his plate twice
With 'I'm really ashamed, but—another small slice!
Your dishes from Russia are really *so* nice!'

Then the prime dish of all!   'There was nothing so good in
   The whole of the Feed'   One and all were agreed,
'As the great Lumpoff Icywitz' Nesselrode pudding!'
Sir Alured Denne, who'd all day, to say sooth,
Like Iago, been 'plagued with a sad raging tooth,'
Which had nevertheless interfered very little
With his—what for my rhyme I'm obliged to spell—vittle,
   Requested a friend   Who sat near him to send
Him a spoonful of what he heard all so commend,
And begg'd to take wine with him afterwards, grateful
Because for a spoonful he'd sent him a plateful.
Having emptied his glass—he ne'er balk'd it or spill'd it—
The gallant Knight open'd his mouth—and then fill'd it!
You must really excuse me—there's nothing could bribe
Me at all to go on and attempt to describe
   The fearsome look then   Of Sir Alured Denne!
—Astonishment, horror, distraction of mind,
Rage, misery, fear, and iced pudding—combined!
Lip, forehead, and cheek—how these mingle and meet;
All colours, all hues, now advance, now retreat,
Now pale as a turnip, now crimson as beet!
How he grasps his arm-chair in attempting to rise,
See his veins how they swell! mark the roll of his eyes!
Now east and now west, now north and now south,
Till at once he contrives to eject from his mouth
   That vile 'spoonful'—what
   He has got he knows not,
He isn't quite sure if it's cold or it's hot;
At last he exclaims, as he starts from his seat,
'A SNOWBALL by ——!' what I decline to repeat,—
'Twas the name of a bad place, for mention unmeet.

Then oh what a volley!—a great many heard
What flow'd from his lips, and 'twere really absurd
To suppose that each man was not shock'd by each word;
A great many heard too, with mix'd fear and wonder,
The terrible crash of the terrible thunder,
That broke as if bursting the building asunder;
But very few heard, although everyone might,
The short, half-stifled shriek from the chair on the right,
Where the Lady of Bonnington sat by her Knight;
And very few saw—some—the number was small,
In the large ogive window that lighted the hall,
A small stony Saint in a small stony pall,
With a small stony mitre, and small stony crosier,
And small stony toes that owed nought to the hosier,
  * L 185

Beckon stonily downward to *someone* below,
As Merryman says, 'for to come for to go!'
While everyone smelt a delicious perfume
That seem'd to pervade every part of the room!

Fair Edith Denne,   The *bonne et belle* then,
Never again was beheld among men!
But there was the *fauteuil* on which she was placed,
And there was the girdle that graced her small waist,
And there was her stomacher brilliant with gems,
And the mantle she wore, edged with lace at the hems,
Her rich brocade gown sat upright in its place,
And her wimple was there—but where—WHERE WAS HER FACE?
'Twas gone with her body—and nobody knows,
Nor could anyone present so much as suppose
How that Lady contrived to slip out of her clothes!
But 'twas done—she was quite gone—the how and the where,
No mortal was ever yet found to declare;
Though inquiries were made, and some writers record
That Sir Alured offered a handsome reward.

King Edward went o'er to his wars in Guienne,
Taking with him his barons, his knights, and his men.
        You may look through the whole
        Of that King's muster-roll,
And you won't find the name of Sir Alured Denne;
But Chronicles tell that there formerly stood
A little old chapel in Bilsington Wood;
   The remains to this day,   Archaeologists say,
May be seen, and I'd go there and look if I could.
   There long dwelt a hermit remarkably good,
   Who lived all alone,   And never was known
To use bed or bolster, except the cold stone;
But would groan and would moan in so piteous a tone,
A wild Irishman's heart had responded 'Och hone!'
As the fashion with hermits of old was to keep skins
To wear with the wool on—most commonly sheep-skins.
He, too, like the rest was accustom'd to do so;
His beard, as no barber came near him, too, grew so,
He bore some resemblance to Robinson Crusoe,
In Houndsditch, I'm told, you'll sometimes see a Jew so.

   He lived on the roots,   And the cob-nuts and fruits,
Which the kind-hearted rustics, who rarely are churls
In such matters, would send by their boys and their girls;

They'd not get him to speak,
  If they'd tried for a week,
But the colour would always mount up in his cheek,
And he'd look like a dragon if ever he heard
His young friends use a naughty expression or word.
How long he lived, or at what time he died,
'Twere hard, after so many years to decide,
But there's one point on which all traditions agree,
That he *did* die at last, leaving no legatee,
And his linen was marked with an A and a D.

Alas! for the glories of Bonnington Hall!
Alas, for its splendour! alas for its fall!
  Long years have gone by
  Since the trav'ler might spy
Any decentish house in the parish at all.
For very soon after the awful event
I've related, 'twas said through all that part of Kent
That the maids of a morning, when putting the chairs
And the tables to rights, would oft pop unawares
In one of the parlours, or galleries, or stairs,
On a tall female figure, or find her, far horrider,
Slowly o' nights promenading the corridor;
But whatever the hour, or wherever the place,
No one could ever get sight of her face!
  Nor could they perceive Any arm in her sleeve,
While her legs and her feet too, seem'd mere 'make-believe,'
For she glided along with that shadow-like motion
  Which gives one the notion
Of clouds on a zephyr, or ships on the ocean;
And though of her gown they could *hear* the silk rustle,
They saw but that side on't *ornée* with the bustle.
The servants, of course, though the house they were born in,
Soon 'wanted to better themselves,' and gave warning,
While even the new Knight grew tired of a guest
Who would not let himself or his family rest;
  So he pack'd up his all, And made a bare wall
Of each well-furnished room in his ancestors' Hall,
Then left the old Mansion to stand or to fall,
Having previously barr'd up the windows and gates,
To avoid paying sesses and taxes and rates,
And settled on one of his other estates,
Where he built a new mansion, and called it Denne Hill,
And there his descendants reside, I think, still.

Poor Bonnington, empty, or left, at the most,
To the joint occupation of rooks and a Ghost,

Soon went to decay,   And moulder'd away,
But whether it dropp'd down at last I can't say,
Or whether the jackdaws produced, by degrees, a
Spontaneous combustion like that one at Pisa
    Some cent'ries ago,   I'm sure I don't know,
But you can't find a vestige now ever so tiny,
'*Perierunt*,' as someone says, '*etiam ruinae.*'

MORAL

The first maxim a couple of lines may be said in,
If you *are* in a passion, don't swear at a wedding!

Whenever you chance to be ask'd out to dine,
Be exceedingly cautious—don't take too much wine!
In your eating remember one principal point,
Whatever you do, have your eye on the joint!
Keep clear of side dishes, don't meddle with those
Which the servants in livery, or those in plain clothes,
Poke over your shoulders and under your nose;
Or, if you *must* live on the fat of the land,
And feed on fine dishes you don't understand,
Buy a good book of cookery!   I've a compact one,
First rate of the kind, just brought out by Miss Acton,
This will teach you their names, the ingredients they're made of,
And which to indulge in, and which be afraid of,
Or else, ten to one, between ice and cayenne,
You'll commit yourself some day, like Alured Denne.

'To persons about to be married,' I'd say
Don't exhibit ill humour, at least on The Day!
And should there perchance be a trifling delay
On the part of officials, extend them your pardon,
And don't snub the parson, the clerk, or churchwarden!

To married men this—For the rest of your lives,
Think how your misconduct may act on your wives!
Don't swear then before them, lest haply they faint,
Or what sometimes occurs—run away with a Saint!

THE BROTHERS OF BIRCHINGTON

A Lay of St Thomas à Becket

You are all aware that   On our throne there once sat
A very great King who'd an Angevin hat,
With a great sprig of broom, which he wore as a badge in it,
Named from this circumstance, Henry Plantagenet.

Pray don't suppose   That I'm going to prose
O'er Queen Eleanor's wrongs, or Miss Rosamond's woes,
With the dagger and bowl, and all that sort of thing,
Not much to the credit of Miss, Queen, or King.

The tale may be true,   But between me and you,
With the King's escapade I'll have nothing to do;
But shall merely select, as a theme for my rhymes,
A fact, which occurr'd to some folks in his times.

If for health, or a 'lark,'   You should ever embark
In that best of improvements on boats since the Ark,
The steam-vessel call'd the *Red Rover*, the barge
Of an excellent officer, named Captain Large,

You may see, some half way
   'Twixt the pier at Herne Bay
And Margate, the place where you're going to stay,
A village called Birchington, fam'd for its 'Rolls,'
As the fishing-bank, just in its front, is for Soles.

Well—there stood a fane
   In this Harry Broom's reign,
On the edge of the cliff, overhanging the main,
Renown'd for its sanctity all through the nation,
And orthodox friars of the Austin persuasion.

Among them there was one,
   Whom if once I begun
To describe as I ought I should never have done,
Father Richard of Birchington, so was the Friar
Yclept, whom the rest had elected their Prior.

He was tall and upright,   About six feet in height,
His complexion was what you'd denominate light,
And the tonsure had left, 'mid his ringlets of brown,
A little bald patch on the top of his crown.

His bright sparkling eye   Was of hazel, and nigh
Rose a finely arch'd eyebrow of similar dye,
He'd a small, well-formed mouth with the *Cupidon* lip
And an aquiline nose, somewhat red at the tip.

In doors and out   He was very devout,
With his *Aves* and *Paters*—and oh, such a knout!!
For his self-flagellations! the Monks used to say
He would wear out two penn'orth of whipcord a day!

Then how his piety   Shows in his diet, he
Dines upon pulse, or, by way of variety,
Sand-eels or dabs; or his appetite mocks
With those small periwinkles that crawl on the rocks.

In brief, I don't stick   To declare Father Dick—
So they call'd him, 'for short'—was a 'Regular Brick,'
A metaphor taken—I have not the page aright—
Out of an ethical work by the Stagyrite.

Now Nature, 'tis said,   Is a comical jade,
And among the fantastical tricks she has play'd,
Was the making our good Father Richard a Brother,
As like him in form as one pea's like another;

He was tall and upright,   About six feet in height,
His complexion was what you'd denominate light,
And, though he had not shorn his ringlets of brown,
He'd a little bald patch on the top of his crown.

He'd a bright sparkling eye   Of the hazel, hard by
Rose a finely arch'd *sourcil* of similar dye;
He'd a small, well-shaped mouth, with a *Cupidon* lip,
And a good Roman rose, rather red at the tip.

But here, it's pretended,   The parallel ended;
In fact, there's no doubt his life might have been mended,
And people who spoke of the Prior with delight,
Shook their heads if you mentioned his brother, the Knight.

If you'd credit report   There was nothing but sport,
And High Jinks going on night and day at 'the Court,'
Where Sir Robert, instead of devotion and charity,
Spent all his time in unseemly hilarity.

He drinks and he eats   Of choice liquors and meats,
And he goes out on We'n'sdays and Fridays to treats,
Gets tipsy whenever he dines or he sups,
And is wont to come quarrelsome home in his cups.

No *Paters*, no *Aves*;   An absolute slave he's
To tarts, pickled salmon, and sauces, and gravies;
While as to his beads—what a shame in a Knight!—
He really don't know the wrong end from the right!

So, though 'twas own'd then   By nine people in ten,
That 'Robert and Richard were two pretty men,'
Yet, there the praise ceased, or, at least the good Priest
Was consider'd the 'Beauty,' Sir Robert the 'Beast.'

Indeed, I'm afraid   More might have been laid
To the charge of the Knight than was openly said,
For then we'd no 'Phiz's,' no 'H. B.'s,' nor 'Leeches,'
To call Roberts 'Bobs,' and illustrate their speeches.

'Twas whisper'd he'd rob,   Nay murder! a job
Which would stamp him no 'Brick,' but a 'Regular Snob'
(An obsolete term, which, at this time of day,
We should probably render by *Mauvais Sujet*).

Now if *here* such affairs   Get wind unawares,
They are bruited about, doubtless, much more 'downstairs,'
Where Old Nick has a register-office, they say,
With Commissioners quite of such matters *au fait*.

Of course when he heard   What his people averr'd
Of Sir Robert's proceedings in deed and in word,
He asked for the ledger, and hastened to look
At the leaves on the Creditor side of this book.

'Twas with more than surprise
     That he now ran his eyes
O'er the numberless items, oaths, curses, and lies,
Et cetera, set down in Sir Robert's account,
He was quite 'flabbergasted' to see the amount.

'Dear me! this is wrong!   It's a great deal too strong,
I'd no notion this bill had been standing so long—
Send Levybub here!' and he filled up a writ
Of '*Ca sa*,' duly prefaced with 'Limbo to wit.'

'Here Levybub, quick!' To his bailiff, said Nick,
'I'm "ryled," and "my dander's up," "Go a-head slick"
Up to Kent—not Kentuck—and at once fetch away
A snob there—I guess that's a *Mauvais Sujet*.

'One De Birchington, knight—'Tis not clear quite
What his t'other name is—they've not enter'd it right,
Ralph, Robert, or Richard? they've not gone so far,
Our critturs have put it down merely as "R."

'But he's tall and upright, About six feet in height,
His complexion, I reckon, you'd calculate light,
And he's farther "set down" having ringlets of brown,
With a little bald patch on the top of his crown.

'Then his eye and his lip, Hook-nose, red at tip
Are marks your attention can't easily slip;
Take Slomanoch with you, he's got a good knack
Of soon grabbing his man, and be back in a crack!'

That same afternoon, Father Dick, who as soon
Would 'knock in' or 'cut chapel' as jump o'er the moon,
Was missing at vespers—at compline—all night!
And his monks were, of course, in a deuce of a fright.

Morning dawn'd—'twas broad day,
   Still no Prior! the tray
With his muffins and eggs went untasted away;—
He came not to luncheon—all said, 'it was rum of him!'
—None could conceive what on earth had become of him.

They examined his cell, They peep'd down the well;
They went up the tow'r and looked into the bell,
They dragg'd the great fish-pond, the little one tried,
But found nothing at all, save some carp—which they fried.

'Dear me! Dear me! Why, where can he be?
He's fall'n over the cliff?—tumbled into the sea?'
'Stay—he talk'd,' exclaimed one, 'if I recollect right,
Of making a call on his brother, the Knight!'

He turns as he speaks,
   The 'Court Lodge' he seeks,
Which was known then, as now, by the queer name of Quekes,
But scarce half a mile on his way had he sped,
When he spied the good Prior in the paddock—stone dead!

Alas! 'twas too true!   And I need not tell you
In the convent his news made a pretty to do;
Through all its wide precincts so roomy and spacious,
Nothing was heard but 'Bless *me*!' and 'Good Gracious!!'

They sent for the May'r   And the Doctor, a pair
Of grave men, who began to discuss the affair,
When in bounced the Coroner, foaming with fury,
'Because,' as he said, ''twas pooh! pooh! ing his jury.'

Then commenced a dispute,
    And so hot they went to't,
That things seem'd to threaten a serious *émeute*,
When, just in the midst of the uproar and racket,
Who should walk in but St Thomas à Becket.

Quoth his saintship, 'How now?
    Here's a fine coil, I trow!
I should like to know, gentlemen, what's all this row?
Mr Wickliffe—or Wackliffe—whatever your name is—
And you, Mr May'r, don't you know, Sirs, what shame is?

'Pray what's all this clatter
    About?—what's the matter?'
Here a monk, whose teeth funk and concern made to chatter,
Sobs out, as he points to the corpse on the floor,
''Tis all dickey with poor Father Dick—he's no more!'

'How!—what?' says the saint,
    'Yes he is—no he ain't,[1]
He can't be deceased—pooh! it's merely a faint,
Or some foolish mistake which may serve for our laughter,
"He *should* have died," like the old Scotch Queen, "hereafter."

'His time is not out;   Some blunder, no doubt,
It shall go hard but what I'll know what it's about—
I shan't be surprised if that scurvy Old Nick's
Had a hand in't; it savours of one of his tricks.'

When a crafty old hound
    Claps his nose to the ground,
Then throws it up boldly, and bays out, 'I've found!'
And the Pack catch the note, I'd as soon think to check it,
As dream of bamboozling St Thomas à Becket.

---

[1] *Cantise*, for 'is not'; St Thomas, it seems, had lived long enough in the country to pick up a few of its provincialisms.

Once on the scent,   To business he went,
'You Scoundrel, come here, Sir' ('twas Nick that he meant),
'Bring your books here this instant—bestir yourself—do,
I've no time to waste on such fellows as you.'

Every corner and nook   In all Erebus shook,
As he struck on the pavement his pastoral crook,
All its tenements trembled from basement to roofs,
And their *nigger* inhabitants shook in their hoofs.

Hanging his ears,   Yet dissembling his fears,
Ledger in hand, straight 'Auld Hornie' appears,
With that sort of half-sneaking, half-impudent look,
Bankrupts sport when cross-question'd by Cresswell or Cooke.

'So, Sir-r-r! you are here,'   Said the Saint with a sneer,
'My summons, I trust, did not much interfere
With your morning engagements—I merely desire,
At your leisure, to know what you've done with my Prior?

'Now, none of your lies,   Mr Nick! I'd advise
You to tell me the truth without any disguise,
Or-r-r!'   The Saint, while his rosy gills seem'd to grow rosier,
Here gave another great thump with his Crosier.

Like a small boy at Eton,   Who's not quite a Crichton,
And don't know his task but expects to be beaten,
Nick stammer'd, scarce knowing what answer to make,
'Sir, I'm sadly afraid here has been a mistake.

'These things will occur,   We are all apt to err,
The most cautious sometimes as you know, holy Sir;
For my own part—I'm sure I do all that I can—
But—the fact is—I fear—we have got the wrong man.'

'Wrong man!' roar'd the Saint—
    But the scene I can't paint,
The best colours I have are a great deal too faint—
Nick afterwards own'd that he ne'er knew what fright meant,
Before he saw Saint under so much excitement.

'Wrong man! don't tell me—   Pooh!—fiddle-de-dee!
What's your right, Scamp, to *any* man!—come, let me see;
I'll teach you, you thorough-paced rascal, to meddle
With church matters, come, Sirrah, out with your schedule!'

In support of his claim The Fiend turns to the name
Of 'De Birchington' written in letters of flame,
Below which long items stand, column on column,
Enough to have eked out a decent-sized volume!

Sins of all sorts and shapes,
From small practical japes,
Up to dicings, and drinkings, and murders, and rapes,
And then of such standing!—a merciless tick,
From an Oxford tobacconist,—let alone Nick.

The Saint in surprise Scarce believed his own eyes,
Still he knew he'd to deal with the father of lies,
And 'So *this*!—you call *this*!' he exclaimed in a searching tone,
This!!! the account of my friend Dick de Birchington!'

'Why,' said Nick, with an air
Of great candour, 'it's there
Lies the awkwardest part of this awkward affair—
I thought all was right—see the height tallies quite,
The complexion's what all must consider as light;
There's the nose, and the lip, and the ringlets of brown,
And the little bald patch on the top of the crown.

'And then the surname, So exactly the same—
I don't know—I can't tell how the accident came,
But *some* how—I own it's a very sad job,
But—my bailiff grabb'd Dick when he *should* have nabb'd Bob.

'I am vex'd beyond bounds
You should have such good grounds
For complaint; I would rather have given five pounds,
And any apology, Sir, you may choose,
I'll make with much pleasure, and put in the *News*.'

'An apology!—pooh! Much good that will do!
An "*apology*" quoth a!—and that too from you!—
Before any proposal is made of the sort,
Bring back your stol'n goods, thief!—produce them in Court!'

In a moment, so small It seem'd no time at all,
Father Richard sat up on his what-do-ye-call—
Sur son séant—and, what was as wondrous as pleasing,
At once began coughing, and sniffing, and sneezing.

While, strange to relate,   The Knight, whom the fate
Of his brother had reach'd, and who'd knocked at the gate,
To make further inquiries, had scarce made his bow
To the Saint, ere he vanish'd and no one knew how!

Erupit—evasit,   As Tully would phrase it,
And none could have known where to find his *Hic jacet*—
That sentence which man his mortality teaches—
Sir Robert had disappear'd, body and breeches!

'Heyday! Sir, heyday!   What's the matter now—eh,'
Quoth A'Becket, observing the gen'ral dismay,
'How, again!—'pon my word this is really too bad!
It would drive *any* Saint in the calendar mad.

'What, still at your tricking?
    You *will* have a kicking?
I see you won't rest till you've got a good licking—
Your claim, friend?—what claim?—why you show'd me before
That your *old* claim was cancell'd—you've crossed out the
    score!

'Is that the way you'd Jew one?
    You've settled the true one?
Do you mean to tell me he has run up a new one?
    Of the thousands you've cheated
    And scurvily treated,
Name one you've dared charge with a bill once receipted!
In the Bankruptcy Court should you dare to presume
To attempt it, they'd soon kick you out of the room,
—Ask Commissioner Fonblanque, or ask my Lord Brougham.

'And then to make under   So barefaced a blunder
Your caption!—why, what's the world come to, I wonder?
My patience! it's just like his impudence, drat him!
—Stand out of the way there, and let me get at him!'

The Saint raised his arm   But Old Nick, in alarm,
Dash'd up through the skylight, not doing much harm,
While, *quitte pour la peur*, the Knight, sound on the whole,
Down the chimney came tumbling as black as a coal!

Spare we to tell   Of what after befell!
How the Saint lectured Robert de Birchington well,
Bade him alter his life, and held out as a warning
The narrow escape he'd made on't that morning.

Nor need we declare   How, then and there,
The Jury and Coroner blew up the May'r
For his breach of decorum as one of the Quorum,
In not having Levybub brought up before 'em.

Nor will you require   Me to state how the Prior
Could never thenceforth bear the sight of a fire,
Nor ever was heard to express a desire
In cold weather to see the thermometer higher.

Nor shall I relate   The subsequent fate
Of St Thomas à Becket, whose reverend pate
Fitzurse and De Morville, and Brito and Tracy
Shaved off, as his crown had been merely a jasey.[1]

Suffice it to say   From that notable day
The 'Twin Birchington Brothers' together grew grey:
In the same holy convent continued to dwell,
Same food and same fastings, same habit, same cell.

No more the Knight rattles   In broils and in battles,
But sells, by De Robins, his goods and his chattels,
And counting all wealth a mere Will-o'-the-Wisp,
Disposes of Quekes to Sir Nicholas Crispe.

One spot alone   Of all he had known
Of his spacious domain he retain'd as his own,
In a neighbouring parish, whose name, I may say
Scarce any two people pronounce the same way.

Re-*cul*-ver some style it,   While others revile it
As bad, and say Re-culver—'tisn't worth while, it
Would seem, to dispute, when we know the result immat-
erial—I accent, myself, the penultimate.

Sages, with brains   Full of 'Saxon remains,'
May call me a booby, perhaps, for my pains,
Still I hold, at the hazard of being thought dull by 'em,
Fast by the quantity mark'd for *Regulbium*.

[1] '*Nec satis fuit eis sanguine sacerdotis et nece ecclesiam prophanare, nisi, coronâ capitis amputatâ, funestis gladiis jam defuncti ejicerent cerebrum*' ('Not satisfied with profaning the church by the blood of a priest and by murder, they cut off the top of his head and with their deadly swords spilt out the brains of the dead man').—MATT PARIS.

Call't as you will,   The Traveller still,
In the voyage that we talk'd about, marks on the hill
Overhanging the sea, the 'twin towers' raised then
By 'Robert and Richard, those two pretty men.'

Both tall and upright,   And just equal in height;
The Trinity House talked of painting them white,
And the thing was much spoken of some time ago,
When the Duke, I believe—but I really don't know.

Well—there the 'Twins' stand
   On the verge of the land,
To warn mariners off from the Columbine sand,
And many a poor man have Robert and Dick
By their vow caused to 'scape, like themselves, from Old Nick.

So, whether you're sailors   Or Tooley-street Tailors,
Broke loose from your masters, those sternest of jailers,
And, bent upon pleasure, are taking your trip
In a craft which you fondly conceive is a ship,
      When you've passed by the Nore,
      And you hear the winds roar
In a manner you scarce could have fancied before,
      When the cordage and tackling
      Are flapping and crackling,
   And the boy with the bell   Thinks it useless to tell
You that's 'dinner on table,' because you're unwell;

   When above you all's 'scud,'
   And below you the flood
Looks a horrible picture of soap-suds and mud,
      When the timbers are straining,
      And folks are complaining,
The dead-lights are letting the spray and the rain in,
   When the helmsman looks blue,
   And Captain Large too,
And you really don't know what on earth you shall do.
   In this hubbub and row,   Think where you'd be now
Except for the Birchington boys and their vow!
And while o'er the wide wave you feel the craft pitch hard,
𝔓𝔯𝔞𝔦𝔢 𝔣𝔬𝔯 𝔶𝔢 𝔰𝔬𝔴𝔩𝔢𝔰 𝔬𝔣 ℜ𝔬𝔟𝔢𝔯𝔱𝔱𝔢 𝔞𝔫𝔡 ℜ𝔶𝔠𝔥𝔞𝔯𝔡.

MORAL

It's a subject of serious complaint in some houses,
With young married men who have elderly spouses,
That persons are seen in their figures and faces,
With very queer people in very queer places,
So like them that one for the other's oft taken,
And conjugal confidence thereby much shaken:
Explanations too often are thought mere pretences,
And Richard gets scolded for Robert's offences.

   In a matter so nice,   If I'm ask'd my advice,
I say copy King Henry to obviate that,
And stick something remarkable up in your hat!
Next, observe, in this world where we've so many cheats,
How useful it is to preserve your receipts!
If you deal with a person whose truth you don't doubt,
Be particular, still, that your bill is cross'd out;
But, with any inducement to think him a scamp,
Have a formal receipt on a regular stamp!

Let every gay gallant my story who notes,
Take warning, and not go on 'sowing wild oats'!
   Nor depend that some friend   Will always attend,
And by 'making all right' bring him off in the end;
He may be mistaken, so let him beware,
St Thomas à Beckets are now rather rare.

Last of all, may'rs and magistrates, never be rude
To juries! they are people who *won't* be pooh-pooh'd!
Especially Sandwich ones—no one can say
But himself may come under their clutches one day;
   They then may pay off.   In kind any scoff,
And, turning, their late verdict quite '*wisey wersey*,'
'*Acquit* you, and *not* recommend you to mercy.' [1]

[1] At a Quarter Sessions held at Sandwich (some six miles from Birchington), on Tuesday the 8th of April last, before W. F. Boteler, Esq., the recorder, Thomas Jones, mariner, aged 17, was tried for stealing a jacket, value ten shillings. The jury, after a patient hearing, found him 'not guilty,' and 'recommended him to mercy.'—See the whole case reported in the *Kentish Observer*, 10th April 1845.

THE KNIGHT AND THE LADY

A Domestic Legend of the Reign of Queen Anne

'Hail wedded love! mysterious tie!'

THOMSON—OR SOMEBODY.

The Lady Jane was tall and slim,
  The Lady Jane was fair,
And Sir Thomas, her Lord, was stout of limb,
But his cough was short, and his eyes were dim,
And he wore green 'specs,' with a tortoiseshell rim,
And his hat was remarkably broad in the brim,
And she was uncommonly fond of him,—
    And they were a loving pair!—
      And the name and the fame
      Of the Knight and his Dame
Were ev'rywhere hail'd with the loudest acclaim;
And wherever they went, or wherever they came,
      Far and wide,   The people cried,
Huzza! for the Lord of this noble domain,—
Huzza! Huzza! Huzza!—once again!—
    Encore!—Encore!—   One cheer more!—
—All sorts of pleasure, and no sort of pain
To Sir Thomas the Good, and the Fair Lady Jane!!

      Now Sir Thomas the Good,   Be it well understood,
Was a man of a very contemplative mood,—
    He would pore by the hour,   O'er a weed or a flower,
Or the slugs that come crawling out after a shower;
Black-beetles, and Bumble-Bees,—Blue-bottle flies,
And Moths were of no small account in his eyes;
An 'Industrious Flea' he'd by no means despise,
While an 'Old Daddy-long-legs,' whose 'long legs' and thighs
Pass'd the common in shape, or in colour, or size,
He was wont to consider an absolute prize,
Nay, a hornet or wasp he could scarce 'keep his paws off'—he
    Gave up, in short,   Both business and sport,
And abandon'd himself, *tout entier*, to Philosophy.

Now, as Lady Jane was tall and slim,
  And Lady Jane was fair,
And a good many years the junior of him,—

And as he,   All agree,
        Look'd less like her *Mari*,
As he walk'd by her side, than her *Père*,[1]
There are some might be found entertaining a notion
That such an entire and exclusive devotion
To that part of science, folks style Entomology,
    Was a positive shame,   And, to such a fair Dame,
Really demanded some sort of apology;
    No doubt, it *would* vex   One half of the sex
To see their own husband, in horrid green 'specs,'
Instead of enjoying a sociable chat,
Still poking his nose into this and to that,
At a gnat, or a bat, or a cat, or a rat,
    Or great ugly things,   All legs and wings,
With nasty long tails arm'd with nasty long stings;
And they'd join such a log of a spouse to condemn,—
    One eternally thinking,   And blinking, and winking
At grubs,—when he ought to be winking at them.—
    But no!—oh no!   'Twas by no means so
With the Lady Jane Ingoldsby—she, far discreeter,
And, having a temper more even and sweeter,
    Would never object to   *Her* spouse, in respect to
    His poking and peeping   After 'things creeping';
Much less be still keeping lamenting, and weeping,
Or scolding at what she perceived him so deep in.

    Tout au contraire,   No lady so fair
Was e'er known to wear more contented an air;
And,—let who would call,—every day she was there
Propounding receipts for some delicate fare,
Some toothsome conserve, of quince, apple, or pear,
Or distilling strong waters,—or potting a hare,—
Or counting her spoons and her crockery-ware;—
Or else, her tambour-frame before her, with care
Embroidering a stool or a back for a chair,
With needlework roses, most cunning and rare,
Enough to make less-gifted visitors stare,
    And declare, where'er
    They had been, that, 'they ne'er
In their lives had seen aught that at all could compare
With dear Lady Jane's housewifery—that they would swear.

[1] My friend, Mr Hood,
        In his comical mood,
Would have probably styled the good Knight and his Lady—
Him—'Stern-old and Hopkins,' and her 'Tête and Braidy.'

Nay more; don't suppose   With such doings as those
This account of her merits must come to a close;
No;—examine her conduct more closely, you'll find
She by no means neglected improving her mind;
For there, all the while, with air quite bewitching,
She sat herring-boning, tambouring, or stitching,
Or having an eye to affairs of the kitchen,
   Close by her side,   Sat her kinsman, MacBride,
Her cousin, fourteen-times removed,—as you'll see
If you look at the Ingoldsby family tree,
In *Burke's Commoners*, vol. xx, page 53.

All the papers I've read agree,   Too, with the pedigree,
Where, among the collateral branches, appears
'Captain Dugald MacBride, Royal Scots Fusileers';
And I doubt if you'd find in the whole of his clan
A more highly intelligent, worthy young man;—
   And there he'd be sitting,   While she was a-knitting,
Or hemming, or stitching, or darning and fitting.
Or putting 'a gore,' or a 'gusset,' or 'bit' in,
Reading aloud, with a very grave look,
Some very 'wise saw' from some very good book,—
   Some such pious divine as   St Thomas Aquinas:
   Or, equally charming,   The works of Bellarmine;
   Or else he unravels   The 'voyages and travels'
Of Hackluytz—(how sadly these Dutch names *do* sully verse!)—
Purchas's, Hawksworth's, or Lemuel Gulliver's,—
Not to name others, 'mongst whom there are few so
Admired as John Bunyan, and Robinson Crusoe.—
   No matter who came,   It was always the same,
The Captain was reading aloud to the Dame,
   Till, from having gone through half the books on the shelf,
They were almost as wise as Sir Thomas himself.

Well,—it happened one day,   —I really can't say
The particular month;—but I *think* 'twas in May,—
'Twas I *know*, in the Springtime,—when 'Nature looks gay,'
As the Poet observes,—and on tree-top and spray
The dear little dicky-birds carol away;
When the grass is so green, and the sun is so bright,
And all things are teeming with life and with light,—
That the whole of the house was thrown into affright,
For no soul could conceive what was gone with the Knight!

It seems he had taken   A light breakfast—bacon,
An egg—with a little broiled haddock—at most
A round and a half of some hot butter'd toast,
With a slice of cold sirloin from yesterday's roast.

And then—let me see!—   He had two—perhaps three
Cups (with sugar and cream) of strong Gunpowder tea,
With a spoonful in each of some choice *eau de vie*,
—Which with nine out of ten would perhaps disagree.—
   In fact, I and my son   Mix 'black' with our 'Hyson,'
Neither having the nerves of a bull, or a bison,
And both hating brandy like what some call 'pison,'
   No matter for that—He had call'd for his hat,
With the brim that I've said was so broad and so flat,
And his 'specs' with the tortoiseshell rim, and his cane
With the crutch-handled top, which he used to sustain
His steps in his walks, and to poke in the shrubs
And the grass, when unearthing his worms and his grubs—
Thus arm'd, he set out on a ramble—alack!
He *set out*, poor dear Soul!—but he never came back!

'First dinner-bell' rang   Out its euphonous clang
At five—folks kept early hours then—and the 'Last'
Ding-dong'd, as it ever was wont, at half past,
   While Betsy, and Sally,   And Thompson, the Valet,
And everyone else was beginning to bless himself,
Wondering the Knight had not come in to dress himself.—
—Quoth Betsy, 'Dear me! why, the fish will be cold!'—
Quoth Sally, 'Good Gracious! how "Missis" *will* scold!'—
   Thompson, the Valet,   Look'd gravely at Sally,
As who should say 'Truth must not always be told!'
Then, expressing a fear lest the Knight might take cold,
         Thus exposed to the dews,
      Lamb's-wool stockings, and shoes,
   Of each a fresh pair,   He put down to air,
And hung a clean shirt to the fire on a chair.—

Still the Master was absent—the Cook came and said, 'he
Much fear'd, as the dinner had been so long ready,
   The roast and the boil'd   Would be all of it spoil'd,
And the puddings, her Ladyship thought such a treat,
He was morally sure, would be scarce fit to eat!'
   This closed the debate—   ''Twould be folly to wait,'
Said the Lady.   'Dish up!—Let the meal be served straight;
And let two or three slices be put on a plate,
And keep hot for Sir Thomas.—He's lost, sure as fate!
And, a hundred to one, won't be home till it's late!'
—Captain Dugald MacBride then proceeded to face
The Lady at table,—stood up, and said grace,—
Then set himself down in Sir Thomas's place.

Wearily, wearily, all that night,
That livelong night, did the hours go by;
And the Lady Jane,   In grief and in pain,
She sat herself down to cry!—
And Captain MacBride,   Who sat by her side,
Though I really can't say that he actually cried,
At least had a tear in his eye!—
As much as can well be expected, perhaps,
From very 'young fellows,' for very 'old chaps';
And if he had said   What he'd got in his head,
'Twould have been, 'Poor old Buffer! he's certainly dead!'
The morning dawn'd,—and the next,—and the next
And all in the mansion were still perplex'd;
No watch-dog 'bay'd a welcome home,' as
A watch-dog should, to the 'Good Sir Thomas';
No knocker fell   His approach to tell,
Not so much as a runaway ring at the bell—
The Hall was silent as Hermit's cell.

Yet the sun shone bright upon tower and tree
And the meads smiled green as green may be
And the dear little dicky-birds caroll'd with glee,
And the lambs in the park skipp'd merry and free—
—Without, all was joy and harmony!
'And thus 'twill be,—nor long the day,—
Ere we, like him, shall pass away!
Yon Sun, that now *our* bosoms warms,
Shall shine,—but shine on other forms;—
Yon Grove, whose choir so sweetly cheers
Us now, shall sound on other ears,—
The joyous Lamb, as now, shall play,
But other eyes its sports survey,—
The Stream we loved shall roll as fair,
The flowery sweets, the trim Parterre
Shall scent, as now, the ambient air,—
The Tree, whose bending branches bear
The One loved name—shall yet be there;—
But where the hand that carved it?—Where?'—

These were hinted to me as   The very ideas
Which passed through the mind of the fair Lady Jane,
Her thoughts having taken a sombre-ish train,
As she walk'd on the esplanade, to and again,
With Captain MacBride   Of course, at her side,
Who could not look quite so forlorn,—though he tried,
—An 'idea,' in fact, had got into *his* head,
That if 'poor dear Sir Thomas' should really be dead,

It might be no bad 'spec.' to be there in his stead,
And, by simply contriving, in due time, to wed
   A Lady who was young and fair,
    A Lady slim and tall,
  To set himself down in comfort there
    The Lord of Tapton [1] Hall.—

Thinks he, 'We have sent   Half over Kent,
And nobody knows how much money's been spent,
Yet no one's been found to say which way he went!—
   The groom, who's been over
    To Folkestone and Dover,
Can't get any tidings at all of the rover!
—Here's a fortnight and more has gone by, and we've tried
Every plan we could hit on—the whole countryside,
Upon all its dead walls, with placards we've supplied,—
And we've sent out the Crier, and had him well cried—
   "MISSING!! Stolen, or stray'd, Lost, or mislaid,
A GENTLEMAN;—middle-aged, sober, and staid;—
Stoops slightly;—and when he left home was array'd
In a sad-coloured suit, somewhat dingy and fray'd;—
Had spectacles on with a tortoiseshell rim,
And a hat rather low-crowned, and broad in the brim.—
   Whoe'er Shall bear, Or shall send him with care
(Right side uppermost) home;—or shall give notice where
The said middle-aged GENTLEMAN is; or shall state
Any fact, that may tend to throw light on his fate,
To the man at the turnpike, called TAPPINGTON GATE,
Shall receive a REWARD of FIVE POUNDS for his trouble,—
(☞ N.B.—If defunct the REWARD will be double!! ☜)

'Had he been above ground
   He *must* have been found.
No; doubtless he's shot,—or he's hang'd,—or he's drown'd!—
   Then his Widow—ay! ay!—But, what will folk say!—
To address her at once—at so early a day!
Well—what then?—who cares?—let 'em say what they may—
A fig for their nonsense and chatter!—suffice it, her
Charms will excuse one for casting sheep's eyes at her!'

When a man has decided As Captain Macbride did,
And once fully made up his mind on the matter, he
Can't be too prompt in unmasking his battery.

---

[1] The familiar abbreviation for Tappington Everard still in use among the tenantry.—*Vide* Prefatory Introduction to the INGOLDSBY LEGENDS.

He began on the instant, and vow'd that 'her eyes
Far exceeded in brilliance the stars in the skies,—
That her lips were like roses—her cheeks were like lilies—
Her breath had the odour of daffy-down-dillies!'—
With a thousand more compliments equally true,
And expressed in similitudes equally new!
   —Then his left arm he placed
    Round her jimp, taper waist—
—Ere she'd fix'd to repulse, or return, his embrace,
Up came running a man, at a deuce of a pace,
With that very peculiar expression of face
Which always betokens dismay or disaster,
Crying out,—'twas the Gardener,—'Oh, Ma'am! we've found
   Master!'—
—'Where? where?' scream'd the lady; and Echo scream'd—
   'Where?'
  —The man couldn't say 'There!'
  He had no breath to spare,
But, gasping for air, he could only respond,
By pointing—he pointed, alas!—TO THE POND!!

—'Twas e'en so—poor dear Knight!—with his 'specs' and his
   hat
He'd gone poking his nose into this and to that;
  When, close to the side Of the bank, he espied
An 'uncommon fine' Tadpole, remarkably fat!
   He stooped;—and he thought her
   His own;—he had caught her!
Got hold of her tail,—and to land almost brought her,
When—he plump'd head and heels into fifteen feet water!

   The Lady Jane was tall and slim,
    The Lady Jane was fair,
  Alas, for Sir Thomas!—she grieved for him,
  As she saw two serving-men, sturdy of limb,
    His body between them bear.
She sobb'd, and she sigh'd; she lamented, and cried,
  For of sorrow brimful was her cup;
She swoon'd, and I think she'd have fall'n down and died,
   If Captain MacBride Had not been by her side,
With the Gardener; they both their assistance supplied,
  And managed to hold her up.—
   But, when she 'come to,'
   Oh! 'tis shocking to view
  The sight which the corpse reveals!
   Sir Thomas's body, It look'd so odd—he
Was half eaten up by the eels!

His waistcoat and hose, and the rest of his clothes
   Were all gnawed through and through;
      And out of each shoe An eel they drew;
And from each of his pockets they pull'd out two!
And the Gardener himself had secreted a few,
      As well we may suppose;
For, when he came running to give the alarm,
He had six in the basket that hung on his arm.

     Good Father John Was summon'd anon;
      Holy water was sprinkled, And little bells tinkled,
      And tapers were lighted, And incense ignited,
And masses were sung, and masses were said,
All day, for the quiet repose of the dead,
And all night no one thought about going to bed.

    But Lady Jane was tall and slim,
      And Lady Jane was fair,—
And, ere morning came, that winsome dame
Had made up her mind—or, what's much the same,
Had *thought about*—once more 'changing her name,'
   And she said, with a pensive air,
To Thompson, the valet, while taking away,
When supper was over, the cloth and the tray,—
     'Eels a many I've ate; but any
  So good ne'er tasted before!—
They're a fish, too, of which I'm remarkably fond.—
Go—pop Sir Thomas again in the Pond—
  Poor dear!—HE'LL CATCH US SOME MORE!!'

MORAL

All middle-aged Gentlemen let me advise,
If you're married, and have not got very good eyes,
Don't go poking about after blue-bottle flies!—
If you've spectacles, don't have a tortoiseshell rim,
And don't go near the water,—unless you can swim!

Married Ladies, especially such as are fair,
Tall, and slim, I would next recommend to beware
How, on losing *one* spouse, they give way to despair;
But let them reflect, 'There are fish, and no doubt on't—
As good *in* the river as ever came *out* on't!'

Should they light on a spouse who is given to roaming
In solitude—*raison de plus*, in the 'gloaming,'—
Let them have a fix'd time for said spouse to come home in!
And if, when 'last dinner-bell' 's rung, he is late,
To insure better manners in future—Don't wait!—

If of husband or children they chance to be fond,
Have a stout iron-wire fence put all round the pond!

One more piece of advice, and I close my appeals—
That is—if you chance to be partial to eels,
Then—*Crede experto*—trust one who tried—
Have them spitchcock'd,—or stew'd—they're too oily when
    fried!

THE HOUSE-WARMING!!

A LEGEND OF BLEEDING HEART YARD

'Did you ever see the Devil dance?'—OLD QUERY.

SIR CHRISTOPHER HATTON he danced with grace,
He'd a very fine form and a very fine face,
And his cloak and his doublet were guarded with lace,
    And the rest of his clothes,   As you may well suppose,
In taste were by no means inferior to those;
    He'd a yellow-starch'd ruff,   And his gloves were of buff,
On each of his shoes a red heel and a rose,
And nice little moustaches under his nose;
    Then everyone knows   How he turned out his toes,
And a very great way that accomplishment goes,
In a Court where it's thought, in a lord or a duke, a
Disgrace to fall short in 'the Brawls'—(their Cachucha).
So what with his form, and what with his face,
And what with his velvet cloak guarded with lace,
And what with his elegant dancing and grace,
    His dress and address   So tickled Queen Bess
That her Majesty gave him a very snug place;
And seeing, moreover, at one single peep, her
Advisers were, few of them, sharper or deeper
(Old Burleigh excepted), she made him Lord Keeper!

I've heard, I confess, with no little surprise,
English history called a farrago of lies;
 And a certain Divine, A connection of mine,
Who ought to know better, as some folks opine,
 Is apt to declare, Leaning back in his chair,
With a sort of a smirking, self-satisfied air,
That 'all that's recorded in Hume, and elsewhere,
 Of our early "*Annales*" A trumpery tale is,
Like the "bold Captain Smith's," and the "Luckless Miss
   Bayley's"—
That old Roger Hoveden, and Ralph de Diceto,
And others (whose names should I try to repeat o-
ver, well I'm assured you would put in your veto),
 Though all holy friars, Were very great liars,
And raised stories faster than Grissel and Peto—
That Harold escaped with the loss of a "glim"—
—That the shaft which killed Rufus ne'er glanced from a
   limb
Of a tree, as they say, but was aimed slap at *him*,—
That Fair Rosamond never was poisoned or spitted,
But outlived Queen Nell, who was much to be pitied;—
That Nelly her namesake, Ned Longshanks's wife,
Ne'er went crusading at all in her life,
Nor suck'd the wound made by the poison-tipped knife!
   For as she, O'er the sea,
   Towards far Galilee,
Never, even in fancy, march'd carcass or shook shanks,
Of course she could no more suck Longshanks than Cruik-
   shanks,
But, leaving her spindle-legged liege lord to roam,
Stayed behind, and suck'd something much better at home,—
 That it's quite as absurd
 To say Edward the Third,
In reviving the Garter, afforded a handle
For any Court-gossip, detraction, or scandal,
 As 'twould be to say That at Court t'other day
At the fête which the newspapers say was so gay,
His Great Representative then stole away
Lady Salisbury's garters as part of the play,—
—That as to Prince Hal's being taken to jail,
By the London Police, without mainprize or bail,
 For cuffing a judge, It's a regular fudge;
And that Chief-Justice Gascoigne, it's very well known,
Was kicked out the moment he came to the throne,—
Then that Richard the Third was a "marvellous proper
   man"—
Never killed, injured, or wrong'd of a copper, man!—
 M 185

Ne'er wished to smother   The sons of his brother,—
Nor ever stuck Harry the Sixth, who, instead
Of being squabashed, as in Shakespeare we've read,
Caught a bad influenza, and died in his bed,
In the tower, not far from the room where the Guard is
(The octagon one that adjoins Duffus Hardy's);
—That, in short, all the "facts" in the *Decem Scriptores*,
Are nothing at all but sheer humbugging stories.'

Then if, as he vows, both this country and France in,
Historians thus gave themselves up to Romancing,
Notwithstanding what most of them join in advancing
Respecting Sir Christopher's capering and prancing,
     'Twill cause no surprise   If we find that his rise
Is *not* to be solely ascribed to his dancing!
The fact is, Sir Christopher, early in life,
As all bachelors should do, had taken a wife,
A Fanshawe by family—one of a house
Well descended, but boasting less 'nobles' than *nous*;
     Though e'en as to purse   He might have done worse,
For I find, on perusing her Grandfather's will, it is
Clear she had 'good gifts beside possibilities,' [1]
     Owches and rings,   And such sort of things,
Orellana shares (then the American Stocks),
Jewell'd stomachers, coifs, ruffs, silk-stockings with clocks,
Point-lace, cambric handkerchiefs, nightcaps, and—socks—
(Recondite apparel contained in her box),
          —Then the height of her breeding
          And depth of her reading
Might captivate any gay youth, and in leading
Him on to 'propose,' well, excuse the proceeding:
Truth to tell, as to 'reading,' the Lady was thought to do
More than she should, and know more than she ought to do;
     Her maid, it was said,   Declared that she read
(A custom all staid folks discourage) in bed;
     And that often o' nights   Odd noises and sights
In her mistress's chamber had giv'n her sad frights,
After all in the mansion had put out their lights,
And she verily thought that hobgoblins and sprites
Were there, kicking up all sorts of devil's delights;—
Miss Alice, in short, was supposed to 'collogue'—I
Don't much like the word—with the subtle old rogue, I
've heard call'd by so many names—one of them's 'Bogy'—
     Indeed 'twas conceived,   And by most folks believed,
—A thing at which all of her well-wishers griev'd,—

---

[1] 'Seven hundred pounds and possibilities is good gifts.'
                                        SIR HUGH EVANS.

That should she incline to play such a vagary,
Like sage Lady Branxholm, her contempo-rary,
(Excuse the false quantity, reader, I pray),
She could turn a knight into a wagon of hay,
Or two nice little boys into puppies at play,
Raison de plus, not a doubt could exist of her
Pow'r to turn 'Kit Hatton' into 'Sir Christopher';
But what 'mighty magic,' or strong 'conjuration,'
Whether love-powder, philtre, or other potation
   She used, I confess, I'm unable to guess,—
   Much less to express By what skill and address
She 'cut and contrived' with such signal success,
As we Londoners say, to 'inwiggle' Queen Bess,
   Inasmuch as I lack heart To study the Black Art;
Be that as it may,—it's as clear as the sun,
That, however she did it, 'twas certainly done!

Now, they're all very well, titles, honour, and rank,
Still, we can't but admit, if we choose to be frank,
There's no harm in a snug little sum in the Bank!
   An old proverb says, 'Pudding still before praise!'
An adage well known I've no doubt in those days,
And George Colman the Younger, in one of his plays,
Makes one of his characters loudly declare
That 'a Lord without money,'—I quote from his *Heir-
At Law*—''s but a poor wishy-washy affair!'
In her subsequent conduct I think we can see a
Strong proof the Dame entertained some such idea,
   For, once in the palace, We find Lady Alice
Again playing tricks with her Majesty's chalice
      In the way that the jocose, in
      Our days, term 'hocussing';
The liquor she used, as I've said, she kept close,
But, whatever it was, she now doubled the dose!
   (So true is the saying 'We never can stay, in
Our progress, when once with the foul fiend we league us.')
—She 'doctor'd' the punch, and she 'doctor'd' the negus,
Taking care not to put in sufficient to flavour it,
   Till, at every fresh sip That moisten'd her lip
The Virgin Queen grew more attach'd to her Favourite.

'No end' now he commands Of money and lands,
And as George Robins says, when he's writing about houses,
'Messuages, tenements, crofts, tofts, and outhouses,'
Parks, manors, chases, she 'gives and she grants,
To him and his heirs, and his uncles and aunts';

Whatever he wants, he has only to ask it,
And all other suitors are 'left in the basket,'
　Till Dudley and Rawleigh　Began to look squally,
While even grave Cecil, the famous Lord Burleigh,
Himself, 'shook his head,' and grew snappish and surly.
　All this was fine sport,　As our authors report,
To Dame Alice, become a great Lady at Court,
Where none than her Ladyship's husband look'd bigger,
Who 'led the brawls'[1] still with the same grace and vigour,
Though losing a little in slimness and figure;
For eating and drinking all day of the best
　Of viands well dressed,　With 'Burgess's Zest,'
Is apt, by degrees, to enlarge a man's vest;
And, what in Sir Christopher went to increase it, he
'd always been rather inclined to obesity;
—Few men in those times were found to grow thinner
With beefsteaks for breakfast and pork-pie for dinner.

Now it's really a difficult problem to say
How long matters might have gone on in this way.
If it had not unluckily happened one day
　That NICK,—who, because
　He'd the gout in his claws,
And his hoofs—(he's by no means so young as he was,
And is subject of late to a sort of rheumatic a-
-ttack that partakes both of gout and sciatica,)—
All the night long had twisted and grinn'd,
His pains much increased by an easterly wind,
Which always compels him to hobble and limp,
Was strongly advised by his Medical Imp
To lie by a little and give over work,
For he'd lately been slaving away like a Turk,
On the Guinea-coast, helping to open a brave trade
In Niggers, with Hawkins[2] who founded the slave-trade,
So he call'd for his ledger, the constant resource
Of your Mercantile folk, when they're 'not in full force';
—If a cold or catarrh makes them husky and hoarse,
Or a touch of gout keeps them away from 'the BOURSE,'
They look over their books as a matter of course.

---

[1] 'The grave Lord Keeper led the brawls,
　　The seals and maces danced before him.'—GRAY.

[2] Sir John Hawkins for 'his *worthye* attempts and services,' and because 'in the same he had dyvers conflights with the Moryans and slew and toke dyvers of the same Moryans,' received from Elizabeth an *honourable* augmentation to his coat armour, including, for his crest, '*A Demi-Moor sable, with two manacles on each arm, or.*'

Now scarce had Nick turned over one page, or two,
Ere a prominent item attracted his view,
A Bill!—that had now been some days overdue,
From one Alice Hatton, *née* Fanshawe—a name
Which you 'll recognize, reader, at once as the same
With that borne by Sir Christopher's erudite dame!
The signature—much more *prononcée* than pink,
Seem'd written in *blood*—but it might be red ink—
   While the rest of the deed   He proceeded to read,
Like ev'ry 'bill, bond, or acquittance' whose date is
Three hundred years old, ran in Latin.—'*Sciatis
(Diaboli?) omnes ad quos haec pervenient*'—
—But courage, dear Reader, I mean to be lenient,
And scorn to inflict on you half the 'Law-reading'
I picked up 'umquhile' in three days' Special-pleading
Which cost me—a theme I 'll not pause to digress on—
Just thirty-three pounds six and eightpence a lesson—
'As I 'm stout, I 'll be merciful,' therefore, and sparing
All these technicalities, end by declaring
   The Deed so correct   As to make one suspect,
(Were it possible any such person could go there)
Old Nick had a Special Attorney below there:
'Twas so fram'd and express'd no tribunal could shake it,
And firm as red wax and *black* ferret could make it.

   By the roll of his eye   As Old Nick put it by,
It was clear he had made up his mind what to do
In respect to the course he should have to pursue,
When his hoof would allow him to put on a shoe!!

No, although the Lord Keeper held under the Crown, house
And land in the country—he 'd never a Town-house.
   And, as we have seen,   His course always had been,
When he wanted a thing, to solicit the Queen,
So now, in the hope of a fresh acquisition,
He danced off to Court with his 'Humble Petition.'

   'Please your Majesty's Grace,   I have not a place
I can well put my head in, to dine, sup, or sleep!
Your Grace's Lord Keeper has nowhere to *keep*,
   So I beg and intreat,   At your Majesty's feet,
That your Grace will be graciously pleas'd for to say,
   With as little delay   As your Majesty may,
Where your Majesty's Grace's Lord Keeper's to stay—
—And your Grace's Petitioner ever will pray!'

The Queen, when she heard   This petition preferr'd,
Gave ear to Sir Christopher's suit at a word;—
'Odds Bobs, my good Lord!' was her gracious reply,
    'I don't know, not I,   Any good reason why
A Lord Keeper, like you, should not always be nigh
To advise—and devise—and revise—our supply—
A House! we're surprised that the thing did not strike
Us before—Yes!—of course!—Pray, whose House would you
    like?
When I *do* things of this kind, I do them genteelly,
A House?—let me see! there's the Bishop of Ely!
A capital mansion, I'm told, the proud knave is in,
Up there in Holborn, just opposite Thavies' Inn—
Where the Strawberries grow so fine and so big,
Which our Grandmother's Uncle tucked in like a pig,
King Richard the Third, which you all must have read of—
The day,—don't you know?—he cut Hastings's head off—
And mark me, proud Prelate!—I'm speaking to you,
Bishop Heaton!—you need not, my lord, look so blue—
Give it up on the instant!   I don't mean to shock you,
Or else by——!—(The Bishop *was* shocked!)—I'll unfrock
    you!!'

The Queen turns abruptly her back on the group,
The Courtiers all bow as she passes, and stoop,
To kiss, as she goes, the hind flounce of her hoop,
And Sir Christopher, having thus danced to some tune,
Skips away with much glee in his best rigadoon!
    While poor Bishop Heaton,
    Who found himself beaten,
In serious alarm at the Queen's contumelious
And menacing tone, at once gave him up Ely House,
With every appurtenance thereto belonging,
Including the strawberry beds 'twas so strong in;
Politely he bow'd to the gratified minion,
And said, 'There can be, my good lord, in opinion
    No difference betwixt yours   And mine as to fixtures
    And tables, and chairs—   We need no survey'rs—
Take them just as you find them, without reservation,
Grates, coppers, and all, at your own valuation!'
    Well! the object is gained!
    A good Town-house obtained!
The next thing to be thought of, is now
The 'house-warming' party—the *when* and the *how*—
    The Court ladies call,   One and all, great and small,
For an elegant 'Spread,' and more elegant Ball,

So, Sir Christopher, vain as we know, of his capering,
No sooner had finished his painting and papering,
  Than he sat down and wrote   A nice little pink note
To every great Lord whom he knew, and his spouse,
  'From our poor place on Holborn-hill (late Ely House),
Lord Keeper and Dame Alice Hatton request
Lord So-and-so's (name, style, or title exprest)
  Good company on   The next Eve of St John,
Viz.: Friday week, June 24th, as their guest,
  To partake of pot-luck,   And taste a fat buck.
N.B. Venison on table exactly at 3,
Quadrilles in the afternoon, R. S. V. P.
For my good Lord of So-and-so these, and his wife;
Ride! Ride! for thy life! for thy life! for thy life!'
Thus courtiers were wont to indorse their expresses
In Harry the VIIIth's time, and also Queen Bess's.
The Dame, for her part, too, took order that cards
Should be sent to the mess-rooms of all the Hussards,
The Household troops, Train-bands, and horse and foot
      Guards.

  Well, the day for the rout   At length came about,
And the bells of St Andrew's rang merrily out,
As horse-litter, coach, and pad-nag, with its pillion
(The mode of conveyance then used by the 'Million'),
  All gallant and grand,   Defiled from the Strand,
Some through Chancery (then an unpaved and much wetter)
      Lane,
Others through Shoe (which was not a whit better) Lane;
Others through Fewtar's (corrupted to Fetter) Lane;
Some from Cheapside, and St Mary-le-Bow,
From Bishopsgate Street, Dowgate Hill,[1] and Budge Row.
  They come and they go,
  Squire and Dame, Belle and Beau,
Down Snore Hill (which we have since whitewashed to Snow),
All eager to see the magnificent show,
And sport what some call 'a fantastical toe';
  In silk and in satin,   To batten and fatten
Upon the good cheer of Sir Christopher Hatton.

      A flourish, trumpets!—sound again!—
        He comes, bold Drake, the chief who made a
      Fine hash of all the pow'rs of Spain,
        And so serv'd out their Grand Armada:
      With him come Frobisher and Hawkins,
      In yellow ruffs, rosettes, and stockings.

      [1] Sir Francis Drake's house, 'The Arbour,' stood here.

Room for my Lord!—proud Leicester's Earl
  Retires awhile from courtly cares,
Who took his wife, poor hapless girl!
  And pitch'd her neck and heel downstairs;
Proving, in hopes to wed a richer,
If not her 'friend,' at least her 'pitcher.'

A flourish, trumpets! strike the drums!
  Will Shakespeare, never of his pen sick,
Is here—next Doctor Masters comes,
  Renown'd afar for curing men sick,—
Queen's Serjeant Barham [1] with his bums
  And tipstaves, coif, and wig forensic
(He lost, unless Sir Richard lies, his
Life at the famous 'Black Assizes').

Room! Room! for great Cecil!—place, place, for his Dame!—
Room! Room! for Southampton—for Sidney, whose name
As a *Preux Chevalier*, in the records of Fame,
'Beats Banagher'—e'en now his praises, we all sing 'em,
Knight, Poet, Gentleman!—Room! for sage Walsingham!—

Room! for Lord Hunsdon!—for Sussex!—for Rawleigh!—
For INGOLDSBY!! Oh! it's enough to appal ye!
    Dear me! how they call!
    How they squall! how they bawl!
This dame has lost her shoe—that one her shawl—
My lord's got a tumble—my lady a fall!—
  Now a Hall! a Hall! A Brawl! a Brawl!
Here's my Lord Keeper Hatton, so stately and tall!
Has led out Lady Hunsdon to open the Ball!

Fiddlers! Fiddlers! fiddle away!
Resin your catgut! fiddle and play!
  A roundelay! Fiddle away!
Obey! obey!—hear what they all say!
Hip!—Music!—Nosey!!—play up there!—play!
Never was anything half so gay
As Sir Christopher Hatton's grand holiday!

The clock strikes twelve!—Who cares for the clock?
Who cares for——Hark!—What a loud Single-knock!
  Dear me! dear me! Who can it be?—
Why, who can be coming at this time of night,
With a knock *like that* honest folk to affright?—

---

[1] Called by Sir Richard Baker 'The famous Lawyer.'—See his CHRONICLE.

'Affright?'—yes *affright*!—there are many who mock
At fear, and in danger stand firm as a rock,
Whom the roar of the battle-field never could shock,
Yet quail at the sound of a vile 'Single-knock'!
Hark!—what can the Porter be thinking of?—What!—
If the booby has not let him in I'll be shot!—
    Dear me! how hot The room's all at once got!—
      And what rings through the roof?—
      It's the sound of a *hoof*!—
It's some donkey a-coming upstairs at full trot!
Stay!—the folding-doors open! the leaves are thrown back,
And in dances a tall *Figurant*—ALL IN BLACK!!

Gracious me what an *entrechat*! Oh, what a bound!
Then with what an *a-plomb* he comes down to the ground!
    Look there! look there! Now he's up in the air!
Now he's here!—now he's there!—now he's no one knows
      where!—
See! see!—he's kick'd over a table and chair!
There they go!—all the strawberries, flowers, and sweet herbs,
    Turn'd o'er and o'er, Down on the floor,
Ev'ry caper he cuts oversets or disturbs
All the 'Keen's Seedlings' and 'Wilmot's Superbs'!
    There's a pirouette!—we're
    All a great deal too near!
A ring!—give him room or he'll 'shin' you—stand clear!
There's a spring again!—oh! 'tis quite frightful!—oh dear!
His toe's broke the top of the glass chandelier!!
Now he's down again!—look at the *congées* and bows
And salaams which he makes to the Dame of the House,
Lady Alice, the noble Lord Treasurer's spouse!
    Come, now we shall view A grand *pas de deux*
Perform'd in the very first style by these two
—But no!—she recoils—she could scarce look more pale if
Instead of a Beau's 'twas the bow of a Bailiff!—
He holds out his hand—she declines it, and draws
Back her own—see!—he grasps it with horrid black claws,
Like the short, sharp, strong nails of a Polar Bear's paws!!
      Then she 'scream'd such a scream!'
      Such another, I deem,
As, long after, Miss Mary Brown [1] scream'd in her dream.
Well she might! for 'twas shrewdly remark'd by her Page,
A sharp little boy about twelve years of age,

---

[1] *Vide* the celebrated ballad of 'Giles Scroggins.'—Catnach's ed. *Seven Dials*, London, 1841.

Who was standing close by
When she utter'd her cry,
That the whole of her arm shrivell'd up and grew dry,
While the fingers and thumb of the hand he had got
In his clutches became on the instant RED HOT!!

Now he whirls and he twirls
Through the girls in their curls,
And their rouge, and their feathers, and diamonds, and pearls;
Now high,—now low,— Now fast, and now slow,
In terrible circumgyration they go,
The flame-coloured Belle and her coffee-faced Beau!
Up they go once! and up they go twice!—
Round the hall!—round the hall!—and now up they go thrice!
Now one grand pirouette, the performance to crown!
Now again they go UP!!—and they NEVER COME DOWN!!!

The thunder roars!   And the rain it pours!
And the lightning comes in through the windows and doors!
Then more calling, and bawling,
And squalling, and falling,
Oh! what a fearful 'stramash' they are all in!
Out they all sally,   The whole *corps de ballet*—
Some dash down Holborn-hill into the valley,
Where stagnates Fleet Ditch at the end of Harp Alley,
Some t'other way, with a speed quite amazing,
Nor pause to take breath till they get beyond Gray's Inn.
In every sense of the word, such a rout of it,
Never was made in London, or out of it!

When they came the next day to examine the scene,
There was scarcely a vestige of all that had been;
The beautiful tapestry, blue, red, and green,
Was all blacken'd and scorch'd, and look'd dirty and mean,
All the crockery broken, dish, plate, and tureen!
While those who look'd up could perceive in the roof
One very large hole in the shape of a *hoof*!

Of poor Lady Hatton, it's needless to say
No traces have ever been found to this day,
Or the terrible dancer who whisk'd her away;
But out in the courtyard—and just in that part
Where the pump stands—lay bleeding a LARGE HUMAN HEART!
And sundry large stains   Of blood and of brains,
Which had not been wash'd off notwithstanding the rains,
Appear'd on the wood, and the handle and chains,

As if somebody's head with a very hard thump,
Had been recently knock'd on the top of the pump.
That pump is no more!—that of which you've just read,—
But they've put a new iron one up in its stead,

   And still, it is said,   At that 'small hour' so dread,
When all sober people are cosy in bed,
There may sometimes be seen on a moonshiny night.
Standing close by the new pump, a Lady in White,
Who keeps pumping away with, 'twould seem, all her might,
Though never a drop comes her pains to requite!
And hence many passengers now are debarr'd
From proceeding at nightfall through Bleeding Heart Yard!

MORAL

   Fair ladies, attend!   And if you've a 'friend
At Court,' don't attempt to bamboozle or trick her!
—Don't meddle with negus, or any mix'd liquor!—
Don't dabble in 'Magic!' my story has shown
How wrong 'tis to use any charms but your own!

Young Gentlemen, too, may, I think, take a hint
Of the same kind, from what I've here ventured to print,
All Conjuring's bad! they may get in a scrape
Before they're aware, and whatever its shape,
They may find it no easy affair to escape.
It's not everybody that comes off so well
From legerdemain tricks as Mr Brunel.

Don't dance with a Stranger who looks like a Guy,
And *when* dancing don't cut your capers too high!
   Depend on 't the fault's in   Your method of waltzing,
If ever you kick out the candles—don't try!

   At a ball or a play,   Or any soirée,
When a *petit souper* constitutes the '*Après,*'
If strawb'ries and cream with CHAMPAGNE form a part,
Take care of your HEAD!—and take care of your HEART!

   If you want a new house
   For yourself and your spouse,
Buy, or build one,—and honestly pay, every brick, for it!
Don't be so green as to go to Old Nick for it—
—Go to George Robins—he'll find you 'a perch'
(*Dulce domum*'s his word) without robbing the Church!

The last piece of advice which I'd have you regard
Is, 'don't go of a night into Bleeding-Heart-Yard,'
It's a dark, little, dirty, black, ill-looking square,
With queer people about, and unless you take care,
You may find, when your pocket's clean'd out and left bare,
That the *iron* one is not the *only* 'PUMP' there!

THE FORLORN ONE

AH! why those piteous sounds of woe,
  Lone wanderer of the dreary night?
Thy gushing tears in torrents flow,
  Thy bosom pants in wild affright!

And thou, within whose iron breast
  Those frowns austere too truly tell,
Mild pity, heaven-descended guest,
  Hath never, never deign'd to dwell.

That rude, uncivil touch forgo,
  Stern despot of a fleeting hour!
Nor 'make the angels weep' to know
  The fond 'fantastic tricks' of power!

Know'st thou not 'mercy is not strain'd,
  But droppeth as the gentle dew,'
And while it blesseth him who gain'd,
  It blesseth him who gave it too?

Say, what art thou? and what is he,
  Pale victim of despair and pain,
Whose streaming eyes and bended knee
  Sue to thee thus—and sue in vain?

Cold, callous man! he scorns to yield,
  Or aught relax his felon gripe,
But answers, 'I'm Inspector Field!
  And this here Warmint's prigg'd your wipe!'

UNSOPHISTICATED WISHES

By Miss Jemima Ingoldsby, aged 15

(Communicated by her Cousin Tom)

Oh! how I should like in a Coach to ride,
  Like the Sheriffs I saw upon Lord Mayor's day,
With a Coachman and little Postilion astride
  On the back of the leader, a prancing bay.

And then behind it, oh! I should glory
  To see the tall serving men standing upright,
Like the two who attend Mister Montefiore,
  (Sir Moses I should say) for now he's a Knight.

And then the liveries, I know it is rude to
  Find fault—but I'll hint as he can't see me blush,
That I'd not have the things I can only allude to
  Either orange in hue or constructed of plush;

But their coats and their waistcoats and hats are delightful,
  Their charming silk stockings—I vow and declare
Our John's ginger gaiters so wrinkled and frightful,
  I never again shall be able to bear.

Oh! how I should like to have diamonds and rubies,
  And large plume of feathers and flowers in my hair,
My gracious! to think how our Tom and those boobies,
  Jack Smith and his friend Mister Thompson, would stare.

Then how I should like to drive to Guildhall,
  And to see the nobility flocking in shoals,
With their two-guinea tickets to dance at the ball
  Which the Lord Mayor gives for relief of the Poles.

And to look at the gas so uncommonly pretty,
  And the stars and the armour all just as they were,
The day that the Queen came in state to the city
  To dine with the whole Corporation and Mayor.

Oh! how I should like to see Jane and Letitia,
  Miss Jones and the two Misses Frump sitting still,
While dear Ensign Brown, of the West Kent Militia,
  Solicits my hand for the 'Supper' Quadrille.

With his fine white teeth and his cheek like a rose,
  And his black cravat and his diamond pin,
And the nice little moustache under his nose,
  And the dear *little* tuft on the tip of his chin.

And how I should like some fine morning to ride
  In my coach, and my white satin shoes and gown,
To St James's Church, with a Beau by my side,
  And I shouldn't much care if his name was Brown.

AS I LAYE A-THYNKYNGE

THE LAST LINES OF THOMAS INGOLDSBY

As I laye a-thynkynge, a-thynkynge, a-thynkynge
Merrie sang the Birde as she sat upon the spraye
    There came a noble Knyghte,
    With his hauberke shynynge brighte,
    And his gallant heart was lyghte,
        Free and gaye;
As I laye a-thynkynge, he rode upon his waye.

As I laye a-thynkynge, a-thynkynge, a-thynkynge,
Sadly sang the Birde as she sat upon the tree!
    There seem'd a crimson plain,
    Where a gallant Knighte laye slayne,
    And a steed with broken rein
        Ran free,
As I laye a-thynkynge, most pitiful to see!

As I laye a-thynkynge, a-thynkynge, a-thynkynge,
Merrie sang the Birde as she sat upon the boughe;
    A lovely Mayde came bye,
    And a gentil youth was nyghe,
    And he breathed many a syghe
        And a vowe;
As I laye a-thynkynge, her hearte was gladsome now.

As I laye a-thynkynge, a-thynkynge, a-thynkynge,
Sadly sang the Birde as she sat upon the thorne;
    No more a youth was there,
    But a Maiden rent her haire,
    And cried in sad despaire,
        'That I was borne!'
As I laye a-thynkynge, she perished forlorne.

As I laye a-thynkynge, a-thynkynge, a-thynkynge,
Sweetly sang the Birde as she sat upon the briar;
  There came a lovely childe,
  And his face was meek and mild
  Yet joyously he smiled
    On his sire;
As I laye a-thynkynge, a Cherub mote admire.

As I laye a-thynkynge, a-thynkynge, a-thynkynge,
And sadly sang the Birde as it perch'd upon a bier;
  That joyous smile was gone,
  And the face was white and wan,
  As the downe upon the Swan
    Doth appear,
As I laye a-thynkynge—oh! bitter flow'd the tear!

As I laye a-thynkynge, the golden sun was sinking,
O merrie sang that Birde as it glitter'd on her breast
  With a thousand gorgeous dyes,
  While soaring to the skies,
  'Mid the stars she seem'd to rise,
    As to her nest;
As I laye a-thynkynge, her meaning was expressed:—
  'Follow, follow me away,
  It boots not to delay,'—
  'Twas so she seem'd to saye,
    'HERE IS REST!'   T. I.